HERO
OF THE
PACIFIC

Also by James Brady

The Coldest War: A Memoir of Korea
Why Marines Fight
The Scariest Place in the World: A Marine Returns to North Korea
The Marines of Autumn: A Novel of the Korean War
The Marine: A Novel of War from Guadalcanal to Korea
Warning of War: A Novel of the North China Marines
Designs
Nielsen's Children
The Press Lord
Holy Wars
Fashion Show, or The Adventures of Bingo Marsh
Paris One
Superchic

The Hamptons Novels

Further Lane
Gin Lane
The House That Ate the Hamptons
A Hamptons Christmas

HERO
OF THE
PACIFIC

THE LIFE OF MARINE LEGEND
JOHN BASILONE

James Brady

WILEY

John Wiley & Sons, Inc.

Library of Congress Cataloging-in-Publication Data:
Brady, James, date.
    Hero of the Pacific : the life of Marine legend John Basilone / James Brady.
        p.   cm.
    Includes bibliographical references and index.
    ISBN 978-0-470-37941-7 (cloth: alk. paper)
    1. Basilone, John, 1916–1945.   2. Medal of Honor—Biography.   3. United States. Marine Corps—Biography.   4. Guadalcanal, Battle of, Solomon Islands, 1942–1943. 5.   Iwo Jima, Battle of, Japan, 1945.   6. World War, 1939–1945—Biography.   7. Marines—New Jersey—Biography.   8. Soldiers—New Jersey—Biography.   9. Raritan (N.J.)—Biography.   I. Title.
    VE25.B36B73 2009
    940.54'5973092—dc22
    [B]

                                                                                2009015922
Printed in the United States of America

10   9   8   7   6   5   4   3   2

To all who put themselves in harm's way, especially the men and women of the United States Marine Corps—then, now, always.

To absent friends and family, who are loved so well.

And for Sarah, Joe, Nick, and Matthew—your Pop Pop loves you so much!

Contents

Acknowledgments

The day after completing this book, Jim Brady died, suddenly and unexpectedly. Because he had not yet written the acknowledgments, we, his daughters, have done so for him.

Near the end of this book, our dad describes himself as "neither a scholar nor a historian, just another old newspaperman who once fought in a war." This is true enough, and yet the statement is not entirely genuine. Jim Brady was a man fiercely proud of his bond with the Marine Corps and of the extraordinary experiences and friendships that he amassed over those six decades. He was also unabashedly delighted at having made a success in journalism. He grew up wanting to write and was a working writer to the last. As difficult as his loss has been for those of us left behind, there is a true sense of joy in knowing that he was doing what he absolutely loved right up to the end.

While our dad did not have the opportunity to compose his own thank-you list, he left stacks of notes and references. Clearly, a great many people gave generously of their time, knowledge, and insights. Some are mentioned in the text, while others remain unsung. Among those we would especially like to recognize are Stephen S. Power of John Wiley & Sons, who first proposed the idea of doing the book; USMC historian Robert Aquilina, who provided what our dad called a "Rosetta Stone of sorts" in primary-source materials from within the Corps' History Division at Quantico; *Leatherneck* magazine's executive editor, Colonel Walt Ford, USMC (Ret.); Colonel John Keenan, USMC (Ret.), editor of the *Marine Corps Gazette*; Colonel Bill White, USMC (Ret.); Raritan's John Pacifico, for his invaluable ad hoc reporting skills; the *Newark Star-Ledger's* Vinessa Ermino and Jeanette Rundquist; Marine Lou Piantadosi; and Marine Clinton Watters, John Basilone's best man. Sincere thanks to *all* who contributed to the making of this book.

Fiona Brady and Susan Konig

Marine platoon sergeant "Manila John" Basilone of Raritan, New Jersey, proudly wears the Congressional Medal of Honor, May 21, 1943.

Prologue

Whatever the century, whatever the war, machine gunners have always been a different military breed, focused and lethal warriors armed with and operating a terrible weapon in a risky trade, very competent at killing en masse, pretty good at getting killed themselves.

F. Scott Fitzgerald, who came of age in the appalling slaughter that was then called the Great War, understood this, which may be why he made his iconic hero Jay Gatsby a machine gunner. We first learn about Gatsby's war as the mysterious but glamorous bootlegger reveals himself bit by tantalizing bit to narrator Nick Carraway while the two young men speed toward Manhattan in Gatsby's cream-colored roadster. Nick listens, fascinated, not sure just how to respond or what to believe, as Jay goes on in his strange, mannered style of speech:

> "Then came the war, old sport.
> "In the Argonne Forest I took two machine gun detachments so far forward that there was a half mile gap on either side of us where the infantry couldn't advance.

We stayed there two days and two nights, a hundred and thirty men and sixteen Lewis guns, and when the infantry came up at last they found the insignia of three German divisions among the piles of dead.

"I was promoted to be major and every Allied government gave me a decoration—even Montenegro, little Montenegro down on the Adriatic Sea."

A generation and a world war later, in the 1940s, another young roughneck of a machine gunner, not a character in a book but an actual Marine from Raritan, New Jersey, was similarly piling up the dead of famous enemy divisions before his guns. He would be awarded the most illustrious decoration for gallantry that we have—the Congressional Medal of Honor—for what he did in the historic battle for Guadalcanal, and later, posthumously, the prized and nearly as rare Navy Cross, for his actions on the first day ashore at Iwo Jima. This man was Sergeant John Basilone.

Basilone was for several years during World War II one of the most recognizable celebrities in the country, a national hero and quite a famous man—young, laughing and roistering, unmarried and, in contemporary terms, quite sexy. Yet today, except among the hard men of the Marine Corps, which so reveres tradition, and in blue-collar, Italo-American Raritan, where the people of his hometown still tend the flame, few Americans could tell you who Basilone was or what he did in our desperate war against the Japanese in the Pacific.

Basilone's feats of arms became such lore that nowhere in the world is there a Marine base that does not boast a building or a street named for him. At huge, sprawling Camp Pendleton, California, where all Marines including Basilone received their final combat training before shipping out to Asian wars from World War II to Korea, Vietnam to Afghanistan, a two-lane stretch of macadam called Basilone Road starts at the commanding general's house and meanders for thirteen miles. Intersecting with Vandegrift Boulevard (generals are awarded "boulevards";

sergeants get "roads"), crossing the Santa Margarita River, and finally exiting the base near San Onofre to merge into and lose its identity amid the humming multiple lanes of Interstate 5, Basilone's modest road disappears just as surely as the man himself has largely vanished from the American consciousness.

He appeared just as suddenly at a time when the Japanese, edging ever closer to our West Coast with each battle, had been, to be candid, beating the crap out of the United States of America in fight after fight, and we sorely needed heroes.

Nonetheless it took the Marines, understandably distracted by war, until May 1943 to award Basilone the first of his medals for what he'd done seven months earlier on Guadalcanal. And it was late June before the vaunted Marine publicity machine even bothered to put out a press release. A story ran in the *New York Times* under the headline "Slew 38 Japanese in One Battle; Jersey Marine Gets Honor Medal." It was a one-day story that without a little hype soon faded. Basilone returned to a pleasant obscurity and the routine of wartime garrison life near Melbourne, Australia, drilling the troops, going on wild liberty weekends, just another good, tough sergeant in a Corps full of them.

Then some bright boys in Washington realized there might be pure promotional gold in Basilone. There were already a couple of Medal of Honor commissioned officers from Guadalcanal, General Alexander A. Vandegrift and Colonel "Red Mike" Edson. How about an enlisted man? Preferably unmarried (women would like that), somewhat colorful, younger? Maybe they could put this Jersey kid Basilone, a nobody from nowhere, to even better purpose than he had shown he was capable of in a foxhole.

Despite desperate battles yet to come and a shooting war raging in the Pacific, orders were cut, and as his buddies gaped and a few fellow soldiers griped about favoritism, Basilone was ordered to the States as an officially anointed hero. He was to go on tour with a handful of other heroic soldiers and sailors, supported by a troupe of Hollywood stars—traveling salesmen assigned to show the flag, boost morale, and sell war bonds.

Needless to say, it wasn't his idea, nor did he want to leave his "boys." Reluctantly, and reportedly in tears, Basilone left Melbourne, sailed to the West Coast, and was swiftly flown east by military aircraft to New York City where the media were—the big radio networks, major newspapers, *Time* and *Life* and *Newsweek* and the other national magazines, as well as the smooth boys of the Madison Avenue ad agencies. And following a crash course, it would be there in Manhattan that Basilone would face the only formal press conference he had ever attended.

It was his first real exposure to the American public. Terrified, he turned to a Marine colonel for help. "Just tell them your story, Sergeant," the colonel said. Tell them how it was." Basilone began to talk about that terrible Guadalcanal night he fought through, barefoot and bare-chested, the tropical jungle rain coming down, the Japanese crying "Banzai!" and "Marines, you die!" and coming on toward his machine guns. Always coming on.

Basilone was a smash hit. In his halting but modest and untutored answers, he responded to the shouted questions of cynical reporters who had seen it all, and won them over with his sincerity. In the end he had them queuing up to shake his hand and say thanks. And so the road show began.

If the press and just plain civilians were impressed by their first glimpses of the heroic Marine, and they were, Basilone was overwhelmed by the enthusiastic "well dones" of his fellow Americans. In the next few months of 1943, he would learn just how supportive they were. General Douglas MacArthur, who had long ago been Basilone's commanding officer in Manila—where the young soldier achieved a first small fame as an undefeated Army boxer, earning the sobriquet "Manila John"—was jollied into issuing a statement calling Basilone "a one-man army," a brand of enthusiastic cheerleading the general usually reserved for his own greatness.

Dozens of press conferences, some orchestrated, others ad hoc and on the run, were laid on with their hurled questions: "Hey, John, how many Japs ya kill?" New York mayor Fiorello LaGuardia, "the Little Flower," welcomed him to city hall, asking where his father came from in Italy. The *New York Times* did an interview. Damon Runyon wrote a piece. *Life* magazine did an elaborate photo spread. John would be photographed wherever he went, often out of uniform and in cock-eyed or clowning poses to please the cameramen, and appeared on magazine covers, bare-chested and firing a heavy machine gun cradled in his arms. One of these pictures, a painting on the June 24, 1944, issue of *Collier's* (ten cents a copy), was the most lurid, in the grand tradition of the pulp magazines.

Basilone was trotted out by his military handlers (peacetime press agents and Madison Avenue ad men in wartime uniform) to one radio station interview after another. Famed, best-selling war correspondent Lowell Thomas, who spent World War I trekking Arabia with Colonel T. E. Lawrence, got into the act, talking about Basilone on the newsreels, mispronouncing his name to rhyme with "baloney." The sergeant was saluted from the White House by President Franklin D. Roosevelt in whose name the medal had been awarded.

As Basilone read, rather bashfully, a canned speech cobbled for him by the handlers, he got a standing ovation from nineteen thousand at Madison Square Garden on Eighth Avenue, where he had once hoped to box. He was headlined in newspapers large and small, often as "Manila John, the Jap Killer." Newspaper columnist Ed Sullivan, always on the lookout for a new sensation to co-opt, took him up, wrote a piece, and did a radio show, basking in the hero's reflected glory. Celebrity saloonkeeper Toots Shor, a notorious front-runner, got on board the "Basilone Express," buying the drinks and glad-handing him around, introducing the kid to the athletes and glamour girls, the wealthy debutantes and chinless wonders of Café Society, the showbiz people and literary types among his boldface regulars. The Navy Department and Marine handlers got him past the velvet ropes and maîtres d'hotel of the Stork Club, "21," and El Morocco, and under the El on Third Avenue, Johnny was welcomed by the barmen and serious drinkers of P.J. Clarke's. Everyone wanted a piece of Manila John.

To the people of Raritan, though, Basilone was already theirs and always would be. They renamed streets and the American

Legion post, and in time they would erect a magnificent bronze statue of him holding his favorite weapon, the heavy water-cooled Browning .30-caliber M1917A1 machine gun, which he had loved to the point of obsession.

The Basilone family was transported into Manhattan to be interviewed. A *Manila John Basilone at War* comic book for kids was published (not a dime in royalties was ever paid). Two members of the Basilone clan would write their own books, amateurish and fanciful, admiring but brief on fact. John's sister Phyllis Basilone Cutter did a fourteen-part serialized account in a local newspaper, the *Somerset Messenger-Gazette*, and her son, Jerry Cutter, and a hired writer named Jim Proser published a book titled *I'm Staying with My Boys*—Cutter admitted that when they got stuck, they "made things up." Best-selling author Quentin Reynolds wrote a magazine piece. An ambitious writer began hanging around the family home hoping to win the hero's cooperation if not collaboration on an "authorized" book, until Basilone himself told the pest to "scram."

The federal government set up a city-to-city "Back the Attack!" war bond–selling tour of the country, first in the East and eventually to go national, with Basilone supported by a handful of other decorated servicemen (he was clearly the star turn) and Hollywood actors volunteered for the task by their movie studios. It would be, said FDR's friend Louis B. Mayer of MGM, excellent, patriotic, and quite free publicity for Mayer's next releases. Joining the tour were Gene Hersholt, John Garfield, Keenan Wynn, Eddie Bracken, and a pride of actresses, beautiful young women including one fairly well-known performer, Virginia Grey, who promptly fell for the young Marine over drinks and cigarettes in a dark hotel bar their first night out on the road.

That plotline alone would have made a swell Hollywood romance of the period, the juvenile dream of every obscure young man who comes out of nowhere, becomes an overnight sensation of one sort or another, and encounters the beautiful princess, or in this case the movie matinee equivalent of royalty, a movie star, the beauty who falls in love with the clean-cut young war hero.

Garfield, one of the troupe, might not have been bad in the role of the fighting Marine.

Basilone was credited by the tour organizers for drawing crowds that bought millions of dollars' worth of bonds. In Newark and Jersey City, where Basilone and Grey first shared a moment, and at New Haven, where Yale undergrads turned out to hail the young man who never even went to high school, in Pittsburgh, Albany, and all over the East, they organized parades: mayors, aldermen, governors, retail merchants drumming up trade, leading citizens and schoolchildren lining up to touch or even just to see Manila John.

He shook hands at factory gates and inside armaments and munitions plants. At a gala black-tie dinner at the Waldorf sponsored by the National Association of Manufacturers, Sergeant Basilone was seated on the dais, mingling with influential and wealthy men, captains of industry and other tycoons, the onetime laundry delivery boy fired for napping on the job atop the soiled laundry bags. A movement was launched to get his face on a postage stamp (eventually issued well after his death). Raritan gave him a parade of its own with tobacco heiress Doris Duke throwing open her estate to handle the overflow crowd. Catholic mass was said by Basilone's old priest, Father Amadeo Russo. The snob membership of the Raritan Valley Country Club turned out, remembering fondly, they claimed, the teenager who'd worked out of their caddy shack, lugging their golf clubs for tips. Basilone was invited to address a Bar Association lunch. He visited elementary school classrooms, signed autographs, kissed pretty girls in the crowd, and greeted old soldiers from earlier wars dating back to the Spanish-American, who approached to pay their respects and, perhaps, to bore the Marine with hoary war stories of their own.

At the family home in Raritan where Basilone grew up with his nine siblings, with only three bedrooms and two baths, they were inundated with fan mail, thousands of cards and letters, mostly from women, including a number of mash notes, and even marriage proposals from girls who had never met the machine gunner. One young woman wrote, "I always wanted to marry a hero." Basilone's brother marveled, "Johnny, everybody in the country loves you." An unsubstantiated rumor surfaced, courtesy of ribald Marine tattle, and possible enlisted men's jealousy, that when a USO show came through the islands of the South Pacific during Manila John's campaigning days, he had "bedded one of the Andrews Sisters." No one held it against either him or Miss Andrews, if the anecdote was true, because in wartime such "showing the flag" might justifiably be considered patriotic.

Basilone got married, but not to a movie star. His wife was another young Marine, a cute sergeant named Lena Riggi whom Basilone met in a Camp Pendleton mess hall.

Then he was gone again, without a honeymoon, back to the fight, back to his boys. He had been offered, and stubbornly turned down, an officers' rank and posh duty stations, politicking instead for just the opposite: to get back to the Pacific. Finally, the Marines had relented and reluctantly cut new orders reuniting him with the Fleet Marine Force Pacific.

Then he was gone for good, the "unkillable" hero of Guadalcanal dead on Iwo Jima, torn apart that first February morning by Japanese fire in the shadow of Mount Suribachi, a hero once again. Then he was forgotten.

How this could happen goes beyond the passage of time simply blurring and obscuring his image. Within the violent priesthood of the Marine Corps, there has long been contention and controversy, and some doubt, surrounding Basilone. There are contradictory and incorrect accounts about what exactly he'd done that dreadful night in the rain on the ridgelines of Guadalcanal in October 1942, starting with the official record in the *History of U.S. Marine Corps Operations in World War II*, volume 1, *Pearl Harbor to Guadalcanal*:

> The Japanese continued to assault out of the jungle and up the slopes. A small group forced a salient in the Marine line to fall upon a mortar position, and further to the front [General] Nasu's soldiers worked close to a water-cooled machine gun and knocked out all but

two of its crew. Marines near the mortar position won back the tube from the enemy, and in the machine gun section Sergeant John Basilone took rescue matters into his own hands. For this action and later heroism in braving Japanese fire to bring up ammunition, Basilone became the first enlisted Marine in World War II to win the Medal of Honor.

In fact, the first enlisted Marine to earn the medal was another sergeant, Clyde Thomason of the 2nd Raider Battalion, killed in the small-scale (and ill-fated) raid in August on Makin Island. But the brief record above does convey some of the savagery and chaotic nature of the fighting that night along the ridgelines, with infantrymen of both sides grappling in the dark over a single mortar tube, and a lone Marine (Basilone) risking hostile fire to sprint out and fetch more ammo for the machine guns, the heavy ammo belts slung about his neck and bare shoulders glistening in the rain. So began the legend of Manila John.

And what really happened later on Iwo? Had Basilone destroyed an enemy blockhouse single-handedly with demolitions, while contemptuously brandishing a knife at the Japanese? In the end, how did he die, on the beach or attacking Motoyama Airfield #1? Was he hit by an artillery or mortar shell and killed instantly as his Navy Cross citation reads? Or did he bleed slowly to death from small-arms fire, as the Marine casualty report has it? Shot up with morphine by a corpsman, had he left messages for his brother, smoked a cigarette, and lived for hours? Was the Navy Cross he received posthumously awarded to make up for the near-unprecedented second Medal of Honor he was thought by some to be chasing?

Then there's this: so hard up were we for heroes that there were suspicions the government had turned to "manufacturing" them. How else to explain the convenience of Basilone—a Marine under orders who would do what he was told, including a war bond tour and morale-boosting visits to war plants? This has clearly happened in more recent wars. Remember feckless young private Jessica Lynch and Arizona Cardinals football star Pat Tillman? Both became the innocent tools of a military publicity apparatus that ambitiously turned an understandably terrified young woman and a tragic victim of friendly fire into heroic but essentially synthetic symbols of American courage under fire. The *New York Times* editorial page savaged the Pentagon's misinformation campaign for conjuring up "the false story that PFC Jessica Lynch had been captured in Iraq after a Rambo-like performance," when she'd actually been injured in a truck crash. And Tillman's mother, Mary, in a book about her son, wrote that "officials tried to hide details about the incident because . . . it made the Army look bad." Ergo the cover-up, trying to persuade a nation that Tillman "had been killed by the enemy in Afghanistan (in a battle that won him a questionable Silver Star) long after the military knew he had been killed accidentally by fire from American forces."

But even suggesting half a century later that Basilone's heroics might similarly have been concocted infuriates contemporary keepers of the Basilone flame. Men such as Deacon John Pacifico of St. Ann's Roman Catholic Church in Raritan seem ever vigilant and ready to stand up to defend the Basilone name and his legend. In May 2007, sixty-five years after the Marine's death, Deacon Pacifico angrily told Vicki Hyman of the state's largest newspaper, the *Newark Star-Ledger*, "That's not what the Army was like in World War II. That's not what the Marines were like."

Having been a Marine myself and still a working journalist and writer of books about Marines at war, I thought Basilone's story was worth telling, worth a search for the real Basilone. I've grown fascinated by Manila John, sometimes puzzled by him, and I'm still trying to get a grip on him—not the bronze statue but the real man, not the marketing image but the real hero—and what made him tick.

In the Corps, you meet natural-born warriors, live with them, fight in the next hole to them, men like Basilone. Sometimes you understand them, frequently you don't. Or there's nothing to understand; he's just another Marine you serve with but never really know. In ways, we're all the same, we're all different. Maybe you're a cowboy, a kid off the farm, a young tough, an inner-city smartass, or a college boy like me, a young lieutenant, as mysterious to the other fellow as he is to you. You have nothing in common, you and he, only the one thing: you're both Marines. You have that, and when you both have also fought in combat, you very much have that, too.

Fighting a war, especially alongside other soldiers, fighting together, you learn the password, you know the secret handshake of combat, of the Few, the Proud, the Marines. Which is why it was conceivable that before I finished writing this book I might eventually get to know a man I never met, who died when I was a schoolboy, get to know him almost as well as all those folks who loved him so.

His story begins on an island few people had heard of before 1942.

PART ONE

GUADALCANAL

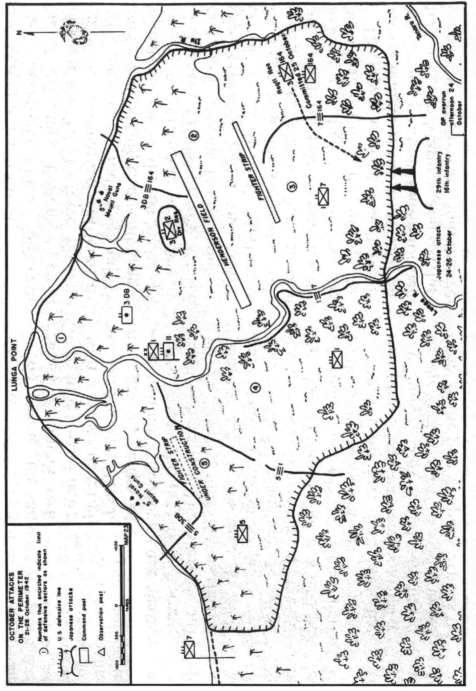

Guadalcanal. On the evening of October 24, 1942, then sergeant John Basilone made a stand on the strategically important high

1

Like Johnny Basilone, the country itself back then was big and brawny, a bit wild and sure of itself, had never been defeated in war, and was accustomed to winning; still young and tough, not effete or decadent like all of those tired Europeans being bullied by dictators, caving in to and being overrun by the loathsome, menacing Adolf Hitler. Our purported allies, fellow democracies Belgium, Norway, the Netherlands, Denmark, and Greece, were already lost or in peril, and the French Army, the greatest in the world it was often boasted, had been thrashed in six weeks and Paris occupied. Britain, even with its powerful Royal Navy and gallant Royal Air Force, was isolated, under siege, its great cities ablaze, its schoolchildren evacuated, its people sheltering in the Underground.

We were different, though. This country didn't lose wars. In eight terrible years of bloody revolution the ill-trained farmers and shopkeepers and frontiersmen of colonial militias had defeated the great British Empire, with the aid of the French fleet had forced the famous Lord Cornwallis to surrender, marching out of Yorktown with his band playing "The World Turned Upside

Down." In 1812 the British were back, burning Washington, but again beaten in the end. In 1848 we rolled over the Mexicans. In the most terrible war Americans ever fought, the country defeated Robert E. Lee, who was perhaps our greatest general but did not possess quite the army of Ulysses S. Grant. Spain in 1898 was a walkover, San Juan Hill, Manila Bay, and all that. In 1917–1918 we came to the rescue of the Allies in Flanders fields and the Argonne Forest.

Yet despite our pride, despite our history and sense of destiny, for the seven months since December 1941 American Marines had done little more than die gallantly in losing causes or surrender, as they had done under fire at Wake Island, or peacefully, striking flags and stacking rifles in humiliating parade formation at the legation of Peking. Except for the air and naval battles at Midway and the Coral Sea, we had been losing and, worse, not to the powerful German army with its Luftwaffe and panzers, its economic machine, its science and technology, or to Mussolini, but to a lesser foe.

They were, to American eyes, the short, skinny warriors of a small island nation with a third of our population, a strange, derivative people known in world markets largely for manufacturing dinnerware and porcelains, knockoff gadgets, china, fine silk textiles, and cheap, colorful children's gimmickry and tin toys, a third-world country of comic-book figures stereotyped and mocked in B-movies as sinister "Oriental" villains or farcical heroes like Mr. Moto, portrayed by Mittel-European Peter Lorre as a clever little detective with outsized horn-rimmed glasses and a mouthful of false teeth, grinning and bowing and given to hissing absurd lines like, "So solly . . . yes, pliss," appealing, like the rest of our view of Japan, to our most facile racist and xenophobic chauvinisms.

What we didn't see was a people with a grand martial tradition who at the opening of the twentieth century in blizzard-swept Siberia and at sea had defeated the czarist fleet and the great peasant armies and Cossack cavalry of the vast Russian empire. And who, since 1937, had been waging another, consistently and appallingly victorious war against the corrupt but much larger

China. Instead we dismissed them as colonial snobs told us that "the Japs," or "the Nips" (lifted from their own name for their country, Nippon), as it was then permissible to call them, were cunning little fellows but not very imaginative. For instance, having years earlier purchased an old surplus Royal Navy destroyer from the British in order to learn how to build modern warships, they had then duplicated the thing precisely, right down to the dent in its bow occasioned by some forgotten collision with an inconvenient pier.

In addition, we were fighting a war like none we or the world had ever seen nor may ever see again, one we couldn't lean on our history for lessons in how to fight. Sprawled across seven thousand miles of great ocean, it featured powerful naval armadas and air forces on both sides and pitted soldiers against one another in murderous ground combat in jungles and on coral beaches, atop mountains and deep in swamps. These were some of the finest light infantry in the world, ours and theirs, Japanese regulars with their samurai traditions of courage and barbarity, their screaming banzai assaults, battling hundreds of thousands of American GIs, sailors, and airmen, and six divisions of United States Marines, who on island after deadly island were living up to their own motto of Semper Fidelis, "always faithful."

A half dozen years after that war, a young New Yorker, a Marine replacement platoon leader, a college boy turned second lieutenant, flew west out of San Francisco bound for the winter mountains of North Korea. The obsolescent Navy C-54 Skymaster carrying the replacement draft took seven days to cross the great ocean, conveniently breaking down or pausing for fuel each night, on Kwajalein, Guam, touching en route Marine holy places such as Iwo Jima of that far greater war. The young lieutenant had never seen combat, knew but secondhand about the South Pacific, beyond seeing the Rodgers and Hammerstein musical in 1949 and attending college with men who had actually fought that war. Now he would be serving alongside many of the seasoned Marines who had defeated the Japanese. For the next year the young officer would fight with the 7th Marines (Basilone's old regiment) against the Koreans and the Chinese army, and would himself come of age in combat at the other end of that greatest of oceans, the Pacific.

In the snowy wartime autumn of 1951, I was that kid lieutenant. A Marine tracking the steps of other, earlier Marines, including Manila John Basilone, but never in war or in peace getting to the obscure Pacific island where his story really begins.

Guadalcanal, whose name derives from the hometown of a long-ago Spanish adventurer, is nearly three thousand miles southwest of Hawaii and one of the larger of the Solomons. It was an appalling place to fight a war, but it was there that we would finally take the ground war to the enemy, give Japan its first land defeat in a half-century of combat against westerners and prove that, mano a mano, American troops were as good as the Japanese Imperial Army.

According to the official records of the United States Marine Corps, the *History of U.S. Marine Corps Operations in World War II*, volume 1, *Pearl Harbor to Guadalcanal*, "Not a single accurate or complete map of Guadalcanal or Tulagi [the tiny neighboring island] existed in the summer of 1942. The hydrographic charts, containing just sufficient data to prevent trading schooners from running aground, were little better."

Aerial photography might have been helpful, *Marine Ops* conceded, but there was a shortage of long-range aircraft and suitable air bases from which they could take off. A lone flight was made, "the beaches appeared suitable landing," another aerial-strip map was scraped up in Australia, and that was deemed it. Estimates of enemy strength were put at 1,850 men on Tulagi and 5,275 on Guadalcanal. "Both estimates were high," Marine historians later admitted. As for the place itself, and its stinking climate, "Rainfall is extremely heavy, and changes in season are marked only by changes in intensity of precipitation. This, together with an average temperature in the high 80s, results in an unhealthy climate. Malaria, dengue, and other fevers, as well as fungus infections, afflict the population." The well-traveled novelist Jack London was once quoted as saying, "If I were king, the worst punishment I could afflict on my enemies would be to banish them to the Solomons."

By the autumn of 1942, "banished to the Solomons" to join that "afflicted population" of those unhappy islands were nearly 20,000 Marines and a smaller number of American soldiers, fighting the equivalent number of Japanese troops. One of those Marines, Robert Leckie, gives us a more intimate and personal description of the place in his book *Challenge for the Pacific*: "Seen from the air, it was a beautiful island, about ninety miles in length and twenty-five wide at its waist, and traversed end to end by lofty mountains, some as high as eight thousand feet." In domestic terms, the place was roughly the size and shape of New York's Long Island but with mountain peaks far taller than any New England ski resort. It was when you got closer up that you recognized the differences.

Leckie quotes one of the local "coast watchers," brave men who stayed behind to report back by radio after the first Japanese landed in the midsummer of 1942, an event that caused most Europeans and Chinese to flee. The coast watcher, British district officer Martin Clemens, described the place for Leckie: "She was a poisonous morass. Crocodiles hid in her creeks or patrolled her turgid backwaters. Her jungles were alive with slithering, crawling, scuttling things; with giant lizards that barked like dogs, with huge, red furry spiders, with centipedes and leeches and scorpions, with rats and bats and fiddler crabs and one big species of land-crab which moved through the bush with all the stealth of a steamroller. Beautiful butterflies abounded on Guadalcanal, but there were also devouring myriads of sucking, biting, burrowing insects that found sustenance in human blood; armies of fiery white ants. Swarms upon swarms of filthy black flies that fed upon open cuts and made festering ulcers of them, and clouds of malaria-bearing mosquitos. When it was hot, Guadalcanal was humid; when the rains came she was sodden and chill; and all her reeking vegetation was soft and squishy to the touch."

Clemens does not mention the big sharks, cruising just offshore and feeding on the bodies, American and Japanese, of sailors, soldiers, Marines, and airmen who fell, alive or dead, into the coastal waters. With about two dozen warships and other vessels of each side going down during the five-month battle, there was plenty for the thriving sharks.

It was the coast watchers who reported that the Japanese were building an airstrip there with Korean slaves, one that would endanger both Australia and New Zealand, our allies whose own forces were largely in action against the Germans half a world away, the famed ANZAC divisions fighting Rommel in North Africa. So they needed our help here on their own doorstep. The Japanese had northern Australia in their path, especially if enemy airpower and the Imperial Navy controlled the shipping routes and opened the way for their infantry.

The U.S. Navy had against all odds defeated the Japanese fleet at Midway, and now it was the turn of American Marines to do the job on land—*if* they were up to the challenge. On August 7 the 1st Marine Division landed by surprise and unopposed. Within a day it encountered and skirmished with Japanese infantry, igniting a terrible battle that would rage for the next five months on land, in the air, and on the surrounding sea.

2

Neither Lieutenant Colonel Lewis B. "Chesty" Puller nor Sergeant Basilone of his 1st Battalion of the 7th Marines had been on Guadalcanal when the 1st Marine Division invaded the island and began their grueling campaign. Fearful that the Japanese were still on the move elsewhere, perhaps against Fiji or the Samoan islands, elements of the 7th Marine Regiment, including Puller's battalion, were dispatched in late summer to defend Samoa against possible invasion. That was where Basilone and his mates groused about having missed the fun, if that's what it was, during those early weeks on the 'Canal.

Samoa wasn't bad duty, though entirely antithetic to the Marine culture of attack. The Marines in Samoa weren't anywhere near the enemy, nor were they about to launch a first offensive against the Japanese; their mission was strictly defensive. And why not? The Japanese were pitching a shutout in the western Pacific, taking one island, one battle after another, and why would they stop short now? No one in Washington or the Pacific knew just where the enemy would strike next. Samoa was certainly a potential target. So the Marines detached to defend it against a proximate invasion dug in and set up their gun emplacements, not only artillery and mortars but those heavy machine guns of Basilone's platoon. When and if the Japanese arrived at Western Samoa, the Marines would be ready to defend the islands, to hold the islands. They'd stacked arms and surrendered at Peking, gallantly lost Wake, burned their colors and asked for terms in the Philippines; they weren't going to lose Samoa without a fight.

Guadalcanal wasn't yet on anyone's charts. No intelligence had come in about the Solomon Islands. And the Japanese had not made up their own minds. They might not yet have recognized the strategic value of the 'Canal for an airstrip. In May when the Marine defense forces landed at Apia, Samoa, there were intelligent men both Japanese and American studying the situation, assessing the region, marshaling their forces, moving prudently closer to each other, but neither side knew precisely what was going to come next.

The Japanese moved first, landing on Bougainville, in the northern Solomons, and then on May 4 taking undefended and minuscule Tulagi, twenty miles across the water from Guadalcanal. In June, they finally made their decision: they would build that famous airstrip in the jungle.

Samoa knew nothing of this. Meanwhile, the Marine defense detachment's job had its fringe benefits. Samoa was "cake . . . a piece of cake," as Marines of the time put it. Basilone, having seen duty in tropical outposts as a younger man while in the Army, would have a basis for comparison. According to his sister Phyllis's serialized newspaper account, Basilone remarked, "Compared to Tent City [in North Carolina], our five month stay in these beautiful islands was a luxury. Not that we didn't continue our training. We got it every day, only now it was real jungle warfare, camouflage, the works." After all, "the Japs were coming, the Japs were coming." Weren't they?

Well, yes, or they had been. Those had been the Japanese plans. But when American naval and air forces defeated the enemy at Midway, June 4–7, Imperial General Headquarters in Tokyo scrapped plans to invade Midway, Fiji, New Caledonia, *and* Samoa. Meanwhile, on Samoa, which was now *not* being invaded, Basilone remarked, "There were some good times. The native women were eager to help the Americans and for months I don't think a single Marine had to do his laundry. Fresh eggs and butter were plentiful and for once the griping subsided.

"By this time I had been promoted to sergeant and my boys were the best damn machine gun outfit in the Division. All sorts of scuttlebutt was drifting into the boondocks and the men were getting restless. We all had thought we would see action first. One morning about the middle of August 1942 word trickled back that our buddies from Quantico and Tent City had already locked grips with the legendary and superhuman Japs."

That last we can take as Basilone sarcasm, but the fact was that a week earlier, on August 7, elements of two Marine infantry regiments, the 1st and 5th Marines, and the 11th Marine artillery regiment, the 1st Marine Raider Battalion, and the Parachute Battalion had landed on the islands of Guadalcanal, Tulagi, and nearby Gavutu. While at Samoa and other backwaters and aboard transport ships, Basilone's own 7th Marine Regiment was scattered over miles of the Pacific and had not yet been committed to battle. Needless to say, the 7th Marines were not happy. When Basilone complained to a Captain Rodgers about his men's impatience, he was told, "For the next few days we are going to run the men ragged. I know they'll bitch and gripe but I still want to hear them gripe *after* their first action."

The captain was true to his word. Said Basilone, "The next few days were hell. All day long we practiced storming caves, then were routed out in the middle of the night to repel imaginary Japs behind our lines. While the men complained bitterly, this practice paid off handsomely in the months to come. Instead of the confusion our buddies ran into, we profited by their misfortunes. I have no doubt many lives were saved with the series of codes and signals we adopted. We became so proficient that not a man of our outfit was shot at by one of his buddies as had been the case during the initial landings on the 'Canal."

August wore on, yet for Manila John and his mates this was not yet even the overture to battle. Guadalcanal was still about twelve-hundred miles away to the west, three or four days by ship, and even there the war had scarcely begun, while on Samoa most of these young Marines were combat innocents. That included Sergeant Basilone, the crack machine gunner Manila John, the salty veteran of three years in the prewar American Army and a few skirmishes with bad men in the backcountry of the Philippines.

We tend to think today of the 1st Marine Division by its nickname, "the Old Breed," salty, battle-tested vets, hard men who broke the Japanese in the Pacific, and later fought desperate battles in North Korea against Chinese regulars at the Chosin Reservoir. They would fight still later in Vietnam, and more recently in the Middle East. But in 1942 they were only kids, young Marines largely untried. In point of fact, the division had only been created in February 1941, eighteen months before it hit the beaches of Guadalcanal, with few of its 20,000 members blooded in actual combat, just some older officers and senior NCOs who had fought in France in 1918, and a few regulars who had chased bandits and fought rebels in Haiti or Nicaragua during the so-called Banana Wars of the later twenties and early thirties. Basilone himself must have been painfully aware of how little fighting had actually gone on outside the boxing ring during his U.S. Army tour in the 1930s in Manila.

Everything changed for John and his machine gunners on September 18, when, some five weeks late, the 7th Marine Regiment, plus some smaller units, went ashore on Guadalcanal to be greeted with the usual catcalls and derision from men who'd been there and fighting since early August. The 7th had been the first regiment of the division to go overseas but ironically the last to go into combat. Their arrival brought the Marine count on the island up to authorized strength, and the division's commander, General Alexander A. Vandegrift, wasted no time throwing these fresh troops into action. Historian Henry I. Shaw Jr. tells us in his monograph *First Offensive* "Vandegrift now had enough men ashore on Guadalcanal, 19,200, to expand his defensive scheme. He decided to seize a forward position along the east bank of the Matanikau River, in effect strongly out-posting his west flank defenses against the probability of strong enemy attacks from the area where most Japanese troops were landing, First, however, he was going to test the Japanese reaction with a strong probing force. He chose Puller's fresh 1st Battalion, 7th Marines, to move inland along the slopes of Mount Austen and patrol north towards the coast and the Japanese-held area."

But what was all this about Vandegrift's being on the defensive? Hadn't he and his division landed against light or no opposition? How were the Japanese now holding much of the coastline of Guadalcanal? What had happened since August 7 when the invading Marines seemed to have gained the initiative?

Shaw, who wrote about those early days and weeks on the 'Canal, explains the situation. "On board the transports approaching the Solomons, the Marines were looking for a tough fight." Estimates of Japanese strength ranged from 3,100 to just over 8,400. In actual count, there were only a total of 3,457, and of those 2,500 were mostly Korean laborers, not actual fighting men. Said Shaw, "The first landing craft carrying assault troops of the 5th Marines touched down at 0909 [9:09 a.m.] on Red Beach. To the men's surprise (and relief), no Japanese appeared to resist the landing. . . . The Japanese troops . . . had fled to the west, spooked by a week's B-17 bombardment, the pre-assault naval gunfire, and the sight of the ships offshore [those twenty-three transports and their escort vessels]." The U.S. assault troops were reported to have moved "off the beach and into the surrounding jungle, waded the steep-banked Ilu River, and headed for the enemy airfield." That airfield was the point of the entire operation, and on their very first day ashore the U.S. troops were nearly there.

But the Japanese enemy was nothing if not resilient. Heavy combat raged on the small nearby island of Tulagi where the enemy consisted of the Japanese equivalent of Marines, what they called "special naval landing force sailors," and those babies weren't running from anyone. On Tulagi that first day the Raider Battalion suffered ninety-nine casualties; a rifle battalion had fifty-six. When night fell on Gavutu, the enemy stayed in caves as the first wave of parachute Marines came ashore, and brisk fighting ensued as they emerged, with the Marines having to fall back for a time. On August 8, the airfield was taken, but more Japanese forces were on their way, by air and naval surface ships. On the several small islands near Guadalcanal in one day the Americans had suffered 144 dead and 194 wounded. On the second day Japanese airplanes sank the destroyer *Jarvis*, and in dogfights over the two days twenty-one Marine Wildcats were lost. Guadalcanal was not going to be a walkover. But there was worse to come, and swiftly.

On the night of the eighth an enemy cruiser-destroyer force off Savo Island proved themselves our superior at night fighting, sinking with no loss to themselves four Allied heavy cruisers, three American and one Australian, and knocking off the bow of a fifth heavy cruiser. About 1,300 U.S. and Aussie sailors died that night, with another 700 badly wounded or severely burned. These losses were such a shock that a panicky Admiral Jack Fletcher asked for and got permission to withdraw his carrier force. The supply and other amphibious support vessels were also pulled from the area, in effect leaving the Marines ashore on their own and without the heavy artillery that had been due to be landed, to follow the assault waves and reinforce the lighter field artillery already ashore. As for ammo and rations, the 1st Marine Division had only a four-day supply of ammunition for all weapons and, even counting captured Japanese food, only seventeen days' worth of chow.

All this as still half-filled supply ships steamed away from the beaches, fleeing the island and the enemy at flank speed. Their departure was so hasty that several small Marine units that should have been landed were still on board and didn't rejoin the division until October 29. Worse still, on August 12 a sizable Japanese force of reinforcements for Guadalcanal was massing at the huge Japanese base of Truk, only a thousand miles away in the Carolines. On Guadalcanal through August and into September there was heavy fighting, continued combat and recon patrolling, strongpoints and beachheads that changed hands several times over, nightly bombing, naval shelling by ships of both sides, and mounting Marine casualties, as well as the first cases of malaria. No wonder Vandegrift had gone over to the defensive before the 7th Marines, and Sergeant Basilone, even got to the 'Canal and the war.

On that first battalion-sized "probing" by Puller and his men on the 'Canal, what would be for many their first firefight, Marine historian Shaw gives us the details: "Puller's battalion ran into Japanese troops bivouacked on the slopes of [Mount] Austen on the 24th [of September] and in a sharp firefight had seven men killed and 25 wounded. Vandegrift sent the 2nd Battalion, 5th Marines, forward to reinforce Puller and help provide the men needed to carry the casualties out of the jungle. Now reinforced, Puller continued his advance, moving down the east bank of the Matanikau. He reached the coast on the 26th as planned, where he drew intense fire from enemy positions on the ridges west of the river. An attempt by the 2nd Battalion, 5th Marines, to cross was beaten back."

Heavy machine guns are defensive weapons that don't usually play much of a role in a probing patrol like this one in rough enemy country, but if this was Basilone's first serious combat, it wasn't dull. What had begun as a "probe" was becoming something else. The 1st Raider Battalion was now involved, and so was Colonel Red Mike Edson, the former Raider who now commanded the 5th Marine Regiment. Vandegrift on the twenty-seventh ordered Edson to take charge of the expanded force that included Puller's fresh but inexperienced battalion. When faulty intelligence caused Red Mike to believe that one of his battalions was advancing when in actuality it had been stopped by Japanese who crossed the river by night, he ordered Puller to take his men by small boats around the enemy flank to land and move inland.

It was a clever tactical idea, but too complicated, and the relatively green 1st Battalion soon found itself cut off on the beach and, covered by gunfire from a convenient American destroyer, was forced to evacuate by sea (Puller himself having gone out in a small boat to the destroyer *Ballard* to make the arrangements and signal back to his men on the beach) and find its way back to the perimeter. The fighting was confused and uncoordinated, and along with the newly arrived 7th Marines (Basilone and his comrades), both the Raiders and the 5th Marines also were forced to pull back from the Matanikau. It was typical of combat at that stage on Guadalcanal that the three-day battle didn't even rate a name. But all the to-ing and fro-ing gained no ground and cost sixty Marine dead and a hundred wounded. The newly arrived Marines were learning, and it was a painful schooling.

Welcome to the war, Manila John.

3

In September 1942, a month after the fight began, Manila John and the 7th Marines finally left Samoa, sailing in convoy to join up with the other two Marine regiments fighting on Guadalcanal. For Basilone's arrival at the war we have to turn from the historian Henry Shaw to Basilone's sister Phyllis Basilone Cutter's serialized newspaper account, written well after the fact and by a civilian who didn't seem to understand the difference between the 7th Marine Regiment, which was John's outfit, and the 7th Marine Division, which never existed, then or now. Such criticism may seem trivial and somewhat hard on a family member, but since numerous articles, one monograph, and a hardcover book have been published that are to an extent reliant on Phyllis's recollections, an analysis of her work is justified. Here then, caveats established, is how she describes, supposedly in her brother's words, the time just before he reached the island: "The Japs were putting reinforcements in nightly and now the talk was maybe our boys would be driven off the island and into the sea. We could not understand where our Navy was. Why couldn't they have stopped the Jap transports? We didn't know our Navy had taken quite a beating, even though they won the sea battle, the losses were costly and the Japs were still pouring in." If John here is referring to the battle of Savo Island, our Navy didn't win the sea battle; it had been massacred, losing four heavy cruisers.

"Suddenly on Friday morning September 18, 1942, the loudspeakers blared," Basilone recalled on the transport, "'All Marines go to your debarkation stations!' We climbed the narrow ladders to positions on the deck above the cargo nets draped over the side and heard the squeaking of the davits as they were swung out and landing craft lowered. The whole length of the ship was swarming with Marines scrambling down the nets into the boats. One by one the boats scooted off to the rendez-vous areas where they awaited, circling. Breaking out of the tight circles, wave after wave sped for the beach.

"Our landing was unopposed and we poured in."

Marine Ops reports simply, "The reinforced 7th Marines unloaded its 4,262 men," as three other transports, also peacefully, delivered aviation fuel, ammo, engineering equipment, and the like along the same tranquil stretch of coastline.

Phyllis's account of her brother's landing makes it sound dramatic, while the official account dismisses it as a mere "unloading." Her newspaper series, with Basilone now ashore on the embattled island, then wanders into pulp magazine fiction, and it seems reasonable to suggest that some of the Basilone lore about his combat experiences from this point on derives from his sister's fanciful journalism and not necessarily from the facts. If there are Marines and others who question any of Basilone's feats of arms, they should consider that the man himself wasn't making these absurd claims; it was his loving sister many years later who conjured up the theatricals.

A week would pass before the 1st Battalion, 7th Marines, was sent into concerted action (on September 24), in the so-called probe by Chesty Puller, as recounted by Shaw. With so many men involved and in rough country, there surely must have been a few earlier skirmishes and spontaneous firefights and shelling. But

Phyllis has young Johnny Basilone, new to battle, starting to take over the war. Still quoting her brother: "This was the morning of the 24th [a week or so after their landing] and after about five hours of the toughest trail-breaking imaginable, we halted for a breather. Our advance scouts sent word back that a heavy patrol of Japs was on the trail ahead. We had not expected to encounter the enemy this side of the Matanikau River."

Here is where the writing really takes glorious flight: "Captain Rodgers [the company commander, it appears] felt we could try to entrap this patrol by encircling them with a ring of machine gun fire. At the same time being fully aware of the enemy's reputation for trickery, he decided he would call on the 2nd Marines for help. Calling me to his side, the Captain said, 'Sergeant, take three machine gun crews up to try and clean up that nest of Japs.'"

This entire passage is ridiculous. Marine company commanders issue their orders through their lieutenants, not their machine-gun sergeants, unless in extreme circumstances. Why would a Marine officer send out three heavily burdened machine-gun crews in thick jungle country to encircle or ambush anybody, especially a number of enemy troops described as "a heavy patrol"? They would send lighter-burdened, faster-moving riflemen, possibly a four-man fire team or squad, depending on the situation. Once the riflemen located the enemy, the machine guns could be brought up or sited on high ground to support an assault on the enemy with overhead fire. To use heavily laden machine-gun crews as scouts far out ahead of the swifter riflemen goes against reason.

And no Marine captain would confide to a sergeant that he was about to go outside the chain of command and his own battalion commander to ask yet another regiment, the 2nd Marines, to back him up—especially not with a battalion commander as fearsome as the terrible-tempered Puller.

The rest of Phyllis's account has Basilone wiping out enemy soldiers right and left. He had been a week on the island, and already "all the newness was worn off by now. We were dirty, tired and mean." The generally sensible Bruce W. Doorly, in his monograph about Basilone, the privately published *Raritan's Hero*, seems to have bought into the Phyllis Cutter version in his own variation on the incident:

"A U.S. patrol had spotted a small group of Japanese on a scouting mission. John was told to bring three machine gun crews and wipe out the enemy, hopefully leaving no survivors that would bring information back to enemy headquarters. Guadalcanal was jungle with low visibility. John and his group snaked their way quietly [dragging those heavy guns?] toward the location where the U.S. patrol had seen the Japanese. Luckily the Marines spotted them undetected. Basilone led the group, moving in closest to observe that the Japanese had stopped to eat, obviously unaware of his presence. Moving back toward his men, John instructed them to set up in a half-circle around the unsuspecting enemy. He cleared his forehead, wiped his eyes. Then started firing his machine gun. The rest of his group also opened fire. John observed the Japanese reacting as they were shot. He later said, 'They seemed to be dancing up and down. I forgot to realize the impact of heavy bullets was jerking them into all sorts of crazy contortions.'"

The new-to-combat Marines had been warned about treachery and enemy tricks, playing dead, for one. "John decided to take no chances. He walked around, finishing off the enemy, making sure they were dead by firing a short burst from his machine gun. One of John's men, Bob Powell, said, 'Jesus, Sarge, what the hell are you doing? Why waste ammo on dead ones?' Just as Bob finished his words, a supposedly dead Japanese soldier jumped up with his gun in hand. Another of John's men quickly shot him down."

Wrote Doorly, "On the way back to camp two of his men got sick. This was everyone's first taste of war. They were very fortunate . . . they suffered no casualties."

While Doorly's version of that first real firefight is more controlled than that of sister Phyllis, there appears to be a need here among Basilone chroniclers, fans if you will, to make him even from the very start somewhat larger than life, bigger, braver, deadlier. But neither account of a first Guadalcanal firefight by Basilone rings true.

Manila John needed none of this tarting up. He was an authentic hero, the real goods. He was a warrior who fought with an extraordinary courage and resolve, with strength and an instinctive canniness far beyond what might be expected of a man of his background and age (he was twenty-five at Guadalcanal), killing a lot of seasoned enemy troops, and he would be rewarded by a nation with medals and gratitude. But people apparently felt they had to create a Basilone of their own, to concoct and exaggerate, regardless of the hard reality, however difficult it was to ascertain entirely who John really was. And phony yarns gained currency, when really there was no need, only this compulsion to inflate and imagine. It may be that units of Puller's battalion, possibly including John and some of his gunners under Captain Rodgers, did actually stumble across some Japanese carelessly eating lunch without any perimeter security and wiped them out with machine-gun fire, but it borders on the fantastic to accept that the action came about when a machine-gun unit was sent on a combat patrol unaccompanied by riflemen, or that one of Puller's captains would breach the chain of command, asking support from another regiment. And in a machine-gun platoon, their sergeant doesn't have "his" machine gun. He directs the fire of others. But here Basilone does most of the firing himself. In that far-fetched "first fight," if it ever happened, the legend of Manila John began to emerge.

He and his gunners were certainly part of that very real and quite bloody "probe" by Puller's battalion in which the Marines took 160 casualties. But with versions of the incident surfacing here and there that have the Japanese caught at lunch, you have to consider the possibility that Basilone had gotten through at least one efficient if rather one-sided firefight *before* Puller's battalion completed its somewhat screwed-up first probe.

Battle, especially for green troops, is always confused, chaotic, frightening, and few men remember its details in precisely the same way. Quite possibly not even Manila John, still new to combat, could tell you precisely what happened in his first firefight and when. The problem is simply that the vision of Basilone wielding a fifty-pound heavy machine gun delivering the coup de grâce to wounded enemy soldiers, firing bursts into their prone bodies, is patently absurd. No Marine with any combat experience will fail to recognize gaps in the narrative. And there is no mention of the incident in Shaw or *Marine Ops*.

There would be more heavy fighting for the lately arrived Marines on October 9 when they crossed the Matanikau River and attacked north. In a three-day fight Puller's battalion (with Basilone) and other units were credited with killing or wounding 799 members of the Japanese 4th Infantry. General Alexander Vandegrift knew the Japanese were building up for a major offensive—reinforcements were being landed on the 'Canal almost every night under cover of darkness—yet another attempt to retake Henderson Field, as the Marines had named their captured Japanese airfield (to honor Marine pilot Captain Lofton R. Henderson, killed flying against the Japanese fleet at Midway).

As has long been Marine infantry philosophy, Vandegrift intended to use constant aggressive combat patrols, raids, and probes in force to upset Japanese plans, unbalance the enemy, render it more difficult for them to build up and attack in great force. Of Basilone's regiment, the official USMC operations history notes, "In the short time that men of the 7th Marines had been ashore on the island, they had earned a right to identification as veteran troops. So with a complete combat-wise Marine Division of three infantry regiments, the 1st, 5th, and 7th by now on hand, plus an artillery regiment, the 11th—and Army reinforcements on the way [their good 164th Infantry commanded by Colonel Robert Hall was already on the island and being gradually fed into the line]—Vandegrift and his staff made plans to meet the strong Japanese attack that was bearing down on them." It would likely be a defensive battle with General Vandegrift and his officers relying on heavy machine guns, such as those of Basilone's platoon.

Thus was the situation in mid-October, the awful terrain and even the weather, with two powerful forces roughly in balance and about to clash, as summed up in the *History of U.S. Marine Corps Operations in World War II*, volume 1. The Japanese moved toward Henderson Field along the jungle track named, rather grandly, the "Maruyama Trail," for their apparently vain new general, scratched out of the inhospitable bush by Japanese engineers. At the terminal of the trail Japanese troops would assemble for their assault on what would come to be known as Bloody (or Edson's) Ridge, where Puller's battalion and other Marine units would make their stand. From *Marine Ops* here is the situation from the enemy's point of view: "Heavy rain fell almost every day. The van of the single-file advance often had completed its day's march and bivouacked for the night before the rear elements were able to move. Troops weakened on their half-ration of rice. Heavy artillery pieces [vital to the siege tactics lying ahead] had to be abandoned along the route, and mortars also became too burdensome to manage. Frequently unsure of their exact location in the jungle, the Japanese by 19 October still had not crossed the upper Lunga, and Maruyama [their new commander] postponed his assault until the 22nd. Meanwhile, General Sumiyoshi's fifteen 'Pistol Petes' [Japanese aircraft] pounded the Lunga perimeter, air attacks continued, and Imperial warships steamed brazenly into Sealark Channel almost every night to shell the airfield, beaches, and Marine positions."

Now, from our side's vantage point, according to *Marine Ops*: "The tempo of action was obviously building up for the counteroffensive, and Marines and soldiers worked constantly to improve their field fortifications and keep up an aggressive patrol schedule. Patrols did not go far enough afield however to discover Maruyama's wide-swinging enveloping force, and recons to the east found no indications of a Japanese build-up on that flank. Thus General Vandegrift and his staff were aware only of Sumiyoshi's threat along the coast from the west. There the first probe came on 20 October."

It was in the Bloody Ridge area on the Lunga River line that the Japanese began testing the Marine lines and outposts, searching for soft spots and lack of security, with infantry patrols and a few tanks. An early probe on the west bank of the Matanikau turned back when one tank was hit by 37mm fire from the 3rd Battalion, 1st Marines. For weeks General Hyakutake had tried but failed to take Henderson Field and so end the thing, and now a new general, Maseo Maruyama, who had flown in to command the 17th Japanese Army, was determined that this offensive would be successful. He was confident he would retake the airfield and swing the battle for Guadalcanal his way. He commanded a famous Japanese outfit, the crack Sendai Division freshly arrived from the big enemy base of Rabaul, to spearhead the effort, and at noon on October 24 he issued a battle order that contained an ominous, if somewhat grandiose, sentence: "In accordance with plans of my own, I intend to exterminate the enemy around the airfield in one blow."

One of the units waiting for him, and for that menacing "one blow," was Chesty Puller's 1st Battalion of the 7th Marines.

4

On the twenty-third, the Japanese attack on the Matanikau River had been beaten back, the attackers cut to pieces. Ironically, 1st Marine Division commanding officer Alexander Vandegrift wasn't even on Guadalcanal during the crucial fighting of October 23–25. Instead, he was in Noumea for a meeting with Admiral "Bull" Halsey. In his stead, Major General Roy Geiger, though an aviator, but being senior man on board, was left in command. And Geiger knew that despite the enemy's appalling losses of the twenty-third, they would be coming back, however many times it took. That was how the Japanese operated and one reason they were so formidable. Everyone knew the little airfield was at stake, the battle was now in the balance and could swing either way—and with it might go the entire Guadalcanal campaign.

At sea the heavyweights were also squaring up. Admiral William "Bull" Halsey, having succeeded a dilatory commander (Robert Ghormley), was now running the overall Guadalcanal campaign, land and sea, and senior Marine officers who knew his hard-charging reputation were delighted. With Halsey on the case, the Navy and Washington itself would be paying attention to a distant front too often on short rations and a slim budget. Halsey and his fleet were now at sea following the parley at Noumea, steaming toward the Solomons with two carriers, two battleships, nine cruisers, and twenty-four destroyers. Arrayed against them, Admiral Isoroku Yamamoto, Japan's top naval commander, had sailed with four carriers, five battleships, fourteen cruisers, and forty-four destroyers. Aircraft from both sides were up. Clearly some sort of major clash of arms was coming, on the island and in the air and sea above and around it.

Chesty Puller's 1st Battalion of the 7th Marines had a mile and a half of ridgeline front to defend. Such a long front held by a single Marine rifle battalion, a thousand men or so, was painfully stretched, with little depth. Out in front of the main line of resistance, the MLR, Chesty had a few outposts, and he was nervous about those. The 2nd Battalion of the regiment (my own outfit eight years later in North Korea), commanded on the 'Canal by Colonel Herman Hanneken, had been pulled out of the line guarding Henderson Field on the south and sent toward the Matanikau, which was why Puller was spread so thin. Hanneken, a former enlisted Marine, soft-spoken but dangerous, an officer who would himself pull a weapon (Mitchell Paige in his book reports that Hanneken once shot a sniper out of a tree with a single shot from a handgun), had previously fought side by side with Puller, the two men so very different in style and temperament but both of them fighters.

Robert Leckie in his *Challenge for the Pacific*, describes Puller's demeanor before the battle as he worked to get everyone in the battalion except the mortarmen up into the thin green line of his lightly held front: "In the morning and afternoon [of October 24] Puller roved his lines, chomping on his cold stump of pipe, removing it to bellow orders ('We don't need no communications system,' his men boasted, 'we got Chesty!'), or speaking through teeth clamped firmly around the stem. Puller's manner was urgent because a young Marine who had fallen behind a patrol that morning had seen Japanese officers studying his position through field glasses. Puller urged his men to dig deeper, but when he came to one position he pulled his pipe from his mouth, pointed at the hole with it, and grunted: 'Son, if you dig that hole any deeper, Ah'll have to charge you with desertion.'" The Marine grinned, and Puller strode on, pleased to see that Manila John Basilone had fortified his "pair of machine guns almost in the exact center of the line."

This is an interesting moment. Leckie, who fought on Guadalcanal and later wrote about it, may have recorded the first interaction of Puller, the legendary battalion commander, with Basilone, the machine-gun sergeant. Marine battalion commanders usually know, or know of, most of their men at least by sight, but such precise recognition by a colonel of a single sergeant on the eve of battle is hardly typical. Given that machine guns play such a crucial role in a battalion's tactics on defense, however, Puller would understandably take more than a casual interest in Basilone and the placement of his weapons. In any event, that is what Leckie reports happened early in the day of what would be, for Manila John, the climactic moment of his young life, and for the colonel, one of the epic combat commands of the war so far. And for anyone who questions just how professional a Marine Basilone had been, that perfect positioning of his guns is telling.

In the Marine Corps a battalion commander holding a defensive line is personally responsible for the location of all of his machine guns. No platoon commander or even company commander has that responsibility, and certainly no sergeant. But here we have the veteran Puller with all his combat savvy, his Navy Crosses, his experience in the "Banana Wars," approving Basilone's placement of his machine guns at precisely the right spot. Where did Manila John pick up that much tactical know-how? Maybe the son of a peaceful Italian tailor in Raritan was just an instinctive warrior. Back home, at Gaburo's Laundry or the country club's caddy shack, who would have thought?

Unknown to the Americans, Japanese general Maruyama had issued orders for the attacking assault troops to jump off against the Marine line of resistance that afternoon at five p.m. Leckie continues reporting on Puller's behavior as the fight neared: "Colonel

Puller returned to his 'command post'—not much of a place but simply a field telephone hardly ten yards behind his line—to repeat his request for permission to withdraw his outpost platoon. He was convinced the enemy was coming, and he feared that the forty men on outpost would be needlessly sacrificed. But his argument— couched in ungentle roars—was unavailing. The men stayed outside the line. "Finally, Puller had all of the field phones opened so that every company and platoon could hear every message. And then the rain came down."

To those of us who open umbrellas when the first drop falls, the sheer weight, volume, and shattering noise of a tropical rain squall is likely beyond our experience. The rain blurred vision and intensified the jungle gloom. Under its battering, men blinked and ducked, squinting as daylight turned to premature dusk, the ground beneath their feet becoming slippery and then viscous slime, and soon sucking, clotting mud. The rain fell that afternoon not only on the Marines but on the Japanese preparing their offensive. And the newly arrived General Maruyama had no conception of what the downpour might do to confuse and disconcert a large body of troops traveling by foot through hard country on their approach march to battle in dense jungle conditions and fading light.

Five o'clock came and went without the scheduled and anticipated attack. It's possible to imagine the thoughts of rain-soaked Marines as they waited for their rendezvous with the enemy and with their own fate. The 7th Marines knew the quality of the Japanese troops they were fighting, and were by now reasonably confident of their own abilities and resources; John Basilone's tactical placement of his guns was evidence of how Puller's battalion had matured to veteran status.

Combat soldiers can rarely agree on just what happened and when in a firefight. And consequently there exist different versions of just what Basilone and his machine gunners did and how they performed in the crucial battle about to commence.

5

Can a single night define a man's entire life? There are a half dozen accounts of just what John Basilone did that Saturday night on Guadalcanal on October 24, 1942, some conflicting, others confused and contradictory. Let's assess them all and pass our own judgments. But take in and remember what his battalion commander, Lieutenant Colonel Lewis B. "Chesty" Puller, believed he saw and to which he later attested in his recommendation for a medal. You may even choose to argue with Chesty, although few Marines would.

Here is the situation. Late in the afternoon the 1st Battalion, 7th Marines, learned they were not only facing General Tadashi Sumiyoshi's command but another, and unexpected, flanking move by Maseo Maruyama, when an enemy officer was spotted on high ground south of the airport studying Bloody Ridge with field glasses, and then a scout-sniper report came in from that same quarter of "many rice fires" two miles south of Puller's extended line. *Marine Ops* acknowledges that at this moment, with the fight not yet begun, the Marines seemed to hold a significant advantage in heavy weapons. As noted, the Japanese had left behind, strewn along the difficult Maruyama Trail, all of their heavy artillery and had even discarded most of their mortars. While the entrenched Marines were supported by all of their own mortars and heavier guns, there was some early hope of moonlight to aid the gunners in zeroing in on enemy targets. But though the rains slackened briefly toward seven p.m. (according to Robert Leckie), heavy rains came again and full darkness settled in on the front. Yet it was then that Maruyama ordered his left-flank regiment, the 29th Infantry, forward toward the main line of resistance.

Leckie reports that Sergeant Ralph Briggs Jr. called in from the outpost and reached Puller. Speaking softly, Briggs said, "Colonel, there's about three thousand Japs between you and me."

"Are you sure?"

"Positive. They've been all around us, singing and smoking cigarettes, heading your way."

"All right, Briggs, but make damned sure. Take your men to the left—understand me? Go down and pass through the lines near the sea. I'll call 'em to let you in. Don't fail, and don't go in any other direction. I'll hold my fire as long as I can."

"Yes, sir," Briggs said, and hung up. Crawling on their bellies to the left, he and most of his forty-six outpost men got out. The Japanese caught and killed four of them. This was about nine-thirty p.m. Soon the enemy had reached the tactical barbed wire in front of the 1st Battalion and began to cut lanes through it.

Toward eleven o'clock, still in heavy rain, the main body of the Japanese force attacked Puller's line amid the usual screaming of "Blood for the Emperor!" and "Marines, you die!"

The Marines responded with, "To hell with your goddamned emperor!" and, hilariously, "Blood for Franklin and Eleanor!"

Writing years later in New Jersey, Bruce Doorly provides us a first mention of Basilone that crucial night about ten o'clock: "The field phone rang. Having waited for days, they thought it must be just another outpost getting lonely. However, when John answered the phone he heard trouble. It was one of his men from a post closer to the front line. He screamed, 'Sarge, the Japs are coming.' In the background John could hear the sound of explosions and gun fire. 'Thousands of them, my God! They just keep coming, Sarge, they just keep coming.' The phone went dead."

This reputed exchange doesn't entirely make sense. Basilone headed a two-machine-gun section of perhaps six or eight men total. Why would he have an outpost of his own reporting to him? Wouldn't an outpost Marine with the enemy that close have whispered and not screamed?

Doorly then writes, "John Basilone took control. He turned to his men and said, 'All right, you guys, don't forget your orders. The Japs are not going to get through to the field. I'm telling you that goes, no matter what!'"

Doorly cites battle descriptions by Basilone that "were often very descriptive and at times comical." Doorly pictures the first assault wave this way: "They could soon hear the Japanese cutting the barbed wire. Unfortunately, they could not see the Japanese in the dark as they had hoped. Their first line of defense, the barbed wire, was already falling. Basilone set the strategy for his unit. He told his men to let the enemy get within fifty yards and then, 'let them have it!' They fired at the first group of attacking Japanese, successfully wiping them out." He quotes Basilone as saying, "The noise was terrific and I could see the Japs jumping as they were smacked by our bullets. Screaming, yelling, and dying all at the same time. Still they came, only to fall back, twisting and falling in all sorts of motions, as we dispatched them to their honorable ancestors."

That first enemy charge was only the beginning of the overall attack. The enemy charged again. The dead began to pile up. "One thing you've got to give the Japanese, they were not afraid to die, and believe me, they did," Basilone is quoted as saying. Grenades flew into the Marine lines and "one Japanese soldier got to within five feet of Basilone—here Basilone used his pistol, killing the attacker."

Leckie picks up Basilone's fight:

"Now the attack was veering toward dead center. The Japanese hordes were rushing at Manila John Basilone's machine guns. They came tumbling down an incline and Basilone's gunners raked them at full-trigger. They were pouring out five hundred rounds a minute. The gun barrels were red and sizzling inside their water jackets—and the precious cooling water was evaporating swiftly. 'Piss in 'em. Piss in 'em!' Basilone yelled and some of the men got up to refill the jackets with a different liquid.

"The guns stuttered on, tumbling the onrushing Japanese down the incline, piling them up so high that by the time the first enemy flood had begun to ebb and flow back into the jungle, they had blocked Basilone's field of fire. In the lull Manila John ordered his men out to push the bodies away and clear the fire lanes. Then he ducked out of the pit to run for more ammunition. He ran barefoot, the mud squishing between his toes. He ran into Puller's CP and ran back again, burdened with spare barrels and half a dozen 14-pound belts slung over his shoulders."

By now, the enemy was drifting west, overrunning the guns to Basilone's right. "They stabbed two Marines to death and wounded three others. They tried to swing the big Brownings on the Americans but they only jammed them. They left the [gun] pit and drove further to the rear. Basilone returned to his pit just as a runner dashed up gasping. 'They've got the guys on the right.' Basilone raced to his right. He ran past a barefoot private named Evans and called 'Chicken' for his tender eighteen years. 'C'mon you yellow bastards!' Chicken screamed, firing and bolting his rifle, firing and reloading. Basilone ran on to the empty pit, jumped in, found the guns jammed and sprinted back to his own pit. Seizing a mounted machine gun, Basilone spread-eagled it across his back, shouted at half of his men to follow him—and was gone."

It must be noted here that a "mounted machine gun," the gun and tripod mount, exclusive of ammo, weighs 49.75 pounds—the gun 31 pounds, the tripod, pintle, traversing, and elevating mechanisms the rest—not including the 14-pound belts of ammo, and Manila John was running around in the rain and mud lugging this thing on his bare back. As Basilone and his squad ran they blundered into a half dozen Japanese and killed them all. Then, at the pit, Basilone dropped one gun and lay flat on his back trying to unjam the other guns and get them working again. It isn't clear here (via Leckie) just how many machine guns he had by now, two or three.

By one-thirty in the morning Basilone had the guns fixed. And by now the Sendai Division was attacking once more. Puller phoned the artilleryman Colonel Pedro del Valle for support and was told the big guns were running short of ammo and when what they had was fired there would be no more shells for tomorrow. Puller informed the artilleryman coldly, an infantryman chiding a gunner, "If they get through here tonight, there won't be a tomorrow." And when a Captain Regan Fuller told Puller he was running out of small-arms ammo, Puller responded, "You've got bayonets, haven't you?" "Sure, yes, sir." "All right then, hang on."

The fight went on all night despite the staggering loss of life, especially on the attackers. Bit by bit American Army soldiers were fed into the cauldron as reinforcements for the Marines, firing the new eight-shot semiautomatic Garand rifles the Marines had not yet been issued (they were still armed with the five-cartridge-clip, bolt-action World War I '03 Springfield). There was a wonderful exchange between Puller and his Army counterpart Colonel Robert Hall, who arrived at Puller's post, guided through the darkness by a Navy chaplain named Father Keough who was ministering to his Marines. Puller thanked the cleric for his assistance and then turned to Colonel Hall. Leckie gives us this dialogue: "Colonel, I'm glad to see you. I don't know who's senior to who right now, and I don't give a damn. I'll be in command until daylight, at least, because I know what's going on here and you don't."

Said the sensible Hall, "That's fine with me."

6

Fresh troops were arriving, but the deadly night was decidedly not yet finished, and Manila John Basilone was still fighting. Using the heavy machine gun cradled in his arms, apparently still attached to the tripod, he killed several infiltrating Japanese, the hot barrel burning him as he did so. At another point some enemy infantry were wriggling toward him on their bellies through the long grass. To get lower and in a more effective firing position, Basilone took the big heavy off its tripod and steadied it in his arms, his own belly flat to the ground, and from that prone position fired bursts as low as he could to chop down the Japanese snaking toward him. As he later remarked, he had "mowed down the crawlers." At the same time the professional machine gunner who knew the gun better than most, in the dark, in the rain, and in combat, continued coolly to instruct his men on using the other guns, finding a jammed gun and reminding them, almost pedantically, "the head spacing is out of line." This is pretty cool stuff under fire, as the Japanese mounted yet another charge, shouting their banzais as they came. One Marine, perhaps not yet a true believer, asked Basilone as the long, exhausting night wore on, increasingly lethal, "Sarge, how long can we keep this up?"

According to Bruce Doorly, Basilone himself was wondering the same thing. And ironically, considering the downpours, they were short of drinking water, some canteens holed by shrapnel, with Marines running dry.

"The attacks kept coming, even in the heavy rain. John told two of his uninjured soldiers, Powell and Evans, to keep the heavy machine guns loaded. He would roll to one machine gun and fire until it was empty, then roll over to the other one that had been loaded while he was firing the first one. When that one was empty he went back to the first one which had now been reloaded. The tactic was used against the remaining Japanese attacks. Just when the Marines could not keep up the pace any longer, the Japanese would retreat to regroup. The enemy would then predictably charge again, in groups of 15 or 20, Basilone letting them get close and then mowing them down. As they were hit, screams filled the night.

"Another Japanese soldier managed to sneak up to their position and jumped right at them with a knife. Again, John got him with his pistol [it must have been a .45, the standard-issue side-arm for a machine-gun sergeant]. The pistol would see more action through the night, as it was the best weapon for those who crept in close by crawling. Some grenades exploded close to John and his fellow Marines, but none hit them. It was a long night and some of the early kills started to decompose. It brought on a nasty stench."

This sounds to me like rather rapid decomposition, but it was, after all, the tropics and these were the dead.

"Later in the night, Basilone saw an incredible sight. The Japanese had taken their dead and piled them up high in front of them to form a wall to protect the living Japanese soldiers who set up their machine guns behind the pile of their dead comrades. To counter the new enemy 'wall,' John decided to move his position to get a better angle. Later, in a break in the fighting, John sent one of his men to push over the wall of dead bodies."

It's worth noting that Bob Leckie has the Japanese bodies piling like a wall in the course of action, while Doorly has them being piled up deliberately. According to Robert V. Aquilina, head of the Marine Corps History Division reference branch at Quantico, and Colonel Walt Ford of *Leatherneck* magazine, there is ample historical precedent, going back to antiquity, for the former, and the piles would have included dying as well as dead enemy soldiers. As for the latter, yes, it could well have happened, but Colonel Ford suggests that it's "more the sort of detail that somebody only knows from having been there." Such variations are illustrative of the challange inherent in accurately reporting accounts of battle—the so-called "fog of war."

By three a.m. the Marines were once more running short of ammo. And the Japanese kept coming. Here is what Basilone's nephew Jerry Cutter and writer Jim Proser have to say about what Basilone did that night, the genuine heroism he displayed, the losses of men close to him that he suffered. While much of their book is inaccurate and somewhat misleading, it does convey something of the chaos and has its moments: "Evans fed the ammo and tried to keep mud off the belts. He also kept an eye on the rear of our position where we turned our .45s on the Japs coming up behind us. A hail of TNT and grenades fell all around us and our ears rang from the explosions so we couldn't hear ourselves yelling from inches away. The concussion was like getting socked in the head by a heavyweight and made it hard to keep your vision clear."

Basilone knew about being "socked," having boxed, often against harder-hitting men. Proser wrote, quoting Basilone, "We were seeing double, and things were moving around. So that we couldn't draw a clear bead on a target. The dead piled up in front of us obscuring the firing lanes. Both guns jammed. I tore mine open and cleared the receiver of mud. Powell did the same. In the process, Evans yelled just in time and we shot two more Japs coming at us from behind. Garland was frantically trying to clean the mud off the belts but it was tough work. We were getting low again on ammo and were out of water completely. The water jackets were smoking again which meant they were low or out of water too. If we didn't get water for the guns the barrels would burn out and never last the night. I got mine firing again but I was hitting only corpses piled high in front of us and others hanging on the wire further back."

"Hanging on the wire." The lethal phrase may sound innocent, meaningless, but men "hanging on the wire" are usually dead attackers, shot to pieces by the machine guns of the defense. The war doesn't matter—the trenches of Flanders in the Great War, so many other infantry battles in World War II. Maybe Grant's and Lee's men had to clear the dead as well. The first dead men I ever saw in combat, five or six North Koreans, were "hanging on the wire" of snow-covered Hill 749 in November 1951. Basilone's and Powell's and Evans's and Garland's dead happened to be Japanese of the Sendai Division. And when there are too many of them obscuring your aim, it is the gunners who have just killed them who are forced to do the undertaking as well, the tidying up of corpses. Listen to what are said to be Basilone's words:

"I ordered Garland to go down and clear the firing lanes. He looked at me and I looked back at him. It could easily be a suicide mission. The latest assault backed off. I didn't have to tell Garland twice. He was up and out of the hole. Evans and I covered him in bursts of fire that kept the field clear on either side of him. He slid down the hill on his butt and pushed the piles of bodies over with his feet, keeping his head below the pile. That did the trick. He slid over to another pile and did the same maneuver. We had a clear field of fire again. He slithered back up the hill while we sent streams of bullets a few inches over his head. For the life of me I didn't know why we hadn't been cross-haired by artillery and concentrated mortar fire by now, but I guess that's where luck comes into it."

Obviously John wasn't aware of all those heavier weapons discarded by the enemy struggling through the jungle along the Maruyama Trail and unable to keep moving under the load. If that was luck, it was what infantrymen pray for, who know the damage good artillery and big mortars can do to men in trenches or foxholes open to the sky and vulnerable to the vertical fall of high-trajectory weapons.

"Garland got back in the hole. I was out of ammo. The boys all needed water as well as the guns. Powell was back on duty sighting down the ridge [with machine guns the most effective killing fire is not straight ahead but across the front, *along* the ridgeline, hitting the enfiladed attackers on their flanks]. The latest wave had retreated. I had to make another run for ammo, and this time for water, too. Down the ridge, there was movement. The Japs had almost the same idea I did. They crept up to the piles of their dead comrades and pulled them on top of each other like sandbags. They had a machine gun up behind the human barricade.

"'Move out,' I ordered. We scraped our weapons out of the mud and hopped out to the left to get an angle on the new advance position of the enemy. Within a few minutes, they had our hole cross-haired and landed mortars on the bulls-eye, but we weren't there anymore [so the Japanese had gotten a few mortars up the Maruyama Trail after all]. We concentrated fire on the new position and wiped out the gunners. There was no fire coming from Bullard's hole over to the left, and I led what was left of my squad over there. When we got there, all my boys were dead. We pulled Bullard and the rest out and took up firing positions in the new hole. The field phone was still open to the CP and I called in our situation—no water, no ammo, the position to our right flank was now out of the fight. We were all that remained of C Company." This surely is an exaggeration, as along the length of an extended company front of perhaps eight hundred yards, no one machine gunner would know his entire company was gone. And according to post-battle casualty reports, the assertion that C Company had been wiped out is false.

"I told Powell, 'If I ain't back in ten minutes, put an ad in the paper for me.' I left the three in the new hole and took off again toward the rear.

"Sniper and mortar fire was constant now and half the time I couldn't tell if the shadows across my path were enemy or not [*what shadows at night in heavy rain?*]. I just kept running. A grenade or mortar knocked me to the ground but didn't knock any more holes in me that I could tell. I was bleeding from several places but none seemed too serious. I got up again and kept moving."

Again there are contradictions here. As for his being hit several times and "bleeding from several places," other accounts marvel that Basilone came out of the fight surprisingly unscathed. Bruce Doorly writes that when Basilone and his remaining men left the field next day to rest, Basilone "realized he had not eaten for 72 hours" and at Henderson Field wolfed down what they had, crackers and jam, and ate them "like it was Thanksgiving dinner." There is no mention of seeking out a corpsman and having his "wounds" treated. The records show no Purple Heart being awarded Basilone. Mitch Paige, in contrast, was awarded both decorations in the continuing fight the next night.

Basilone's account, via Cutter and Proser, goes on: "At the ammo depot I pried open ammo boxes and draped six of the fourteen pound ammo belts [about eighty pounds!] over my shoulders. I picked up another of the boxes and started moving out. Then I remembered the water. I was a fully loaded mule and couldn't do much better than a fast walk with all the weight hanging on me. I passed the CP and called in for water. Someone came out and draped a few canteens on belts around my neck."

This is confusing. Puller's CP was previously described as being nothing more than a field phone on the reverse slope of the ridgeline. What was the "out" someone came out of? There were no structures or caves on the ridge that we know of.

Basilone does describe overhearing "Chesty . . . giving hell to someone over the phone." This sounds about right. The Cutter and Proser book continues in Manila John's voice: "I was back onto the trail in the darkness with my heavy coat of bullets banging against my knees, my hands full with the ammo box. I shuffled along as fast as I could. If I ran into Tojo in the dark, I'd have to drop the ammo box to reach my .45 on my hip. I ran behind the ridge crest but that didn't stop sniper fire from whining past my head. They were behind our lines and by the amount of fire, there must have been quite a few of them. I thought, if they can't hit a slow-moving target like me, that must mean my number isn't up, at least not tonight. I soon couldn't think about anything but about somehow making it a few more feet. The whole trip was about six hundred yards and I didn't stop once for a breather. Every thought and scrap of strength I had, was focused on just making a few more feet down the trail. I slipped under the weight several times, covering the belts with mud.

"I made it to the hole and made the call sign, 'Yankee Clipper,' as I came up from the rear so they wouldn't shoot me thinking I was a Jap infiltrator. I dropped what I had, 1500 rounds, and jumped in behind it. Powell was out of ammo on his gun. He grabbed a belt and I took over his trigger just in time. The next wave was on its way up the ridge. With Garland and Evans covering our flanks with their rifles, Powell and I leap-frogged from one gun to the other. The water wasn't nearly enough to fill the water jacket of even one of the guns, so I had to fire one of the guns while the other one cooled, and while Powell cleaned the next ammo belt and reloaded. We were able to keep a fairly constant rate of fire doing this and also make the Japs shift their targeting from our right gun to our left. It was hours after the first attack and they were still coming, wave after wave screaming 'Banzai!' and 'Marine, you die!' and we kept killing them. Evans and Garland threw grenades down the hill until they were barely able to lift their arms [it is unlikely there would have been that many grenades in a single machine-gun position]. The boys drank all the water in the canteens and when they could, pissed into the water jackets. Another wave of men ran up the ridge, broke and died in front of us. Some had gotten through. We could hear the firing to our rear. I wasn't sure our guns would hold up under another attack."

As the night fight continued, Basilone is said to have made yet another run to the rear, a water run, this time to A Company on C Company's flank. "Who the fuck are you?" someone demanded when he called out the password. Typical Marine response. But when Basilone returned to his own position and the guns, "Garland was dead. He was a big boy, a quiet type and brave."

Page 212 of Cutter and Proser's account reports Garland's death as a fact, but Doorly's book lists Garland, with "Powell, Evans and La Pointe," as having been ordered by Basilone the morning after the fight to return to Henderson Field while he remained behind "at his post in order to help the new men," who must have been replacements, during the less severe fighting and mopping up that continued on October 25.

At my request Bob Aquilina at Quantico looked up Garland's "death." He found seven or eight Marines named Garland who died during various Pacific campaigns, but none on Guadalcanal in October 1942. The "death" of Garland remains an enigma.

Young Marine officers and NCOs are taught, "Don't over-identify with your men. Know their military strengths and weaknesses, but not which guy has a kid, or an old gray-haired mother at home. When you send a man out on the point, the riskiest position, you send the best point man, the sharpest-eyed, canniest scout you have. Otherwise, you weren't going to lose just him to enemy action, but maybe your own life."

There was also the inarguable truth that every death of one of your men, a "Garland," tears a piece out of your own psychological hide, diminishes you as surely as one of John Donne's clods: "If a clod be washed away by the sea, Europe is the less." Clearly, as his NCO, Basilone would mourn Marine Garland, his man, his machine gunner. You hear it in his words: "a big boy, a quiet type and brave." We recall his assessment of the man, and the professional: "That night, when I told him to go down the hill, he hesitated just long enough to read my face. He looked to me just long enough to know I wasn't kidding, then off he went." But had Garland really died that night? It remains one of the narrative's puzzles.

Now, unexpectedly, on the twenty-fifth fighting erupted again with new massed Japanese assaults. This time it wasn't Puller's and Basilone's turn but the 2nd Battalion of the same regiment, the 7th Marines, commanded by Lieutenant Colonel Herman Henry Hanneken, that found itself grappling with the attacking Japanese infantry in lethal close combat, and it would be

Mitchell Paige, another, and quite different, machine-gun sergeant whom Basilone actually knew, who would be at the heart of the most horrific fighting and would himself be nominated for a Congressional Medal of Honor. More on that later.

About four on Sunday morning, the twenty-fifth, the Japanese punched another hole in the Marine lines between Basilone's C Company and A Company, but that was the end to his hard fighting for the moment. Proser describes his getting the crackers and the jam, and quotes Basilone as saying of himself and his handful of hungry but surviving men, "We were all wounded." I find no independent proof of this. Customarily, unless a wounded man is treated by a medic (a Navy corpsman) who notes the fact, no Purple Heart is awarded. Myriad cuts, burns (Basilone's scorched arms, for example), and scratches are often ignored, overlooked by the Marine himself. Despite his words about being "wounded," the records indicate he earned only the one Purple Heart for wounds, for those suffered at his death on Iwo Jima on February 19, 1945, some three years later. Nor does his citation for the Medal of Honor mention his being wounded on the 'Canal, which such carefully vetted citations customarily do.

Marine Ops doesn't break out daily USMC casualties for each night of the three-day battle of Bloody Ridge but says "sources" put the entire three-day cost to the 7th Marine Regiment at 182 dead. Basilone's reference to C Company's having been wiped out and his handful of men the only ones left is clearly an exaggeration. And his service record book notes that Basilone "joined Company D, 1st Battalion, 7th Marines May 29, 1941," while Puller's own written citation for the Medal of Honor calls Basilone a member not of C Company but of D Company. It seems to me axiomatic that Puller would know one of his rifle companies from another. And surely Basilone would have no such doubts about his own outfit. Blame confusion in battle, but family and other reminiscences are replete with such perplexing errors of fact.

As for the Japanese, their losses at Basilone's machine-gun position are put at thirty-eight dead by PFC Nash W. Phillips of Fayetteville, North Carolina, who was in Basilone's company on the 'Canal. Total enemy losses on October 23–26 are recorded as 3,500 dead, including one general, Yumio Nasu, and his two regimental commanders. Puller's citation for Basilone's medal (countersigned by Chester Nimitz himself) refers to a thousand dead Japanese buried or left unburied in front of 1st Battalion's position.

7

Basilone's own terrible night was succeeded only hours later by the equally desperate nightlong fight by the 2nd Battalion in which Mitchell Paige distinguished himself and would be written up for a Congressional Medal by his own commanding officer, Colonel Herman Hanneken. In a 1975 book by then Colonel Paige titled *A Marine Named Mitch*, he recalled a temporary lull in the aftermath of the October fighting, including his own, on the Guadalcanal ridgelines: "The next day Chesty Puller came up to see me. He sat down next to me after we shook hands and he told me about the big attack they had down at the airport on the night of the 24th [Paige's own battle was fought late on the twenty-fifth]. He also told me he had just seen Colonel Hanneken at the Division Command Post before he came to visit with me. He told me that he read a report that Colonel Hanneken was preparing, recommending me for a medal. 'Chesty' went on to tell me that that [*sic*] his sergeant was also a machine gunner and that our actions were similar. I said, 'wonderful, is this sergeant someone I may know?' 'I don't know,' he said, 'but his name is Basilone.'

"I said, 'Johnny Basilone?' And he said, 'Yes.' I had made platoon sergeant just before we left the States and I told Chesty that I had recently seen Johnny when we were moving positions and I had asked him when he expected to be made platoon sergeant, and he said soon he hoped. I told Chesty that I hoped this would help Johnny get promoted to platoon sergeant. I had met Johnny originally back in New River, North Carolina, just after he joined the 1st Battalion, 7th Marines. He told me he was better known as 'Manila John,' and then I said, 'you must have been in the Philippines,' and we had a lot to talk about as I told him I had been stationed in Cavite [the big U.S. naval base on Manila Bay] for some time. Johnny had been in the Army and was stationed in Manila, thus the name 'Manila John.' We had a friendly greeting when I would call him 'Doggie Manila John,' and he would jokingly call me 'Cavite Mitch.'"

There are suggestions that in the months between the time both sergeants were "written up" for decorations and the day months later when they actually received their awards (the Medal of Honor) in Australia, someone up the line of command in Washington decided these two enlisted men had legitimate "hero" potential. After all, two Medals of Honor for Guadalcanal heroics had already been awarded to senior officers, and wasn't it time for enlisted men to be recognized for what the Marines had accomplished in handing the Japanese their first defeat since ground fighting began?

John Basilone's sister Phyllis takes up the story in her brother's voice, recounting his telling of what happened on Guadalcanal and how Chesty Puller had recognized not only Paige's but also Basilone's own pivotal role:

"As dawn came, the last frenzied attack, preceded by their now familiar cries, 'Marines you die, Banzai, Marines you die!' By now we were all light-headed as we sent back our songs of death . . . towards the end I had to stand up with my 'chopper' [the heavy Browning] cradled in my arms to fire out over the rising pile of dead. The attack was growing weaker and weaker and suddenly the last desperate charge petered out at the wire. I rested my head on the ledge of the emplacement, weary, tired and grateful the Lord had seen fit to spare me. Then I heard my name being called. Looking up I saw Lieutenant Colonel Puller, my command-ing officer, standing with his arm outstretched. He shook hands with me and said, 'I heard you came back for ammunition. Good work.'"

There was considerable hard fighting left on Guadalcanal for Manila John's outfit, but on the following night, a Sunday, the brunt of it would fall not on Puller but to the east, where Colonel Hanneken and his 2nd Battalion, 7th Marines, fought off another all-night assault by the Japanese, and where Paige, though wounded, held his position as tenaciously as Basilone had.

Basilone has his own, surprisingly modest, count of casualties on the night fight for which he will ever be remembered and on which he won the famous Medal of Honor. Compared to the ear-lier inflated estimate that C Company (of perhaps two hundred men) was "wiped out," the Jerry Cutter and Jim Proser book once again contradicts itself. Here is their quote from Basilone: "In the whole 1/7 [1st Battalion, 7th Marines] we lost 19 boys that night. Another 30 were wounded and 12 were missing." Then John says, "Twelve of my boys were dragged out of the mud that day, some of them in pieces. They were just about everybody I knew on the island." Does this account, supposedly in his words, really make any sense? Nineteen Marines in the entire battalion dead and twelve of them were Basilone's "boys," his machine gunners? Out of the other eight hundred or thousand men in Puller's 1st Battalion, there were only seven Marines killed who didn't work with or for John Basilone? Despite the bloody setback those two nights, the Japanese had not quit.

In postwar depositions in 1946, Japanese senior officers cava-lierly swapped insults and blamed one another for the loss of Guadalcanal, for failures in strategy and tactics during the period of October 23–26, but no one, especially not the Americans, sug-gested the enemy couldn't fight. October phased into November, when there was more bloody combat with both Puller's 1st Battalion (Basilone included) and Hanneken's 2nd (with Mitch

Paige) again engaged in heavy fighting. At sea, the two fleets fought, usually out of sight of the other, trading heavy losses to air attacks. In one battle, seventy-four American planes and more than a hundred Japanese aircraft were lost, warships went down, and the coastal sharks feasted. On land, the fighting ebbed and flowed, men continued to die, and Henderson Field was bombed and shelled and threatened again on the ground, but it never fell.

Tokyo must at last have been having second thoughts about whether this one relatively insignificant island was worth the loss of so many ships, planes, and irreplaceable pilots, to say nothing of thousands of veteran infantry. Gradually as November ran its course, the Japanese brass stopped sending in reinforcements, no longer dispatched their capital ships in harm's way, and in the end began to evacuate. The battle became one of hot pursuit, as the Americans, Marines and soldiers, chased and attempted to trap the remaining enemy infantry. Every Japanese soldier who died on the 'Canal would be one man they wouldn't have to fight on some other hostile shore. There were fewer pitched battles, fewer banzais screamed.

The American Army was in growing numbers taking over the Marine positions, and on December 7, the first anniversary of Pearl Harbor, elements of the 1st Marine Division began leaving the island. The last Japanese to quit Guadalcanal, harried and pursued by American GIs, were evacuated on the night of February 7–8, 1943. No one knows how many died, but sources say more than 14,000, with another 9,000 missing and presumed dead. And these were only the ground forces. Japanese naval and aviation casualties are not included.

The official history of *Marine Ops* compiled the following casualty figures for the 1st Marine Division from the landing on August 7 to early December: 605 officers and men killed in action, 45 died of wounds, 31 MIA and presumed dead, 1,278 wounded in action. Another 8,580 "fell prey to malaria and other tropical diseases." As is often the case in war, illness took more lives than combat.

Speaking of which, as early as October General Alexander Vandegrift at the Noumea conference was already lobbying to get the 1st Marine Division "to a healthier climate" as soon as possible. The Japanese offensive of October 23 and the following days rendered consideration of that a purely academic exercise; the Marines couldn't be spared. But now that the Army had arrived and the Japanese were trying to leave, where the division would go next had become a concern. Phyllis Basilone gives us some insight into her brother's state of mind toward the end there on the 'Canal. Basilone, for all his heroics, was now having nightmares.

During the firefight on the long night of October 24, a lone Japanese soldier somehow broke through their position. Someone shouted, "Look out, Sarge," and Basilone saw the man disemboweled by a Marine's machete and Basilone and his gun were splattered with the man's red blood "and blue guts." Despite all he'd seen and experienced already, this particular incident seemed to have shaken Basilone. According to his sister, he threw up and was trembling uncontrollably. The machete killing was but a single event during a night of such horrors. But this one shocking moment among so many had its impact, coming back to haunt his dreams. The previously imperturbable sergeant was shaken, having trouble sleeping, and haunted by wild dreams of combat, drenched with night sweats and shivering. Was this malaria or what they call battle fatigue? Phyllis tells us that Basilone himself wondered.

The scuttlebutt was that the division was headed for Australia, which, with its "people like us," the girls, the cold beer, and especially the temperate climate, sounded to the Marines like Eden, and especially to Manila John with his tour in the Philippines and memorable R&R in neighboring New Zealand, where the young Americans fell in love with the people and the land. As Basilone waited to ship out, away from the 'Canal and its horrors, he sounded pensive, waxing philosophic, which would be something new for him, a facet of his makeup not previously remarked on at Raritan, the Philippines, or in his Marine experience. Combat can do that.

Listen to Basilone in his sister's account as the troopship carried him and his unit out of the war zone and toward what they expected to be a period of rest, refitting, and getting well: "Looking about me during the long voyage to Australia was heart-rending. Where only a few short months ago they were only boys in their teens, now they appeared old, far beyond their years. Their sunken eyes reflected the pain and misery they had been subjected to. I was no different. My family on seeing me at this moment wouldn't even recognize me. The only thing that kept us from just collapsing on the deck and going into a shell was the gratifying thought we had met the feared enemy, defeated him on his own ground, and poured the flower of his troops back into the earth and sea."

This sounds a bit poetic for Basilone, but his sister goes on with his description: "After a long trip during which we soaked up the sunshine and fresh sea air, with nary a Jap sub to bother us, we dropped anchor off Brisbane, Australia, the city we had been told would be our rest camp." Located on the northeast coast of the continent, it was hundreds of miles closer to the tropics than the other big Aussie cities of Sydney, Canberra, and Melbourne, with their more moderate climate in the country's south. It was hardly the cooler, healthier "temperate" rest camp area Vandegrift had requested.

Some rest. Some camp.

8

D own Under, the Marines might have expected to go "Waltzing
Matilda," but Australia turned out to be a shock to men you'd
think were beyond shock.

"None of us realized the weakened condition we were in,
and that the camp set up outside Brisbane was only temporary,"
Basilone is reported to have said. Instead of a rollicking good liberty
or a more extended leave, the Marines were marched to a hastily
thrown-up military tent city. "We soon learned we were supposed
to set up permanent defense positions along the Australian coast."
Where they would presumably confront a Japanese invasion, if and
when. And this would be along the hot, fevered, mosquito-blown
northern Australian coast, only a hundred miles from New Guinea
where the enemy was already established. In the inverted world of
the Southern Hemisphere, the south was cool, dry, and moderate,
while the north was hot and pestilential like the 'Canal. On top of
that, Australia both needed the Americans and resented them.

Here is John's account of that first, disillusioning view the
Marines would have of their new home, as recorded by Phyllis
Cutter: "Coming all that distance cramped in transports, we could

hardly believe our eyes when we finally marched and were carried into our rest camp. If we bitched about 'tent city' we were sorry. This was even worse. Guadalcanal was paradise compared to this swamp [surely this is typical Gyrene hyperbole!]. Goony birds and mosquitoes made sleep impossible. Our breaking point was not far off. General Vandegrift was furious and after having southern Australia scouted for a more suitable location, he proposed the Division be moved to Melbourne where the climate was cooler and free of the giant mosquitoes. Having decided on the new location, Vandegrift found that the Army could not spare any ships for transporting the men."

Marines are celebrated for the profane eloquence of their wrath, and Vandegrift was a celebrated Marine. These were *his* men who for months had been abiding in hell and, despite everything, had met and defeated the Japanese and captured one of their islands after nearly a year of seeing the Japanese invade and occupy our islands. And now this worn-down, fevered corps of heroes had been billeted in a swamp and barred from more salutary precincts by a lack of Army shipping! The situation did nothing to endear the U.S. Army to the Gyrenes or to their general officer commanding. Alexander Vandegrift's righteous rage swiftly reached the United States Navy, and more to the point, it got to Bull Halsey, a man who appreciated a good exchange of oaths, who on the spot issued orders to send Navy transports to Brisbane to pick up the 1st Marine Division and deliver it to Melbourne. When the Marines out there in the swamp heard the news, they cheered Halsey's name.

Said Basilone, "Our first sight of Melbourne as we docked in the harbor brought tears to our eyes, it seemed so much like home. That is, the home we knew, the Golden Gate in Frisco, the Statue of Liberty in New York Harbor, Chicago on the Great Lakes, St. Louis and the mighty Mississippi. We disembarked and with the Division band in the foreground, we paraded through Melbourne to the cheers of thousands of friendly people. During our march through the city our eyes drank in the sights. We had forgotten what a simple thing like a wide city street looked like."

To men who for months had been slogging through swamps and along narrow jungle trails, such things were startling in their commonplace loveliness, as were the lighted streetlamps of a city not blacked out by night, to say nothing of the dry barracks and clean bunks following the morass of "tent city" Brisbane.

And the girls, the girls! Basilone marveled at them as well. "They weren't jealous like girls back home, they'd simply ask each other if they'd had a nice time. It was a little confusing, don't get me wrong, they were nice girls and wonderful company even if your ego was dropped a bit."

"We had by now gotten over the first flush of liberty," Basilone is quoted as saying, which sounds rather tame considering that, even today when Marines are asked how a liberty weekend had gone, the cheerfully vulgar but standard response might be, "I got screwed, blew-ed, and tattooed." Basilone added that he and his buddies now, for the first time, "began to look around and enjoy the people. They were without question the most honest and sincere people we had ever met. They threw open their homes to us and most of the men took advantage of their generous hospitality. Some of the boys fell in love, some lived with families, especially the boys from the Midwest, who really had a ball. They did all the farm chores and, while exhausted, they enjoyed it."

One local favorite to which the Marines never got accustomed was mutton for breakfast, or pretty much at any meal and anytime. But as Basilone noted, despite mutton, "We were slowly but surely getting back our strength and, with it, our desire to live." Part of that desire, naturally, was sex.

"There were never enough girls to go around and it was a rat race to get a date and hold it. I did pretty well." At this somewhat modest boast from the newly arrived but hardly bashful Marine sergeant, it might be well to go to Basilone's nephew Jerry Cutter on the subject. Cutter quotes Basilone about those early days at Melbourne: "Strangers were buying us drinks, taxicabs gave us free fares and women came out of their houses to meet us. Now the women, what can I say about the women? To begin with they weren't shy. They stood up square to a man and told him straight out what they liked, didn't like, and how they expected things to go. And things certainly did go. One of the things going around camp after that [first] night was, 'what they say about Atabrine [that it rendered a man impotent] ain't true.' One thing I learned about nearly dying is that it gave me a hell of an appetite—for everything. The last time I had anything close to this much sex, I was nineteen years old and paying for it. I ate, drank, and screwed like a wild pig, and didn't feel bad for one second about any of it."

The good times wouldn't roll forever. They lasted, in Basilone's words, "until the Ninth Australian Division returned home from the Middle East. They were a wonderful bunch but you couldn't blame them for flaring up. Here we were solidly entrenched in their homeland, had the market on their women, the corner on money and we spent it, how we spent it, as if there was no end to our supply." After all, for those months on the 'Canal, there was nothing to buy, nowhere to spend a man's pay. "As a result, fights flared up all over town. Many a pub was wrecked in short, furious fist fights. The Aussies were hard fighters, and once we understood their methods, we more than held our own. They were clean fighters in the sense they did not use anything but their fists but they would not fight alone."

Apparently if you duked it out with one Australian, you had to fight every Aussie in the room. "The whole situation was well on its way towards getting entirely out of hand. We got so we wouldn't travel alone. While this cut down on the number of fights, there were still plenty of bad ones. Finally the whole mess was laid before [Marine] General Rupertus. The general, in an effort to ease the situation, decided that the 1st Marine Division would host the Aussies with the biggest party they had ever seen. The only precaution Rupertus took was the directive be issued that the beer was to be served in paper cups. He even had the courage and conviction to order that the MPs not attend. This party, more in the nature of a peace conference, was a huge success. At least ten thousand men attended, half of them Australian. For the occasion, the Melbourne cricket grounds were turned over to both armies. We got to know the Aussies better and believe it or

not the fights in the pubs stopped. Shortly after the 'peace conference,' the Aussie Ninth was pulled out and sent to New Guinea
[where the enemy held perhaps half the vast island, the second
largest in the world]. With all the fuss and fights, we were sorry
to see them go. Our money was getting low and the Aussies were
always good for a beer or two."

Bruce Doorly in his monograph, *Raritan's Hero*, recalls one
of those earlier evenings, before the pacifying beer bust at the
cricket grounds: "One night John got into a situation over a girl
in a bar, with an Australian soldier, John tried to back off but the
other guy would not. Using his boxing experience, John hit him
with a straight left causing the Australian to fall to the floor. He
got back up and came at John again, this time with two of his
friends. Basilone's buddies joined in and a small riot erupted.
Military police got the riot under control relatively quickly."

Considering Basilone's boxing prowess (nineteen wins in nineteen fights at Manila for his Army unit before the war), his fear-
lessness, his appetite for women and their obvious interest in him,
and his adventures in the Marines and civilian life, you wonder at
how few brawls there were. The man was a fighter, in every sense,
but not your usual barroom brawler, bellicose or easily riled. There
was an admirable prudence, the realization that his fists could be
considered lethal weapons, and he disciplined himself in their
use, which probably made him even more effective and dangerous
when he did occasionally lash out.

Wartime Australia, menaced by the Japanese, was hardly a
normal situation for a young soldier from any country. There were
rational and understandable reasons for a love-hate relationship.
The Yanks were here and their own boys weren't. As the Brits put
it when Americans flooded into the United Kingdom by the hundreds of thousands in the buildup to D-Day, "The trouble with the
Yanks is, they're overpaid, oversexed, and over here." The British
understood we were there to help them beat the Germans. That
still didn't make the reality entirely palatable. The Australian situation was analogous. Tens of thousands of young Australians, including their best troops, weren't here facing the Japanese, protecting

their own country, their wives, the kids, and their homes. But the Yanks *were* here, and that wasn't quite the same thing.

"The bloody Japs aren't a hundred miles away across the Torres Strait, their planes are bombing Darwin [on the northern coast], and our lads are half a world away fighting the bloody Eyeties [Mussolini's Italians]." There was considerable truth to all of this. It was late 1942, early 1943, and the Americans had landed and fought their way through the Vichy French at Oran and Casablanca and near Algiers to open a second front against the Germans and their increasingly insignificant Italian partners. The Aussies (and New Zealanders) were also in North Africa with the British Eighth Army, and soon to be joining up with the new Allied invaders to the west. But in the meanwhile, the Brits and their empire were fighting full-time against Rommel and his Afrika Korps. So until their own 9th Division sailed home for a break, the only sizable forces back home Down Under would be the "bloody Yanks."

And waiting for them the glories and creature comforts of Melbourne, with its lonely, lusty, and compliant women, to welcome the nearly 20,000 men of the recently landed 1st Marine Division, malaria-ridden, exhausted, wasted, haunted, but randy, womanless, and by now battle-hardened. These Yanks, at least, had proved themselves able to "kill Japs." A mixed blessing indeed!

There is no indication that Manila John understood such dynamics or cared. All he knew was that he and his machine gunners were out of hell and, like Sydney Carton, in "a far, far better" place, a civilized country much like their own, where, drained and tired and haunted as they were, they could expect to recover and live once more as men and not animals of the field. But just how thin, in wartime with its stresses and losses, might be this veneer of civilization, even in a country as lovely as Melbourne and its agricultural environs? These were a grand people and this Australia a gorgeous place; there was beer to be drunk, liberty to be enjoyed, girls to be loved, money to be spent. Cutter reports further on "Uncle John" Basilone's revels amid the hospitable people of Melbourne: "They'd find a bald-headed Marine dead drunk, planted face-first in their petunias, and they'd bring him into their home, clean him up, and introduce him to their daughter."

Basilone had singular memories of his own. "I woke up one morning in my bunk and had no idea how I got there. I didn't remember the trip back or how I got my arm all bloodied. Somebody had wrapped it in white gauze so I figured I must have been in the sick bay at some point. All I knew was that my head hurt like hell. My mouth felt like mice had made a nest in it, and my arm hurt as bad as my head. I got myself cleaned up and had to shave with my left arm because my right was so sore. I still couldn't remember how I had banged it up. At chow Powell looked up at me over his coffee and smiled like the cat that just shit in the corner. 'Death Before Dishonor, sarge,' he said.

"'What the hell was that?' I was thinking but didn't say anything.

"'Let's take a look at it,' he said.

"'At what?' I said. I still wasn't too fast on my feet before coffee. Then it all started to come back to me. The drinking contest on Flinders Street, the cab ride and the little shop by the docks with drawings of dragons in the window. Powell nodded at my arm. Then I saw the rest; the tray of black inks, the needles, and the bald top of a man's head bent over my arm as pain shot through me. Powell was kissing a very heavy, brown-skinned girl and watching us. I peeled back the bandage on my arm, and saw the scabbed-over letters in blue ink, 'Death Before Dishonor' and some other design that was covered in dried blood. I liked it.

"'Death Before Dishonor,' I repeated to Powell. 'Who paid for it?' I asked because I didn't remember that part.

"'Beats me, but somebody did,' he said. It was done now and I was pleased with it."

Not every night was tattooed, drunken, or lecherous. The local girls also loved the new American dance, the "jitterbug," and were mad to learn more about it and work on their technique. There were families that took in some of the boys for domestic, warm, family-style meals and small, relatively sober parties. Men fell in love and got married, some were "adopted" by families and helped out the households with a little cash, and they learned to drink tea, sitting around the kitchen table as they'd done at home. They taught the Aussies our songs and learned theirs. To this day Marines who served Down Under can recite the lyrics of all four stanzas of "Waltzing Matilda" and do a pretty good job on its close harmony. American farmboys vanished for days at a time and then wandered back to the base explaining they'd been helping a local farmer get the crops in. Basilone fell for the younger children of one family and found himself playing on the floor with a little girl who reminded him of a niece in the Reisterstown, Maryland, home of his sister Phyllis Cutter and her husband, Bill.

The Marines who came to Australia, as well as others who went to New Zealand in those days, were there for rest and relaxation and recuperation, to cure the malaria and purge the intestinal worms. To come back from the dead. So that soon they would be sufficiently fit to fight the Japanese all over again on some other lousy island. Or maybe right here up north in the swamps and on the beaches of the northern coast with its malaria and crocodiles. Military bases thrive on rumor, on scuttlebutt; gossip was the circulating blood of every-day garrison life, and here at Melbourne the talk was of when they might be leaving, where they would be going next, about the order of battle and terms of engagement the next time out.

And now, in the spring of 1943 (which was autumn Down Under), other rumors began to circulate through the 1st Marine Division, not about the future but about its so recent past, some of it about Manila John Basilone and his exploits last October on Guadalcanal. There had already been some talk, earlier rumors, the morning after the fight on Bloody Ridge, especially about how Chesty Puller himself had gone out of his way to recognize Manila John and give him a "well done" for having gone back for ammo under fire at the worst of the enemy attack. Basilone heard the talk, of course, but refused to put much stock in it. After all, as he said, "There were thousands of boys fighting and dying. Why should I be singled out?"

Then in May 1943 the scuttlebutt ramped up.

9

Perhaps the best account of the time and the place comes not from Basilone family accounts or from neighbors and boyhood chums at Raritan, and certainly not from the taciturn John himself, but from another Marine who was there, the "other" Marine machine-gun sergeant from Guadalcanal, Mitchell Paige.

In January 1943, Paige, a more buttoned-up NCO than the casual, carousing Basilone, had been commissioned a second lieutenant in the United States Marine Corps, his date of rank backdated to October 1942, which meant a nice packet of back pay. Basilone, only slightly junior as sergeant to Paige, was not offered a commission. Later, he would be given several such opportunities, but not in early 1943. Not that he wanted or had politicked for an officer's gold bars. Manila John was happy being a sergeant. Paige, in his own postwar book, writes about that May in Melbourne where some quite extraordinary things had begun to happen. Fortunately for us, if Basilone wrote very little, Paige took notes or had an exceptional memory.

"One day we received word that a very distinguished person would be visiting our camp at Mount Martha. We were all busy with our machine guns when we saw the inspecting party coming through our area. We were instructed to continue our work. This was a great departure from the standard practice of a troop formation and formal inspection for a visiting dignitary. But Eleanor Roosevelt, the President's wife, only wanted to see the camp and see the troops in training. She stopped by our platoon and shook hands with us. I never dreamed that again one day I would shake hands with the First Lady in the White House in Washington.

"[Another] day the entire camp went on parade. There were to be presentations and awards. A group of us were assembled along the parade ground waiting for instructions when Colonel 'Chesty' Puller came smartly over to us as we all came to attention and rendered a snappy salute. Chesty grabbed me by the arm and said, 'Sergeant Paige, you're senior here, oh, yes, now you're a looie,' as he twisted his jowls to one side and with a warm smile said, 'You'll always be a sergeant to me. You know the backbone of the Corps is the non-commissioned officer.' Then he said, 'Sergeant Basilone, you will march next to Paige,' and then he lined up the rest of our group. The band struck up a march number and Chesty marched us front and center as my spine tingled with pride, being with such men. Chesty halted us directly in front of the Division commander, General Vandegrift. My citation was read and then in the name of the Congress and of the President of the United States, General Vandegrift placed the Congressional Medal of Honor around my neck. After which, I stepped over next to Colonel Merrill 'Red Mike' Edson and I continued to stand at attention as Johnny Basilone's citation was read and he, too, received the Congressional Medal of Honor from General Vandegrift. The 1st Marine Division Band and all the troops then passed in review as General Vandegrift, Colonel Edson, myself and Johnny Basilone received the honors—all four of us with the Congressional Medal of Honor and all for Guadalcanal."

Here, from the official records, is how Basilone's citation read:

For extraordinary heroism and conspicuous gallantry in action against enemy Japanese forces, above and beyond

72 HERO OF THE PACIFIC

the call of duty, while serving with the First Battalion, Seventh Marines, First Marine Division, in the Lunga Area, Guadalcanal, Solomon Islands, on October 24 and 25, 1942. While the enemy was hammering at the Marines' defensive positions, Sergeant Basilone, in charge of two sections of heavy machine guns, fought valiantly to check the savage and determined assault. In a fierce frontal attack with the Japanese blasting his guns with grenades and mortar fire, one of Sergeant Basilone's sections, with its gun crews, was put out of action, leaving only two men able to carry on. Moving an extra gun into position, he placed it in action, then, under continual fire, repaired another and personally manned it, gallantly holding his line until replacements arrived. A little later, with ammunition critically low and the supply lines cut off, Sergeant Basilone, at great risk of his life and in the face of continued enemy attack, battled his way through hostile lines with urgently needed shells for his gunners, thereby contributing in a large measure to the virtual annihilation of a Japanese regiment. His great personal valor and courageous initiative were in keeping with the highest traditions of the United States Naval Service.

The citation was signed by Franklin D. Roosevelt.

Chesty Puller, that legendary Marine, would eventually, in the time of Korea, win his fifth Navy Cross, but he never possessed what Paige and John Basilone now had, the Medal of Honor.

That night, tired of being gawked at in the barracks, Basilone and his closest buddies visited their old haunts on Flinders Street and, in Basilone's words, "got shit-faced" as he clowned about, wearing his cap sideways and mugging. Newly minted second lieutenant Paige, now an officer and gentleman, presumably celebrated in more decorous fashion.

Paige continued, "A couple of days later Johnny came to see me and said, 'Listen, we've got a ticket home right away.' That afternoon a jeep pulled up to our battalion headquarters and I was summoned to Colonel Amor LeRoy Sims' office to see General Vandegrift and Colonel Edson. The general told me that Basilone was going home and that we had another campaign coming up. For several days following my visit with General Vandegrift, Colonel Edson and Colonel Sims, reporters and war correspondents continued writing stories about me. I was advised my picture was going to appear on the cover of LIFE magazine [then a very big deal, *Life* being that era's print version of network television, with one of the largest circulations in the business] while holding a machine gun in my arms with a belt of ammunition over my shoulders, as had been told them by Captain Ditta and others whom they had questioned about our action on Guadalcanal. . . . For some reason, my picture never appeared."

A note of possible jealousy here? There would be many such photos and a sculpture of John Basilone in a similar pose, machine gun cradled in his arms, the ammo belt slung across his shoulders. Paige continued, "I always felt hesitant about talking with them [the journalists], as I wasn't interested in publicity, and medals had never really entered my mind." Within days Puller would be awarded a third Navy Cross and another lieutenant colonel named Conoley was also given the cross. At the ceremony, Paige stood with Conoley and Basilone with Puller. In this section of Paige's book, he goes into no additional detail on why Basilone may have been selected to go home and why it was assumed Paige himself would stay in the Pacific for that "next campaign." All Paige would add about his friend Johnny was a gracious little passage of *l'envoi*: "Manila John went home to sell war bonds and two years later he had volunteered to go back overseas. Johnny joined the 5th Marine Division which went to Iwo Jima. A few minutes after they hit the beach in the opening assault, on February 19, 1945, Johnny and four of his men were caught by Japanese mortar fire and were killed. My good friend, Manila John Basilone, was awarded the Navy Cross posthumously for that action."

Almost three weeks went by at Melbourne before, on June 12, Basilone bothered to write home about the famous medal, and he did so briefly and simply: "I am very happy, for the other day I received the Congressional Medal of Honor, the highest decoration you can receive in the armed forces. Tell Pop his son is still tough. Tell Don [John's kid brother] thanks for the prayer they say in school [for soldiers overseas]."

For all the talk about "a ticket home," the famous medal around his neck, and the brief flurry of publicity, as May became June and then July, Basilone was still in Australia, routinely drilling his machine gunners, marching in step, and dutifully saluting officers, including brand-new shavetails, young second lieutenants who'd never heard a shot fired in anger. They, too, were saluted and were to be obeyed. The more sensible young officers knew how absurd the situation was and restrained themselves, playing it cool and trying to learn from these salty and combat-hardened enlisted Marines and NCOs, not throwing their rank around with guys like Basilone. Basilone's new and raw young machine gunners were impressed by their betters, the veterans of the 'Canal, and were eager to listen and to learn—which was what Sergeant Basilone wanted, young men to be taught the hard, deadly lessons of combat.

Manila John had announced prematurely to Paige in May that they had that "ticket home." But in July he was still there, training troops, making formation every morning, doing whatever it was he did each night as the weeks passed. And the Pacific war went on. For a time it wasn't really a Marines war at all. The only substantial fighting by late May was in far-off Attu in the Aleutians where the Japanese had dug in and the American Army, the GIs as they were now widely called in the headlines, were taking significant losses trying to dig them out. The Aleutians were cold and windswept, isolated and only thinly populated, really not very strategically important. But they were part of territorial Alaska and therefore American ground. And that was sufficient emotional and political reason to take them back, regardless of the cost. Fighting continued in the Solomons, though not on the 'Canal, and it was mostly a naval fight and an aviator's war. Henderson Field remained vital, and the once tiny, beleaguered, potholed little airstrip was now capable of launching a hundred American warplanes at a time to harass and sink Japanese shipping, to shoot down Zeroes, to take the bombing war to other of the Solomons still in Japanese hands. Henderson Field had indeed been worth fighting for.

On May 30, Attu fell. The ghastly count read 600 Americans dead, 1,200 wounded. True to their tradition, only 28 Japanese troops, all of them wounded, survived, with 2,350 dead, many of those suicides. Across the world the Russians were chewing up the Germans in fierce spring fighting, Tunisia still held out against the Allies, while plans firmed up for the invasion of Sicily, Patton and Monty and all that. In the Atlantic we were now sinking German U-boats in almost equal numbers to Allied losses in the convoys.

Closer to Australia and New Zealand where the Marines like Basilone trained, played, and waited, the island-hopping resumed with GIs and Aussies fighting in increasing numbers on New Guinea, and the 4th Marine Raider Battalion prepared to land on New Georgia, the first real confrontation of U.S. Marines and Japanese infantry since Guadalcanal was finally "secured," Marine terminology for "job well done." As was said in wise-guy USMC lingo, "There's no cure like see-cure!"

Basilone, in the Jerry Cutter and Jim Proser account, takes up the story: "We were back on maneuvers, gearing up for some scheme they were cooking up with Mac's [Douglas MacArthur's] 6th Army stationed up in Brisbane, probably the same swamp we left behind [an ironic note of delight to the Gyrenes, surely]. The wheels were turning again, slowly. Each day new equipment arrived and more shaved-head 'boots' a few weeks out of Basic filled out our ranks. It was a good mix in a way because we could fill in the new boots on the real world of jungle warfare, not what they heard in scuttlebutt. I wished somebody like us had been there on the 'Canal to take us aside and tell us the real dope. I could tell we were going to keep a few of these kids from getting killed because they listened to every word and we never had to tell them something twice."

Reading such sensible, and even rather noble, stuff from Manila John, you have to wonder as he drilled these kids on his beloved heavy Brownings, stripping and reassembling them in the dark, had he earned a few bob competing with them, as he had done during his Army days, stateside as a Marine, or on Samoa?

There is another reference to home: "George [another of John's brothers] had joined the Marines. He was headed to the Pacific, too, so maybe we'd meet up somewhere. Everyone was doing fine and they were praying for me every day. The whole town was. That was supposed to make me feel better because a lot of angels were watching over me. If that was true, I'd have a few things I had to answer for when I got to heaven. *If* I got there."

There is a new, uncertain tone here, pensive, less impulsive. He was getting older, maybe growing up. In May, when he was awarded the medal, he'd declared, almost in glee, that the famed medal meant a "ticket home." That moment was now forgotten, the jubilation vanished. He was reconciled to the idea of going back into combat, taking on another campaign, landing on another hostile beach. That was what Marines did. And Basilone was certainly a Marine before he was ever a Medal of Honor laureate. Paige would be going back to war, Puller would be going, Bob Powell and the rest of them, and this "mix" of youngsters fresh out of boot camp and old stagers from the 'Canal would be going to the war. And why wouldn't Manila John be with them?

The warrior in Basilone seemed at peace with the notion of another fight. He was not at all restive or apprehensive.

Suddenly in Melbourne, there arrived new orders. Manila John was being pulled out of his battalion, was leaving the division and shipping out for the States, where an entire country at war was about to meet and embrace him. Many there were as yet unaware of just who the guy was, where he came from, and what he had done in his short and eventful life beyond killing people and winning medals.

If you really want to know about Johnny Basilone, though, you start with a small town in New Jersey.

PART TWO

HOMETOWN

Basilone in his service uniform.

10

John Basilone's family boasted no martial tradition, and John was a fairly unruly kid, not overly given to discipline, so he had no reason to believe, not then, that he just might have been born to soldier.

In fact, his boyhood was unremarkable small-town stuff. According to Bruce Doorly: "Basilone's mother Dora Bengivenga grew up in Raritan, born in 1889 to parents Carlo and Catrina, who had recently emigrated to America from Naples, Italy. Carlo was a mill worker. In 1901 Dora's parents purchased a house in Raritan at 113 First Avenue for $500. This would later be where John Basilone grew up. The house was built in 1858 and in 1901 was a single family home, but later additions would [make] it a two-family house. John's father, Salvatore Basilone, had come to America from just outside Naples in 1903 when he was 19. He went to work in Raritan and made friends among the other Italian Americans."

There were church parties and neighborhood gatherings, and it was at one of these that Salvatore met Dora. They dated for three years, saved some money, got married, and moved in with Dora's parents on First Avenue. Salvatore worked as a tailor's assistant, and their first five children were born in the family home. Looking for more work than Raritan offered, they moved north to Buffalo, New York, where young John, sixth of the Basilone children, was born not in a proper hospital but at home, very much in the family tradition, on November 4, 1916. But the Buffalo interlude was brief. Whether it was the long winters or a slump in the tailoring trade, the family returned to Raritan in 1918. By now Salvatore had a tailor shop of his own, and they were living in one-half of the two-family house. There was one bedroom downstairs for the parents, and two more upstairs, one for the girls, the other for the boys. There were usually several kids to a bed and the house had a single bathroom. The Basilones certainly weren't living grandly.

Growing up, John enjoyed the usual scrapes, black eyes, tossing rotten tomatoes, swimming "bare-ass" in the Raritan River, silent movies, later talkies, mostly westerns and serials, in a local movie theater kids called the "Madhouse" for its boisterous matinees punctuated by loud boos, hisses, cheers, and thrown popcorn. Half a dozen sources recall one Basilone caper that was hardly ordinary. At age seven and eager for adventure, he climbed a pasture fence and was promptly chased and knocked over by a bull. No damage was done to either boy or bull.

Doorly reports that St. Bernard's parochial school yearbook described John as "the most talkative boy in the class" and that "conduct was always his lowest mark." His sister Phyllis admitted the boy had difficulty in grammar school, couldn't seem to "buckle down" to his studies. When he graduated, at age fifteen (most graduated at thirteen or fourteen), Basilone opted to drop out, not to go on to high school. He confessed, apparently to his adviser, Father Amadeo Russo, that he might be a "misfit," that school just wasn't for him. John's father objected strongly to the idea of working at the local country club, but the boy assured him he could make a little money caddying at the club, shrewdly pointing out he'd be outdoors getting exercise and plenty of fresh air. At the Raritan Valley Country Club, according to the Cutter and Proser book, it was while caddying for a Japanese foursome that young John had one of his early "premonitions," of a war one day when the United States would have to fight the Japanese. No one else in Raritan can recall Basilone's ever having spoken of such a premonition. "He wasn't that sort of fellow," one said. On rainy days or when caddying was slow, John and the other boys played cards. John turned out to be a natural at it, becoming a lifetime gambler, canny and adept, winning more than his share of the usually small stakes.

When the golf season ended, John got a "real" job, working as a helper on a truck for Gaburo's Laundry at the corner of Farrand Avenue in Raritan, delivering clean clothes, a job he actually held on to for a year before being canned for sleeping on the job. According to Doorly, future Raritan mayor Steve Del Rocco, who knew Basilone, called him "a happy go lucky . . . [who] enjoyed everything he did."

But John was restless. And with his lack of education and difficulty with books, in a down economy, at some point he must have concluded that going into the Army (a private received twenty-one dollars a month; a uniform; a pair of stout, hard-soled shoes; and three squares a day) might be a way of escaping depressed and jobless Raritan. Not yet eighteen, he needed parental approval, and that took considerable convincing. According to sister Phyllis, their father, Salvatore, "tried to reason with him. 'Johnny, you're crazy. You're only a kid. There's no war, why do you want to join the Army?'" Raritan was a small town, and John's mother was reluctant to see her boy leave home and go out into a very large and unknown world. He argued, though without any evidence, "I'll find my career in the Army."

Wrote Phyllis, "He explained to papa that with the Depression all about us, it was almost impossible to get a job. Army life might be just what he was looking for, he said. Then again, when his enlistment ran out, conditions might be better." On that point, Salvatore, an employed tailor but very well aware of the lousy job market, who'd been pressuring John to start a career in something, *anything*, reluctantly had to agree with his son. Doorly writes that the senior Basilones may have concluded the military could be "a good match" for a strong, active, out-of-doors kid like their son.

We know to the day the date on which John would later join the Marine Corps, but there is a debate on when, even in what year, he earlier joined the prewar U.S. Army in the mid-1930s. Doorly believes John joined up in June 1934. Cutter tells me that by his reckoning, John enlisted "about three months before he turned eighteen [on November 4], which would have been August of '34. I know his parents had to sign on." His Marine Corps records insist he had joined the Army early in 1936. His 1935 Army service in the Philippines, thoroughly documented, indicates the Marine data is incorrect. But the military records that might solve this small and perhaps unimportant question were destroyed by fire in 1973 at the Military Personnel Records Center in St. Louis, Missouri, where the archives were held. According to Marine historian Bob Aquilina, Marine and U.S. Navy records went untouched in the fire but Army records of the time were burned.

There may have been additional arguments within the family about John's enlistment, some fits and starts along the way, since with the requisite records missing, some contradictory evidence suggests that John didn't actually enlist until he was nineteen. The Marine Corps, which apparently keeps files on just about everything, even the other military services, reports on John's military service record that he joined the Army on February 5, 1936, and served on active duty with consistently excellent fitness reports until being discharged back into civilian life and the U.S. Army Reserve on September 8, 1939. Since there is reasonable proof that as a young soldier still on his first enlistment John arrived in the Philippines in March 1935 to start a two-year overseas tour of duty, we can conclude that, at least this once, the Marine Corps got it wrong.

All we get is a fanciful line or two supposedly from "Johnny" to Phyllis Basilone as he left home for the Army. She describes his getting on the train at Raritan for Newark and then traveling under the Hudson River into Manhattan, no date given. "Well, Sis, I'm on my way. I wonder if this is what I really want; everybody's advice is still ringing in my ears." After all, the boy may not yet have turned eighteen.

11

When the Raritan Valley local pulled into its last stop one January morning in 2008, the three local men were waiting for me out in the cold in a red Lincoln truck because the station's waiting room was locked. We'd arranged for me to meet with some people in New Jersey who could tell me about John Basilone, his home and family, his roots. The men were John Pacifico, a Roman Catholic deacon for twenty-five years at St. Ann's Church on Anderson Street; Herb Patullo, who was driving the truck and who owns a historic piece of high ground in the nearby Watchung Mountains on which Washington and the Continental Army once encamped in a blocking position to mask Philadelphia from the British; and Peter Vitelli, a large, talkative man who used to be in sales and marketing in Manhattan and recalls that at age six at St. Joseph's parochial school in Raritan, he once shook Basilone's hand when the nuns trooped the returning hero around to the classrooms to greet the children in 1943.

Pacifico, Vitelli, and Patullo, are members of the Basilone Parade Committee, three of those who tend to Basilone's memory and reputation and still stage the march in his honor every September, commemorating the day he returned on leave from the Pacific wearing the Congressional Medal of Honor. Raritan erupted (no other word will do) in a spontaneous welcome as he took a jubilant stroll through the town, the kid who once delivered their laundry, carried their golf bags, and had now become an American folk hero.

The men saw to it that I got a place in the truck, and it turned out they knew me from the page I wrote every Sunday for *Parade* magazine, a sort of accreditation as a professional that gave them a small assurance that I wasn't just another nosy parker but a reporter who *might* be trusted. I was hoping there would be a station coffee shop where I might get a wake-up cup of coffee, but no such luck. These men were focused, however, and they knew precisely why I was there, and so we drove on.

Our first stop was the Raritan Public Library, a small, trim white-framed building where on the second floor up the carpeted wooden staircase is the Basilone Room. It is nothing fancy, just a place where they collect and keep memorabilia about him. On a table were three white leather-covered photo albums filled with mostly black-and-white photographs: Basilone, in uniform and out, at various stages of youth (after all, he was still in his twenties when he died), pictures of his family, of friends, of the more or less famous movie stars who traveled the war bond sales route with him. I recognized John Garfield, who would play a Marine in a wartime picture, Eddie Bracken, Louise Allbritton. Vitelli leaned over my shoulder to identify people. He pointed out Virginia Grey. She was the woman who had caught Basilone's eye, and he hers. There were casual shots set in a soda shop. Basilone, they said, was known to be "the biggest ice-cream soda drinker" in town, while his schoolboy hobby was "chewing gum," and his ambition was "to be an opera singer"—if not a heavyweight boxing champ appearing in Madison Square Garden like his hero, a huge, strong, but awkward Italian fighter named Primo Carnera. There were pictures of Basilone in uniform, sometimes squared away and crisply tailored, or more casual on liberty with his "piss-cutter" overseas cap jauntily cocked or turned sideways. Beneath the uniform, there were two tattoos: "Death Before Dishonor" and a heart pierced by a sword.

We then took off in Patullo's red truck for a tour of the place where Manila John Basilone grew up, crossing the John Basilone Veterans Memorial Bridge over the Raritan River. "That's the Doris Duke estate over there," someone said, indicating a smooth, grassy, handsomely treed lawn that seemed to go on and on without ever a house in view. The place was so large you could hide a mansion on it. It had been a relatively warm and damp winter, and for January, everything was very green.

"He was actually born in Buffalo," someone said, "November 4 in 1916." Halfway through World War I, I calculated hastily to orient the time frame we were discussing, "and at twenty-eight he was dead." My guides showed off buildings where Basilone family or friends had at one time lived, other places of significance to Basilone, anxious to be helpful and at the same time to provide me a positive slant on their town. But not phonying it up. They took turns at talking or sometimes all spoke at once. I scribbled notes.

"New York City police commissioner Ray Kelly (also a Marine, of the Vietnam era) was here for the Basilone Parade one September, and he called Raritan 'a Norman Rockwell sort of town.' It's really a blue-collar town. Back then most people worked at Johns Manville. Or the Raritan Woolen Mills. Raritan started out Dutch, then it was Irish, and at the turn of the century the Italians and Slovaks came in. The Irish controlled all the justice system. Oh, sure, there was bias (established Irish versus the arriviste Italians), a couple of incidents.

"There's the statue, at Somerset Street and the Olde York Road, the stagecoach road between New York and Philly."

We pulled over and got out of the truck to look at the town's big monument, the outsized statue of John Basilone, a few yards from the Raritan River. "How tall was he?" I asked one of the men. "Five eight, five nine." Someone else said, "Maybe five ten."

Proud of their hometown boy, I think they kind of wanted him to be taller. The statue itself was big and bronze, maybe seven or eight feet high, a muscular young man, bare-chested as he had been in that fight on the Lunga River on Guadalcanal. His arms cradled a heavy machine gun, the weapon he loved, his weapon for killing.

He fought that night barefoot in the mud for better traction, but the sculptor had added what looked to me like modern Army combat boots. The replicated Medal of Honor on the statue was also, alas, a mistake, the Army version of the award, not the slightly different Navy version, as is appropriate for a Marine. Patullo pointed out for my tutelage the minor design distinctions in the two versions of the medal. That's how sensitive these men are about "their guy" John.

Next, we swung by Bridgewater-Raritan High and parked at John Basilone Memorial Field. We went into the athletic building and were greeted by a huge mural, maybe ten feet wide and about eight high, of Gunnery Sergeant Basilone. Out the other side of the building we walked onto the athletic field made of artificial turf, and the impressively modern composition running track surrounding it. Some boys in the infield played touch football while other kids, boys and girls both, in running shorts or sweats, sprinted or jogged laps. On the exterior walls of the athletic building looking out at the field were replicas of the two citations, the one for the Medal of Honor, the other for the Navy Cross Basilone was awarded posthumously on Iwo Jima.

We stood there reading the citations. Once again, talking up Raritan as a fine place, someone said, "Out of six thousand people in Raritan, nine hundred or a thousand went into the service during the war." They meant World War II, it was clear, not Iraq.

It was obvious that Raritan remembers almost everything about its hero. "He went to St. Bernard's grammar school. It burned down years ago. St. Ann's was his parish. Father Russo was his priest. Amadeo Russo." I noticed no one bothered to use Basilone's name with me anymore. They realized by now I know who "he" was. As in, "He never went to high school."

After grammar school Basilone caddied at the Raritan Valley Country Club. "Could I see that?" I asked. "Will they let us in?" The answer was, "Sure."

"Raritan Valley C.C. was very elitist then," I was informed, once again with a possessive local pride about *their* country club. "And the only way kids could make a living was to caddy. It was the Depression." I was interested in knowing more about the caddying, about Basilone's own golf. "John was good, but his brother Carlo was better." I'd also read that the young Basilone had premonitions, that he foresaw things, including his own death in war. And that when he was caddying for a foursome of Japanese businessmen in the 1930s, he had one of his premonitions. Because the men were taking snapshots, Basilone sensed there was going to be a war one of these days and America would have to fight Japan. "Ever hear any of that stuff?" I asked. No one I spoke to in Raritan was buying it.

Nor did they see anything sinister about the golfers. "Johnson and Johnson [of nearby New Brunswick] was just getting started off the ground and they built here. That's why there were Japanese here then. They were okay." Vitelli interrupted. "Tony Farese was the pro back then so he might know about premonitions, but he died recently at ninety-five. There was also a story Basilone once caddied for David Niven when he played Raritan. Niven told that to Pete, the bartender at P.J. Clarke's, and Pete told it to me. Niven was supposed to have said it might have happened, but he couldn't swear to it. Raritan was a very social club. A lot of people played here."

The Basilone house at 605 First Avenue (Basilone's Marine service records insist 113 First Avenue) in Raritan is now a small office building housing a fire alarm company, All-Out Fire Protection. What kind of house was it then? I asked. "Just a normal up-and-down house." How did they fit ten kids in there? My guides shrugged. It was Depression time, people made out somehow. We looked over the house and drove past sister Mary's home and where brother Alphonse used to live over there on the right, on to Gaburo's Laundry, the outfit that canned young Basilone from a delivery job for crapping out on the job, literally napping atop some piled-up laundry bags. Our next stop was at Basilone Place, a short residential street with small, neat houses on each side and carefully tended lawns, all of them very green in winter. This was where Joe Pinto still lived, and we were going to see Joe.

My guides had phoned ahead and Mr. Pinto came to the door and welcomed us. He is a slender, very small man bent nearly double at the waist, and very old. In the old days, I was told, he owned the Raritan Liquor Store.

We all took chairs and Mr. Pinto began to talk. "I grew up with him, more or less," he said of Basilone. "I'm ninety-nine years old now, and there couldn't have been a better guy. When he came home from Guadalcanal there was a parade here. He wore his uniform and he went all around town, and I was one of the guys he hung out with, his father and Chief Rossi of the police, Rocky Calabrese whose family had the department store." I asked what Basilone drank. "Beer, soda, not so much wine, but he'd drink anything. We went up to Villa Firenze one night, a regular night, John and me and two girls, and I was driving a car I'd just bought [probably used, since wartime Detroit wasn't making any new automobiles] and we had a flat up front. No jack, no lights, and two in the morning after a night of drinking. We're standing around there, lighting matches so he could see, and John's pumping the front tire with a hand pump, and we got going again. He was a regular guy, he'd do anything. A happy-go-lucky guy, about twenty-six years old.

"He left to go back [to the war] and got married out in California. He never brought his wife back."

What was it like when you heard he was dead? I asked the old gentleman.

"It was as if everyone in town went to hell. Everyone knew him, from his time as a laundry deliveryman," he said. "I had a business, ran a liquor store, came up here in thirty-six. So I knew him, a happy guy, always razzing with the kids." When I asked, Joe said, "No, he didn't find the laundry job demeaning." I asked other questions, about John's boxing, reports that Madison Square Garden wanted him, that a promoter wanted him to go pro, did he and Pinto ever box? I asked again about his supposed premonitions. For a man his age, Pinto was very crisp in his responses.

"I never sparred with him, and don't think he ever gave a thought to turning pro. As for premonitions, no, I never heard any of that. And he was not a guy to brag about the past, what he did [in the Pacific]. A handsome guy, but he didn't have much time for girls [others disagree bluntly on that point], and not a fancy dresser. I think he had one suit, and his father was a tailor, a man who would fix anything, no charge. His mom was a good looker and very nice. A nice, close family. I don't think you will ever find another man like John. A good guy, and anyone saying 'not' ought to be shot. John was the kind of guy some people can hate because he was so right. They had a funeral mass right here for him at St. Ann's."

On that exit line, we shoved off to meet the man who buried John Basilone, Raritan undertaker Anthony Bongiovi, ninety-six years old, whose home is attached to the funeral parlor and who received us in his blue wool bathrobe while reclining on a settee in the living room. He began by apologizing. "I've got this breathing thing." He paused to take a breath. Then he went on with a long rambling story, not about Basilone but another wartime casualty, an Air Corps officer killed in a plane crash and how his mother was hysterical and demanded the mortician open the sealed coffin. "The mother is screaming, 'I want to see my son, I want to see him!' In those days they held a wake at home, in the living room. So I didn't want to see that with the Basilones. But I get a call from the Basilone family and I know [Mrs. Basilone's] not going to be able to see her son." It was three and a half year's after his death before he was disinterred from an Iwo grave and sent home. So obviously there was nothing left that a mother should be shown.

"I go to see the family at their home and I say, 'What the hell!' This is a local guy and the only one ever receiving a Medal of Honor, so I said, why not bury him right here at Raritan? At the house I calmed Mrs. Basilone. I said we could have John right here at home on the first floor [for a viewing of the casket]. I knew it would be a lot of work for me but what the hell. So I had the body shipped from Dover, Delaware."

This is confusing. The evidence indicates the body was sent directly from Delaware to Arlington, Virginia, site of the big national cemetery, with the government and the undertaker making the arrangements, the idea of burying John in Raritan having been scrapped. Bongiovi went on, at least in part clarifying the situation. "The funeral mass was said at St. Ann's in Raritan with the burial to follow at Arlington."

The old man paused again to catch his breath. This was clearly tiring him, but he wanted to keep going. He was very clear about the last part of his story.

"I had my own limo and the chief of police drove another car and the family rode with me and some others drove behind. I had it timed out so that in three hours [Bruce Doorly says it was four hours] we would meet at Arlington. I had never met John Basilone but it had to be right. We got to the cemetery and expected to see a firing squad and a casket with the flag on it, but when we arrived we got the Marine Corps band and a firing squad and a lot of generals, who they were I don't know, and I said to myself, 'What is this?' I introduced the family to the higher-ups and we had the funeral. And that's why, ever since, we celebrate this young guy's death."

We thanked Bongiovi for his time and help and said our good-byes, his daughter graciously apologizing for not having her dad all dolled up for us. There were cars and limos pulling up outside his funeral home now for another wake as we left the old undertaker and went out into the midafternoon sun. The following month I got a phone call from Raritan that Mr. Bongiovi himself, the undertaker who buried John Basilone, had died on February 1 at nearby Somerset Medical Center.

Before I left Raritan on the late afternoon train into Manhattan, I also learned about Basilone's "double-dating with a buddy named Augie Sena at Chichi's pizzeria in nearby Bound Brook before he left for the Army," and about "a red-haired girl named Josephine Cianciella, a local babe who went out with John in the late thirties, after he got out of the Army. He was dating Josephine and then he left to go back to the war. Her father was the local druggist."

But when we phoned, Augie Sena wasn't available, nor were several other promising sources, so I provided Pacifico a list of questions for the deacon to ask if he could nail any of the sources down and convince them to sit still for a tape-recorded grilling.

12

As good as his word, later that month John Pacifico sent from Raritan an audiotape of three interviews he'd conducted.

First was ninety-four-year-old Augie Sena, who said he'd lived all his life in Raritan. As to when he and Basilone met, he said, "In the late thirties at the Raritan Valley Country Club, we both caddied there together. I didn't know him that good. We lived on different streets. He was very friendly, made friends with a lot of people." About sports, Sena said, "I knew him as a football player out there. No, I never knew him as a fighter." Nor did he remember any premonitions about the Japanese golfers. "We caddied for the Japs because they played a lot of golf there. I think [he went into the Army] for the excitement. He wanted to travel. But [contradicting Joe Pinto] he had a lot of girls. He was a good-looking fella. So he had a lot of girls as far as I know."

Sena remembered Basilone when he came back from Guadalcanal with his medal. "I knew him back then, knew him pretty good. He used to deliver my laundry. A lot of times we used to meet at the Checker Diner around the circle in Somerville and we used to talk a lot. They had a big parade for him and then after that we were having coffee one day together and he was telling me he was going back [to the Pacific war] and I told him he was foolish. He would sever a lot of bonds like that. He told me he had to go back, wanted to go back. I don't think he changed much from when he went in and when he came back [from the war]. He liked to go back to the Army [Augie meant the Marines], he told me. He had an easy go and was selling bonds and he didn't have to go back, and I asked him why he wants to go back. He said he had to go back. That's what he told me."

Pacifico asked Sena whether he and Basilone discussed combat. "No, we never talked about that." Was it patriotism that had John out selling war bonds with movie stars? "No, he didn't think it was patriotic. He'd rather go back and fight. He'd rather go back with his buddies, he said. That's what he told me. He was anxious to go back, he told me. I told him he was foolish but that's what he said, that he wanted to go back. He really wanted to go." Augie kept stressing that. And when the brass said okay? "He really wanted to go back. It was the last time we had coffee and he was telling me he was leaving the next day, and that was the last time I seen him and I never seen him no more after that."

And when Sena learned his friend and neighbor had been killed? "I think Steven Del Rocco told me. He told me John Basilone got killed on Guadalcanal [actually Iwo Jima]. I'm pretty sure Steve told me on Anderson Street." And his memories of Manila John? "That he was a good person, that's all. He fought for the country. He had to go back. He died for his country. He was a good man, that's all I could tell you."

Former mayor Steve Del Rocco is eighty-nine years old and a lifelong Raritan inhabitant. He recalls, "I grew up with John and the whole family and got to know John pretty well on the golf course at Raritan Valley C.C. where he excelled in golf and he was a very good golfer. He was a very ambitious kid. [The family certainly didn't think so, and his father was forever asking John what he was going to do with his life.] He was always looking to do something, like he had ants in his pants and he couldn't stand still. Always looking to do something. Times were tough then. It was during the Depression, the biggest depression of our lifetime. The sport that I know he was the best in was golf. One of the best golfers in town. Every Monday was caddies' day and John would always be there, playing golf. He was a real good golfer. He played for a little bit of money and the more he played for, the better he was. Other sports, I'm not familiar with."

Did Del Rocco believe Basilone went into the Army because there were no jobs, or for excitement and travel? "I think he went in because [he] wanted to do something and there was nothing [here] to do. It was a depressing time those years in the thirties and I think it was a great challenge for him to go into the Army." And after that tour in the Army? "We knew him. He used to hang around what they called the joint down Ellison Street, and that's the last time I saw John [before the war]. We were playing cards there that night and he was leaving the next day to join the Marines, and that's the last time I saw him. He looked like he was anxious to get in the Marines, he thought it was something a little tougher, or something better. He would like it better than the Army, and I'm sure that he found it a better place to go. That is, for him. What motivated him, you know, he worked in the laundry, and I remember he got the job there and he stayed around for a while, and he got a little tired of the job and I think that's why he left."

And after Guadalcanal and the medal? Was he still one of the boys or distant? Scarred by the war or something like that? "Well, he wasn't scarred by the war. The only thing I can say about that is that I knew he missed it. He wanted to go back to it. He wasn't very happy selling war bonds. That wasn't his forte. He couldn't wait to get out of here and go back into the Marines. He never talked about combat. We never, one of us, brought it up. I think that was what drove him back to the Marines that he didn't want to sell war bonds. He just didn't want to do it. He wasn't up to it. He'd much rather be with the boys he left behind. Very anxious to get back, to get back in the worst way. He had a chance to spend the rest of his life as a Marine without going back to battle, but he chose to go back to battle to be with his friends, and that's something you got to admire."

And when the future mayor learned his local pal was dead? "I got a telephone call from I forget who it was who called me and told me about it and I didn't know anything about it until this phone call, and of course the next day it was all over the papers. That's when I knew for sure. There's not much I can say except to say his love for his country, to go back when he didn't have to go back. He could have stayed here and laid around and lived a good life, but he chose to go back and sacrificed his life for his country."

Del Rocco was one of the pallbearers, "the last pallbearer still alive. The big regret," he said, "that John's mother passed away before his body came back to Raritan or was taken to Arlington. [Not so; Dora Basilone attended her son's funeral at Arlington.] But when anybody was killed or died in the service, ten thousand dollars was given out to the family, and at that time John was married to a Marine girl from California and when she got the check for ten thousand dollars she turned it over to the Basilone family in respect of John Basilone. "She returned ten thousand dollars to the family."

Lena Riggi's niece later confirmed that story to me that her aunt, John's widow, gave the ten thousand dollars to the family. That didn't mean there wasn't some family hostility toward the widow, for whatever reason. Later I would get some insight into that.

Pacifico also got another neighbor on tape. Joe Sian is also eighty-nine and a lifelong friend of the Basilone family but one with a special perspective: "During the war when he got killed at Iwo Jima, I was there at the time [aboard a Navy warship providing naval gunfire support to the Marines ashore]. Yes, I heard it the same day because I was in the radio gang and when it came over our speaker I knew about it. It was the same that day as every day with that invasion. You were there two days of bombarding, day and night. And then we went back to the Philippines."

How did Sian feel about the news, knowing Basilone as he did? "I knew about him because when he came to Raritan [in 1943 after Guadalcanal] I was at the parade and all that stuff when they had the big time at Duke's Park. Everybody was buying bonds. My father bought bonds. Then we all went to [Doris] Duke's and had a big ceremony. I only met him once, when we were kids. I saw him in town. I was no friend of his. I just knew of him."

Pacifico pressed Sian, but he didn't know much. "Because, like I said, he's on the other end of town so we were not friends."

And about Basilone's selling war bonds? "Well, he didn't care too much for that. He didn't care for the big shots because he was going to Orlando's bar a lot with Gaburo. Al Gaburo was with him at that time, from when he was delivering laundry for Gaburo's Laundry. He was pretty cocky later, let's put it that way. I used to see him around town, not that I was friends with him."

Did he talk then about combat, or about going back? "Combat, no, and yes, he really wanted to go back." And at Iwo, did Sian ever land or remain aboard ship? Stayed on board. "Bombarded for two days and two nights. I knew he wanted to go back because he was going around this bar a lot and that's when he used to talk about it a lot. I didn't know he was on the island when we were bombarding and we found out he got killed when we got it on the radio."

Pacifico continued asking about Joe's relationships with the Basilones after the war. "Well, Dolores was a good friend of mine. She lived with me for a few months. She was the second youngest of the family. She went someplace. She had to take Donald with her. Donald's the youngest and he's still alive in Florida, and Dolores died. She died four and a half years ago. And that's about it."

There's an authentic small-town American feel to much of this, my own interviews and what's on the Pacifico tape, really less a profile of the most celebrated man in town than a last-century portrait of a provincial town and its people, a modest place only an hour from Times Square. In Raritan, if you lived at the other end of town, or on a different street, you weren't friends. You met people at bars. You worked local jobs, attended Catholic schools. You didn't belong to the country club but probably caddied there. In Basilone's town almost everyone seemed to have an Italian surname, they prayed at the same churches, drank at the same bars, had the same favorite Italian restaurants, dated some of the same Italian girls, fell for a guy's sister, worked at some of the same jobs. And most of the boys joined up during the various wars. They all knew who John Basilone was and remembered him. But how many really knew the man, the machine gunner who in passing through a damp tropical hell killed so many enemy soldiers and became famous?

The other thing about these Raritan interviews was the insistence over and over that Basilone hated the war bond tour, and wanted sincerely to return to the Pacific, to the fighting, to his Marine buddies. Everyone noted it.

Over the past year or two I searched for Basilone, for which of several overlapping or contradictory versions of the man and his war might be the real one, the true John Basilone. I visited Marine bases where he is anything but forgotten, the local libraries, museums, the archives of New Jersey's largest daily newspaper— the *Star-Ledger* in Newark—and other newspapers, local and large. I interviewed friends, his fellow Marines, the citizenry of Raritan, his old neighbors, schoolmates, drinking buddies, the mayor, and then in a phone call, the one surviving of ten Basilone children, seventy-eight-year old Donald in Florida.

"So you're the youngest of the Basilones," I said as we began, and Donald responded, somewhat amused by the irony, "The youngest and the only."

As noted, I'd gotten to see even the old undertaker, Anthony G. Bongiovi Sr., who buried John at Arlington. And, yes, Jon Bon Jovi was of the same family, albeit with a different spelling, but according to my Raritan guides, definitely a cousin. There had been something of a family falling-out early in Jon's career, a disagreement over his dropping a family marketing and commercial connection as his reputation grew. A neighbor in Raritan congratulated me for having been just about the last reporter to see the undertaker, to ask about Basilone and do an interview. And now I was going to have somehow to arrange an interview with Donald Basilone in Florida, the kid brother, the only Basilone left.

That subsequent, gracious, rather sad phone call reminded me not to dawdle. The people I had still to talk with or to visit (mostly Marines) weren't getting any younger (nor was I myself, to be candid). And gradually, as I went, a picture was emerging of small-town 1930s America where their hero came of age.

13

John Basilone, for all his restlessness, turned out to be a dream recruit. He was strong, tireless, not homesick, and for once, eager to learn. Once the drill instructor realized the young boot wasn't just brown-nosing, he took note of and encouraged the lad. Basilone's first outfit was Company D of the 16th Infantry stationed not on some hostile frontier or distant military post, but perched right out there in the middle of New York harbor, on Governor's Island at Fort Jay. According to retired Marine Colonel John Keenan, editor of the *Marine Corps Gazette*, in the United States Army between the world wars, and specifically in the thirties, there was little or no formalized recruit depot or boot camp such as in the Marines. Recruits were usually assigned to an existing regiment of the regular Army, there to be trained and then incorporated into the ranks of the regiment, depending on its needs and the new soldier's aptitude and skills, if any. This, on Governor's Island, was to be whatever recruit training he would receive.

Jim Proser quotes Basilone as delighted with Governor's Island, comparing the place to a country club, noting that it even had a small golf layout where he might hit a few balls. I'm not sure anyone ever filled him in on the island's history, purchased hundreds of years earlier from the Indians for two ax heads and a few iron nails, and then doubled in size to 172 acres by landfill from the excavation of tunnels for the city's brand-new subway system. In World War I a small airfield was built and pilots trained there to fly military aircraft. At some point German sailors were interned here.

But it was also on Governor's Island that, for a variety of reasons, Basilone fell in love with his weapon of choice, the water-cooled .30-caliber heavy machine gun. For the usual enlisted grunt, the gun is far too heavy to be at all lovable or to become a man's personal weapon as it would become Basilone's. The Jerry Cutter and Jim Proser book takes up Basilone's affection for the weapon, purportedly quoting him: "All through the summer [of 1934] I worked on my two specialties, machine gunning and poker. I also had a very active hobby across the harbor in Manhattan when we had passes [recruits aren't usually issued many passes] off the base. This involved young ladies who seemed to be attracted to men in uniform. All in all, the Army was shaping up to the kind of life that was tailor-made for me.

"Even my specialty, machine gunner, suited me down to the ground. When I imagined myself in some future battle, even though I had no idea what a real battle was like, I only knew what I'd seen in the movies. I knew I wanted to be behind a machine gun. Outside of a tank, I figured that was the most powerful weapon on a battlefield, and I was damned if I was getting into a tank if I could help it. I couldn't stand even being in a room all that much. I wouldn't last ten minutes inside a tank."

Was there a suggestion of claustrophobia? "The first time we rolled our 1917A Browning water-cooled .30 calibers out of the old fort's magazine on their caissons, they looked to me like something I could handle. They were human-sized. They weren't complicated. We rolled them out to the gunnery ranges and spent the next six weeks of our boot camp learning the weapon."

No one else refers to Fort Jay as a boot camp. But Cutter and Proser press on, describing John's passion for the weapon: "You could see the rest of the boys getting excited as the sarge went through the ins and outs of the machine. He seemed to go on forever—by the book. The 1917A, its military purpose, capabilities, operating procedure, safety procedure, parts, and assembly—it went on all day. By the afternoon we were ready to get our hands on one and try it out. Sarge went on, the strategy of infantry assault, interlocking fields of fire, trajectory, care and maintenance. Just before chow, we set them up on the range and squeezed off our first rounds."

In 1951 in North Korea with Dog Company, 2nd Battalion, 7th Marines, commanded by Captain John Chafee (the future senator), I was briefly in charge of a Marine machine-gun platoon, and this account of a first day's training with the heavy guns sounds like nonsense. This is not to blame Basilone but the family amateurs who wrote about him. For a young soldier, after less than a full day's training in a weapon as complex and deadly as the machine gun, actually to be firing live rounds without even the usual dry runs and "snapping in" without live ammo doesn't ring true. Or is this simply my being a Marine and overcritical of Army procedure? To be sure, I checked with one of my own former machine gunners, Charles Curley, at his home in Olean, New York. After I read him the passage, he went into detail on the education of a machine gunner. "Oh my God, lieutenant. In my case we were trained at Camp Pendleton on the gun, and then before I ever fired a live round, I had to work my way up, from ammo carrier to assistant gunner to gunner. It was never accomplished in just one day. You had to drill on the gun, take the gun apart, reassemble it, name all its parts, even tell them how many air holes cooled the jacket of the air-cooled gun. You learned all that, then you lugged the ammo, before you ever fired a round of live ammo." Maybe during the ensuing six weeks of machine-gun drill, Basilone actually fired the damned thing, but it surely wasn't that first afternoon.

Basilone, in the Cutter and Proser book, goes on: "For me, it was a God-given moment [those first rounds squeezed off]. It was pure thunder in my hand. The most awesome personal weapon ever built. With correct technique, the gun could fire almost continuously for days before the barrel had to be replaced. It could fire in all weather, in all directions and accurate at 150 yards [This is also silly. The gun's sights are graduated to 2,400 yards and the effective maximum range almost half that and not the meager 150 yards impressionable recruit Basilone supposedly believed.] I was safe and nobody else was. I was like the God who throws thunderbolts." The mock literary allusion doesn't really fit the Basilone we know.

His enthusiasm wasn't feigned, however. This wasn't just a kid's normal excitement over a new and elaborate toy. Basilone truly loved the machine gun. The passion began right there on Governor's Island and would continue through his army years, the first overseas tour at Manila, his Marine Corps hitch, on the 'Canal, and he would still be lugging a Browning machine gun, fiddling with its head space, fretting over its care and feeding, using it to kill people, up until Iwo Jima, on the last day of his young life.

But long before then, there was that other youthful enthusiasm which also sounds genuine; there were the girls. Just a pleasant ferry ride away, the city of New York, with its millions of women, its Third and Sixth Avenue bars under the elevated trains, the Greenwich Village joints, the German beer cellars, the brauhauses of Yorkville on the Upper East Side. So passed a pleasant season, machine-gun drill, poker, ferry rides, and Manhattan honeys.

And sometime early in the new year of 1935 the young soldier was, for the first time, about to travel at government expense, to begin seeing something of the great world beyond Raritan and neighboring New York City. Basilone was being transferred, first sent to the West Coast, and then overseas, to the distant shores of the faraway Philippines. Had a restless small-town kid really found a home in the Army?

14

John Basilone had been a soldier long enough by now to have put aside any youthful illusions. You think it was easy earning that twenty-one dollars a month in the Depression-era Army? The corporals and sergeants chivvied and hassled you from reveille to Taps, the officers lorded it over you, and if you cursed back, hit out, or even gave anyone ranked higher than you a sour look, the MPs beat the shit out of you and you went to the stockade where they beat up on you some more. But what were the options? Where were you going to go? There was no money and little hope or opportunity beyond the CCC (Civilian Conservation Corps) or the Army, only the unemployment lines, the soup kitchens, and the hobo jungles with the rest of the tramps, where the strong screwed boys and weaker men, because there were no women, and thugs would beat a man to death for a pint of rye whiskey or his mulligan stew. As hard as the soldier's life was in the thirties, were you really going to give it up for that and go out on the tramp?

Phyllis Basilone Cutter's story details her kid brother's travels as he departed the garrison at Fort Jay for California and then across the Pacific to Asia. She makes it sound a pleasant idyll.

"The group of us were herded into buses for the quick trip to the Pennsylvania Station in New York. Arriving at this tremendous station our sergeant for the trip counted noses as we filed out of the buses and stood at attention on the walk. To the curious onlookers we must have presented quite a sight as we marched through the station, down the steps to the lower level where our train lay waiting. I was anxious for a window seat as I had never traveled much before and did not want to miss the view. Approaching the vestibule of the Pullman car, I broke ahead and ran for a window seat which I fortunately got. In a few minutes we heard the conductor's 'all aboard,' the peep-peep of the signal, and we were on our way. I got into my seat, hunched back and munched on my goodies, and we were on our way.

"Reaching Chicago, we passed over a maze of tracks and had a tiresome three-hour layover waiting for the West Coast Limited. Finally we were made a part of this super train and heading westward. Looking back, the huge buildings and skyscrapers of Chicago faded in the distance as our train picked up speed. The trip was uneventful. As I watched the countryside speeding by, milepost after milepost, I was amazed and felt small indeed as the vast panorama spread itself before my eyes. I had never been on such a long trip. I soaked up the ever-changing landscape like a dry sponge, for which, during the dark and anxious days still to come, I thanked God because it gave me strength when I needed it most. Just to feel that I was a tiny part of a vast country that we all more or less take for granted, until we sense the danger of losing it, was the spark that kept us going in the face of odds that seemed insurmountable. So you see, folks, we young-uns do think seriously on occasion."

There is much in this passage that's both phony and yet quite sweet, natural, and rather innocent. Maybe it was just a protective big sister's efforts years after the fact to shape the narrative in ways to make her kid brother sound better. The phony part isn't simply that self-consciously corny "young-uns" line, but the reference to those "insurmountable odds." In 1935 as John set off for the coast on his first serious travels, there was no war going on; that was still six years ahead. Such passages, written long after Basilone's much later voyage to a real war in which he would fight heroically and be killed, suggest that his sister was imagining what a boy on his way to war might have felt, translating his wartime emotions to a much earlier, long but essentially uneventful peacetime train ride across a tranquil nation. But some of the passage does ring true: a young man's excitement at embarking on a long trip and seeing the big country for the first time, hustling to find a window seat, munching his goodies—chocolate bars and peanut brittle—gawking at the landscape speeding past, marveling at a first glimpse of Chicago. He was, after all, still a boy, but if it was all a long way from Raritan, Johnny Basilone was to travel farther, and further, much, much further.

The Jerry Cutter and Jim Proser parallel account of that same train ride is juicier, somehow more credible, even when contradictory. In their book, Basilone leaves for California from Grand Central Station instead of Penn Station. Here's their account leading up to and of his trip west following a couple of days leave in Raritan:

"In July there was a machine gun competition on the base. My unit, D Company, walked away with the pennant. I was in a company of 58 winners. I could easier spend a year with these guys than a weekend at home. They were my family now. This was my home and the army was my life. I was a soldier.

"We shipped out to San Diego on the Super Chief out of Grand Central Station. You might have thought of it as the Wild West by what went on in the saloons in the station. The closer it got to 'all aboard' the wilder things got. Fellas who never smoked or drank in their life were doing two at a time. That went for women, too. I'm not proud of the way we acted but I won't pretend we were choirboys either. We were warriors and likely off to war [once again, a war that wouldn't begin for them until 1941]. Orders were for the Philippines. Soon enough, the MPs cleaned the places out and got us on the train. They were some of the roughest sons of bitches I ever met, those MPs. If you didn't hear them the first time they said something you might never hear anything again. They used those white batons the way Ted Williams used a ball bat. [Williams was at this time, in 1935, still an unknown schoolboy, not the major league star who hit .400, so the reference simply doesn't work.] Five or six boys got dumped into the train bleeding or doubled over with the wind knocked out of them. I hadn't really seen that kind of rough stuff before. In camp nobody was ever gotten beaten like that, that bad. In a way, after all the ceremonies, and speeches after basic training, this was the real graduation. We were trained for violence and here it was. Every one of us who could still walk wanted to jump off that train and smash those MPs in the face. That's who we were now. We were violent men. We were a hunting pack and our blood had been spilled. We were ready for our first kill."

What first kill? No one was fighting; there was no war.

"A long train with soldiers holding full pay envelopes was like a dream come true. The first crap game started before we cleared Grand Central. I was in no hurry because the money wasn't leaving this train for the next four days. I wanted to see the country since I'd never been outside New York and New Jersey.

"We slept in our seats and washed over a basin the size of a soup bowl with one foot wedged against the bathroom door so we wouldn't get knocked around by the swaying of the train. By the second day we were starting to smell like goats. Civilians who got on the train didn't stay around us long. We were irritated as hell from not getting any decent sleep and arguments were breaking out every hour or so. If it weren't for gambling, I'm sure we would have been at each other more than we were. The fact we still had three days to go didn't help. We had our choice of three kinds of sandwiches, ham, cheese, or ham and cheese. Pretty soon we weren't a crack fighting force, we were a gang of squabbling chiselers and malcontents. The Army made sure we were going to get to California alive, but they weren't worried about morale. The unfunny joke going around was they were going to put down straw for us and give us hay instead of sandwiches at the next stop. I lost interest in the passing scenery. It all looked the same. I just wanted to get off that train and away from my brothers-at-arms. After the third day of sleeping sitting up and eating stale sandwiches, we were all miserable. Liquor bottles,

puke, and cigarette butts covered the floor in some cars. The por-
ters wouldn't come near us anymore, and neither would any civilians. We were stuck with each other in our filth and stench. We
sat shoulder-to-shoulder unshaven and hung over. All we thought
about was getting off that train. Fights broke out and almost
nobody tried to stop them."

Then, suddenly and miraculously, everything changed. They
were in California, and after getting off this cross-country train,
they traveled south along the coast. As Basilone is supposed to have
said in his nephew's postmortem account, "The Pacific Ocean slid
into view and I'd never seen anything quite as beautiful before."

The Pacific. Where John Basilone would come of age, where he
would fight the Japanese in two pivotal battles, where he would
become a living American legend, a famous man, where he
would return a second time to the battle, where he would die and
be buried. Did any of this occur to the restless kid from Raritan,
still a teenager and an untried soldier, or did he marvel only at the
great ocean's splendor?

Phyllis's account resumes. "The arrival at San Diego, California
was quiet. After a few days of getting settled and outfitted, we
started our basic training."

Can this possibly be correct? Basilone had already been in the
Army for months, probably since the previous summer, had served
with an established outfit at Fort Jay, Company D of the 16th
Infantry. Whatever training they did at San Diego soon came to a
close, and one night (the date is elusive) at eight p.m., machine gunner John Basilone and his outfit were mustered and marched aboard
the USS *Republic*, a military transport that would take them to the
Philippines. The Jersey boy had crossed the country by train and
now would be leaving it entirely by ship to continue his Army career
on the other side of the Pacific, 8,000 miles away. A band played, the
transport slipped its lines, and the lights of San Diego slowly fell off
and faded astern. Stifled by the close quarters below, Basilone slept
that first night on deck, at a vacant spot near the stern.

"Making myself as comfortable as was possible, I stretched
out. Looking up I could see the sky with its thousands of stars

blinking, so close you felt you could reach up and touch them. Well, I thought, this is better. Outside of one rainy night, that was my bedroom the remainder of the trip." He was eighteen years old, a child of the Great Depression, on the first leg of a long voyage en route to an eventual glory.

15

The Philippines had become an American territory following the Spanish-American War with a promise eventually to be granted independence. But in the mid-1930s with an elected president of their own, they were still very much subject to Washington's wish and whim, so much so that a retired American general, Douglas MacArthur, now cruelly considered a back number, commanded their armed forces, such as they were—a handful of what were romantically called "Filipino Scouts" and some 16,000 U.S. Army regulars and naval personnel—a "corporal's guard" to a man of General MacArthur's towering and magisterial self-opinion. His actual title was Military Adviser to the Commonwealth Government and his rank that of a lieutenant general in the Philippine army. For MacArthur, this was something of a professional and career comedown, since he had fought famously in World War I, and in the last hours of that war to end all wars had been promoted to flag officer rank as a brigadier general by his commanding officer, General of the Armies "Black Jack" Pershing. (It was said MacArthur had desperately twisted arms for that eleventh-hour promotion, on the grounds that once the fighting ended, so too would all promotions to general officer in the shrunken peacetime Army sure to come.)

MacArthur had later in the uneasy peace between the world wars been promoted our own Army's commander as Army chief of staff, in which role and on the president's orders he had brutally smashed the so-called Bonus Army of aggrieved war veterans camped out in the parks and streets of the national capital. Now, himself abruptly among the unemployed, the man on horseback had been stunningly dismounted.

But for MacArthur, Manila was hardly an unpleasant exile. There were powerful family ties to the islands. His own father, Arthur MacArthur, had commanded in the Philippines, and the son had lived there when he was a little boy. Now another Arthur MacArthur was growing up there with *his* parents, Jean MacArthur and "the General," as Mrs. MacArthur habitually called him, in vice regal comfort in postcolonial Manila. There was always with MacArthur, even in economically straightened times and on a more modest scale, plenty of "pomp"; it was the "circumstance" that was missing in the Philippines.

Now in March 1935, John Basilone of Raritan who had the circumstance but hardly the pomp, was about to join the MacArthurs. Not, of course, as anything approaching a social equal, but more the equivalent of a young caddy carrying for wealthy and select country club members.

Aboard the USS *Republic*, Basilone sailed into Manila Harbor past landmarks that would within a few years be sandblasted into the American consciousness, the fortified island of Corregidor, the Bataan Peninsula, the big naval base at Cavite, delivering the young soldier to his duty station for the next two years, as a machine gunner under one of the most celebrated of all American warriors, Douglas ("Gawd Almighty Himself") MacArthur. But here also young John would flirt for the first time with the idea of marriage, to a local girl named Lolita, and he would make something of a reputation as a fighter, not in war but in another arena, as a jock on the boxing team of a peacetime Army garrison.

Eight thousand miles from San Diego, and in a time of strained military peacetime budgets, the replacement draft that included Basilone was short of just about everything: proper uniforms, decent rations, and, for some reason, soap. (Since there was no rationing, the shortage of soap must have been the result of a logistics foul-up or an incompetent supply officer, or a supply sergeant down the line who was on the chisel and selling soap to the locals for cash.) The undersupplied troops were armed not with the old bolt-action 1903 Springfield rifles of World War I (Sergeant York, and all that) but the even older Boer War Enfield.

Out of sheer hunger, soldiers fleshed out mess hall chow with Filipino fare, goat meat becoming a staple. Some of the troops were adopted by local Philippine families or got part-time jobs in Filipino shops and businesses, or moved in with native girls. Others started up local, off-base businesses of one sort or another, of which Jerry Cutter and Jim Proser quote Basilone as saying, "For the first year or two I didn't go in for that. I was still U.S. Army and kept my nose clean as far as all that." Some troops took up wearing Philippine civilian clothes, a few deserted entirely, or cracked, "went Asiatic." Not Basilone, though he complained that only the constant card games got him through the boredom of that first year in country.

There were bandits up in the hills and a few rebels of one persuasion or another, and you might think that MacArthur would have had his troops constantly out in the field, aggressively patrolling, in order to train and season his men and eliminate boredom, if not the bandits. No such luck. Perhaps budgetary constraints limited such exercises and prohibited the general from issuing orders that would have benefited both his men and his entire command. These were hard times, and this was an Army on the cheap. They counted cartridges, so that firing-range practice, something you'd think to be essential, was curtailed. Or maybe MacArthur was simply getting older, saw little future in his career, and, inertia being what it was, just didn't bother ordering units into the field.

Basilone recalled that from time to time shots were fired at the Army encampments from beyond the perimeter security. There might then be a halfhearted attempt to track down and capture the "guerrillas," but the Americans never caught anyone in the rough terrain of the countryside. And there might have been the odd firefight, though how did you chase bandits through the bush lugging a Browning water-cooled heavy machine gun, basically a defensive weapon, and with its tripod, water jacket, elevating and aiming devices, and the pintle on which everything turned, weighing when loaded nearly a hundred pounds? The answer was, you didn't, so it is highly unlikely the young machine gunner ever fired a shot in anger in the Philippine years.

For the bored, card-playing, womanizing, and randy young Basilone, there were, however, the attractive charms of the petite, dark-haired, dark-eyed local women, who he thought resembled some of the handsome Italian-American girls he'd known at home in Raritan. There were plenty of compliant "amateurs," and there were the favorite girls at the local bordellos. According to a few dubious, entirely unproven allegations, Basilone actually became a junior partner in running one of these establishments of easy virtue. I found no credible evidence of that, but almost surely he patronized the brothels. The whorehouse "management" rumors may have derived from the small "nightclub" he and his girl, Lolita, set up inside her uncle's bicycle shop, which sounds colorful and fun but reasonably innocent.

All of MacArthur's troops looked forward to their R&R stints every six months in New Zealand, with its temperate climate, pretty girls, local beers, and "people a lot like us." Some of the farmboys and ranchers among the enlisted men spent their R&R, and voluntarily so, living with families and working without pay and happily on farms and cattle stations (ranches). The Yanks found New Zealanders wonderful, but really they would have welcomed almost anything to get them out of the Philippines for a time. Some of Basilone's fellow soldiers, their enlistments up, instead of going home to the States returned to New Zealand to marry local girls.

Beyond his acknowledged skill as a machine gunner, there was at first little to distinguish Basilone's first overseas tour of duty, apart from his card-playing expertise and a penchant for going barefoot in monsoon season. Army-issue wool socks, when wet, itched, and men developed fungus and jungle rot. Cotton socks sent from home rotted quickly. Basilone had a simple cure—go without—and was regularly chewed out about it. But his feet toughened up, he developed surer footing, and he didn't itch anymore. Going barefoot was just about all that set him apart from his mates—or it was until he began to box.

In the jock-happy prewar regular Army, service athletes, especially competent boxers, might do pretty well for themselves. MacArthur, who served once as superintendent of the Military Academy at West Point, understood the constructive role military athletics could play in a bored peacetime Army and encouraged the athletic culture. James Jones wonderfully (and tragically) portrayed the scene in prewar Hawaii in *From Here to Eternity* with fighter and trumpeter Robert E. Lee Prewitt as his hero. Young Basilone's experience was more rewarding. He began boxing, horsing around at first in ad hoc fights. "A lot of steam had been building up in my head."

Part of that "steam" was a professional and rather patriotic frustration. The soldiers had been told that if the Japanese (the closest, perhaps the *only* potential enemy) ever attacked, the plan was for American regulars of MacArthur's little Army to retreat to Corregidor and fight it out from there. As Jerry Cutter reported the situation from Basilone's point of view, "I didn't like sitting around waiting for an attack just so we could run for it. And I didn't like that we were stuck on this island [Luzon] and we weren't even important enough to get soap. Sparring let me blow off steam and kept me sharp. Being a fighter got you privileges sometimes like an inside bunk and credit at card games—which I didn't usually need." Based on his success in those pickup bouts, he volunteered for the unit's organized boxing squad, and as a muscular young athlete in good shape, he began fighting in service bouts as a 160-pound middleweight. He was now nineteen, and thanks to being physically more mature, a year older, and with regular workouts, conditioning, and better chow, had soon grown into and was fighting as a light heavyweight (175 pounds). He soon caught on to the racket. "Once I started winning I started getting steaks and pork chops stolen from the Officers' Club. My fellow soldiers began to see me as a money-making enterprise."

Soldiers, and especially other gunners and his buddies, not only backed him with cash in side bets but volunteered as sparring partners, medics as cut men, others as corner men, trainers, managers, and cheering squads. Gambling picked up and money changed hands. Basilone was becoming a popular local character on whom a man might make a buck.

There were organized bouts twice a month, and Basilone won them. Never lazy, he trained hard, running up hills or in the soft, yielding sand of the shoreline of Manila Bay. Parallels to the much later and fictional Rocky Balboa are irresistible. For all Basilone's casual, card-playing ways, there is an impressive discipline about the slimly educated youngster, the newly minted soldier. One weekend when a fellow soldier named Smits was arrested for being intoxicated, Basilone and some buddies conjured up a scheme to break him out of the drunk tank of a Filipino police station by ramming a stolen truck into the prison wall early on a Sunday morning, the clever reasoning being that the cops, being Roman Catholics, would be at their devotions and attending mass. Whether the Sunday-morning ploy was Basilone's or a group decision, they got Smits out and weren't caught themselves. The plan worked.

Following two knockouts in Basilone's first three winning formal bouts, the brass began coming by to see him fight, even MacArthur on one occasion stopping by to wish him luck. He eventually ran his record to eighteen wins, no losses. According to Cutter and Proser, the adulation went slightly to Basilone's head, and he started thinking of his undefeated record and himself as a sort of "mascot" for the general, someone to whom MacArthur, with his ego, could justifiably point in an otherwise unimpressive little command. Reputedly, word of Basilone's ability trickled back to the States, and offers to turn professional came in from New York fight managers and promoters, though no one I spoke with in Raritan could provide any names or details about what probably was just wishful thinking. But a fighting nickname, "Manila John," seems to have stuck. And MacArthur was pleased as the kid's perfect ring record improved, with a big possible fight against a Navy boxer coming up.

It was always an occasion, the whores and the saloons especially rejoicing, when the fleet sailed into Manila, and with Army and Navy rivalry heightening, officers trading boasts and placing bets, they staged Basilone's last Army bout, matching him as a soldier against a formidable American Navy tar, "Sailor Burt," a tough machinist's mate, "a fucking Dane . . . a shoveler of shit," as the troops rudely put it. Manila John's buddies placed their own bets, warning him he'd "better win" or they'd be broke till next payday. He tried, prudently, to warn them off. Sailor Burt was tough and Manila John could guarantee nothing. But the soldiers didn't listen.

The day of the big fight arrived, and with it a lunch that wasn't the usual dreary mess hall chow for the gladiator, but a steak, French fries, sliced Bermuda onion, topped off by apple pie, and steaming black coffee. With a cheering, foot-stamping audience of sailors and soldiers, including the brass from both services, Basilone and Burt went at it, trading knockdowns, both men nearly out. In the end it was a twelve-rounder and yet another knockout, as "Manila John" won again, running his record to 19–0. His commanding officer was jubilant, and even the disappointed admiral came back to the lockers to congratulate the foe, the Army boy who knocked out Sailor Burt.

With his Army hitch nearing its end, the young man was torn. He hated the boredom, the weather, not enough to eat even of the usual lousy food, the malaria, the bugs, the chiggers, the snakes, but most of all those "standing orders to retreat" in case of war, the prospect of a fallback to Corregidor if and when the Japanese came ashore. And John *knew* they were coming. He liked the discipline and much of the structure and purpose he found in the Army but hated some of it. He's quoted on how enlisted men were handled: "They trained us to be fighters and treated us like convicts."

John thought he might be in love with Lolita, even considered staying in the islands with her and starting a real business outside the bike shop cum nightclub. But in the end when his sergeant asked if Basilone planned to re-up for another tour, he said no. Twenty-one years old, he headed home to Raritan, as adrift as he had been three years before, as directionless and unfocused, as unskilled in civilian terms. And even worse, having returned home, he realized already that he missed some aspects of Army life—the machine gun, the boxing, the camaraderie. His nephew Jerry Cutter summed it up, supposedly in his uncle's words: "I had lost the life, the calling I had found. I wasn't a soldier anymore. I was lost."

16

B ack home, again a civilian, John Basilone recognized swiftly, pragmatically that "there's not much use for a machine gunner in New Jersey." If he expected much out of his hometown, he was mistaken. He went to see and seek counsel from his old priest/adviser Amadeo Russo at St. Ann's. The men talked with the old familiarity, but there were no easy answers. At home Basilone self-consciously told stories of the Philippines but not about Lolita, whom he sloughed off as just another of the generic native girls he'd encountered. Asked about the Army, he didn't feel that he could explain it very well, not so they would understand—the contradictions, the pull it had on him still, and the other, less appealing aspects of garrison life—not so that anyone "got" his mixed emotions. It was frustrating.

The Depression had eased marginally, and some of Basilone's boyhood friends were settled down and doing well. Others were as adrift as he was. No high school, no marketable skills, nothing beyond being able to field-strip and rebuild a Browning water-cooled heavy machine gun. Basilone was a good boxer in amateur circles but was sufficiently savvy to know that was a long way from being a professional paid to fight like his old idol, Primo Carnera, in Madison Square Garden. There was always the caddy shack at the Raritan Valley Country Club. As an adult, he was caddying again that summer over his father's objections: "You can't be a caddy your whole life," his father said. For a time he drove a laundry delivery truck for Gaburo's Laundry (his sleeping atop the laundry bags apparently forgiven). Then he took a job in nearby Bound Brook with the Calco Chemical Division of American Cyanamid. That job lasted a year.

Basilone's sister Phyllis and her husband, Bill Cutter, were living in Reisterstown, Maryland, near Baltimore, and Bill convinced John to become an installation mechanic for his gas company employer, the Philgas Company. Basilone moved in with the Cutters. He seemed to enjoy the work and was good at it, but after about eight months the old restlessness was working at him.

In a way he missed the orderly, organized misery of an enlisted man's daily routine on a military post, no matter how distant or alien. And he was again sensing that war was coming to his country, his home, as it had to so many other nations around the world. It got him thinking about again enlisting. But this time he wouldn't go Army.

Basilone was now twenty-three years old, a veteran, a traveled man, strong and aware of his own highly specialized skills and strengths, a solid 180 pounds, a formidable amateur boxer, and considerably larger than his father. But he didn't know quite how to break the news to his parents that civilian life wasn't working out for him and that he was going back into the service. That in fact, and without telling anyone, on July 11, 1940, the day on which Marshal Pétain, now virtually a Nazi puppet, became president of Occupied France, John had gone into Baltimore and enlisted in the Marine Corps. The Marines were apparently glad to have a man with three years of Army service behind him and a veteran machine gunner at that. Phyllis was stunned, but Bill seemed to understand and be supportive, agreeing to help smooth things over with the family and especially with the patriarch, the Old Man, Salvatore the tailor.

The two men and Phyllis drove north the next day to Raritan. The situation promised to be awkward. John seemed to have grown tranquil now that he'd made a decision and taken action. He thought he now knew how to appeal to his father, through the old man's love of his adopted country, his patriotism, and though his mother might "carry on," she would eventually fall in line. The ploy worked. Over a smoke he told his father he was concerned about threats from the country's enemies. Who would dare attack us? the senior Basilone demanded. John was prepared. "The Japs, Pop." Maybe he was still thinking of that golfing foursome at the country club, those Japanese golfers taking photos.

At Sal's insistence, John agreed to remain in Raritan for a round of leave-taking with family and friends. At first he resented these duty calls. But as the visits went on, seeing pals and relations, with the well-wishing, the ritual glass of wine, the gifts, usually money, pressed into Basilone's hands, he felt better about things. And to be candid about it, he could use the dough. His appointed date with the Marines arrived, and he left Raritan for the South, reporting to boot camp at what was then the Marine Corps recruit depot at Quantico, Virginia, just thirty-five miles south of Washington, D.C.

In her serialized newspaper account of her brother's adventures, and in his voice, this is how Phyllis describes John's formal introduction to the Corps: "A hot sweltering humid day. The processing didn't help any, however. Looking back I can truthfully say the first night at Quantico was the only night I found it difficult to fall asleep. If I thought Army training was tough, it was soon put out of my mind. When they train you to become a Marine, you either fall by the wayside or you emerge as the best damn fighting man in the service. We trained and went through exercises at Quantico until we were razor sharp. Our sergeant was a holy terror and if only one-tenth of our bitching came true, he'd never have a restful night's sleep. Later on we thanked God for our training under Sarge. It certainly paid off. Maybe he knew; he always hollered, 'Come on you guys, get the lead out of your asses. What'd you think, you're in the Army? Set up these guns, on the double.' It got so we could set them up in seconds flat. Secretly, I had the feeling he was satisfied, even proud of us."

All this may have dismayed Phyllis, but to most Marines the drill sounds familiar, routine, and rather tame. If "asses" was the worst language and "hollering" the worst treatment that boot camp drill instructors passed out back in 1940, Manila John was a fortunate man. One can assume this business of "setting up guns" dealt with the Browning heavy machine guns on which Basilone had been already thoroughly checked out during his Army hitch. As for that "hot sweltering humid" Quantico weather, I can testify as a Marine who spent three summers there (1948, 1949, and 1951) that heat and humidity was commonplace. For an American with two years in the tropical Philippines, the climate of northern Virginia shouldn't have been a shock. And for an enlisted man and trained athlete with three years of Army service behind him, a Marine recruit depot would be tolerable if not posh. Yet as Phyllis sums up in John's voice his Quantico experience, "If we thought boot training was tough, we soon discovered that compared to our training and exercises at Guantanamo Bay, Cuba, it was duck soup."

According to Basilone's USMC military service record, he boarded ship, traveling "tourist class" aboard the SS *McCawley* on September 28, 1940, and was ashore at Guantanamo on October 2. Nothing much was going on there, just a handful of peacetime Marines in canvas leggings toting Springfield '03s, guardians of one of the modest and most enduring outposts of American colonialism, held ever since the Spanish-American War. Teddy Roosevelt may have landed at or embarked from here. And in Basilone's words, "There we put in seven miserable months of maneuvers. For this we earned the title of 'Raggedy-Ass Marines.'"

Some of those maneuvers weren't at Guantanamo itself but at the Puerto Rican Island of Culebra where, as early as the winter of 1923–1924, the Marine Corps had begun a concentrated and very serious program of amphibious warfare, training troops to land on hostile beaches under fire, from small boats launched beachward from transports, destroyers, or other larger craft. By

1940 and 1941, Basilone was one of many Marines readying for amphibious warfare. There were as yet no specially designed landing craft, and photos of the time show Marines jumping into shallow-water beaches from Chris-Craft speedboats, civilian-style 1920s motorboats of one sort or another, rifles at high port to keep them dry and out of the corroding saltwater.

In a still young country like ours, it's fascinating the way history can compress and fold in on itself. Here we were in the 1940s training troops on islands and beaches won by Teddy Roosevelt and his generation at the end of the last century during the Spanish-American War, incorporating new assault tactics developed in the 1920s, to be put into action against the Japanese in the mid-twentieth century in World War II.

On New Year's Day 1941 Basilone joined the outfit with which he would first see combat, D Company, 1st Battalion of the 7th Marine Regiment of the Fleet Marine Force (FMF). On March 1, 1941, he was transferred to D Company of the 1st Marines, a different regiment. There is no explanation for this transfer. Perhaps someone was short of a machine gunner, and indeed Basilone would soon land back in the 7th Regiment.

He wrote little, nothing that came down to us through family and friends or through the years. Instead, we get the spare official record of his service, the flawed memories of his folks, most of them now dead, and beyond that, a frustrating silence.

The paucity of letters from Basilone to the family, or to anyone, is frustrating. The nuns at his grammar school and Father Russo, his mentor, must share the blame for Manila John's failure to write, even to the family, or keep some sort of informal diary. He must have had some informed, interesting things to say, one young man's commentary on being in a peacetime American military while much of the cultured and civilized Old World was at war, a war that was maybe coming, and soon, to a still peaceful, complacent America. Why should we be immune? If France with its greatest army in the world could fall, London burn, and Poland, the Low Counties, Norway, and Denmark be conquered, why would we stand untouched?

Or might not machine gunner Basilone have made pungent comparisons between the Marines and his previous employer, the U.S. Army? Did he miss General Douglas MacArthur and his paternalistic cheerleading, yearn for the boxing, ache for Lolita? Was Marine chow better than the crap they fed him in Manila? Or was there anything else from his previous enlistment and two years in a foreign country from which he took lessons? From which fellow Marines might have learned something? When he read the papers, if he did, was he following with even a narrow professional interest what was happening in Europe and North Africa? When he heard of growing tensions in the Pacific, did he once more recall that foursome of Japanese golfers he once took as spies? Might Basilone not have taken scribbled notes, worried about the future, concerned himself about a possible American war, drawn and mulled obvious conclusions?

From Guantanamo Bay, sandy, hot, wind-dried, and peaceful Gitmo, the Marines moved on to more promising exercises, those landing maneuvers at Culebra. Basilone and his heavy machine gun moved on. There were other Marine Corps "stately pleasure domes" to come. On April 19, 1941, "Patriots Day" in Boston, where they were still celebrating the battles of Concord and Lexington, Basilone and Company D arrived aboard the good ship *George F. Elliott* at Parris Island, South Carolina, later to become the East Coast's recruit training depot. It was there on May 15 that Basilone was promoted, the same day the Germans were preparing to drop their paratroopers on Crete, including old heavyweight champ Max Schmeling, to take the island from the Brits, whose numbers included Royal Marine commando officer and author Evelyn Waugh and some battered Greeks.

Basilone had been rewarded with a promotion by temporary warrant to corporal, a swift promotion in those days, which must say something about his performance, professional skills, and attitude as a relatively new Marine. When you think back to those three years of consistently "excellent" fitness reports during Army service, he seems to have been a born soldier.

There was a brief stop at his old boot camp at Quantico, a base now expanding rapidly. A short furlough later that month was followed by what sounds like seagoing duty, aboard the *Harry Lee* from June 7 to July 23 and then aboard the *Fuller* from July 24 to August 13. On September 30, 1941, Basilone arrived in North Carolina and went ashore at a new and growing base called New River. Also on that day, in Russia, Kiev having been taken, Guderian's panzer army wheeled toward Moscow. It looked as if the Soviets were next to finished, the Germans closing on victory. There was no comment on this that we know of from Basilone.

Phyllis in her account has her brother touching not on the world war but about his latest duty station in the Carolinas: "If we thought Cuba and Culebra were bad, our first look at New River made them look like the Riviera."

Marine Barracks, New River, North Carolina, what is now known as Camp Lejeune (or in Marine jargon, "Swamp Lagoon"), was a new East Coast Marine base on a big river flowing into the nearby Atlantic. In 1941 the Navy Department and Marine brass, increasingly concerned about the Japanese, were considering an expansion of the Marine Corps from a mere 7,000 troops and 500 officers to something a lot bigger, a Corps that would have need of large new bases. Basilone is quoted as describing New River this way: "Picture if you can over 100,000 acres of plains, swamps, water infested with snakes, chiggers and sand flies. No mountains or hills, just flat, swampy terrain, and you get an idea of what our playground was."

With winter coming on, Basilone's outfit was still housed in tents in the cold and damp, the heating supplied by smelly stoves prone to starting fires and very good at putting out soot, with lighting mostly limited to candles. The training concentrated on amphibious warfare drill, men climbing down cargo nets into small boats, much of the time using mockups on dry land since neither large transports or landing barges were available, though cargo nets were plentiful. There were no USO shows coming to New River, the only medium was the local weekly newspaper, and perhaps out of sheer boredom,

Basilone resumed boxing, again going undefeated, though against what quality of competition isn't clear. He enjoyed a week's furlough that ended with his return to New River on November 26, two weeks before the attack on Pearl Harbor, a shattering and historic event about which, by my reckoning, Basilone has absolutely nothing to say. The Japanese had surprise-attacked us, and Corporal Basilone issues no comment, displays no reaction.

The United States had been attacked and was now at war, the entire country was up in arms, our military men and bases were on alert, Basilone was a serving Marine, yet there is nothing at all recorded of letters or calls or any exchanges whatsoever between him and his folks. Its is tempting to say that this is vexing, but perhaps in the new wartime situation Basilone may simply have been kept busy. After all, the Marines were supposed to be "first to fight."

On January 23, 1942, Basilone was promoted, again by temporary warrant, to sergeant-line, once more a rapid promotion perhaps reflecting not only on his outstanding record but the accelerating expansion of the Corps. In the Pacific the Japanese were winning almost everywhere and rolling up American and Allied forces. And on that very date of Basilone's promotion, Japanese troops landed on New Britain, New Ireland, Borneo, and in the Solomons, on the big island of Bougainville. An enemy sub had shelled the oil fields of Long Beach, just south of Los Angeles. Incendiary balloons launched in Japan floated across the ocean on prevailing winds toward the forested slopes of Oregon and Washington State, fortunately setting no fires. But the bastards did have a helluva nerve, didn't they?

In March, reacting to continued enemy pressure and new landings in the Pacific, a detachment of Marines, Basilone among them, was assigned to the defense of American Samoa, and the entire 1st Marine Division, which had been created only thirteen months earlier, got its orders for service overseas. On April 10 Basilone's bunch embarked from Norfolk for the Pacific, and after a long, leisurely voyage, "Our convoy reached Apia, Western Samoa on May 8, 1942 and set up camp." The Battle of the Coral Sea was fought that day. A few days earlier in the Philippines, where Basilone once served, the historic 4th Marines had burned their regimental colors and sent off two officers, a field music (probably a bugler), and an interpreter to ask the victorious Japanese for terms, and then surrendered, shortly to set off on the long death march to the camps.

In peaceful Samoa, Sergeant Basilone was just barely en route to the war and, eventually, a shot at the enemy. Neither he nor anyone else could have predicted that within months he would fight heroically in desperate battles on Guadalcanal, be shipped to Australia, awarded the grandest medal we have, and then confronted with a hard choice to make, to "stay with his boys" and go back into combat, or accept a free ride home to the States as an anointed hero.

PART THREE

HOME FRONT

Major General Alexander A. Vandegrift, Colonel Merritt A. Edson, Platoon Sergeant Mitchell Paige, and Sergeant John Basilone after receiving their Congressional Medals of Honor at Camp Balcombe, in Australia, May 21, 1943, for their heroism at Guadalcanal.

17

The Marine Corps finally, in midsummer of 1943, after much backing and filling, made up its mind. John Basilone was being sent back to the States.

"The day officer came in one day and handed me orders, [to] separate from my unit. I was shipping out, going home. I was to report to Marine headquarters in New York City. There were no further instructions. Talking about coming from left field, I had to read the damn thing three times. I was going home. It didn't make any sense. My guys are gearing up for operations and I'm shipping out? [Bob] Powell looked at me as if I was Jesus H. Christ himself. He gave me his folks' address in New Haven and for a minute I thought he was going to cry. Nobody even thought seriously about home and not even in a dream. But here it was in front of me and I was going. . . . The orders said now, so I packed my sea bag." Basilone's mood had changed, his earlier elation over the medal's being a sure "ticket home" had evaporated. He would be going home, but now reluctantly.

It's exasperating that nowhere do we have a date for the man's departure. It probably was July. Basilone's service record book shows that he was promoted to temporary platoon sergeant on June 1, 1943, and the entry on the next line, partly illegible, indicates he sailed on the twenty-seventh (it had to be July) via the ship *Rochambeau*. In the next service record book entry, Basilone reports into Marine barracks at the Washington, D.C., Navy Yard on August 31, 1943. Furloughs might logically fill in the gaps covering most of August. The medal ceremony had been on May 21, 1943. Yet there was no official news about it until June 23 when it was released to the national press. The *New York Times* ran its front-page story on June 24, under a headline that read, "Slew 38 Japanese in one battle; Jersey Marine gets honor medal." The lead read, "The son of an Italian-born tailor in New Jersey took his place tonight among the great American war heroes, when a Marine Corps platoon sergeant, John Basilone of Raritan, 26, one of a family of ten children, was cited for the Congressional Medal of Honor, the highest tribute the nation can bestow on its fighting sons." John's letter to the family telling about the medal was dated June 12, and they received it June 21, did not understand its significance, and therefore didn't really react until the news broke in newspapers on the twenty-third or (as in the *Times*) the twenty-fourth of June.

Bruce Doorly in his monograph notes, "In July of 1943, John was notified that he was being sent home, but there was a catch to it. John would have to go on a 'bond drive' and on a 'speaking tour,' to war plants.

"This wouldn't be the first of these bond-selling caravansaries of Hollywood stars and actual decorated heroes to tour the country. In 1942 the luminous Carole Lombard, a glamorous figure and gifted film comedienne, the wife of Clark Gable (himself now an Air Corps officer), was killed in a plane crash during just such a trip. As John loaded up to go home he told his buddies he would be back, but they did not believe him. . . . John arrived back in the U.S., landing in California in August of 1943."

Jerry Cutter, Basilone's nephew, attempts to nail down his uncle's return to the continental United States, starting with this account, in John's voice, of the press reception at Roosevelt Base, a wartime operation on Terminal Island off Long Beach, California, possibly where the *Rochambeau* docked following its long crossing from Melbourne: "They swarmed over us, snapping pictures and yelling questions, everybody calling to me, 'Manila John, how d'ya feel when ya got the medal?' 'Hey, Johnny, were ya scared?' 'Have ya called home yet?' 'How'd ya feel when you killed all those Japs?' Talk about being in the spotlight, it was like the whole country turned its headlights on me and wanted me to tell them every last thing down to what I had for breakfast."

Sounds like the celebrity press of today, the paparazzi, the shouted questions about whether he liked being called "Manila John, the Jap Killer"? Would he be going back into the ring?

This was a guy who hated to be "gawked at" in his own barracks by Marines he knew, let alone total strangers doing a job. But here's how Phyllis Cutter reconstructed the time following the May 21 award presentation at Melbourne, in Basilone's voice, including a brief reference on a fairly important official matter. During his California sojourn in August 1943, she quotes him, fed up by all the press, as saying, "Turning down a commission, I asked to be sent back into action with my buddies and was promptly refused."

This is new, the mention of a possible commission, the Corps finally offering him an opportunity to become an officer, just as they had earlier with Platoon Sergeant Mitchell Paige. There would later be similar offers in Washington, but this reference is the earliest such bid of commissioned rank that I can find. In Phyllis's article, Basilone goes on: "I think it was during the latter part of July 1943 [while still with his unit in Australia] I was being briefed on my return to the States. Yes, I was being given leave. However, there was a hitch to it. I was given a faint idea of what was expected of me and told I would be filled in at HQ in New York City."

Phyllis describes Basilone's departure from Melbourne with one Marine, on seeing John crying, sneering to another, "I thought you said he was a tough guy." There is no account of his voyage home aboard, the records say, the *Rochambeau*, or his brief August stay in California with its welcoming if rowdy press events. There was a quick authorized visit to Camp Pendleton at Oceanside, California, to see his brother George, who was now a young Marine there in training. "A big fuss" was made, and George was given time off (he was later sent home on leave to be with his brother).

While Basilone was still in California the Marine Corps was already briefing him on an upcoming tour with movie people to sell war bonds around the country. "We kept hearing that this bond tour was going to get going but one thing or another held up the show. First it was some movie star couldn't get away, and then it was a scheduled event that was delayed and would throw the whole schedule off. So we ended up sitting in our barracks with absolutely nothing to do except waiting to be called for interviews with newspaper or radio people. They all asked pretty much the same questions. So I started telling them they could read the other newspaper and get all the answers they wanted."

So Basilone was starting to mouth off, wise-guy style. "My shadow [his guide and monitor on the tour] lit into me after that. These were all important people from important places. If I didn't toe the line he'd see about getting me shipped back to that jungle. That was definitely the wrong thing to say. He said it like being in the jungle fighting was a place where you went if you couldn't get a soft desk job like him, and his important people."

You wonder why Manila John didn't just deck the creep. Apparently the significant next step in his journey was the order to report to the senior Marine at 90 Church Street in Manhattan. Maybe they were finally getting started on the war bond tour.

Phyllis picks up Basilone's story in New York, at the Marine Corps office there, where the returning warrior would again be trotted out for the press, his first organized Manhattan press conference. A comic book called *War Heroes* had been released, his story as a superhero garishly reported in detail. There is no suggestion anyone in the Corps or in publishing even bothered to ask Basilone's clearance on the comic. He was a serving Marine and, medal or no medal, he was expected to do what he was told.

Wrote Phyllis in her brother's voice: "It was mid-morning on September 4, and sitting in the Corps office nervous, with the perspiration rolling down my brow, I remarked, 'Geez, this is something.' Well, anyway, I told the reporters who had jammed the press room my story exactly as it happened. As I once again related my experiences, I seemed to have drifted back to the 'Canal, bringing home the realization that as long as I had to repeat the experience time and time again, it would take a long time to erase its memory from my mind. Maybe that's the price a hero pays. I didn't know." You sense the confusion in the young man's mind, the understandable stage fright, almost a longing for military routine, for the structure of the unit, the outfit, his pals, the Marine Corps itself. Yet this was in a Marine office in Manhattan and the Marine Corps was more or less running the show, and the sergeant was going along with it as best he could. Things lightened up that September afternoon.

"At noon I was taken over to City Hall to meet 'The Little Flower,' Mayor LaGuardia. He turned out to be an all-right Joe. Of course the reporters and photographers tagged along, jotting down our every word to the steady pop of the flash-bulbs all over the place." LaGuardia made a little talk about the significance of Basilone's medal and the requisite pitch for Americans to buy war bonds during the bond drive coming up, and then he turned back to Basilone with a question. "Sergeant, where did your old man come from?"

Basilone gave the proudly parochial Italian American mayor chapter and verse about Italy, Naples, the name of the ship on which his father sailed to the States, and his work as a tailor, and the Little Flower beamed. There were other press conferences, with family members participating in some of them, and Marine brother George marveling to John at one point, "The whole country is crazy about you." Then it was off to D.C. and another round of press conferences, including one at USMC headquarters, on or about September 9, a session that would be pleasantly pivotal. Amid the usual shouted questions and flashbulbs going off in his face, Basilone later admitted, "I was sweating, nervous, and turning to an officer, I said, 'This is worse than fighting the Japs.' He patted me on the shoulder and told me to tell the reporters what happened on October 24–25 in my own words."

Apparently a hush then came over the big room, and for the first time the thing was no longer a circus or an adversarial process, a scrimmage between aggressive reporters and photographers and an overwhelmed Marine still unused to any of this. With Marine public affairs officers and noncoms in charge on their own turf, even the cocky press boys calmed down, stopped shouting, settled in to take notes and let the man speak. Basilone, at last and perhaps for the first time, would be able to tell his story quietly and in a measured and orderly fashion, without interruption, as he best remembered it.

"I started to talk and as the words poured out, I became oblivious to the reporters and all the confusion going on about me. I told them how there had been a heavy tropical rain all day long." Then he told them about the fight, starting with that field phone's ringing at about ten that night, warning that a Japanese attack was about to hit their ridgelines, and went on from there, taking a live audience with him through the nightmare hours of darkness and into the welcoming gray half-light of another dawn, trying to explain how an exhausted, stressed man in mortal combat felt about having lived to see yet another day.

Except for an unlikely Manila John word like "oblivious," it almost seems that this would be the press conference where Basilone made some sort of a breakthrough, realizing that if he just told the story in his own way and his own words, he might be able to handle the challenge of speaking in public. And when the machine gunner had wrapped up his story and a colonel called a halt to the proceedings, each of the newspaper reporters, not shouting now but rather subdued, walked up and asked to shake his hand.

"With that they filed out of the press room. I was a little shaken, retelling those terrible hours all over again." Shaken, sure, but he had coped, had talked at some length, and if not articulately then clearly, to hard-bitten professional journalists. He had not only responded to their questions but, it was quite apparent, moved some of those hard-shelled pros. Peter Vitelli, one of my sources in Raritan, supplied me the CD of a Basilone sound bite, so I've actually heard his voice talking to an admiring crowd. He could be an effective speaker.

Now, as Basilone's tour of the United States was about to start, Phyllis's account becomes quite detailed and precise, with dates, places, events, names, and ranks, everything but serial numbers. Her son Jerry's later but parallel version differs somewhat in the racier details of the journey.

According to Phyllis, the same public relations colonel who'd calmed and encouraged Basilone earlier now took him aside in D.C. and briefed him on the coming agenda. The tour would kick off shortly, the month of September 1943, roughly a year after Basilone and the rest of the 7th Marines went ashore on the 'Canal. "The colonel came over to me and told me to sit down and take it easy. He then outlined the coming bond tour. I was assigned to Flight number 5 of the War Veterans Airmadas [you begin to suspect a Madison Avenue ad agency copywriter at work here in the jargon, with that coined word "Airmadas"]. My companions were to be Sergeant Schiller Cohen, Bosun's Mate 2nd Class Ward L. Gemmer, Machinist Mate 1st Class Robert J. Creak, and film stars Virginia Grey, Martha Scott, Eddie Bracken, John Garfield, and Gene Lockhart [Keenan Wynn would be added]." Not precisely the A-list of Hollywood legends, but not bad. The destinations were largely and conveniently in the Northeast to start. "We were to cover the following cities, Newark, Jersey City, New Haven, Conn., Providence, R.I., Pawtucket, R.I., Worcester, Mass., Albany, Utica, and Rochester N.Y., and Allentown, Pa." And though Basilone was only one of four servicemen on the tour it was obvious he was the big catch, with the first stops in his home state. But he had questions and might as well ask them now.

"I said to the colonel, 'Sir, you mean to tell me I have to speak at all of these rallies? What in the world will I talk about?' 'Sergeant, don't worry about it, you will be introduced and asked to say a few words. Just remember, this tour is important to the war effort, in addition to raising money, you will be speaking at war plants and you of all people should know how desperately we need supplies, guns, and ammunition at the front lines. You may not think so now, but you will be serving your country as much as if you were back in the jungle killing the enemy.'"

How much of this Basilone actually bought into is impossible at this remove to say, but as a schoolboy at the time, five years before my own Marine Corps enlistment, I remember how seriously civilians took such patriotic exhortations in wartime. We had rationing and blackouts and casualty lists, so the war was hardly a far-off story. We at home were in ways also living with it. In the daily papers and in the magazines that came to our house, and on the radio and in the movie newsreels, to a boy like me seeing footage of heroic figures like Manila John Basilone mouthing the same or similar words, they meant something. We weren't yet jaded.

18

In Newark, New Jersey, the bond tour's first stop, and only a forty-minute train ride on the Raritan Valley line from his hometown, John Basilone recalled, "There were a lot of speeches by top officials. I remember Mayor Murphy saying how proud he was of what Newark had contributed to the war effort, and how he urged all citizens to buy bonds until it hurt—and then buy one extra. After a wonderful dinner and more speeches we were taken to Proctors Theatre for a showing of 'Mr. Lucky' [with Cary Grant and Leo Durocher's wife, Laraine Day]. Following the showing, the Hollywood stars in the Airmada introduced us service men. We all gave a short talk and urged the audience to 'Back the Attack.' Judging the reception we were given in Newark [where there were surely Basilones and a pride of neighbors and friends in attendance], we knew we were in for a hectic tour. There would be little rest, except for short naps, between our jumps from city to city. We were formally greeted at [Jersey City's] City Hall by the commissioners before proceeding to the Hotel Plaza, where we were the guests of about 300 leading citizens for luncheon. Commissioner Potterton was the toastmaster and thanks to him, the speeches were held down to three minutes each." Whether this was because the commissioner took up all the time with his own verbosity is not explained.

It was also in Jersey City that, according to Jerry Cutter, things started to warm up between the returning hero and one of the Hollywood stars, Virginia Grey. "Mayor Murphy made a good speech. We all got our turn at the microphone. Bracken and Garfield were completely relaxed as they told people how important it was that they support the boys overseas.

"Virginia introduced me and turned to me with a look that was a little different than the look she gave to the other guys. We did another event in Jersey City that afternoon and then a few hours off. Virginia and I managed to separate us from the others and slipped away to a hotel for a few drinks in a dark, back booth. She was from a show business family and grew up in Hollywood. I never met anyone even a little bit like her before. She was just about the funniest lady I'd ever run across, and beautiful, with real movie star looks—honey-colored hair and eyes that were deep blue, cornflower blue. She was thin, must have weighed just over a hundred pounds, and had so much energy I thought she was going to get up and tap dance on the table. We laughed our heads off. She didn't take Hollywood glamour seriously at all because to her, it was just the family business. And could she tell dirty stories on all the big stars going back all the way to the silent movie days when her dad was a big shot.

"She was too good to be true. I couldn't stop looking at her. What really got me was that she was the real McCoy—inside. The tour was more important to her than her Hollywood movies. It wasn't some put-up job just to get her face in the papers, she really put her heart into everything she said out there in front of the people. When I heard that from her and knew she was telling the truth, I was like the dog with a bone. It seemed like green lights all the way for Virginia and me. Being on the road like we were, meant that we were together every day." Clearly, Manila John was a fast worker.

Since Jersey City was only the second stop on the newly launched tour and their drinks and conversation in the back booth of the hotel bar their first hours alone, one marvels at how quickly Basilone "fell for a dame." There was another dinner at a different "fancy hotel," lots of speeches, plenty of big shots, and much pulling out of wallets and checkbooks for war bonds. There then followed at the big Jersey City theater another showing of Cary Grant's *Mr. Lucky*. Virginia had an informed take on that, you can be sure. "We laughed all the way through, even the sappy love story was okay," said Basilone. "Virginia kept whispering funny comments . . . about Cary not knowing what a woman might want."

Less laughingly, and apparently meaning it, Basilone went on: "Virginia and me were falling hard and fast even though we'd just met. It was easy to be around her when we were alone. She never put on airs. And I didn't treat her like some of the girls who just wanted to have a good time with soldier boys for an evening. She was a real first class lady. She made her own money, a hell of a lot more than I did, and didn't need anybody. She was altogether a new deal. Everything was still brand new between us and we were surrounded day and night by wild guys like Eddie Bracken who was just about the funniest guy I'd ever met. He was like me, couldn't sit still. That took the pressure off us when we were out in public because Eddie was always there making jokes and playing tricks on everybody. It was the perfect set-up. Nobody made a big deal about us. It must have seemed like the natural thing.

"We eventually got around to the talk about what I was planning for the future. I hadn't been with one woman for years, and wasn't sure if I was one-woman material any more. It was always love 'em and leave 'em, have a few laughs and then have to ship out or make it back to base. Now I was in a whole new ballgame with Virginia but I couldn't tell her. It would only have made us both feel bad. After the movie the movie stars walked out on the stage in front of the screen and introduced us vets to the other servicemen and people in the audience. The slogan was 'Back the Attack,' and we pumped a few more bond sales out of them.

Virginia was a tiger and would have taken their gold teeth if she could.

"We left the theatre, off for the evening. Orders were to report to the hotel lobby tomorrow morning. Virginia and I walked through the quiet streets for a while and didn't say too much. We got back to our hotel late and went up to our rooms. It was one of the only nights I didn't wake up around midnight and grab for a weapon. Just having her in the same building was enough for me. I slept."

There are two surprises here. This is the first time since Australia that Basilone mentions nightmares of battle, sudden awakenings and a grab for weapons. And there is an admirable discipline on the part of both Grey and himself, that business of going to their separate rooms. Well, the tour was still young. And so were they. Phyllis Cutter picks up the thread: "In Plainfield [another New Jersey town] we went through much of the same. The people listened intently when Max R. Roener, the master of ceremonies, introduced us, we got a wonderful reception and were deeply impressed when the people stood in silent tribute as seaman 1st class Elmer Cornwell, U.S. Navy told how he lost 50 pounds while adrift in a lifeboat for 36 days with rations for only 15 days. It's amazing [Basilone concluded silently, perhaps recalling his own ordeals] how much the human body can take, although I feel there must be a guardian angel that watches over us at times of great stress. How else can you account for any of us being on this platform, instead of in a lonely grave thousands of miles from home and our loved ones?"

From Newark airport, Navy bombers flew the tour group to New Haven, Connecticut for a parade. There were five thousand marchers, plus jeeps, tanks, and scout cars, two bands—one from the Army Air Corps and the other from the Coast Artillery—and the State Guard. Then came time for a freshening-up at a hotel and a big rally that evening at the Arena, a fanfare of trumpets, a parade of flags of the Allied nations, Governor Baldwin, yet another mayor Murphy, the "Hollywood singing star" Miss Edith Fellows handling the national anthem, more speeches, and an honor guard of air cadets training at Yale University. This may well have been Manila

John's first brush against the Ivy League. "Later we were introduced by the Hollywood stars in our group and each of us had a little piece to say, after which we were given a standing ovation." This
was Basilone's first such speaking date outside of his own state, and
apparently it went very well since he mentions "being sorry to leave
this pleasant city."

The PR people were apparently doing their work. At one stop
they arranged to have a general release carrier pigeons in a park. In
Rochester in upstate New York, a stop Basilone had his own personal reasons to anticipate, there was a rally at Red Wings Stadium,
after which he managed to slip away to visit with the family of his
machine-gun buddy on the 'Canal, Bob Powell, meeting his mom
at 98 Garfield Street: "Bob's sister Peggy answered the door and in
seconds I was meeting Bob's mother and sister Vicky. Vicky was 22
and a looker, in fact she was beautiful. Bob had certainly held out
on me [where was Miss Grey?]. Peggy, just eight, was cute and a
little darling. I had quite a talk with Mrs. Powell, telling her all I
could about Bob. She hung on every word. I know she was proud
and thrilled when I told her if it weren't for guys like Bob covering
up for me on the right and left flanks, I'd never have lived to get
my medal. I told her how Bob and I had become close personal
friends, training together at Parris Island, New River, and Cuba."

In Albany John looked up the mother of Jackie Schoenecker,
another Guadalcanal Marine, assuring her Jackie wasn't holding
back when he told her he hadn't been wounded but was simply
suffering from malaria. "I explained that it was a common ailment
in the tropics and as a matter of fact, I was walking around with it.
I know I eased her fears."

The tour was well organized, Basilone noting that the "publicity and fanfare" whipped up before every stop ensured a big
crowd and local enthusiasm before the traveling road show of
heroes and Hollywood stars even came to town. Some of it was
fun, some moving and emotional, some quite frankly a pain in
the ass. As Basilone put it, "No matter where I went, there was
always some guy who would ask a million questions about the
Japs and outside of the job I was now assigned to. I didn't feel like

talking about them. Too many of my buddies were still dying in the stinking jungles, which when I looked around, seemed around a million miles away. Still, they were there, fighting, praying, and dying." He asked himself, "How much longer could I continue feeling like I did?" and got no answers.

Finally, this leg of the bond tour (there were others to come), the Northeast swing, was over, and it was time to go home to Raritan, the little town where Basilone grew up. "I looked forward to spending a few days with my family." But there was still "Basilone Day" to get through.

His hometown's celebrations began the morning of September 19, 1943, at Somerset Street and Route 31, "welcomed by the honorary chairman and mayor Peter Mencaroni, together with chairman William Slattery of the Township Committee. At the welcoming ceremonies I should have expected what was to come. There had already gathered so early in the morning a large crowd, affectionate, wonderful folks all calling my name and crushing in on our car. As I waved back, I spotted some old friends. With my family and buddy, Private 1st Class Steve Helstowski by my side, we entered St. Ann's Church for a high mass, which I had asked to be said for all my buddies still fighting in the South Pacific. All during mass I prayed for my buddies and for God to give me the strength and wisdom to uphold the high honors that were bestowed on me.

"A long time ago, it seemed ages, I had knelt in this very church and prayed the good Lord to help and guide me. Now, I was back again, feeling very small and humble as I realized that God in His wondrous ways had heard my prayers. Not only did I fulfill my promise to Pop to keep his name high, but that God had seen fit to touch me with His magic, lifting me up for the whole world to see."

This was a Basilone we had not seen before, spiritual, meditative, even pious. How much of this was genuine, how much simply a reaction to all of the adulation and love on every hand, the solemnity of mass at St. Ann's, his recalling the Marines still out there in the Pacific, is impossible to say. Phyllis records what are supposed to be her brother's thoughts on his return home after the cauldron of Guadalcanal and the celebrity of the unexpected medal. "I had become a national hero, kids worshipped me, my buddies would give up their lives for me and actually did. I was featured in magazines and comic books. Newspapers had endless articles about my exploits, and the bright light of publicity shone on me day and night. To cap the whole incredible drama, the President of these great United States of America had seen fit to bestow on me the greatest honor this country could give." Does this really sound like Manila John? To me it smacks of press agentry, prepared sound bites provided the young hero by his handlers and dutifully recorded later by Phyllis Basilone Cutter in her newspaper series about her brother John.

Bruce Doorly has his turn at summarizing the war bond tour to date, echoing much of what Phyllis had written, before getting to his own detailed account of the return to Raritan, and including a fascinating insight not previously recorded: even during that first leg of the speaking tour, Basilone was drinking heavily. "The publicity and fanfare did not let up at any of the bond rallies. While Basilone himself said, 'The constant fuss is starting to get on my nerves.' He was not cut out to be a public speaker. He was a soldier, and was starting to wish that he was back in action. On the tour there were constant questions about the battle with the Japanese, which he answered over and over. The pressure of the attention got so bad that John had started drinking. One veteran [presumably another serviceman on the bond tour] said, 'He knocked off a fifth the way you knock off a beer. Whisky, gin, it made no difference.'"

Basilone's last surviving sibling, Donald, who lives in Florida, told me that when he and John shared a bedroom during his brief Raritan respite from the war bond tour, and later when he was on leave, his brother didn't tell him much. But he remembered one thing clearly: "He always had a bottle of liquor on the dresser." Donald was impressed by that.

Manila John had long enjoyed a drink. Was he simply getting back into a normal peacetime routine of social drinking? Or did he now "need" a drink? Were his tour handlers supplying the stuff to keep him relaxed, keep him performing?

Phyllis says a priest named Graham said the mass at St. Ann's; Doorly says it was Basilone's old pastor and guidance counselor, Father Amadeo Russo, which sounds more likely unless somehow a very young Reverend Dr. Billy Graham had shoehorned himself into the moment. Father Russo, in his sermon, said, "God had spared [John] for some important work," a remark that inspired Basilone later to write his sister, "The importance of bringing me back finally sank in; and I resigned myself to the role that had suddenly been thrust on me."

Here is Doorly on that September 19 in Raritan from local accounts by people like Peter Vitelli (also one of my sources), who was then a six-year-old schoolboy: "At 11:30 there was a lunch in Basilone's honor headed by the reception committee at The Raritan Valley Farms Inn, a popular restaurant . . . on the Somerville Circle where the Super 8 Motel is today. Then, at 1 p.m. the parade started. Total attendance was estimated at 30,000 . . . the groups marching included The American Legion, VFW, state and local police, service men on leave, French Navy Soldiers [their Marines, it can be assumed], Coast Guard, drum & bugle corps, Boy Scouts, Girl Scouts, Red Cross units, Air Raid Wardens, The Italian American Society, Raritan First Aid Squad, soldiers from Camp Kilmer, and various marching bands."

The whole catalog shouts quintessential Americana on parade, the local hero, whether Medal of Honor winner or captain of the high school's winning football eleven, passing the home folks in review. In a nice nostalgic touch, one marcher was John Reilly, who had four decades earlier been awarded the Medal of Honor during the Spanish-American War. "John Basilone rode in an open car with his parents Sal and Dora, who beamed with pride throughout the parade," Doorly reported. "Also in his car was Private Stephen Helstowski of Pittsfield, Mass. [who had] fought with John on Guadalcanal and had been injured in the battle."

There's a photo from that parade showing Basilone sitting happily, high atop the backseat of the convertible behind his parents, with Helstowski in the front passenger seat alongside a capped and uniformed chauffeur, Basilone waving at the crowd and the sun-drenched crowd gawking and some waving back, little kids and a few uniformed servicemen and women visible, several people walking behind or beside the slowly moving auto, so slowly that Basilone was able to shake hands with pedestrians even as the open car rolled along without having to stop, some of the handshakers aging vets from World War I.

Flags flew, the weather was perfect, and little Peter Vitelli remembered how orderly the big crowd was as he sat on the curb in front of St. Ann's Church watching the parade pass by and eventually halt and morph into a "rally." At some point, the lovely actress Louise Allbritton was kissing Basilone. There is no mention of Virginia Grey. The disgraced though still popular former New York City mayor James J. "Jimmy" Walker somehow showed up, ubiquitous, beaming and shaking hands, "working the room," so to speak. This had become commonplace, people wanting to be seen with the hero, wanting to be associated with him. To a fallen idol like Walker, this was the sort of event he needed and could use. The crowd, as anticipated, was so great that "local rich girl made good" Doris Duke Cromwell had generously invited the committee to move everyone onto her vast estate, where they'd erected a grandstand, and to continue the festivities, holding the culminating rally right there, which is just what they did. Father Russo gave an invocation. A local girl, Catherine Mastice, who would later sing in the 1949 Radio City Music Hall Christmas show, sang "The Star-Spangled Banner." Anthony Hudek, then wide-eyed and thirteen years old, recalls, "It was as if the world came to Raritan."

A five-thousand-dollar war bond was presented to Basilone, and he responded gracefully, accepting it "for all my buddies overseas on the front lines—they really appreciate everything you wonderful people are doing by 'backing the attack' [he had the advertising agency selling line down pat by now] and buying these war bonds. Today is like a dream to me. Thank you all from the bottom of my heart." Former state senator Joseph Frelinghuysen (from a local family of considerable wealth and distinction and himself a very appealing figure whose own son was a POW in enemy hands) spoke, and Basilone responded again, noting that his medal belonged in part to many others, "the boys who fought by my side."

During the Frelinghuysen remarks, Basilone's small niece, five-year-old Janice, sneaked up onstage to sit with him, drawing a roar in response, and remaining with her heroic uncle throughout. That was the press photo everyone ran the next day, the war hero and the little girl in her party dress on his lap. Fox Movietone News got it all, and the newsreel ran coast to coast the following week, including a recording of Basilone delivering a short speech about the country and its good people and promoting the sale of war bonds. His delivery is a bit stilted, but his voice is deep, almost rich. Catherine Mastice returned to sing a new song entitled "Manila John," composed by the organist of St. Ann's, Joseph Memoli with words by W. A. Jack.

Basilone at times seemed overwhelmed by what organizers called "the biggest day in the history of Raritan." But for some stupid reason, pure military bureaucracy at work, I suppose, Basilone wasn't to be permitted to enjoy the night at home. On orders, and pointlessly, he was hustled back to New York and a Manhattan hotel for the night. Maybe they feared that this close to home and family, he might go AWOL and they'd have difficulty getting their boy back to the tour. By Monday the call of the war plants was heard, and Basilone was back in New Jersey at the Johns Manville factory in Manville, just north of Raritan, meeting war production workers, shaking hands, and talking up war bonds.

The next day Basilone was at Calco Chemical, where he'd worked as a laborer. The Somerset County Bar Association beckoned that same day. One can only imagine what Basilone managed to say to the Bar Association: citing torts and precedents? Then it was off to Pittsburgh for a bond rally at a big steel plant. Within hours he was back in New Jersey, speaking to the Rotary Club at Somerville. It is not clear any of this coming and going so close to Raritan included a trip home to his mother and father's house for a meal or a night with the family. Or what Gene

Lockhart and Eddie Bracken and the actresses thought of small-town and industrial New Jersey as they were trotted around.

Doorly reports that someone, somewhere, finally decided to give the poor guy a break. A thirty-day leave came down from the top. Thirty days of no speeches, no war plants, no bond rallies. And by now Basilone badly needed a rest. He spent the time at home in Raritan, where he played with the local kids and slept late, bunking in with little brother Don, nights where he and his Raritan pals all did a little drinking and admired the local girls. But there was a letdown, a long-delayed reaction. Doorly details it. He quotes Basilone as telling friends in Raritan that as much as he appreciated the admiration and attention, he was a soldier and wanted to get back to the war. This is the first mention of Basilone's yearning for the Pacific.

19

There are men who quite literally love war, the rattle of automatic fire, the crack of a single rifle shot, the song of the bullet's ricochet, the sweet reek of gunsmoke hanging blue in the air, the heightened tension, the living (and too often dying) on the edge, the adrenaline rush, the yelling and shouting, the sound and the fury. Many of such men are Marines, veterans of different wars in different climes and down through the ages. I have myself after a firefight heard Marines coming out of the fight and back inside the wire coarsely enthusing, "Lieutenant, I love this shit." In a book I wrote about motivation, about what draws Marines to the guns rather than, more rationally, away from them, a few Marine critics carped that of all the various reasons Marines fight, I had scanted the sheer love of a fight, the appeal of battle, the call to the guns, the passion warriors bring to battle. Manila John Basilone seems to have been one of those men, one of the war lovers.

By the late summer and early autumn of 1943, Basilone had been for some months distanced from combat, death, and the war, had been home long enough seeing family and old friends, appearing before cheering audiences, consorting with Hollywood movie stars, to understand that the medal had given him some leverage, and that perhaps the time was nearing when he might start using it. He had never been much of a politician, but this could soon be the moment. Perhaps the bond tour had lost its charms, had become boring, the parroted, scripted phrases grown glib, so easily tumbling from the lips. Maybe Virginia Grey's ardor had cooled. The shrewder of the brass may have begun to sense that their pet machine gunner was no longer as docile and instantly obedient, no longer entirely on board. He'd gotten over his stage fright, his anxiety at being the center of attention, the bashful unease of being "gawked at." He'd picked up the sales jargon for the war bond drive—"Back the Attack," that sort of thing—and preached it on demand. Or was that cynical even to suggest?

For the first time, and quite specifically, Basilone bridled at being "Manila John." After all, Manila was no longer the town he once knew, where he found and loved Lolita, where he'd first tasted a small fame as he boxed undefeated, was backed in wagers and cheered on by his fellows, and where General Douglas "Himself" MacArthur, who lorded it over the poor Filipinos, vice regal in style and manner, had still found time to come back to the dressing room to shake his hand after a winning bout over a tough sailor. That Manila no longer existed, wasn't Manila anymore; it had been a "Jap" city for more than eighteen months, "Yokohama South." If there was in Basilone no longer any affinity for the place, why should people still be yammering questions at him as Manila John? Or worse, "Manila John the Jap killer"?

Basilone by now might well have been asking himself, what did civilians, even those who loved or just plain admired him, the home folks, the kids, the reporters, the girls, the fans, with their glib queries about "killing Japs," really know about war, combat, and death? So, to mollify a performer apparently growing antsy and querulous, the brass again offered Basilone a commission as a second lieutenant in the U.S. Marine Corps, the same rank that Mitch Paige, while they were both Down Under, had quickly accepted. And now six months later, the sergeant in Basilone would again turn it down. He was an enlisted man, a noncommissioned officer, and happy to be so. None of this "officer and a gentleman" snobbery for him. The brass then tried another incentive. Would Basilone like to go to Camp Pendleton at the pleasant seaside town of Oceanside in Southern California as a gunnery instructor and run machine-gun training there? He loved machine guns, knew the weapon intimately, was a proven teacher of the weapon's construction, operation, usage, its deadly effect. In a way, this would be a perfect fit, a dream assignment. Thanks, sir, but no thanks.

Then just what did John Basilone want? What would it take to keep him out there visiting war plants, selling bonds, doing interviews, boosting home-front morale? To Basilone, if to few others, the answer was simple: he wanted to return to the Pacific, to go back to the old outfit, to "his boys," to combat and the war. He was starting to mouth off about missing the Pacific, missing being a Marine and being tired of his role as a performing seal.

Every Marine senior NCO or officer who ever served knew guys like Basilone. They could be great Marines, the very men you wanted in the next hole to you in combat, but when it came to the chain of command, the regulations, to getting along, "brown-nosing" a little if he had to, the man could be a pain in the ass. There was the usual old commissioned snobbery at work still in the Corps, the occasional officer's snarl about "shifty-eyed enlisted men" or about "a guy who every morning you ought to punch right in the face because you know damned well before the day is over, that bastard is going to fuck up one way or another." Basilone was hardly that, not a troublemaker or a malingerer, not after three years in the Army with consistently excellent fitness reports, or in combat as a Marine. He was by late 1943 a thorough professional. But he was also a Marine who wanted his way and kept after you until he got it.

Basilone sent in an official request through channels to rejoin the Fleet Marine Force Pacific, the famed FMF PAC for which he had fought as a member of the 7th Marines, 1st Marine Division.

It was just as officially turned down. The Marine Corps didn't see any profit in returning a Medal of Honor man to combat and suffering the angst and second-guessing inevitable in getting a hero killed off.

And, the brass told itself, let's face it, this guy was good at selling war bonds. In a traveling troupe of heroic servicemen and Hollywood stars, Basilone was a movie star himself. The dark good looks, the hint of danger, of a coiled tension, a recklessness that appealed to women sexually and to men who wished they had something of that same aura, these were the qualities that made Basilone so good at what he did on the war bond promotional tour. The best thing about it was that he was a "movie star" who in real life had been as heroic as any Hollywood idol on a make-believe screen.

Basilone was the goods and people got it. They recognized him for the real thing, and when he spoke and cracked that lopsided Italian smile, the crowd understood this wasn't just a practiced performer. This was a genuine American legend come to town or to the gates of the big war plant just outside, to say hello, to shake your hand, to congratulate the shift worker who'd exceeded his or her production goals that month, to the factory manager whose assembly line had earned an "E for Excellence" banner from the War Production Agency, to visit the local grammar school, to kiss the baby and muss the hair of the local kid, and to do it all with an easy grin, a half-bashful hello, a dashing young man in an honorable uniform, and, above all, that pale blue ribbon on his chest or the medal itself suspended from his neck by another matching pale blue ribbon. No wonder the girls and the women loved him, the men admired him, the kids shouted and ran after him. Louis B. Mayer of MGM, President Franklin Roosevelt's close friend and financial backer, couldn't have invented him, no Oscar-winning screenwriter could have written him, the marquee part of Manila John Basilone, a hero of the Pacific. As Basilone's brother George had remarked, "Everybody loves you, John."

Basilone raised money, boosted morale, sold bonds, reaped publicity, did the damned job, a job he was continually told was every bit as vital to the nation's war effort as had been his ferocity in a fight, his mastery of the lethal Browning heavy machine gun, the man's sheer animal endurance, the physical courage, the killer instinct.

Basilone, not educated, naive but hardly stupid, must have been aware this was simply pious, full-blown press pageantry. Peddling war bonds door-to-door was important, of course, the war had to be paid for, but there were plenty of good salesmen in America selling everything else, from Fords to encyclopedias and patent medicines. There were only a relatively few men capable, strong enough, and sufficiently courageous to go into the jungle barefoot and armed in a tropical rainstorm at night and fight hand-to-hand against the flower of Japanese imperial infantry, out to kill you and your buddies, and fully capable, as they'd already shown on island after island, of doing so.

Bruce Doorly gives us this evocative and in ways shrewdly illuminating vignette of the restless hero paradoxically at rest, during that monthlong military furlough back home in Raritan as 1943 neared its end: "After bond tours and visits to war industries, John was granted a thirty-day leave which he was able to spend at home. While most of the attention bothered John, when the attention came from kids, he loved it. John's brother Carlo remembers that kids would gather outside the house at 113 First Avenue, yelling until John came out to talk to them. The kids would swarm over John, which he greatly enjoyed. His old boss from Gaburo's Laundry, Alfred Gaburo, remarked, 'his greatest pride was the kids in the neighborhood. The kids idolized him and he idolized the kids.'"

"During the time that John was home after the big celebration [of September 19] he made special visits that those present will always remember. In between public appearances, John got some relaxation, visiting neighbors, feeling somewhat like a regular guy again.

"One weekday, John took time to pay a special visit to his niece Janice's school. . . . Janice was the niece who climbed on his lap at the rally on Basilone Day and had her picture on the front page of the newspaper. Janice, now 65, when interviewed for this [Doorly's] book, lit up and described how special that day was when her Uncle John, everyone's hero, came to visit 'her' kindergarten class. He talked with kids and shook hands with many teachers. The whole school was excited and she was a very proud five year old. While Janice says she has only vague memories of the parade and rally on Basilone Day, and no specific memories of sitting on John's lap at the rally, she remembers vividly his visit to her school.

"One night on leave, John stopped by the local tavern, Orlando's. The owner, Tony Orlando, was very dedicated to the local servicemen. He posted their pictures on the wall, wrote them letters, sent them packages. To have John Basilone, Raritan's hero, stop in to socialize, was an honor for the Orlando Tavern. All eyes and attention that night were on John. His drinks were, of course, 'on the house.'"

Another favorite local hangout, for Pop Basilone's generation more than the son's, was the Star of Italy Mutual Aid Society building on Anderson Street. This was an outfit that helped recently arrived immigrant Italians to get started in America. Since Basilone was officially still "under orders," even on leave, he was pressed into service, speaking to an audience of a hundred about the appeal, patriotic as well as financial, of war bonds. The club's president, Charles Franchino, recalled young Basilone as "likable, regular" and, according to Doorly, Franchino was surprised to hear Manila John talking during his leave about wanting to get "back into action," and asked why. Basilone, possibly having fun and kidding an older civilian, said, because he liked the feel of firing a machine gun.

It wasn't all small-town, back-home camaraderie, laughter, dinner dates, and drinks on the house. Basilone was no longer on the war bond tour hustling sales, but the publicity mill, like the war itself, ground on.

"Basilone was featured on the radio a few times toward the end of 1943," Doorly recalls. "The NBC show entitled 'Marine Story' had John talk about his experience at Guadalcanal. Legendary Ed Sullivan, who had a variety show on radio, similar to his later

TV show, had John Basilone on the air. Ed and John would come
to know each other as 'friends.' They met at a bond rally at the
Capital Theatre in New York where Sullivan was the master of ceremonies. At this rally, John spoke to the crowd about his Division's
action on Guadalcanal. When he finished he received a standing
ovation that lasted several minutes. Ed Sullivan wrote a few times
about John in his newspaper column for the New York Daily News
[then the biggest circulation newspaper in the country selling
three million copies per day], John wrote that 'Ed went out of the
way to do things for me and he took pleasure in whatever he did. I
shall never forget him and his sincere friendship.' Even years after
John's death, Ed Sullivan continued sending John's family free
tickets to his newly launched and successful TV show. John's sister
Dolores recalled Ed to be very personable and caring."

Phyllis Basilone Cutter recalled her brother's new love affair
with New York, the big city just across the Hudson a few miles (and
a world) east of little hometown Raritan. "New York, supposedly
the city without feeling, took me into her heart. Every door was
open to me. Ed Sullivan of the New York Daily News and Toots
Shor took me in tow. They went out of their way to do things for
me and what I liked about them both was that they took real pleasure in whatever they did. Both are grand fellows and I shall never
forget them and their sincere friendship. It was a privilege and an
honor to know them."

To those who knew Sullivan, then or later, he was a self-
important and rather cynical man mostly involved not with others
but with himself. Basilone's and his family's impressions of Sullivan's
goodness of heart may say more about Basilone and his folks, their
own decency and their essential niceness and authenticity, than
about the worldly Sullivan. Regarding Toots Shor, a large, vulgar man
who ran a "great joint" (his own description), a Marine enlisted
man of Basilone's age and appearance, without the Medal of Honor,
might not have been entirely welcomed by Toots or his doorkeepers.
If you were famous, even marginally, it was, "Come right in, pally.
The drinks are on us." Otherwise it might be, "Beat it, Marine. Try
the joints under the El on Third Avenue."

There is a wonderful small and telling scene in Sydney Pollack's *The Way We Were* burlesquing popular nightspots such as Shor's, the Stork Club, and El Morocco during wartime, where the headwaiter at the velvet rope smilingly welcomes the colonels and the ranking naval officers and then curtly dismisses a GI and his girl, enraging Barbra Streisand's feisty character, the "pinko" scold, who promptly ushers the young couple swiftly past the rope and chews out the flunky, dressing him down as "You fascist rope holder!" That's how it was at Shor's joint back then and would have been for Basilone, had he been just a sergeant on his own, without a medal or an escort of military PR flacks.

By this time, Manila John was a star. With Sullivan and Shor, that was the difference. Basilone's youthful, innocent naiveté was never more evident than in his assessment of these two front-runners, his appreciation of the newspaper columnist and the saloonkeeper, his gratitude and their "sincerity," for the things they did for him. He didn't yet realize, and perhaps never fully would, what *his* heroism and consequent fame did for the sycophantic users around him, the leechlike pilotfish attached to the deadly prowling shark.

As Doorly puts it, "Basilone's life was no longer private. An article appeared in the Sunday Daily News [whose circulation rose to four million on Sundays] including many things about John's life, including that John had a girlfriend. The girl was Helen Helstowski of Pittsfield, Massachusetts . . . sister of John's military buddy Stephen Helstowski." The surprise here is there was no mention anywhere at this time of Hollywood glamour girl and fellow war bond trouper and reputed love Virginia Grey, the well-known if not precisely famous film actress. Where were gossip columnists Hedda Hopper and Louella Parsons at moments like this? Yet here was this publicity about an anonymous Pittsfield girl with a difficult name. John and Helen, with her brother the intermediary, had corresponded, he'd visited her while touring at Albany, not far from Pittsfield, and the two certainly became friends and saw each other several other times. There is no indication it went much beyond that. "While no one said the romance was a wild, passionate affair, John was a celebrity, and the newspapers were going to report and sensationalize the story, writing that, 'He fell in love.'" Maybe the media haven't really changed all that much.

Meanwhile, at the little house in Raritan, fan mail arrived in volume. It was mostly from young women. Some included photos. Some were outright proposals of marriage. According to Doorly, one hopeful girl said, "I think you are wonderful. I always wanted to marry a hero." A writer named James Golden had been trying for some days to get to Basilone and do an interview, to get the hero to talk about himself. When the pestering continued, an irritated Basilone had had enough. "Look, Golden, forget my part. There was not a man on the 'Canal that night who doesn't own a piece of that medal awarded to me."

Basilone had proved himself a natural at war. It was coping with civilians during a peaceful interlude at home that was giving him difficulty.

20

A gala dinner at the Waldorf and there he was on Park Avenue, up on the dais, young, handsome, bemedaled, and dashing, a man's man, somehow larger than life. But some still thought of John Basilone as the aimless, perhaps even shiftless, half-educated, hard-drinking young Italian Catholic Jersey kid with nine siblings but no "family" to speak of. A gambler and a brawler, a misfit who didn't get out of grammar school until he was fifteen, who never attended for a single day the local high school, who caddied for a living at the country club, cadging tips from the rich guys, beating the other caddies at cutthroat poker for their tips, and who was fired from one of the few jobs he ever had, working on a laundry truck. And now here he was, Basilone of the U.S. Marine Corps, sitting up there on the dais in uniform and wearing the famous medal, at the Grand Ballroom of the Waldorf, alongside such industrial giants as Alfred P. Sloan Jr. and others out of the pages of *Forbes* and *Fortune* magazines, a scheduled dinner speaker and an honored guest of the National Association of Manufacturers (NAM).

Those seating arrangements are one of the many paradoxes of this narrative, and was there ever such an absurd dichotomy?

Manila John and the big shots. Seated nearby, the closest thing Basilone ever had to a role model or an icon, a Marine lieutenant general named Alexander A. Vandegrift, honored by President Franklin Roosevelt with the same pale blue ribbon that Basilone wore, a couple of very brave men of disparate backgrounds, the commanding general of the 1st Marine Division (and eventually commandant of the Corps) and the lowly machine-gun sergeant of the same division, but both of them Marines, both of them now, and maybe forever, legends of the Corps. If only Basilone's battalion commander, Chesty Puller, were here, John could brace Chesty with his plaints. Well, then, with no Chesty on board, the "Old Man," Vandegrift, would have to do.

With the timing and instinct that in the Philippines had earned Basilone the reputation and the undefeated record of a feared prizefighter, one who recognized and would exploit an opening when he saw one, and could sense weakness in an opponent, Basilone took immediate advantage of the place and the moment. During a (men's room?) break in the proceedings he pounced on General Vandegrift, who had commanded him on the 'Canal and had that day in Australia pinned the medal on him. Vandegrift wore the same medal and additionally had a flag officer's clout, but on this night Basilone had his ear, and he didn't hesitate. The war in the Pacific raged, Basilone was a Marine who'd been there at the start, and now he wanted in at the finish. How could he get back into the fight when the big shots insisted on parading him around the country like a show pony, a traveling salesman working conventions and formal affairs like this one, when all he really wanted to do was to rejoin the war, again lead troops in the field? Could Vandegrift help? The general promised to look into it.

Maybe he did, but all John subsequently learned was that instead of being sent to join one of the Marine divisions now fighting the Japanese in the Pacific (there would eventually be six before the war ended), he found himself shunted off into the ultimate rear echelons of rear echelons, in a Navy yard a hundred miles from the nearest sea.

On August 31, 1943, while the American carriers *Essex*, *Yorktown*, and *Independence* attacked Marcus Island in the central Pacific, and in Europe the Russians advanced on Smolensk, John Basilone was reporting at and would be pulling guard duty in the Guard Company, Marine Barracks, Washington Navy Yard, with frequent timeouts to address a group or hawk another war bond.

Was this bureaucratic coincidence or was the Corps punishing the audacious SOB for having gone outside the chain of command to pester Vandegrift at the Waldorf? Whatever the situation, Basilone was increasingly pissed off.

"I felt I was still on display," he complained to his family. At another time he compared himself to "a museum piece." By now, the movie stars, including the Virginia Grey he had "fallen for," had all gone back to Hollywood. They had been freed to return to their real jobs as movie heroes, while the one actual hero among them was prohibited from getting back to *his* profession, that of killing Japanese infantry. Surely Basilone grasped the irony.

Try to analyze Basilone's state of mind as he followed in the newspapers what was happening in the Pacific while he manned a duty desk in Washington. The Marines were fighting on Bougainville in the Solomons, his old Aussie "mates" were slogging ahead in New Guinea, on Christmas Eve American naval forces attacked Buin and Buka islands to draw attention from an imminent landing by other Marines on New Britain, and on December 26 those landings took place, as General Rupertus's 1st Marine Division, Basilone's old outfit from the 'Canal, splashed ashore and headed inland as 1943 ended, to capture the Japanese airfield at Cape Gloucester. Basilone, instead of being there, was reading about the Pacific in the *Washington Post* and the *Washington Times-Herald*.

It wasn't as if Basilone had some schoolboy's romantic idea of what combat was all about. He was a realist and had known war. Maybe he felt he was letting his fellow Marines down.

Or maybe it was the country itself and its people who were driving him back to the war—his handlers, the shadows, the PR people and the ad men, the military brass, the war bond lobby, the crowds cheering him, the kids shouting his name, the newspaper reporters and radio broadcasters dogging his steps, the celebrity hunters like Ed Sullivan and Toots Shor, the legendary journalists like Lowell Thomas, the big businessmen of the NAM, like Sloan of GM who put him to use, the clergymen who preached his virtues, the heiress Doris Duke who turned over her acres to a grandstand where he would be saluted, the lovesick but ignorant girls proposing marriage, the authors who wanted to do books about him.

Then in December with the holidays coming, an impatient Platoon Sergeant John Basilone did what Marines in trouble are trained to do. He went to "the man." His commanding officer, knowing Basilone to be something of a ballbreaker, but one with an impeccable combat record and the famous pale blue ribbon, asked irritably what it was this time, what was it the sergeant wanted?

Basilone answered in five words: "Sir, I want the fleet."

Do not be confused by the phrase. Basilone wasn't asking for a shipboard assignment but a transfer to the Fleet Marine Force, to one of the Marine divisions now fighting the Japanese somewhere out there in the vast Pacific theater. And within days (it was just before Christmas), and possibly and belatedly due to General Vandegrift's intervention, Basilone at last got his wish.

Orders were cut dated December 29, sending him off to Camp Pendleton, California, to join the then newly forming 5th Marine Division, to report on January 17, 1944, to the Headquarters and Service Company of the 27th Marines, an infantry regiment. Nine days later, on January 26, he was sent up to HQ Company of the 1st Battalion of the 27th Regiment, one of the three rifle battalions that made up the fighting heart of a Marine regiment, just what he wanted and had been asking for. In November 1942, following his epic fight on the 'Canal, Basilone had been promoted to platoon sergeant, line, and now on March 8, 1944, he would be given his final promotion in the Marine Corps, to (temporary) gunnery sergeant, one of the most highly respected and important ranks a noncommissioned officer could be given, a rating that carried with it the informal and yet revered abbreviated title of "gunny." So that, as a Marine, "Gunny" John Basilone would some ten months later make a final landing on a hostile beach.

21

The Marines gave John Basilone a few days' leave over the holidays to tidy up his affairs at home, see the family, jaw with Pop and his siblings, reassure his mom, have a glass at Orlando's Tavern, say so long to his pals, attend mass in Father Russo's old church, and sing "Auld Lang Syne" on New Year's Eve. Then it was off to the West Coast and a line outfit at Camp Pendleton, a man back where he belonged and very much at ease with the place, the people, the job, and himself, once again a real Marine.

Camp Pendleton, where I've served (most Marines have), is a big, stark, parched, and rather primitive ranchlike spread of hilly brown terrain given to brush fires in the Santa Ana wind season and floods in the rainy time, covered with wartime acres of dun tentage and flat fields dotted with metal Quonset huts and the newer large, spare two-story wood-framed barracks and similar-looking mess halls and outbuildings, some of them still smelling of newly sawn wood. The landscape was populated, except for the Marines, largely by rattlesnakes, coyotes, jackrabbits, and plenty of tarantulas, the husky, hairy spiders mainly visible by night when the headlights of speeding autos or military vehicles pick them up, slow-moving and shimmering, on the brownish hill-sides. Pendleton is situated on the Pacific coast a half hour north of San Diego, an hour south of Laguna Beach and its beachfront hotels and bars, surfers and pretty California girls, and maybe another hour south of LA and Hollywood.

I suppose there is some way to calculate how many Marines have passed through the main gate of Camp Pendleton, California, since John Basilone arrived there in January 1944, men either reporting in for training or prior to shipping out later for the Asian or the Middle Eastern wars. Named for famed Marine general "Uncle Joe" Pendleton, it is a huge base fronting on its west side the Pacific coastline and the garrison town of Oceanside, whose main drags are a kaleidoscope of bars and small restaurants, uniform tailoring and pressing shops, a couple of small churches, filling stations, pawn shops, fast-food joints, barbershops and beauty salons, and tattoo parlors, with plenty of cute young California blondes and the off-duty, on-the-prowl Marines who hunt them.

This chunk of Southern California is an arid stretch of hills, cut by arroyos that flood swiftly after sudden downpours, the terrain reaching mile after rolling mile to the east where further miles away you can see the Southern California coastal range, mountains that for half the year are topped by snow. Marines began going to war from Pendleton in the 1940s when the enemy was the Japanese five thousand miles away, on all those lethal islands. In the summer of 1950 Pendleton started sending another generation of Marines seven thousand miles to Korea, to the Pusan Perimeter, the landing at Inchon, the desperate fight at the Chosin Reservoir in North Korea, and to the bloody Outpost War in which my class of young Marines fought until the truce of 1953. Then came Vietnam and the awful decade in which 58,000 American soldiers and Marines died, most if not all of the Marines direct from Camp Pendleton. In more recent years, the maws of Iraq I, Afghanistan, and Iraq II, were once again being fed through the main gate at Camp Joseph H. Pendleton.

Sensibly, they gave Basilone a platoon sergeant's job with a machine gun platoon. The men of the platoon, most of them young, including a kid named Charles W. "Chuck" Tatum, who would write a good book about that time at Pendleton and the battle for Iwo Jima, all recognized who Basilone was. You could hardly have been a Marine in 1943 or 1944 and not known of Manila John. The legend was now a member of the new 5th Marine Division, but his brother George was also on the base, training with the slightly older 4th Division, which would be heading out to the Pacific and the war before the 5th Division got itself organized. At the moment the 5th was nothing more than a skeleton formation peopled by newly graduated Marine boots and a cadre of seasoned noncoms and a few young officers. Basilone was by far the most famous 5th Division Marine already here.

In the months he'd been away the war itself and even the helmets and the weapons had changed. The new Garand M1 semiautomatic rifles were slowly replacing the old bolt-action Springfields that went into service in 1903, and, more to the point with a machine gunner, there was the relatively new air-cooled version of the .30-caliber Browning machine gun, much lighter. No more pissing into the water jacket with these babies.

But as an Old Breed Marine, an old-fashioned sort of fellow, Platoon Sergeant Basilone took a traditional tack in breaking in the raw Marines of this brand-new platoon in a brand-new division. He requisitioned cleaning gear, buckets, swabs, and pine oil floor cleaner and put his handful of boots to work sweeping and swabbing the wood-frame barracks. It took two days to get the place up to the sergeant's gleaming, polished standards, but that's what boots were for, menial duties, physical labor, snappily delivered orders to keep them busy and out of trouble. And now the new men began to trickle in to fill out the new division's ranks, some of them from a recently disbanded Marine parachute outfit, paramarines, a cocky bunch who thought of themselves as the "elite." Manila John wasn't impressed by what he thought of as "candy-assed" parachute training and wasn't buying much of that crap—including their penchant for tucking their trousers into their boots instead of wearing them loose outside as proper Marines did. Even the paratroopers knew about Basilone, and that in itself defused potential problems. As did the arrival of a couple of salty noncoms Basilone had known before, men who knew their stuff and didn't take any shit either from boots or from boot-wearing paramarines. We are forever being told that "sergeants run the Marine Corps," and as a brand-new and still amorphous division like the 5th was forming up and starting to organize itself, the adage was never more valid.

Basilone and his NCOs soon had his platoon out on the ground working with the two machine guns. Nobody knew the heavy better than Sergeant Basilone, but he was no slouch on the LMG (light machine gun) either. He worked them hard, snapping in (drills without live ammo), prepping them for the real thing on the firing range. Jerry Cutter and Jim Proser, in their book, possibly assisted by brother George Basilone, flesh out the Pendleton episode before, in John's voice, he sailed again for "the fleet": "A young sergeant, Biz Bisonette, checked in at the same time as the paratroopers and assisted with training of the company. [This is a mistake—Basilone had a platoon, not a company.] He was a tough cookie and an expert in hand-to-hand combat. When it came to jungle fighting we learned our lessons on the 'Canal. Any front-line fighter would need hand-to-hand skills as much as any weapon in the arsenal. The first order of business was getting the boys on the firing range with the .30-caliber machine guns, the old water-cooled Brownies and the lighter, air-cooled version. I drilled the boys on the mechanics and took them through the book, my book, on machine gunning . . . the care and maintenance, and of course, blindfold set-up, repair and tear-down, were all chapters in my book that my new boys would learn better than anything they ever studied in their lives. These new boots would also know how to operate all the weapons on the battlefield, ours and the enemy's, in case they had to use them.

"We practiced setting up various pieces of equipment until everyone could recognize any piece of a weapon by its feel and set it up in the dark. A vet sergeant named Ray Windle came on board in the next week or so. He'd seen plenty of action and knew the score on a jungle battlefield. He was a tough talker like Chesty, and a hot head, so I knew he'd be an easy mark in a card game and this gave me hope for off-duty entertainment. I couldn't fraternize with the boys to the point of gambling with them, so I was left with the non-coms. This cut my chances for extra income in half. But I was glad to have Windle with us. He was the kind of battle commander we needed around these boys. They looked so damn young, some of them. They looked like the sons or the kid brothers of the boys in the 1/7 [John's Guadalcanal battalion]. Malaria and combat hadn't touched these boys yet. Entire battalions started arriving. Many were boys who had trained to be paratroopers, like the earlier group. Once Topside caught on that you can't parachute into a jungle, where most of our work was going to be, it became our job to retrain them in amphibious assault tactics and jungle warfare. Basilone was back in business.

The only drawback, according to Cutter and Proser, was "dames." As Basilone said so himself, "Even on base I couldn't get away from the women and the truth was, I didn't want to." There were plenty of Camp Pendleton women, healthy, fit young female Marines working the mess halls, and Basilone had begun looking them over. Despite their shapeless fatigues you couldn't miss the curves.

You have to wonder why, only a two-hour drive from Los Angeles, it hadn't even occurred to Basilone to call Virginia Grey, hop a Greyhound bus north to drop by her place, send her a postcard to say hi. After all, on the bond tour, all those overnight hotel stops and their having fallen for each other, it would have been the natural thing to do. Recall Basilone's determination that there would be no more "love 'em and leave 'em" for Manila John. Not the way he felt about his movie star, Virginia, the lovely, classy, coolly irreverent actress who liked to knock back a drink with him and who made him laugh, the young woman who had nothing of Raritan about her, still less of prewar Manila.

But on her side, Miss Grey must have heard through Hollywood's gossipy bush telegraph that her good friend John Basilone had been transferred to the West Coast a few hours away. Yet she made no move that we know of, even though it would have been the simplest thing to have the studio set up a PR mission to Camp Pendleton starring Miss Grey with a couple of other pretty

actresses along for cover, a singer, and a comedian or two, to entertain the troops. The studios loved to do that stuff. It was good PR,
good community relations, it was free publicity for the next movie
release, the politicians liked it; in the White House Louis Mayer's
friend FDR would show his gratitude to the industry. But Virginia
never came to Pendleton. Basilone never called her. Maybe, on
both sides, their storied love affair had been nothing more than a
flirt, or at a more basic level, a one-night stand.

Or Virginia Grey may have been off on location, making a
movie somewhere, fantasy material; the reality was these mess
hall girls on the same base. And Basilone was feeling horny and
checking out the women Marines, still in that chauvinist time vul-
garly referred to as BAMs, "broad-assed Marines," though not
usually in their earshot. Think of it, all those healthy young men
and strapping, fit young women in their late teens or early twenties, eyeing each other, young hormones raging, while wartime
husbands and wives, fiancées and girlfriends were far away. All
this against the coiled tension of a nation at war and with new battles waiting. Manila John unblushingly admits to his own sexual
frame of mind in early 1944, describing his preoccupation at the
time as that of "a pig in a pastry shop when it came to females."
However many of the mess hall girls he went through—none of
them immune to the fact he was not only handsome and a platoon (soon to be gunnery) sergeant but perhaps the most famous
and openly admired noncom on the sprawling base—there must
have been a few. "There was plenty of whispering about me being
a war hero," he admitted.

Then, and we can be sure about this, along came a BAM who
was different, who cast a spell, who wasn't just another attractive
pastry in the shop. She was sergeant Lena Riggi, a reservist with
one less stripe than John, but with other attributes. And Basilone
was hooked. Here is his account of the meeting: "I saw her as I
came down the serving line. She was dark—Italian or Spanish
kind of dark. Black hair, dark eyes, and she walked around like
she owned the place. Damn, I had to get to know that one. At
first it was just a look between us. There was nothing on it. No

wink or smile like we knew something special between us. It was just her looking at me from a distance taking stock of me and me looking back at her. I nodded and she might have nodded, or not, but she wasn't falling all over herself, to get to know me. I liked this girl. She was tough. And she was a sergeant, the rules against fraternizing [with enlisted female personnel] didn't apply."

Maybe this was the girl he'd been waiting for since Manila and his cockeyed plans to take the bar girl Lolita home to mom, or, alternatively, to stay there in the Philippines with Lolita to start up a good bar or another bicycle shop (and, as things would have turned out, to end up in a Japanese POW camp).

Lena Riggi was a beauty, dark-haired, dark-eyed, like the girls and young women he most admired growing up in New Jersey. She was Italian, probably Catholic (yes, it happened that she was), the daughter of working people like his own, in her case onion farmers back in Oregon. That little nod and look John mentioned was sufficient to get the Pendleton mess hall rumor mill working. "Sergeant Lena Riggi 'heard all from her lady friends about me. They went on and on about what a hero I was, how brave I was and that I knew all the movie stars.' Sgt. Riggi waited for the gossips to tire themselves out, looked at them and said, 'So what?' She was the girl for me. When she saw me again she pretended like no one told her a thing about me and that was just the way I liked it."

Given the exigencies of war and the accelerated training schedule of a brand-new division being formed, the romance wasn't going to be easy. The young lovers had conflicting schedules, there was little privacy, their barracks were several miles apart with very little available transport within the base to shuttle them back and forth. By day he was with his machine gunners, drilling them on both guns, the heavy Brownie of his heart and the more mobile air-cooled light. The pace picked up, the days of battle were coming, and they piled it on the new men and on the 5th Division generally: gunnery, night problems, obstacle courses, leaps into pools to simulate abandon-ship drill. They did underwater rescue and open-ocean distance swims.

Basilone, of course, concentrated on the guns, but as a veteran noncommissioned officer who had plenty of combat time and knew that more was coming, he kept up on the other skills, the intensified training the division was working on. "It was clear to everybody that because of the build-up, that we were headed toward a hell of a fight somewhere. We practiced beach landings and assaulted fortified positions. My machine gunners needed steady hands and cool heads for the work we had assigned to us. Our most important assault exercise was providing covering fire for a demolition man in an attack on a fortified position. We drilled by laying a line of covering fire about a foot over a man's shoulder as he ran toward an objective. One slip or a half second of distraction meant we would shoot our own man. Under bombardment on a beach it would be ten times worse and fatal for both the gunners or the demo man if it failed." On Iwo Jima, these drills would pay off for Basilone's gunners.

Every Marine infantryman understands, and certainly a hardened close-range combat veteran like Basilone knew, the very risky aspect of covering fire, especially overhead fire, where short rounds meant you were hitting your own men in the back. At the same time, Marines assaulting a dug-in enemy loved accurate overhead fire that would kill or distract the men bringing entrenched fire to bear on them, the vulnerable assaulting infantry. The assaulting Marines were willing to take the risk to reap the potential reward of keeping the other guy's head down. These were among the fundamental truths by which the infantry lives—or dies.

Off duty, the next time John and Lena met, he asked for her phone number and got it. They had a movie date. This was hardly the only event on the Pendleton social calendar. The 5th Division would now formally be recognized as an entity, be awarded its regimental colors: the band would play, the generals gather, the regiments march. A few Hollywood people came down—Edmond O'Brien and Ann Blyth among them, but no Virginia Grey. Basilone feared for a time he might be asked to speak, but the idea of an audience of 25,000 Marines chilled him, and he was relieved the issue did not come up. After the festivities, a remainder of the day's liberty would be authorized. Finally, an afternoon free for Sergeants Riggi and Basilone. And it was obvious John's mind was on the young woman and not on the parade, the visiting Hollywood firemen, the brass, the regimental colors, or his newly minted division, but on Lena and the way her body moved. "She walked easy, like a girl walks when she's on her way somewhere important. She didn't have the kind of sway girls can turn on when they want to impress a guy. She walked right up and stood square on her feet with a beautiful big smile. Damn, she had a big beautiful smile with a mouthful of teeth you could see from a mile away."

Evidently, John had seen plenty of women walking before, either with a sway or with a squared decisiveness as they approached him. And he knew the difference. Now, on this sunny liberty afternoon following the ritual formalities of the 5th Division's official entry into the Corps, all over the huge base, wherever there was an empty flat space, ballgames broke out, basketball but mostly baseball with one outfit pitted against another, intramural affairs, but well backed by cash-money wagering, the kind of thing on which Basilone had long thrived, betting on himself mostly. But on this particular Southern California afternoon Manila John had another sort of sporting life in mind.

Here is how in his words this rather sweet and very simple homespun mating dance began between a Marine and his girl, between a hero of the Pacific and the young woman who would become his wife. And just how, supposedly in his own words, it came down over the years through family to his nephew Jerry: "We probably walked several miles going from one ballgame to the next, talking all the way. She came from a big Italian family, onion farmers up near Portland, Oregon. That accounted for the stance she had that I recognized right away. She grew up working hard like the farm kids I grew up with. It generally made for a strong back and square shoulders, even on women. She didn't ask me a thing about the Medal. She didn't even seem much interested in war stories. That was good because I wasn't the guy to tell any. We just walked and talked like any other two people getting to know each other. Both being Italian and Catholic, there was a lot we already knew and didn't have to say. Mostly we talked about our families. She didn't mind walking which was always a good sign because I always had to walk to think clearly."

Basilone and Virginia Grey had also walked for hours the night they met, first for drinks and then back to the hotel. Walking with a girl apparently brought out the talk in the usually reticent Basilone, though this particular stroll on a military base doesn't sound like much of a romantic lovers' lane. "We walked past rows of tanks, trucks, and all types of artillery. She joined the Corps because she wanted to be with the top outfit in the war effort." It may be difficult to accept in a more skeptical age, but during World War II people in the United States actually did talk in patriotic phrases like that. Basilone continues, "It wasn't hard to figure out that with all this hardware around us, and only a few hours left of liberty, that we didn't have all the time in the world to get to know each other. The talk always circled back to family and how much we missed them."

That was February 1944. Basilone was twenty-seven years old and had a year to live.

22

For several months the young lovers saw each other once or twice a week, despite the distance between their barracks. The typical date was a movie on base and a couple of sodas at the PX since John, as he put it, had "stopped boozing," except on a few occasions when he went out with the boys to the Oceanside bars where they drank 3.2 beer, "getting dizzier" and spending more time "pissing" the weak brew than drinking it.

On March 1, 1944, Basilone had earned that other stripe, being promoted (on a temporary basis, which was the norm at the time) to gunnery sergeant. A few more bucks every payday, increased respect, additional responsibility. The promotion surely was welcomed and enthusiastically accepted, unlike those second lieutenant's commissions he'd flatly turned down.

Out in the Pacific as March became spring, fighting came to a bloody end on Bougainville, where 8,000 Japanese died or were wounded in the last-ditch fighting at a cost of only 300 American casualties, and an air and naval war raged in the Carolines with U.S. forces having the upper hand, while the Australians pushed ahead on New Guinea. Everywhere we seemed to be winning and the once "invincible" Japanese enemy losing. The great Japanese base of Truk was hammered. In a single naval and air attack the ever larger and more powerful American Navy could now typically deploy a dozen carriers. Basilone and his pals could recall bitterly when the United States was so short of operational carriers that Admiral Jack Fletcher asked permission to pull back from the Solomons entirely while we still had one or two carriers left, and in so doing left the fighting Marines ashore bereft of air support except for the handful of shore-based "Cactus Air Force" planes at small, battered Henderson Field. To a veteran of those bleak and bloody months on Guadalcanal, Marines, sailors, and GIs, it seemed another war entirely.

Then at Pendleton word went out. Another of the two big new Marine divisions, the 4th, George Basilone's division, was getting its orders and would be headed west to the fleet, to the war, to the Japanese-held islands. And in early June on the other side of the world, a huge amphibious force of Americans, Brits, Canadians, and French landed on the beaches of Normandy. It was D-Day; Europe had been invaded, Hitler would be dead within eleven months, and Germany would surrender soon after. But here in the Pacific, the Japanese would still be fighting, and few of them ever surrendered.

Once the 4th Division had shipped out for the Pacific, Basilone and his mates in the 5th knew their turn was coming. The tempo and difficulty of the training became more intense; the field exercises stepped up even further. And this just as the poor guy had fallen in love and for the first time in his often chaotic life was seriously thinking about marriage and wondering just what it took to have a lifelong and loving relationship like the one he knew at close range between his own mother and father. Was such an enviable life partnership possible for Manila John and his new love, Lena Riggi?

There were no uncertainties about the growing intensity of his daily military training grind, the pounding the Marine infantry was taking in the hardening process. No one knew precisely when or on which new hostile island it might be, but the 5th Division

Marines sensed another landing was coming, and their officers wanted them ready. The Marines themselves wanted to be ready. Basilone summed it up for his machine gunners, who on average had to carry considerably more weight than a mere rifleman, not only the heavier weight of the guns but the ammo boxes, the tripods, the aiming devices, all hard steel, as the men themselves were now hardening into. "We worked a lot on physical training, getting our lungs and legs to the point where we could hump steel and supplies uphill or through deep sand all day." It sounds reminiscent of Basilone's own training runs off Manila Bay in preparation for prizefights against the likes of Sailor Burt.

Basilone drove his men as he had driven himself, knowing how even more demanding combat could be. None of this facilitated a love affair with the girl he wanted to marry. "It was hard to have energy left over to see Lena even though I was thinking of her all the time now. She was thinking of me too and wasn't at all shy about telling me how she felt." By the start of May, John knew that his time with Lena, their time together here at Pendleton, was running out. He was trying for once to think ahead. There was much to talk about, to do, if only there wasn't the pressure of time, the need to rush. "I wanted to know how it was to love somebody the way Pop loved Mama. At least I wanted a few days, or weeks if I could get it, to know what it was like to be married. I wanted to be able to say 'I love you' a few times and mean it. Maybe it was something we wouldn't have done if we weren't in a rush, but Lena agreed to marry me. We set the date for July 10th, 1944."

There were three problems: the Marine Corps, money, and the Catholic Church. There was also John's brother George, now in harm's way. On June 15, the 2nd and 4th Marine divisions had landed on the big enemy-held island of Saipan, and hard fighting raged with heavy casualties on each side. Was George okay? No one could yet say.

Closer to home, Lena was working out things to be done, and laying plans for something she'd always hoped for: a big, white wedding. The duty chaplain, the Catholic padre of course, declared in ex cathedra tones that he needed two weeks of instruction for the bride. As a Catholic myself, I'm not sure why the priest didn't also need two weeks with John. When Lena explained to the chaplain (all Marine chaplains are naval officers, not Marines) that as a serving sergeant in time of war, she couldn't just take off for two weeks to go to wedding school, the good father was tolerant but firm. She would just have to find the time. Rules were rules, and as not only her priest but as her superior officer, he intended to follow them, and she had better as well. Fed up already, an irritated Lena Riggi demanded of the stuffy priest, "What are you going to tell me? You've never been married." And that was that.

John liked this girl better all the time. Like him, she was a bit of the maverick. Together, they went to St. Mary's Church in downtown Oceanside and found themselves a more pragmatic Catholic father, Reverend Paul Bradley, to whom they explained their dilemma, and in the end he agreed to marry the young couple with or without the fortnight's instruction, thereby rendering unto Caesar (the Marine Corps and its chaplains) the things that were Caesar's but rendering to God the things that were God's, a couple of Catholic kids in love and about to be separated by the damned war.

The ceremony was set for three p.m. on July 10 at St. Mary's. Lena was a half hour late, the single-vehicle Oceanside taxicab company having forgotten her reservation. Attending, and patiently awaiting the bride, were John's commanding officer Colonel Justin Duryea, the executive officer, Lena's sergeant, and the women in her outfit. Some local people dropped by to wish the couple well, and a few reporters from Los Angeles showed up. Standing in for her dad, Sergeant Frank Budemy walked Lena down the aisle and gave the bride away.

Father Bradley recited the vows, the couple looked into each other's eyes, John kissed the bride, and yet another wartime marriage had been solemnized in a small-town church just outside the main gate of a military post somewhere in America.

The only difference was that here were two Marine sergeants being wed and one of them was one of the more recognizable people in the country. The small reception was held down the street at the Carlsbad Hotel, a convenient and useful favorite of Hollywood studios making war movies and calling on the Marine Corps for cooperation and the use of facilities and open spaces on the nearby base's tens of thousands of acres. The studios and the Washington big shots knew the value of such films to morale and the war effort, and unless a breach of security were involved, the Marine Corps and the other branches tried to be cooperative, even to the extent of having troops appear as extras. Jerry Cutter and Jim Proser describe in Basilone's voice the place and the moment: "The reception wasn't fancy, with meat and everything else being rationed, but even so we managed to have a pretty decent dinner with some of the people from our units. Most of them didn't stay, making up excuses about a night maneuver or something they had to get back to in camp. None of us had much money. Everybody knew I was pretty well tapped after paying for the ceremony and I'd have to pay for them if they stayed to eat. A few of Lena's girlfriends stayed and a few fellas from my unit got a drink at the bar and sat with us, saying they weren't hungry." Soldiers that age are always hungry, and it's obvious that such men, who liked John and empathized with his financial straits, were giving the groom a gracious out.

"After dinner," Basilone went on, "we spent our honeymoon night in a room upstairs. We were happy together. Even though it was a rush, I know I did the right thing. I think she felt that way, too.

"We were on the train early next day to see Lena's people in Portland. The train was hot, crowded and dirty. We managed to get a seat while most of the Marines and sailors on board had to stand. We traveled until late the following morning, over 24 hours, with no place to sleep except our seats. I thought a lot about the fancy private cars and having our own plane on the bond tour. I wished I could give Lena some of that kind of treatment. She wanted the fancy stuff that women want for their weddings and it was a shame she didn't get most of it. But she didn't complain, I had to give her that. She didn't make a peep and I started to feel lucky I married her. That was our honeymoon, a stopover in Los Angeles on the way and a few days in her parents' home in Portland."

Back in Oceanside, there were no apartments they could afford, their joint income at that time being about seventy bucks a month. "Lena got pissed off after a few days and wanted to use my name and status to pry open a place to live. I was having none of that. I wasn't going to trade on the Medal for anything. It wasn't completely mine anyway. Nine boys also owned it with me. I thought this might be a hard idea for her to understand and I expected we would have our first big fight, but she surprised me again. I said what I had to say about it and we never talked about it again. She was a Marine and she understood what I was saying. It was then that I knew I had married the right one for me. We continued to live in camp in our separate barracks." So much for romance in the middle of World War II.

When the two wangled a seventy-two-hour pass they took a train north to L.A. with less than a hundred dollars between them, zeroing in on Beverly Hills and places that let servicepeople in without a cover charge. When they fell in line outside a joint owned (or fronted) by a former boxer, a very good light heavyweight turned movie comic named "Slapsie Maxie" Rosenbloom, word quickly got out that the young Marine waiting to get into the place was John Basilone, and a flunky murmuring the words "Medal of Honor" began hustling Lena and John toward the head of the line. But John "wasn't having any of that," and he and his bride abandoned the idea of an evening at Slapsie's and went down the street to a different boîte, named for another comedian, Joe E. Lewis, considered more of a "class place," where for some reason the young couple was welcomed without incident. Once inside, however, the two Marines found themselves experiencing the same sort of fuss. Basilone sets the scene: "Joe E. Lewis . . . was there. His routine was all about boozing and losing money on the horses. He had almost everybody in the place almost dying with laughter. A few people who said they were somebody in the movies came over to our table and said hello. They left business cards and told me to give them a call. They wanted to

introduce me around town to movie people. Joe introduced me
from the stage and I had to stand up and take a bow while everybody clapped. Joe was a real patriot. He was close to fifty [to
a Marine in his twenties, apparently quite an antique] but he did
shows for a lot of the fighting boys who were stranded on islands
out on the Pacific."

It's possible that John might have been thinking of himself on
Samoa and the 'Canal or of his brother George that day on Saipan.
Or of his own new 5th Division, which would soon be headed west
to the islands of the Pacific. Of Lewis, he said, "The brass didn't
want him to go [to the war zone] but he needled them until he
got himself flown out on a cargo transport. All he brought along, a
change of clothes and a few cases of good Scotch. He made a lot
of friends and brought a little bit of home out to us. He was a real
good guy so I stood up for Joe and fried under the spotlight for
awhile. He was a good comic for Marines since his two favorite
subjects—drinking and gambling—were pretty much what we
liked to do too. Lena didn't mind all the attention, it was all new to
her, so I stood up there and let her enjoy it. It was our best night
together. We ended up walking back to our hotel as the sky turned
from black to deep blue and the stars faded out. We were getting
used to each other. That 72 hours was our best time together. Our
last day was just rest. We didn't get out of bed until dinnertime."

Two weeks after this Los Angeles idyll, Basilone's new 5th
Division was told it would be shipping out, destination unknown.
These were, of course, the days of patriotic, war-winning slogans:
"A slip of the lip can sink a ship." So people, including the troops,
were supposed to keep their mouths shut about troop deploy-
ments and weren't told much in the first place. One of Lena's pals,
her maid of honor, in fact, a Marine named Ruby Matalon, gave
the couple her Oceanside apartment for their last California night
together. But it wasn't to be, not with the schedule the Marines
were on. Basilone's unit was to leave its area on the base at four
a.m., and there was no transport that could get John back there
by then from Oceanside. So the couple couldn't spend their last
night in a pleasant if borrowed apartment, and had to say their

goodbyes in the place where they had first locked eyes and met, a Camp Pendleton mess hall. "We talked of our life after the war— what we would name the first boy and the first girl," Basilone said. "She held up pretty well while we talked. She didn't cry, and pretended she was okay, but she was no poker player. But I was. I told her, 'I'm coming back,' and she believed me."

At dawn the 5th Marine Division was on the move, shipping out and "in the field," as the orders read, on August 12, 1944, Basilone aboard a tub called the USS *Baxter*, hot, filthy, and crowded, with many of the new men who'd never been at sea before puking, and the chow some of the worst swill Basilone had yet experienced in the Corps. On the day the *Baxter* sailed, in France the U.S. Army crossed the Loire, and on the Eastern Front Soviet troops broke the German lines and advanced fifteen miles in a day. It was becoming clear who was winning the war.

The 5th Division Marines still didn't know where they were ultimately headed, where they would next fight, but it was surely going to be the Pacific, and the islands. The first stop would be decidedly not a hostile beach, but the romantic, lovely Hawaiian Islands, where they would arrive at Hilo harbor on August 18. Neither the voyage from San Diego nor the new base, Camp Tarawa, were the stuff of honeymoons, especially one being taken by the groom without a bride. John still had no word of brother George on Saipan.

Camp Tarawa, named for a bloody and thoroughly screwed-up epic Marine assault that nearly ruined the 2nd Marine Division, had been pitched in the midst of what they called the Great Hawaiian Desert, a tent city in a dusty bowl over which loomed the twin volcanoes of Mauna Loa and Mauna Lea. The nearest swimming beach was a day's hike distant and the division wasn't giving many days off. The intensified training schedule stimulated competition between individual Marines and units, and to boost morale and nurture unit identity, Basilone and his machine gunners shaved their heads.

And then almost miraculously out of the vast Pacific, brother George appeared, unhurt and on the neighboring island of Maui.

John wangled a pass and the brothers reunited. George had for some minor infraction been in the brig on bread and water but bragged that the Corps lost money on the deal, because he ate so many loaves of bread. Word came from Peleliu that Chesty Puller's battalion had taken a terrible beating with very high casualties. For the time being, it was finished as an effective Marine fighting force. The Japanese might be losing the war but they weren't throwing the game. At Camp Tarawa men were being trained to handle the improved and terrifying flamethrower, now an integrated infantry weapon in assaulting fortified positions.

The gunners, riflemen, demolition men, and now the new flamethrowers drilled together as a lethal team with a specific set of new tactics for assaulting blockhouses and other fortified positions. The flaming napalm would do horrific things to human flesh. As the wisecrack went, "an ugly war just got uglier."

But many Marines, including the pragmatic Basilone, welcomed anything to the arsenal that could give the machine gunners an edge, kill the Japanese, and save his men. He drilled the gunners in flamethrower tactics hour after hour, teamwork that would pay off later in the fighting.

John and George got lucky with the coincidental appearance of a Dr. John Fox, who ran the local school district nearest Camp Tarawa and got word to John that he was also from Raritan, New Jersey, and why didn't John come by for an occasional home cooked meal, and if they could spring George, he was invited as well. To men living on field rations, you didn't turn down an offer like that. The Basilone boys and the good doctor enjoyed a jolly Raritan reunion.

In October the first Americans landed in the Philippines, and on October 20 MacArthur splashed ashore in a carefully staged landing for the newsreel cameras following the assault troops by several hours and getting the general's khakis wet. On that same day he broadcast to the Filipino people that, indeed, "I have returned." There is no record of Basilone's response, but considering his prewar years in Manila serving under MacArthur, it is difficult to believe he didn't have some variety of emotional reaction.

All through November fighting continued on various Philippine islands and in the surrounding sea, with Senator John McCain's admiral grandfather one of the key players. The Allies were fighting in and around Sumatra and other of the Dutch East Indies, and in Burma the Brits had seized the initiative from the enemy and were on the offensive. Clearly, the Japanese were being pushed back everywhere.

In December, at Camp Tarawa, the rumor mill was chattering. The 5th Division would soon be on the move. Another island would be taken, perhaps one in the chain of islands that led to Japan itself. No place names were mentioned, even in scuttlebutt form, just that it might be an island with an airfield. On December 27, 1944, two days after Christmas, the division began loading its vehicles and heavier gear and tons of supplies. In mid-January 1945, as the United States entered another new wartime year, American carriers were attacking Formosa, Nationalist Chinese were pushing the Japanese out of Burma, there was heavy fighting on Luzon in the Philippines between invading GIs and Japanese defenders, and in Europe Warsaw fell to the Russians and a Polish unit.

At Camp Tarawa, embarkation orders were cut. The 5th Marine Division, Basilone and company, would be sailing, destination still unknown, on January 17, 1945. Manila John was once again going to the wars.

PART FOUR

IWO JIMA

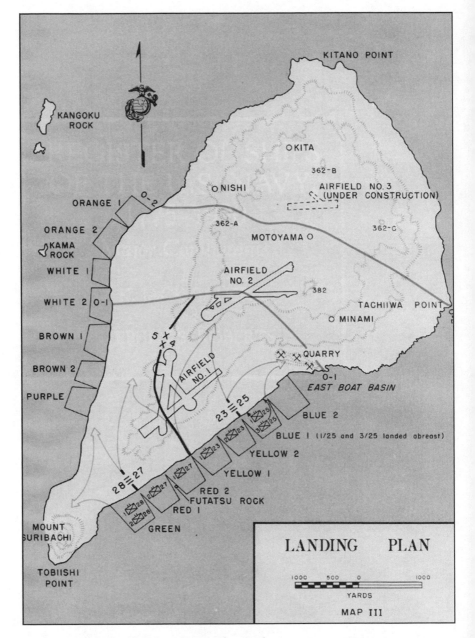

KITANO POINT

KANGOKU
ROCK

OKITA

ONISHI
362-B
AIRFIELD NO. 3
(UNDER CONSTRUCTION)

ORANGE 1   O-2

ORANGE 2
KAMA
ROCK

WHITE 1

362-A
MOTOYAMA O
362-C

WHITE 2   O-1

AIRFIELD
NO. 2
382

TACHIIWA   POINT

BROWN 1

O MINAMI

5 X
X 4

BROWN 2

QUARRY

PURPLE

AIRFIELD
NO. I

O-1
EAST BOAT BASIN

23 ≡ 25

BLUE 2

BLUE 1 (1/25 and 3/25 landed abreast)

YELLOW 2

YELLOW 1

28 ≡ 27

RED 2
FUTATSU ROCK
RED 1

MOUNT
SURIBACHI

GREEN

TOBIISHI
POINT

LANDING   PLAN

1000   500   0   1000

YARDS

MAP III

Iwo Jima. In the Battle of Iwo Jima, John Basilone, now a gunnery sergeant, charged across Red Beach 2 with the 1st Battalion, 27th Marines on D-day, February, 19, 1945. He would die there on that first day of the assault, falling just short of one of his unit's primary objectives, Motoyama Airfield # 1.

23

wo Jima, Japanese for "Sulfur Island," is a volcanic flyspeck in the Central Pacific situated roughly six hundred miles north-northwest of Saipan and Tinian in the Carolines and another six hundred or so miles from Tokyo, the capital and largest city of Japan. It was this equidistant geographical position that gave Iwo any importance whatsoever in the Pacific war. Japanese engineers had built three airstrips on the small island (only ten square miles of sand and rock) from where their Zeroes and other intercep-tors could attack United States B-29 Superfortresses based in the Carolines en route to Tokyo and other mainland Japanese tar-gets. The same Japanese fighters taking off from Iwo could also ambush and shoot down B-29s on their return flights to Tinian and Saipan, especially Superforts damaged by Japanese antiair-craft fire or shot up by Zeroes over the mainland, now limping home, wounded, slowed, and vulnerable, the planes and their ten-man crews. If American forces could take Iwo, the lives of hun-dreds, perhaps thousands of U.S. flyers would be saved and our bombardment of the home islands stepped up in frequency and in bomb tonnage. It would also permit American fighter escorts, with their relatively short range, to accompany the B-29s to Tokyo and back, improving their effectiveness.

Invading and taking the rugged little island from its powerful garrison of good Japanese troops and dangerous aircraft would not be done on the cheap. Major General Harry Schmidt's V Amphibious Corps would be ticketed for the task: three Marine divisions, the 3rd, the 4th (with George Basilone and commanded by Major General Clifton B. Cates), and the brand-new and untested as a unit 5th Marine Division, a blend of raw-to-combat young Marines freshly over from the States and salty and blooded veterans like gunnery sergeant John Basilone, a total of roughly 60,000 men, about half of them having already faced and fought the enemy. There would be casualties, and some senior Marine officers expected them to be heavy.

I have been to the island once, in November 1951, almost seven years after the battle, as a replacement platoon leader being flown out to the 1st Marine Division in North Korea. Our Navy transport plane landed at Iwo to refuel, and we forty or so young officers and senior NCOs had a few hours to stretch cramped legs and wander about and gawk, very much like tourists anywhere—except that, for Marines of any generation, Iwo Jima wasn't a tourist attraction but a sacred shrine. My memory of the place is simple. Mount Suribachi was stark, bare, smaller than I anticipated; the air reeked of sulfur, the sand was black, and the wind moaned. Beyond that, nothing. Only the imagined echoes of muted battle long ago and the sense of other presences, the ghosts of the men of both sides who fought and died here. Those sensations I took with me, along with a sense of awe, long after the stench of sulfur faded. A Japanese source once described Iwo in these words: "no water, no sparrow, no swallow." More prosaically, an American source described it as being shaped like "a porkchop."

Everyone I've asked about the epic battle, from Associated Press photographer Joe Rosenthal, who took the iconic photo of the flag-raising on Mount Suribachi, to combat Marines and one Navy nurse who were there under fire in the famous fight, remembers the shifting sands, difficult if not impossible to dig foxholes in. That sand, the smell, and the wind.

As a twenty-three-year-old lieutenant in 1951, I was hardly an expert on Iwo, but I probably knew more about the island than did Gunnery Sergeant John Basilone as he sailed from Hawaii in late January 1945, one small element of a convoy of 500 ships and perhaps 100,000 men, sailors and Marines both. As he and his machine gunners departed Pearl Harbor on January 26 aboard the USS *Hansford*, it is probable that none of them, Basilone included, had ever even heard the name of their targeted destination and had not yet been told about Iwo. The Marines still took security seriously, and it was standard operating procedure in amphibious warfare not to tell the men where they were headed until they were at sea, unable to blab. Now, on the second day the *Hansford* was out of port, Lieutenant Colonel John Butler got on the horn over the ship's PA system. You know, the old "Now hear this, now hear this" announcement. Said the colonel, "Our destination is Iwo Jima, an objective closer to the Empire of Japan than any other to date." I suspect the saltier of the Marines on board took this as a good news/bad news item of information. Good in that it took us a step closer to winning the Pacific war; bad in that the closer Americans got to the Japanese mainland, the harder and more desperately the enemy would fight and the more Marines would die.

Maybe the best place to start telling about Iwo is with Marine historian Joe Alexander. In his monograph *Closing In: Marines in the Seizure of Iwo Jima*, Alexander begins with a dramatic little vignette, not at the start of the fight but two weeks into the battle, on Sunday March 4.

There was a hot war going on and gunfire everywhere, when a desperately wounded B-29 bomber called *Dinah Might*, crippled during a bombing raid on Tokyo, piloted by Lieutenant Fred Malo and carrying a ten-man crew, came in on an emergency landing. It was crash-land at sea or risk this heavily shot-over landing strip, and Malo piloted her in safe if not precisely secure, everyone glad to be alive but anxious to be swiftly away. The Air Corps was paying its boys to fly, not to get shot at on the ground like ordinary infantry grunts. *Dinah Might* underwent half an hour of very hurried makeshift repairs, took off safely again (every Japanese gunner within range firing at the damned thing), and got back to its base without further distraction. It would be only the first of hundreds of such B-29 emergency landings on Iwo and the first ten of what would be thousands of air crewmen saved, and it proved to at least some of the Marines then fighting there that the place might turn out to have been worth taking.

Colonel Alexander sets the scene, writing that by this date, "The assault elements of the 3rd, 4th and 5th Marine Divisions were exhausted, their combat efficiency reduced to dangerously low levels, the thrilling sight of [the] American flag raised by the 28th Marines on Mount Suribachi had occurred ten days earlier, a lifetime on Sulphur Island. The landing forces of the V Amphibious Corps (VAC) had already sustained 13,000 casualties, including three thousand dead. The 'front lines' were a jagged serration across Iwo's fat northern half, still in the middle of the main Japanese defenses. Ahead, the going seemed all uphill against a well-disciplined, rarely visible enemy."

But to the machine gunners at sea in January aboard the USS *Hansford*, all this was well into the future. And, as Alexander remarked, ten days could be a lifetime on Iwo. Bruce Doorly's monograph about Basilone takes us on board with Manila John and his gunners: "The convoy of U.S. ships was still three weeks and 5,000 miles from arriving at Iwo Jima. They took time to prepare. The men kept in shape by doing exercises. Due to the limited room on the ship each group would have to wait for the limited open space used for calisthenics. John worked his men hard to ensure that they would be ready. By this time their hair started to grow in again [remember those shaved heads that relieved the boredom at Camp Tarawa?]. To keep themselves busy, the 'soldiers' [Doorly uses the word interchangeably with 'Marines'] played cards and read. Books were passed around and traded. A small pocket copy of The New Testament became popular as they neared Iwo Jima. Letters home were written."

Knowing Basilone's tastes, you suspect he played more cards, read fewer Bible passages, and wrote fewer letters than most.

Now that the men were safely unable to pass on the information about their location (there was no way letters could be mailed until after the invasion), officers provided them with more detailed dope about the operation. The fight was expected by some on the staff to last only a few days since the island had already been bombed for two months, and the manpower advantage would be something like four to one. When informed of this optimistic projection, Basilone is quoted as remarking, "Bullshit," out of hearing by officers but loud enough for his men. Having fought the Japanese before, old salt Manila John knew that any fight against more than 22,000 Japanese soldiers prepared to die for emperor and country would be hard and drawn out, anything but a three-day affair.

On February 12, Lincoln's Birthday, and with only another six or seven hundred miles to go, the convoy paused at Saipan, where John's outfit was transferred to another ship, an LST (Landing Ship Tank) carrying a flotilla of smaller landing craft in which the Marines would hit the Iwo beach. On February 16 the LST departed Saipan on the last leg of its long voyage. Men were quieter now. Religious services were well attended.

Medics on some of the smaller ships reported an outbreak of diarrhea. Doorly suggests that some of the "new" men were getting nervy. Had Doorly never heard the popular and often uttered combat phrase "scared shitless," conveying an entirely different situation? And as for only the newer Marines being affected, seasoned Marines with a few firefights under their belts will tell you that the worst time of all is before battle, the anticipation of action, and that once the firing starts, the adrenaline flows and a man's focus becomes more acute and shifts to killing the enemy instead of worrying about oneself. But all of this is small-unit stuff, and those the humble infantrymen, not the planners or decision-makers, but only the traditional raw meat at the end of the stick that prods the enemy.

Alexander provides the bigger picture. General Schmidt, who was expecting a ten-day fight, issued operation plan 5-44 on

December 23. Despite its pre-Christmas timing, says Alexander, there was little gift-wrapping: "The plan offered nothing fancy." Another, slightly junior Marine general, Holland M. Smith ("Howlin' Mad" Smith to his Marines) said of the invasion, "It's a tough proposition," and gloomily predicted "severe casualties unless greater and more effective preliminary naval bombardment was provided." There were two potential landing beaches, both dominated by the 550-foot-high Mount Suribachi. The three thousand yards of black sand beach to the southeast appeared more sheltered and was favored by Schmidt. On D-Day the 4th Division (George Basilone) would land on the right of that black sand beach, the 5th Division (John Basilone) on the left with the 3rd Division held in reserve and to be sent in later. It was the classic triangular USMC setup, two up and one back. Alexander lists the initial objectives: one airfield, the lower one of the three, the western shore, and the hill, Suribachi. A first-night, and probably major, enemy counterattack was expected, and welcomed, cheerfully this time, by Smith. "That's generally when we break their backs," he said pleasantly of the anticipated enemy strike; he was a man who enjoys a good battle.

As Basilone's LST and scores of other ships, large and small, steamed toward Iwo, toward the waiting enemy and the battle to come, it may be that some of the more contemplative Marines reflected on the company of men with whom they sailed and would fight, their Corps, and how during only a few years it had grown. When Basilone and others, including 4th Marine Division C.O. Major General Clifton B. Cates, fought on the 'Canal in 1942, there existed in the entire Corps only the 1st Marine Division in the Pacific, with a 2nd Marine Division still forming up at Camp Lejeune. Now the Marine Corps comprised five divisions with a sixth on the way. There loomed yet another overall goal for the Corps, once Iwo and later Okinawa were digested, when the United States would be invading Japan's mainland, its home islands, probably starting with Honshu, with a huge American Army—an army that was to be spearheaded by six Marine divisions landing abreast, 120,000 men assaulting a hostile beach under fire in one of the greatest battles ever joined. Not that even in a six-division Corps would the intimacy of the Marine Corps ever totally vanish, that comforting sense that even if you personally didn't know another Marine, you knew a guy who did, and that sooner or later you would serve together—at Quantico, Parris Island, "Dago" (San Diego), Pendleton, "Swamp Lagoon" (Camp Lejeune), Twentynine Palms, or on those waiting hostile beaches of the Pacific.

There was still that fellowship, the brotherhood, no matter the overlapping of its generations, the timelessness of its traditions and lore, "the love of one drunken Marine for another." It surely must have seemed that way to General Cates, now sailing in convoy with John Basilone and his machine gunners.

One of the fighting, nonstaff generals commanding the invasion troops, Cates, who had been around for a long time, was a slim, dapper gent who smoked his cigarettes through an elegant holder, and would eventually become commandant of the Marine Corps. As a second lieutenant in World War I on June 6, 1918, he went over the top with his platoon at a place called Belleau Wood where the 5th and 6th Marine regiments would in desperate combat blunt the final thrust by General Ludendorff to take Paris and end the war. Early in the firefight, hit in the helmet by a German machine-gun bullet, Cates was knocked out, only to be revived by one of his men pouring a bottle of red wine over his face and head. "Goddamn it, Tom!" protested Lieutenant Cates. "Don't put that wine over my head, give me a drink of it." Thus revived, Cates pulled himself together, resumed the fight, and led his men into the key French village of Bouresches that was their objective, chased out the Boches, and hung on with only twenty-one men against German counterattacks until relieved. Cliff Cates was nominated for a Medal of Honor and eventually awarded a lesser decoration and fought out the rest of World War I a decorated hero.

On Guadalcanal, as a colonel, Cates commanded troops fighting to hold Henderson Field, and it may have been that Basilone then met, saw, or served under him there in 1942. Six years later, when I reported in to Quantico, Virginia, the Marine Corps Schools, as a college sophomore in the platoon leaders class, Cates was the base's commanding officer before whom all of us passed in review. I still recall seeing him strolling about with that cigarette holder. Now here he was closing in on Iwo with Manila John et al. That's what I mean about the relatively few degrees of separation between Marines of one war or another, one outfit, whatever the decade.

But in February 1945 the two men, one as a two-star general, the other a gunny, Cates and Basilone, would again be in the same fight, the general as one of the senior officers agonizing about how to get their artillery regiments ashore before dark of that first day to help handle those anticipated counterattacks against the first waves of assaulting Marines, of whom Basilone would be one. The aerial and naval bombardment of Iwo Jima was in one sense encouraging to the assault troops of the three attacking divisions. It should soften up the Japanese defenders, cave in and crush their pillboxes and blockhouses, put at least some of their artillery out of action, maybe cut some communications wire, perhaps damage, destroy, or ground some of their planes, hole their runways and break up the tarmac. All this would be good. But what of the famous element of surprise? There could be no great surprise to men being bombed and shelled for weeks. They knew the Marines were coming. And they would even know when, since the bombardment would have to lift before the first waves of Marines hit the beach.

Basilone tried to explain these things to his platoon. The men, even the boots among them, realized he knew this stuff, had fought, and brilliantly so, on an earlier island, and that if any NCO could help them get through the coming fight alive, it would be an old salt like Manila John. Even the nickname, with its suggestion of previous Asian service, of the "Old Breed" and the comforting knowledge that gunny Basilone had been there and come back alive, must have cheered his men, given them a little confidence. So what if Basilone had his doubts about the effectiveness of naval bombardment and what bombs could do or fail to do to an entrenched enemy? As for his "boys," most of them were convinced the gunny would get them through the battle to come, if anyone could.

D-Day would be February 19. Pretty soon now they would be sufficiently close to hear the sixteen-inch guns of the battleships, the heavy bunker-busting bombs of the big planes. The convoy plowed on through chill rain squalls and even sleet. This wasn't the hot and steaming tropical South Pacific Basilone knew so well. Colonel Alexander continues to narrate the story of the Iwo Jima invasion from the point of view not of the infantry and the enlisted men, who would do the fighting, but of the staff and the flag officers, the Marine generals and Navy admirals who had worked up the plan and would now issue the commands.

Like all really good Marine officers, Joe Alexander was not only a student of tactics and the capacity of his own forces, the necessity for speed, but he also believed in "knowing your enemy." He studied the most important subject, the opposing commander. He got to know and understand, and never to underestimate, the foe—in this case, Lieutenant General Tadamichi Kuribayashi, a fifty-three-year-old very senior and high-ranking officer who had once actually lived in the United States, where he was assigned to the Japanese embassy in Washington. This was quite a highly ranked officer for a command so limited and a relatively small force of only 22,000 men. But General Kuribayashi had been handpicked for this job by the very highest authorities because he was a brilliant staff officer destined for great things, as well as a fifth-generation samurai, which in imperial Japan was sort of like being an original DAR, a Son or Daughter of the American Revolution. And this being Japan with its own very particular code of military honor, rather than fail at his mission a samurai was expected to be ready to kill himself by disemboweling in the ritual manner. The Japanese were indeed sui generis.

Kuribayashi was no mindless automaton, however, but a modern and intelligent man, also very much a realist who wrote to his wife six months before the battle, "The Americans surely will invade this Iwo Jima . . . do not look for my return." Think about being a loving wife back home and receiving a cheering little missive like that! Later, during the battle, he would candidly inform his superiors in Tokyo without dramatics and flatly that he could hold the island *only* if they sent him naval and air reinforcement. Otherwise he could not, though he assured the brass he would die there. He had already demanded and received "the finest mining engineers and fortifications specialists in the Empire."

Colonel Alexander details how these experts were used. "When American heavy bombers from the Seventh Air Force commenced a daily pounding of the island in early December of 1944, Kuribayashi simply moved everything—weapons, command posts, barracks, aid stations—underground. These engineering achievements were remarkable. Masked gun positions provided interlocking fields of fire, miles of tunnels linked key defensive positions, every cave featured ventilation tubes and multiple outlets. As an American joker following the battle remarked, 'everything was buried but the airstrips.' One installation inside Mount Suribachi ran seven stories deep. The Americans would rarely see a live Japanese on Iwo Jima until the bitter end." Maybe it was just as well, in the spirit of positive thinking, that the first assault waves to hit the beach weren't too assiduously briefed on the sophistication of the enemy defense system.

Alexander also assesses the strengths and weaknesses of the three assaulting Marine divisions. Of Basilone's 5th, the newest of all, here is Colonel Alexander's reading, including a personal note about Manila John: "The unit's newness would prove misleading. Well above half of the officers and men were veterans, including a number of former Marine parachutists and a few Raiders who had first fought in the Solomons." Agreed a recently arrived battalion commander after observing a live-fire exercise back in Hawaii, "These were professionals." Alexander noted that "among the veterans preparing for Iwo Jima were two Medal of Honor recipients from the Guadalcanal campaign. Gunnery sergeant John 'Manila John' Basilone and Lieutenant Colonel Robert E. Galer. Headquarters Marine Corps preferred to keep such distinguished veterans in the States for morale purposes, but both men wangled their way back overseas—Basilone leading a machine gun platoon, Galer delivering a new radar unit for employment with the Landing Force Air Support Control Unit. The Guadalcanal veterans could only shake their heads at the abundance of amphibious shipping available. . . . Admiral Turner would command 495 ships of which 140 were amphibiously configured, the whole array ten times the size of Guadalcanal's task force." Before it was over, they would need the lot.

24

Before the Navy and the Marine Corps even reached Iwo, they were already feuding, the dispute ignited by an Army Air Corps–Navy rivalry. With a bloody fight like Iwo coming up, you marvel that senior professional officers, the best products of West Point and Annapolis, would permit themselves the luxury of jealous, pride-driven college-boy spats. But they did.

The Air Corps Superfortresses had recently flown a big mission over Japan that failed to destroy the targeted aircraft factories, and Naval Air was out to prove it could do the job. Task Force 58, assigned to batter the island of Iwo Jima with big guns and fleet aviation just prior to the Marine landings, sort of a knockout blow, was instead being lured by a new target of opportunity, within easy reach on Honshu, those Japanese factories the B-29s missed. Ambitious naval leadership allowed itself to be distracted and sent the huge task force steaming away from Iwo toward the Japanese mainland, creating for the Marines two problems. This sudden, last-minute change of plans meant that the Navy was taking away not only its big new battleships and their sixteen-inch guns so effective in shore bombardment, but also the fleet's eight Marine squadrons of specially trained, close air support fighter-bombers, experienced in working with ground air control officers to fly shotgun for the infantrymen hitting the beaches and then heading inland against formidable enemy defenses. In the end, Task Force 58 did its thing on Honshu and then belatedly returned to Iwo in time, if only briefly, to support the landings. It then hurried somewhere else again on yet another mission, not to return to Sulfur Island.

As D-Day (February 19) came closer, the commanders of both sides met with their staffs. Tadamichi Kuribayashi declared that despite all of the bombing and shelling, the bulk of his defenses were intact and functioning, and kept his message to the staff simple: "I pray for an heroic fight."

On board Admiral Richmond Kelly "Terrible" Turner's flagship, Joe Alexander reports, "The press briefing held the night before D-Day was uncommonly somber. General Holland Smith predicted heavy casualties, possibly as many as 15,000, which shocked all hands. A man clad in khakis without rank insignia then stood up to address the room. It was James V. Forrestal, Secretary of the Navy. 'Iwo Jima, like Tarawa, leaves very little choice,' he said quietly. 'Except to take it by force of arms, by character and courage.'" That reference to Tarawa was sufficient to shake any Marine in the room, since it was well-known that Tarawa was a bloody foul-up and losses there, for a three-day fight on such a small island, had been ghastly. Colonel Alexander now takes us to D-Day itself, the nineteenth (as for the brilliant Forrestal, he so exhausted and drained himself, so suffered over the casualty rolls on Iwo and elsewhere in the Pacific as secretary of the Navy, that he would eventually commit suicide). "Weather conditions around Iwo Jima on D-Day morning were almost ideal. At 0645 Admiral Turner signaled, 'Land the landing force.'"

Pulitzer Prize–winning novelist John P. Marquand, the author of best-selling New England tales of manners, covering the invasion as a war correspondent, wrote these first impressions of Iwo: "Its silhouette was like a sea monster, with the little dead volcano for the head, and the beach area for the neck, and all the rest of it, with its scrubby brown cliffs for the body."

And off they went, the 4th and 5th divisions abreast, while the 3rd Division hung back in reserve, a decision later to become controversial. Why hadn't all three powerful divisions hit the enemy simultaneously?

John Basilone and his platoon would hit the beach in the fourth wave about nine-thirty a.m. He would be under fire for the first time in more than two years, since the 'Canal in late 1942.

In Hawaii, John's brother George had questioned him closely about motivation. "You had it made. You could have called your shots. A commission or a soft berth at Pendleton. Why come back to this rat race? You of all people should know what our chances of getting back alive are." According to Phyllis Basilone Cutter, John answered this way: "When I left the theatre of operations on Guadalcanal [it was actually Australia] to come back stateside, I promised my buddies I would return and that promise I didn't make lightly." He didn't make it back, however, not specifically to them. With the brothers in Hawaii, George continued to argue. "You were lucky to get back alive. Why push your luck?" But John wasn't having any. "George, the Marine Corps is my whole life. Without it the rest seems empty. This thing I have to do, something keeps pushing me. I now know what I want. If I don't make it, try and explain to the folks. I know they always loved me. God knows I do them, but this is bigger than family and loved ones and I must do it." This sounds too pious and self-effacing to be convincing. Phyllis, with her brother George surely the source, must have attempted to quote John accurately. Why would she phony up her beloved brother's words on something as serious as the possibility of his own death? It's just that the words are so stilted.

Jerry Cutter and Jim Proser take a crack at describing what it must have been like in that landing craft carrying Basilone to Iwo and his destiny. But how much of this is to be believed? Recall that Cutter once told me that they "made up" some of their reporting.

According to Cutter and Proser, it was a bitter John Basilone who got into the landing craft. "We filed down the gangways into the ship's steel belly. Half of my boys loaded into amphibious tractor 3C27 with me. Amtrac 3C27 was an armor plated rectangular tub made for delivering men onto a beach. It rode low and slow in the water." As the concussions from the big naval guns roiled the ocean and created waves, and the small craft circled slowly waiting for orders, men began getting seasick, including some of the twenty-five Marines in Basilone's boat. And we have the sergeant unsure about whether he should talk straight to his men before they reached the beach. Should he assure them that the big guns and aerial bombing were paving the way to a successful assault, or tell them truly how bad it just might be? According to Cutter, Basilone was ambivalent: "It's going to be all right, boys. They're going to be as dizzy as shit-house rats after we get done pounding 'em. I lied—just as Topside lied to us, when they told us it would be over in 72 hours. All of us vets knew that 72 hours was pure bullshit and said so. It was like an involuntary reaction. The minute it dropped from the C.O.'s mouth, it sounded like a dozen men coughed at once. But it was a dozen mumbled 'bullshits' jumping right off the lips of us vets. We couldn't help it. There were 23,000 [sic] trained Japanese jun-gle fighters straight ahead who had been digging in and calibrating their guns for the last three months." Cutter's book leaves Basilone's dilemma unsolved. What did he actually tell his men? It is not clear that he said anything. And not to quibble, but there was no jungle on Iwo Jima for those "Japanese jungle fighters" to exploit.

The book goes on to describe the landing craft's ride toward the beach, the men puking, the shells passing overhead, Basilone's memories of prewar Japanese golfers at the Raritan Valley Country Club, his premonitions of a war to come. Then it reels off into what seems to be pure fiction in which Basilone, the hardened combat veteran and professional gunnery sergeant, behaves like a clown: "A few more of the boys tossed their steak and eggs as we came around. Tension had been ratcheting up as we turned around in circles at the rally point. This was it, we were going in. I got up behind the .50 caliber machine gun mounted by the driver. Orders were not to fire unless we saw enemy, but I knew we wouldn't see any. After three months of waiting for us, they were dug in too deep, and the Japs were too good at camouflage. We wouldn't see a damn thing. So I planned to shoot everything just to be sure. I chambered the .50 and squeezed off a few rounds. The driver [remember, the 'driver,' a Navy coxswain, was in command of the craft, not a Marine sergeant along as passenger] reminded me of orders not to fire unless we saw something, and I gave him my opinion. 'Fuck orders and fuck you, Mac.'"

This is just crazy. At a time when a veteran platoon leader should be calming and reassuring his seasick, scared, green troops about to hit a hostile beach under fire, and whatever Cutter and Proser's good intentions to show Basilone off at his dynamic, decisive warrior's best, the passage only brings into question his leadership skills, his emotional stability, and his savvy as a combat veteran at a critical moment. First, the small craft was pitching and tossing so wildly that men were "puking," which meant there was no stable platform on which Basilone could stand while firing. They were not in the first wave but in the fourth wave, so that other Marines, several thousand of them, were already ashore and in the sights of that .50-caliber gun he'd just commandeered and was arrogantly threatening to fire beachward, quite possibly at his fellow Marines! And here is the experienced, cool Sergeant Basilone, who should at this point be preparing his men to hit the beach, counseling the reluctant or afraid, soothing the overexcited, doing none of these things. Instead, he's jumping up, cursing out the coxswain, grabbing the .50-caliber to fire off a few random rounds, not at any target he can see but just generally in the direction of the beach where his most likely victims would be fellow Marines. This is not believable and is insulting to Manila John.

Cutter's story of Basilone's arrival on the beach at Iwo grows more bizarre. Now, as the amtrac rolls up on the sand and encounters steep terraces that slow and then halt its progress, the Marines leap out into deep, clinging black sand. As the Marines and their "Doberman war dogs" (first mention of those, by the way) try to dig in, Gunnery Sergeant Basilone issues his first order to the machine gunners, not to organize themselves, and then position, load, and sight their guns, but instead to "Fix bayonets!"

He tells the boys to pull out their scout knives, an order given usually when ammo is short or hand-to-hand combat is about to erupt? This is idiotic. If a machine-gun sergeant expects trouble, an enemy counterattack, he gets his machine guns ready to turn back the oncoming Japanese, wipe them out, and break the attack, what Basilone himself did with such lethal effectiveness on the 'Canal. Neither machine gunners nor assistant gunners even carry bayonets, though ammo carriers who are armed with carbines may do so ("which weren't worth diddily shit," my machine-gun expert Charles Curley assures me). The Japanese counterattack never came, not at the beach, where there were already four Marine waves ashore and a fifth arriving on the heels of Basilone's fourth. The problem now was for NCOs like Basilone to help get the men on the beach unscrambled and to head inland, in Manila John's case, toward an airstrip, Motoyama #1.

Basilone's later words on the beach itself, via Cutter, once we get beyond the just plain silly "Fix bayonets!" sound credible: "They tore us up while we were lying on the beach but me and Lou Plain [a colonel and the regimental executive officer] got this show on the road. We kicked their asses and dragged boys up by the scruffs of their necks. 'Get the fuck off the beach. Move out!' we yelled at them over the incoming fire. They were moving over the terraces now and were finding whatever cover they could in shell craters on the flat land. Bulldozers had punched gaps through the terraces and tanks were on their way up from the beach to support us. A few mixed squads of C and B Company boys were now at the edge of Motoyama #1 Airfield, our first objective. Once we took out the bunker that was slicing open the 4th Division with their cannon, we only had to worry about the snipers, the dug-in artillery looking down on us from Suribachi, and the constant hail storm of mortars that fell from the sky. Other than that, at least we were off the water's edge. Which had turned into a killing field."

25

I've tried to assess which of a number of versions of what happened the morning of February 19 is true. But are any of them?

John Basilone's sister Phyllis has her version. She loves her brother, but has never seen a war. Her son Jerry Cutter, also not a writer, and his cohort, Jim Proser, have their account. The Marine Corps records say one thing. *Leatherneck* magazine has stories by various adepts. Charles W. "Chuck" Tatum, one of Basilone's gunners, has written his own book, *Red Blood, Black Sand*, and the very professional Douglas "Bill" Lansford, a writer and a Marine who was there, has his recollection. Historian Joe Alexander writes at length of that morning. There've been movies with John Wayne and films directed by Clint Eastwood. Dozens of Iwo Jima books. Did Basilone die instantly from a mortar shell? From artillery fire? Did he linger for hours, speaking with a corpsman and even smoking a cigarette? Did he never regain consciousness? Gradually bleed to death of small-arms fire as the official Marine Corps casualty record of the time suggests? His Navy Cross citation says he was killed instantly by a shell. Phyllis says he lived for hours, discussed events, smoked a cigarette. Choose your version.

Maybe the Japanese have theirs. Or did they ever even know who Manila John was? Few survived to say. You have the sense their Sendai Division troops would have liked Basilone, even welcomed him into their own and very special pantheon of warriors—and then killed him before he could kill them, which he surely would have done and happily. General Tadamichi Kuribayashi might conceivably have greeted Basilone as a fellow samurai, gallant, impassioned, fierce, if a bit crude perhaps, a warrior not overly given to politesse or ritual.

I believe this was how it really was on that February morning in 1945: Basilone and other Marines headed down into the hold of the LST to board the smaller landing craft that would actually take them through the surf and up onto the black sand beach, the medium LCMs and the smaller personnel-carrying LCVPs, the tractorlike amphibians they called amtracs. Navy coxswains piloted the assault waves to the shore, backed out, returned to their mother ships, and loaded up again to return with fresh meat for Iwo, men or supplies. There was some wishful thinking in the scuttlebutt men heard that the brass figured it for a seventy-two-hour fight, over in three days, maybe five. "Bullshit," said others, including vets like Basilone. But what the hell, anything was possible.

Historian Joe Alexander sketches the scene. "The massive assault waves [two reinforced infantry regiments from each of the two attacking divisions, the 4th and the 5th] hit the beach within two minutes of H-Hour. A Japanese observer watching the drama unfold from a cave on the slopes of Suribachi reported, 'At nine o'clock in the morning several hundred landing craft with amphibious tanks in the lead rushed ashore like an enormous tidal wave.'" The executive officer of the 28th Marines recalled, "The landing was a magnificent sight to see, two divisions landing abreast; you could see the whole show from the deck of a ship." If you were closer than shipboard, it wasn't all that "magnificent." It was too close. The tracked amphibious vehicles bellied down in the soft sand, and the wheeled vehicles simply spun their wheels. Some of the smaller landing craft swung sideways in the surf, a few capsized, men had to bail out heavy-laden in deeper water, some drowned. But from the distant vantage points on the ships, everything looked great. If you have enough rank, and are far enough from the gunfire, the perspective is always terrific. I attended only one war, a small one, but I was an infantryman, a rifle platoon leader. I never enjoyed that luxury of distance. At that point, from the ships, it was still a "show"—but not for long.

On shore, the enemy patiently waited for orders. Kuribayashi had made only one small blunder so far: when the underwater demolition teams going in before the first wave had been spotted, instead of ignoring the mere handful of invaders, the general had permitted some of his artillery targeting the beach to fire at the demo teams, tipping off their hidden positions to the counterbattery crews of the bigger guns on the battleships, the eight-inch-gun heavy cruisers, Marine aviation, and the big bombers, causing the Japanese guns considerable counterbattery damage. Otherwise, the Japanese were smart. They accepted that the Marines, some of them, maybe a lot, would reach the beach alive and in condition to fight. The enemy had no illusions of stopping them all on the way in or in the surf before they landed. If there had to be Americans on the three-thousand-yard black sand beach, why not withhold fire until there were plenty of them, thousands of Marines instead of mere hundreds of potential targets? Let the first waves land and be reinforced, and then when the narrow beach was clogged with Marines and their weapons and supplies amid the usual chaos, confusion, shouting, and mixed signals, exacerbated by the nerviness of men fresh to the fight, the contradictory orders and wild firing at nothing, hit them hard. Hit them with everything. *That* would be when the Marines were most vulnerable. What a target of opportunity. What a slaughter. The disciplined Japanese held back, held back, held back.

As Kuribayashi assessed his intelligence reports from the many observers, including the handful of Zeroes overhead surveying the scene and dodging the American fighters, he at last gave the orders for his artillery to fire their beach concentrations, target areas already zeroed in on weeks or even months before, crosshatched down to the last square meter of black sand. Sand now covered with American Marines, their weapons, and their packs, their sergeants and officers trying to get the men organized into fire teams, squads, platoons, and companies and saddled up to push inland to engage the enemy. And to get the hell off the soon-to-be lethal beach. It was at that delicate stage of operations that the artillery crashed down murderously on the first four or five waves of Marine infantry, as they admitted, "bare-assed naked," because you couldn't dig foxholes in the soft, shifting and blowing black sand. Shovel with your entrenching tool, watch the sand slide back into the hole, and shovel again. Corporal Ed Hartman, a 4th Division rifleman, said, "The sand was so soft it was like trying to run in loose coffee grounds." Shoveling it was worse; you dug and dug and still didn't have a deep hole to shelter in. And by then you might be dead.

Bill Lansford, a World War II Marine and one of the legendary Carlson's Raiders, later a Hollywood screenwriter, still residing in California, gives us this account of Basilone's and his own first hours on the island. Lansford, an old pal of Basilone's who was by now in a different outfit (a job at regimental HQ) and in a later wave, wrote about it for *Leatherneck* magazine:

"On the morning of 19 February, 1945, we hit Red Beach on Iwo and started climbing its black sides under a storm of enemy mortar and artillery. Basilone had landed one wave earlier and apparently moved in. He didn't know how to stand still. 'Let's go in and set up them guns for firing,' a correspondent later quoted him. Whose guns the correspondent is talking about is hard to imagine. From the moment we landed it was total confusion: platoons and companies mixed up and in the wrong places; men and equipment sinking into the black sand while officers and NCOs drifted about, looking for their men. All that as Kuribayashi's presighted weapons tore our battalions to pieces.

"In the midst of the hellish noise and confusion," Lansford wrote, "two Marines were seen moving among the stalled troops shouting, cursing, and moving them out. One was Colonel Louis C. Plain, the regimental executive officer of the 27th Marines, who would soon be wounded and evacuated, the other was John Basilone. Having cleared a path for the troops on the beach, Basilone gathered several more Marines, set up a base of fire, and ordered them to hold while he went back for more men and weapons. On his way Basilone spotted three M-4 Sherman tanks, their water-cooled V-8s grinding like hell as they struggled up the beach under heavy fire. Knowing their value for knocking out bunkers, Basilone immediately took over."

There is usually a telephone on the exterior rear of tanks, and it may be that Basilone was using that to communicate with the crew inside and give them the benefit of his superior field of vision outside the buttoned-up vehicle.

Lansford continues: "Sergeant Adolph Brusa, a mortar squad leader, remembered he suddenly looked up and there was this lone Marine with those tanks. 'And I said to myself, that's John Basilone! What the hell is he doing standing up when everyone else is hugging the ground?' What Basilone was doing was guiding the tanks through a minefield and pointing out targets while completely exposed to the fire aimed at the Shermans."

We've got to wonder, how would a machine-gun sergeant just off the beach know where the enemy minefields were located? There is no description I can find of Basilone's going ahead of the tanks on hands and knees, probing with a bayonet for the telltale clank of metal on metal as Marines were trained to do when traversing mined areas. And defenders don't usually leave marking stakes to alert an oncoming foe. I accept the other suggestion, his pointing out targets of opportunity to the tankers. Good infantrymen do that.

"Leaving the tanks on high ground, Basilone returned to round up more troops for the assault team he had started building near the edge of Motoyama Airfield #1 (one of his unit's several first-day objectives). To do this he'd have to re-cross the steep volcanic beach where he had met the tanks and where many Marines were still pinned down by Kuribayashi's relentless shelling and well-camouflaged pillboxes." To one who's read descriptions and the citation for what Basilone did on Guadalcanal in October 1942, there is an eerie resonance, this business of going back, under heavy fire, small arms as well as shelling, and more than once, to pick up ammo or water or even a few stragglers he could use in the fight.

Lansford cites one of the officers in the battle who was an eyewitness: "Among those trying to reorganize their scattered units was Major (later Colonel) Justin G. Duryea of the 1st Battalion, 27th Marines. Duryea, who would lose an arm in an enemy mine explosion on D118, (and who) was so impressed by Basilone's heroism that he later recommended him for a second Medal of Honor." The second medal he once joked with buddies about going after?

"Basilone had landed with the fourth wave approximately at 0930. It was now almost noon and throughout the battle he had risked his life repeatedly, disregarding every danger, to restore momentum to the stalled attack. It seemed nothing could touch him [as nothing had touched him on the 'Canal two years before], and yet by ignoring fire that would eventually kill or wound thousands of men, Basilone had finally pushed his luck beyond its limits."

Before the landings George Basilone had warned his brother about pushing his luck. Now Bill Lansford picks up the theme, just before going on with his account of Manila John's death that first day on Iwo Jima. "Many men have said they saw John Basilone fall on the beach, which he did not. One said Basilone's legs were blown off by a mine. Several claim they heard Basilone's final words, and one said Basilone begged to be put out of his misery with his own pistol. Perhaps the most credible witness is Roy Elsner, the headquarters cook who had watched our machine gun drills back at Pendleton and was now on Iwo. He said that when he and some buddies were hunting for their headquarters, 'A few hundred yards from Motoyama Field #1 we heard an explosion, which caused us to look a bit to our right, toward the field. We saw Basilone and the three guys who were with him fall. We reached him almost immediately.'"

There are the other versions, not only from Marines in the Iwo fight but from members of the family, some of which I will cite. First, though, a moving note from Lansford in *Leatherneck* magazine: "Some time after noon I came across a group of blackened bodies on the edge of Motoyama Airfield #1. Company C was advancing half a mile ahead, sweeping the flat field clean, when one of the dead caught my eye. He was a thin, pallid kid. His helmet was half off, and he lay face up, arched over his combat pack. With his jacket torn back and his mouth open I vaguely recognized someone in that lean, lifeless face beneath its dusty stubble of hair. 'That's John Basilone,' said one of the men standing around. 'He just got it.'

"That's bullshit. I know Basilone. We were in the same company. Someone else said, 'That's Basilone.' A guy I knew said, 'Yeah, he was briefing his guys when a mortar scored a direct hit. It killed them all.' I went and studied the dead man closely, but I didn't touch him. The shell had landed at his feet and sent shrapnel into his groin, neck, and left arm. He looked incredibly thin like an undernourished kid, with his hands near his stomach as though it hurt. This was the hero of Guadalcanal, the joy of a nation, the pride of the Marines, and my friend Manila John Basilone."

Reading that, I was unsure whether Lansford really accepted that the "thin" body was John's. So in June 2008 I phoned Bill again in California to ask. He said, "It was about noon of the first day and getting shelled to hell and all of us were in some state of shock. And of course it was John. I saw his pack with his name on it. And when the burial detail came up this cook was in it who knew our outfit and knew John and he made the same ID. I used to stay in touch with him [the cook Elsner] down in El Paso and then we lost contact. And I certainly knew Basilone from our time in the same machine-gun outfit. I was a section leader and he had a squad. We had gone on liberty together, gotten drunk together, and remember how we all shaved our heads that time?"

When I mentioned the several versions of Basilone's death that I'd read, Lansford reacted contemptuously. "There's a lot of scuttlebutt and bullshit out there, a lot of self-promoters. I've seen the different versions."

I then cited the official casualty report from the History Division in Quantico attributing Basilone's wounds to "GSW," gunshot wounds. Lansford wasn't buying that either. "That's absurd. I saw the body." I then mentioned the report's detailing three different hits, right groin, neck, and left arm. Lansford agreed that part sounded like what he'd seen but held to his insistence it was a single mortar shell that did it, not gunshots. We'd both seen dead bodies and knew that shellfire and small arms usually make different-looking entry wounds. He then continued with a last description of the living Basilone from memory. It's worth hearing.

"I was trying to round up all my guys at the foot of Motoyama Airfield #1 and the assault groups had gone through and there were a lot of Japanese dead lying around. It had been raining intermittently and I went over to one of the dead to go through the body for papers or maps or whatever, which we did for intelligence. He was wearing a raincoat and their [Japanese] raincoats were better than our ponchos and we would take things like that. And John Basilone came out onto the plaza near the lip of Motoyama Airfield #1 and he was calling his men together, you know with his hand circling above his head [the 'gather on me' gesture] and five or six guys came over. That was when a mortar shell came in and killed all of them, I don't know, four or five. I saw the medical report from the people who do the examination and it was one mortar shell. Just one."

I said, "One is all it takes," or something like that, and I again thanked Bill Lansford, a wonderful writer, who was writing a new book of his own and had worked on other projects with Ken Burns and Steven Spielberg.

26

There are as many descriptions of John Basilone's last firefight and where and how he died as there are Alamo legends about a wounded Jim Bowie's final fight in the old monastic cell where he lay waiting for the enemy with a knife and a gun or two. In Texas, they tell to this day of platoons of Mexicans found dead around Colonel Bowie's last bed.

I don't mean to be flip about this, but the Basilone family has been of little help in establishing the facts of just how John died and what he accomplished that terrible morning under heavy fire against the Japanese. Phyllis Basilone Cutter provides us perhaps the most colorful and probably the least credible account of her brother's heroics, in her hagiographic depiction of the fighting and of his unspoken thoughts and what he supposedly said and actually did in the battle. This is entirely understandable. Phyllis was a civilian writing about the brother she loved and lost, for a local audience, many of whom knew young John, remembered him as a boy, and revered his memory. Whether in Phyllis's family biography of the Basilones or in the fourteen installments of the same story she wrote for the Somerset County, New Jersey,

Messenger-Gazette newspaper, there is a "lives of the saints" quality to her account of his heroics, the stuff of B-movie, Republic Pictures films of the era when John and his sister were growing up and going to the local movie theater ("the Madhouse") in Raritan.

To begin, Phyllis talks throughout of Basilone's having landed with the first wave of assault troops, as if this makes him somehow braver than men who came later. In fact, Basilone was in the fourth wave, landing at about nine-thirty that morning, perhaps twenty-five or twenty-eight minutes after the first wave, a position every bit as perilous and courageous as the three waves that hit the sand earlier. Phyllis's account of Basilone's Iwo starts as he and his men board their landing craft, first circling, then taking a direct line to the hostile beach, and their landing under fire.

At this point, with battle about to be joined, a platoon to be steadied and encouraged, weapons and gear to be checked, Phyllis imagines, in Basilone's voice, that he isn't focused on Iwo and the battle coming up fast, but on December 7, three years earlier. "We thought of Pearl Harbor and had no compassion for the enemy." There may be Marine gunnies who speak or think like that as they go into combat, but I don't know any. Phyllis has her brother next describing the situation on the beach as the Marines come in for a landing: "The Japs lay stunned and helpless under the curtain of fire. Our landing was met by only weak small arms fire. The beach was coarse volcanic ash which made for a bad landing. We sank deep into the ash, slowing us down, as well as practically miring our vehicles. The boys were all together gathering their equipment so that we could work our way off the beach inland to our predetermined points, when we were suddenly peppered by machine gun fire. 'Down, fellows, hug the beach! Pull your helmets in front of your faces.'" This line is nonsense.

The ostrich buries its head in the sand; Marines in a firefight rely on their vision to target the enemy, to return fire, to figure out what's happened, to look for orders. If you cover your face with a helmet, you're blind. And this is an order given by a seasoned gunnery sergeant to his Marines? Phyllis goes on with her account, quoting Basilone: "As if struck by lightning, we hit the ground fast. Carefully tilting our helmets a bit we could see where the machine gun fire was coming from. It had to be silenced or we would be pinned down indefinitely."

Phyllis picks up Basilone's early moments on the black sand beach of Iwo with her "tale of the blockhouse," a dramatic vignette of which there are multiple versions. And she shifts from first to third person and back, in retelling what Basilone did next to silence the enemy gun. "Telling us to stay put [who is 'us,' who is narrating here?], Basilone crawled in a large semi-circle toward the blockhouse, which was spitting fire and death. He was able to crawl underneath the smoking gun ports. As he rested his back against the wall of the blockhouse, we counted with him the seconds before each machine gun burst. Waiting for the interval, he pulled the pin on his grenade, slammed it in the gun port and ran like hell down the beach. He tripped in the deep ash and as he buried himself protectively we heard the muffled roar of the exploding grenade. The blockhouse was smoking and the gun at the port had disappeared. Basilone ran back, dropping another grenade in for insurance. There were no signs of life, nothing but silence and the sickening smell of burnt flesh and scorched hair. Working his way back to us Basilone yelled, 'well, boys, there's one bunch of slantheads who won't bother anyone. They're fried.'"

Why would a machine-gun platoon sergeant be carrying hand grenades? I don't insist it never happened, but it puzzles me. Riflemen tote grenades, but machine gunners already have such heavy loads that they don't need to pile on additional gear.

Alternating between third and first person, Phyllis continues, describing the heavy enemy bombardment chewing up Marines on the beach. More disconcerting is Basilone himself explaining from the beach what the Japanese strategy is and what orders General Tadamichi Kuribayashi is sending to his various commanders. How the hell can a gunnery sergeant under fire know what's going on with general officers at the enemy headquarters as he and his men attempt to mount up and move on against hostile resistance?

When an American tank passes through Basilone's position and is hit by shells, one of its crew members scrambles out
of the hatch to safety, only to be killed by Japanese small-arms
fire. "Basilone was raging," Phyllis wrote, "rising to his feet as he
charged over to the tank cradling his machine gun in his arms
[machine gunners in the platoon usually carry the guns; the platoon sergeant doesn't]. Spotting a flash from a tree top [were
there many trees on Iwo?] he stood upright and sprayed it furi-
ously. We heard an unearthly scream as the treacherous sniper
plummeted to his death. By this time there were other tanks,
unaware of the heavily mined path. Basilone yelled and waved his
arms, motioning them to follow him. As we watched [who is 'we?']
he led them in a wide circle into the safety of the wooded area."

So now Basilone is commanding a tank platoon, and again,
how does he know where the mines are? "By now Basilone was
as if possessed, ignoring the flesh ripping death all about him he
rushed back to us shouting 'OK, fellows, let's get moving. We got
to get these guns set up.'" Now, either they're going to set up the
machine guns where they'll make a stand or they're going to move
out; they can't do both. "We began to work our way off the beach.
Without warning the whole beach erupted. The enemy had recovered and was fighting back."

This is terrible stuff, and it goes on like this, making little
sense, such as Phyllis's statement at this point that "it was hours
before another Marine landed on the beach." Other sources say
the fifth wave had landed on the heels of the fourth (Basilone's),
adding to the confusion. But Phyllis makes it sound as if Basilone's
platoon was the famous "Lost Battalion" of World War I, abandoned and alone, out in front of the lines, facing 22,000 Japanese
all by itself, when it was actually still on or trying to advance off
the beach with thousands of other Marines. Basilone sends a
scout named Sammy ahead to look over the way ahead and report
back. "Fragments of white, steely death were whining and singing
all about us. It was a miracle that up to this point, any of us had
escaped injury, much less death."

The fevered prose of a bad war movie goes on. And Phyllis is not alone in this. Another Marine, Charles "Chuck" Tatum, a member of Basilone's platoon, in his book *Red Blood, Black Sand*, offers this capsule description of Manila John in a firefight, from the point of view of the assistant gunner who feeds the belted ammo into Basilone's gun. "Basilone's eyes had a fury I had never seen before. Rigid, hard clenched jaw, sweat glistening on his forehead, he was not an executioner but a soldier performing his duty."

This aside, Tatum does tend to clear up questions about Basilone and the famous blockhouse. Tatum's B Company had gotten bogged down, and as the confusion grew worse, Basilone was seen stalking up and down the beach trying, with Colonel Plain, to get his own men and the remnants of the earlier waves organized and heading inland. Tatum and the B Company machine gunners recognized Gunny Basilone and, knowing his reputation, were only too happy to fall in line when Basilone gave the "gather" signal and tried to get everyone moving forward.

Tatum writes that in the beach chaos, while trying to get men from different units organized, Basilone came across a demolitions assault team headed by Corporal Ralph Belt. It was not Basilone, but one of Belt's men, who, on Basilone's order, and given covering overhead fire by Basilone's machine gunners, rushed the looming blockhouse and tossed a heavy satchel charge of C-2 plastic explosive at its steel doors. According to Tatum, no one got up on the roof during the attack. And it was a Marine flamethrower operator, a hulking corporal named William N. Pegg, also on Basilone's orders, who finished off the blockhouse and cooked the men inside, again assisted by overhead machine-gun fire. Those Japanese able to flee, some of them actually aflame, would be shot down by Tatum, PFC Alvin C. Dunlap, PFC Steve Evanson, and Private Lawrence "Cookie Hound" Alvino.

These men and Tatum himself credit Basilone for organizing, ordering, and directing a brilliant blockhouse operation, but not for having carried out the demolition himself. It was a perfect example of carrying out a perfect plan of assault, a Marine Corps "school solution," employing flamethrower and demolitions, the sort of live-fire maneuver Basilone had drilled into his men over and over at Pendleton and later Tarawa. It was a feat of cool, superb leadership that could easily all by itself have earned Basilone a decoration.

Which is why it's exasperating that the Navy Cross citation needlessly includes an imaginary single-handed Basilone appearance on the blockhouse roof. Tatum's book adds clarification on that point, saying that *after* the position had been destroyed, Basilone grabbed Tatum and his machine gun and they took to the roof of the wrecked fortification for a better vantage point from which to pick off fleeing Japanese.

Phyllis now resumes her own version of Basilone's final orders and actions. As Sammy the scout gives the all-clear, the unit prepares to move inland: "Turning to the rest of the boys, Sergeant Basilone snapped, 'Okay, boys, stick close and follow me. Remember, if anyone gets it, the rest keep going. That's an order. We've got to get those guns set up. Let's go.' Single file we followed him. He never once looked back. He knew we were right behind him. Progress was slow. We had to detour and work our way around our knocked-out, still blazing vehicles. Dead Marines in our path received silent salute as we passed them. Every one of them had fallen face toward the enemy, rifles still in their hands." This is an unlikely picture to anyone who has ever walked over a heavily shelled, chaotic field of battle and seen the contorted limbs of the dead.

"The ground was rising and slowly settling back under the thunderous impact of heavy mortars and artillery shells. Slowly, it seemed hours, we crawled for the comparative safety of the first rise of ground. The figure of Sammy loomed larger and larger through the haze as we approached the end of the beach area. A second later, just when we thought we'd make it, suddenly there was a horrible screeching, whining sound picking up in intensity until we thought our eardrums would burst.

"Sergeant Basilone yelled, 'Hit the dirt, boys!'

"As if in rehearsal, we all hit the ash. Just at that moment, there was a terrifying roar, indescribably loud and angry. As we were slammed into the ground, we saw Sergeant Basilone hurled bodily into the air. It was as if a huge hand had reached down, smashed him deep into the volcanic ash. As we picked ourselves up, dazed, groggy and numb from the concussion we saw Sergeant Basilone lying half-buried in the swirling volcanic ash. He was unconscious and from the peculiar position he was in, appeared to have been hit bad. Sammy, who until this moment was too shocked to move, recklessly ran over to Basilone and was trying to rouse him."

There are additional contradictions here. Other accounts have Basilone killed with three other men in a group as they advance on Motoyama Airfield #1, not on the beach. Here he seems to have been the only one in the unit to have been hit. Though later Phyllis has the scout Sammy telling the wounded Basilone, "Sarge, it's horrible. Most of the group got it," the official Marine Corps casualty record blames small-arms fire, not a big shell. In Phyllis's version Basilone is still alive but unconscious. Several of her sentences later, he is awake and trying to shove his intestines back inside his body, and he is speaking. Others say he died instantly. Some say he lived half an hour. Phyllis has him living for hours and his men calling for help: "Medic, medic!" In the Marine Corps the call is always for "Corpsman, corpsman!" our term for a medic.

But these are details, and perhaps I'm nitpicking. Phyllis's account of her own brother's death deserves a hearing. Without my injecting further critical commentary, this is how she narrates the story in the *Somerset Messenger-Gazette* on Valentine's Day 1963, eighteen years after his death, of Manila John's last hours:

"You could see Sergeant Basilone fighting his way back to consciousness. In deep shock and tottering on the brink of complete unconsciousness, the sergeant was fighting back. His face, twisted and contorted with pain, was set in grim determination. By now Sammy was crying as he cradled Basilone protectively in his arms. Basilone slowly and with great effort, opened his pain-wracked eyes and said, 'Sammy, what happened?' Sammy, convulsed with grief, could only mutter, 'Sarge, it's horrible. Most of the group got it.' We watched silently, knowing the rest of us should move on, yet not wanting to leave the two of them alone on this God-forsaken beach. As we leaned over, Sammy was removing Sarge's hands which were clasped tightly over his stomach. The sight before our eyes was horrifying. Basilone's hands were drenched with deep scarlet blood, which trickled back to his wrists when Sammy elevated Sarge's hands over his head. The hot nauseating smell of blood and torn guts swirled slowly under our nostrils. We gulped back hard, but Sammy couldn't take it. He started to heave, horrible, retching, vomiting. It was then Sergeant Basilone displayed the intestinal fortitude he was so noted for. Ever so slowly and with a deftness surprising in such a muscular man, Basilone reached down into the sickening bloody mess that were his intestines, and placed them back into his torn and gashed open stomach. The effort must have been exhausting, as he lay back breathing heavily, biting huge gulps of the dust-laden air. Sammy had reached the dry retching stage. Suddenly, as if propelled from a catapult, he dashed madly down the beach, shouting, 'medic, medic!'

"Don't ever discount the courage and bravery of our medics. This lad was typical. There he was, oblivious to the hell and destruction being showered upon him as he tenderly ministered to the wounded. We watched as Sammy talked to him and gestured in our direction. No doubt Sammy told him the wounded Marine was Sergeant Basilone. It made no difference to the medic. A Marine was a Marine, Medal of Honor or not. To his credit, and keeping in the spirit of the Corps, he calmly finished bandaging his patient. Then, and only after making the wounded youngster as comfortable as possible, did he accompany Sammy back to us and Sergeant Basilone. We watched hopefully as the medic silently, and with tender hands, examined Basilone's wounds. Reaching for his kit, he fished out a hypo and bending loosely to Basilone's ear, he said softly, 'It's OK, Sarge. I'm going to give you a shot of morphine. That'll ease your pain until we can get you to a doctor.' The enemy by this time had succeeded in stopping any more landings.

"Basilone's only chance to live was to be taken back in one of the empty assault boats as it returned for another load. Seeing Basilone tug at the medic's sleeve, we edged closer to hear his words. 'Level with me, Doc. Am I going to make it?' Hanging on for doc's reply we heard him tell Basilone, 'Sarge, I'll give it to you straight. If I can get you back to the hospital ship in a couple of hours, you have a chance. Right now we're pinned to this god-damned beach. Your guess right now is as good as mine. I'm going to stay with you and the first boat that hits the shore will have you and I as passengers on the way back. Meanwhile, when the pain gets unbearable, yell out. I'll give you another shot. That's the best I can do for you now.' Basilone nodded he understood.

"We watched fascinated as his life blood slowly and relent-lessly kept oozing out, trailing brilliant crimson streamers down his side, turning the black volcanic ash into a dark purple spot which spread out ever so slowly. He was bleeding to death before our eyes and we were powerless to stop the flow."

In the Taebaek Mountains of North Korea in January 1952 I watched a Marine bleed to death coming back from a combat patrol. We had him on a stretcher, and it took the wounded man maybe seven hours to die. Toward the end he thought he was Jesus. Loss of blood eventually kills you; along the way it weakens not only the body but the intelligence, the judgment, the brain. Lose enough blood and you don't make much sense anymore. In Phyllis's story, Basilone was not only physically tough, he was still remarkably cogent.

In her account, as hour after hour passes, Sammy and Basilone have a discussion of what Basilone wants the young Marine to tell his brother George when and if George hits the beach. Basilone says he's had it, that he knows there's no chance. Sammy argues with him. Then Sammy pulls out a pencil and takes down Basilone's instructions about his brother. Basilone asks the corpsman, "Doc," for a cigarette. Doc then lights a cigarette for Basilone and places it between his lips. But the wounded ser-geant coughs and the butt comes away soaked with blood. Then Sammy reaches inside the pocket of Basilone's "tunic" and pulls out the miniature Bible many combat soldiers were given and carried during World War II, worn as protection in a pocket over the heart. Sammy begins to read the Lord's Prayer. As he finishes, Basilone's face, "now in peaceful repose, turns toward us." The Marines drop to their knees in prayer, as John Basilone "slipped away." Sammy, unbelieving, tries to rouse him, but the corpsman tells him, "Kid, it's no use. He's gone."

Here is Colonel Joe Alexander's briefer account: "On the left center of the action, leading his machine gun platoon, in the 1st Battalion 27th Marines' attack against the southern portion of the airfield, the legendary 'Manila John' Basilone fell mortally wounded by a mortar shell, a loss keenly felt by all Marines on the island."

Did he die on the beach, on the approaches to the airfield, from a mortar round or gunfire? On this last question, the official USMC casualty report backs up neither the family biographies nor Colonel Alexander. No mortar explosion is cited. Basilone's death in this report, drawn up on March 7, 1945, two weeks after he died, reads like this: "Nature of wound, GSW [gunshot wound], right groin, neck, and left arm." Robert Aquilina of the Corps' History Division reference branch in Quantico concludes that Manila John probably bled to death from these gunshots.

Marine casualties that first day ashore amounted to some 2,400 wounded and 501 killed, and Alexander reports in a small but very human sidebar that survivors of that deadly February 19 still remember how cold it was the first night after the landing, so unlike the tropical Pacific many of them knew from earlier fights.

Jerry Cutter, Basilone's nephew, has his version of his uncle's death, conflicting dramatically with his mother's more detailed version. Here, probably no truer but less flowery and imaginary, is what Cutter and writer Jim Proser wrote: "Sergeant John Basilone was killed by an enemy mortar shell at approximately 10:45 a.m. February 19, 1945. He suffered massive abdominal wounds but lingered for approximately twenty minutes before succumbing from shock and loss of blood. Four Marines died from the same explosion. His last words were spoken to a Navy corpsman who attended to him following the explosion. That corpsman has vowed never to reveal those final words."

So the two Cutters, mother and son, differ. In Jerry's story, no final message to George, no last cigarette, no Lord's Prayer, only twenty minutes of life, no three or more talkative hours, no peaceful look on his face. As to death by mortar shell or small-arms fire, Joe Alexander and the official casualty report are also at odds on that one specific item. There are other versions of his death as well. But it is the family versions that appear to stray furthest from the facts.

Clearly, they love the man, but trying to make a great warrior even better—a superman, an icon, conjuring up dialogue never spoken, prayers never prayed, inventing scenes that never happened, laying it on thick about feats of arms surely within Basilone's competence, but which never happened—is no service to a great man.

The service record book on Gunnery Sergeant John Basilone, his dates of enlistment, promotions, duty stations, transfers, and the like, filed at Marine Corps Schools, Quantico, Virginia, ends with this simple entry on his death: "Killed in action, February 19, 1945, Buried in grave 41, row 3, plot 1, 5th Mar Div cemetery, Iwo Jima, Volcano Islands." That's all there is, no poetry, no flourishes, no heroics.

PART FIVE

COMING HOME

Gunnery Sergeant John Basilone, originally buried on Iwo Jima, was re-buried in 1948 at Arlington National Cemetery with full military honors. Marine comrades are seen holding the American flag during services as members of the family look on. (Seated left to right) Basilone's sister Phyllis (in light jacket); his mother, Dora; and his father, Salvatore.

27

In the traditional Marine Corps protocol of death, the family must be officially notified before any media are contacted. Inadvertently, though quite properly, it was a Basilone clan member who first learned of John's death on Iwo long before anyone at home got the news. George, John's brother, whose Marine unit went ashore several days after the first waves, was approached by a sergeant assigned to seek him out with the bad tidings. The sergeant saw the name Basilone stenciled on a backpack, and according to Bruce Doorly's account, called out, "George, I need to talk to you." Alarms went off, since George had never seen this sergeant before. "How come you know my first name?" A subsequent and famous photo shows George kneeling, a thoughtful, wry half-smile on his face that resembled John's so closely, at the simple white cross marking the temporary grave on Iwo. Coincidentally, another Raritan Marine named Tony Cirello would find John's pack in the sand and return it to George.

When the word finally came to Raritan on March 8, sixteen days after Manila John's death, there was some confusion. A reporter that morning phoned brother Angelo Basilone's house on Second Avenue. His wife answered, then went directly to the parents' home on First Avenue to ask the matriarch of the family, Dora Basilone, if she knew anything. Dora didn't, and for a time the two women took comfort in the possibility that this was all a mistake and the reporter had gotten it wrong. Ten minutes later via Western Union a War Department notification (I suspect it was actually a Navy Department wire, which would be standard operating procedure for a Marine death) arrived, not at the Basilone family's front door, but at Pop Basilone's new place of work at Holcombe & Holcombe (he had sold his own shop). It went to Sal Basilone because he was officially listed as next of kin in John's service record book. This is how the telegram read: "Deeply regret to inform you that your son, Gunnery Sergeant John Basilone, USMC, was killed in action February 19, 1945 at Iwo Jima, Volcano Islands, in the performance of his duty and service to his country. When information is received regarding burial, you will be notified. Please accept my heartfelt sympathy."

It was signed, "General Alexander Vandegrift," who had been John's commanding officer on Guadalcanal and later presented him with his medal. The circle was closed.

In Camp Pendleton, Sergeant Lena Riggi Basilone, John's wife, got a similar wire.

Salvatore immediately phoned home and broke the news. It was official now, official and confirmed—no more comforting doubt, no hope there'd been a mistake. Bruce Doorly writes in his book, "Dora was in a state of shock and described as being on the verge of collapse. Salvatore quickly came home and soon word of John's death sped throughout the town. When a local Raritan boy died in the war, the word always spread quickly. Police Chief Lorenzo Rossi went around town informing people of John's death. The station master at the Raritan Train Station told commuters as they walked to the train. The church bells at St. Ann's were rung. Father Amadeo Russo [the youthful John's mentor] soon arrived at the house to comfort the family. The Basilone house was quickly flooded with visitors offering their sympathy. John's sister Dolores described for Doorly's monograph how she was notified. She was in class at Somerville High School when the principal of the school came in and said her dad had called. She and her younger brother Donald had to go home. No other information was given them but when the principal himself drove them both home, they started to realize that something major had happened. They were informed of John's death when they arrived home."

Both local newspapers, the *Somerset Messenger-Gazette* and the *Plainfield Courier News*, were afternoon papers, and on that same day, March 8, Basilone would be their front-page lead story. On a larger scale, the *New York Times* commented editorially, "Being a Marine fighting man, and therefore a realist, Sergeant Basilone must have known in his heart that his luck could not last forever. Yet he chose to return to battle." Also that day, March 8, Marines were still fighting on Iwo, pushing forward against fierce opposition. In Germany U.S. infantry and armor crowded onto the congested Remagen Bridge across the Rhine while desperate Nazi counterattacks continued. In Burma, British and Indian divisions broke out of their bridgeheads across the Irrawaddy, west of and "on the road to" Mandalay, where in Rudyard Kipling's poem "The Road to Mandalay" "the old flotilla lay."

Back home in Raritan, while everyone mourned John Basilone, the family thought about and prayed for another son, George, still believed to be on Iwo. How dreadful it would be to lose another boy on the same lousy little island. On Saturday the tenth there was a requiem mass at St. Ann's. Town flags flew at half-staff, and the American Legion post changed its name to "Sgt. John Basilone Post 280." Word arrived that Basilone had post-humously been awarded the Navy Cross. One of his officers on Iwo, Justin Gates Duryea, had submitted Basilone's name for a second Medal of Honor, only to be informed by higher echelons that all the Congressional Medals they could give were already gone. Heroism was one thing, bureaucracy remained very much another.

At St. Ann's they held a memorial mass later on Sunday, April 29, 1945, with Father Russo saying the high mass and the chaplain of nearby Camp Kilmer (named for the New Jersey poet killed in World War I), Reverend Raymond Kilmera, there to concelebrate. The Marine Corps dispatched a Marine color guard and a colonel, Harold Parsons. Governor Walter Edge sent the state adjutant general, and other local officials attended, as did people from the VFW and American Legion and the Army and Navy Union. Two Boy Scout troops were on hand, a band from Camp Kilmer, a detachment of troops and WACs from Fort Dix, and civilians from other New Jersey towns—Camden, Perth Amboy, South Orange, Trenton, and Newark.

A month earlier, on March 26, after thirty-six days of battle (remember that optimistic estimate that this might be a seventy-two-hour fight?), combat on Iwo ended with a final suicide attack by 500 Japanese troops against Basilone's 5th Marine Division. By the time the guns fell mute, 25,000 Americans were casualties, 7,000 of them dead. On that day on the Western Front the American 7th Division began to cross the Rhine. In the Philippines 14,000 American soldiers landed against hostile opposition near Cebu City.

When I first went down to Basilone's hometown that January morning all those years later on the early train out of Newark, and those three old boys from the Basilone Parade Committee met me at the depot in the red truck, they told me that when news of Basilone's death came, it was like the world ended in Raritan, just came to an end, not as literally but just as certainly as it had out in the Pacific for Manila John.

But worlds don't come to ends. Amid the grief, life goes on. And the war itself went on, until it eventually ended, too late for Sergeant Basilone and for so many more. Among them were small-town boys from burgs like Raritan where local people put up markers and ever after recalled.

Germany surrendered in May, Japan on August 15, 1945. On that mid-August day an impromptu parade of thanksgiving made its straggling way along Somerset Street in Raritan, and when the VJ Day march ended, the celebrations continued at local places like Orlando's Tavern, where John Basilone used to drink, and where Tony Orlando hosted a victory party. Surely toasts were drunk to Manila John's memory. He would have liked that. One unnamed local serviceman was quoted as saying on that last day of the war, "I keep thinking of my buddies who won't come back." But many of the dead *would* be coming back.

During World War II, we often buried the bodies of our men where they died—Italy or Normandy or the Pacific islands—with the tacit understanding that our people would eventually be brought home and planted here where they grew up and where they belonged. In 1948, three years after he died on Iwo, John Basilone came home from Iwo Jima.

And so it happened that in April of that year Raritan would have yet another opportunity to mourn and celebrate their local hero. The government had begun moving bodies back from Iwo's ad hoc cemeteries, giving families the option of choosing a burial near home or a plot at Arlington. Dora initially preferred to have John buried at Raritan, where the family lived and where he grew up. But local funeral director Anthony Bongiovi, nearly one hundred years old when I interviewed him, told me there was indecision at first. He admitted he didn't want to be in the middle of it, didn't welcome having to handle the job with its possible complications.

Well, after my talk with undertaker Bongiovi I was still getting differing versions of whether the body had passed through Raritan, where a mass was said at St. Ann's Church, several sources insisting they had seen the casket. So I asked Deacon John Pacifico of the church to clear up the mystery. On September 2, 2008, he wrote back: "Dear Jim, Both Anna Marie Bongiovi and Steve Del Rocco have confirmed that the body of John Basilone never came to Raritan. The body was at Arlington."

So at some point the decision had been made to bury their son at Arlington, instead of in New Jersey. Some sources say Bongiovi recommended Arlington. He didn't say that to me but continued telling me what then happened.

According to Doorly it was the undertaker who convinced Dora being buried at Arlington was a big deal, would do honor to her boy, and that Arlington was where Basilone belonged. I don't

believe that any of them, including the undertaker Bongiovi, suspected what was coming. They all expected an intimate little
funeral, a prayer from Father Russo, some friends, the family, a rite
appropriate to a small Jersey town and a blue-collar family and their
boy who never made money or much of a splash when he lived
there, who joined the Marines, and then died in the war.

The burial was on April 20, 1948, but the Basilone funeral was
going to be relentlessly small-town. Police chief Rossi volunteered
to drive the limo, Bongiovi volunteered the undertaking services,
Father Russo drove up front with the chief, with Dora and Sal, the
parents, in back. A couple of other cars made up the cortege, carrying Basilone brothers and sisters and some neighbors. Al Gaburo
the laundryman came, the man who once fired Johnny for goofing
off and sleeping on the laundry bags; the mayor Rocco Miele; a
future mayor, Steve Del Rocco. It was about two hundred miles,
but the traffic was lighter then and they made it in under four
hours.

Bongiovi told me they expected a simple affair, a couple of
guys with rifles, maybe a bugler to play Taps, that was about it.
Doorly gives this account from the family and Raritan vantage
point: "When they arrived, they were amazed. First, they were
picked up from their vehicles and driven in jeeps to the grave site.
There they saw dozens of military dignitaries, a Marine band, and
uniformed soldiers [Marines, surely] who would fire a gun salute.
It was a most impressive, inspiring service, a true tribute to an
unselfish hero. Father Russo blessed the casket. An American flag
had first covered the coffin, and then as is customary, it was later
taken off, folded in the ritual manner, and given to the Basilone
family. Anthony Bongiovi, when he spoke with Doorly, said the
funeral was simply unbelievable. He recalls that it was during
the playing of Taps that everyone became emotional. The family
and friends all drove back the same day."

More than four hundred miles down and back and eight
hours behind the wheel. No one thought to have reserved a couple of hotel rooms or a motel, what was then called a travel court.
Maybe they didn't have the dough. But they had properly buried

their Johnny. Lena Riggi Basilone, the widow, wasn't there. She had come east after the war to meet John's family, though only the once. Her niece, an actress and dancer, lives in New York, where in 2007 I interviewed her.

Doorly contacted Virginia Grey for a comment to use in his monograph, asking if she remembered Basilone. She was eighty-seven by then and still living in California, and she sent a statement: "How I do remember John. Every time I pass Basilone Drive at Camp Pendleton, it brings tears to my eyes."

Curiously, there is very little about Basilone's widow, though there is a photo from 1949 when she and the family attended in Boston the commissioning of the destroyer USS *Basilone* on July 26. Doorly writes this brief passage about her: "Lena did not meet John's parents until after his death when she came to New Jersey. A picture of them together appears in this book. She never remarried, as she was very content with her life. She told a friend 'Once you have the best you can't settle for less.' Lena was described by her friends as a great cook, who enjoyed inviting people over for special dinners. She worked at an electrical plant. Always active in military affairs, she volunteered at the Long Beach Veterans Hospital, the American Veterans Auxiliary, and the Women Marines Association. She died on June [11] of 1999 at the age of 86." Former Marine Clinton Watters, the best man at their wedding in 1944, told me in admiring tones, "When she was in her eighties, she looked fifty."

With the widow so relentlessly offstage in the various accounts of Basilone's life, I contacted her niece, Fiddle Viracola, an Emmy-winning actress, singer, and dancer who appeared on Broadway in such plays as *The Beauty Part* and *The Rose Tattoo*, and who lives in Greenwich Village. She told me she had met with a writer for a new Steven Spielberg–Tom Hanks television series about the Pacific war, and has on her own been collecting material about John and Lena for a screenplay. She's also had an exchange of letters with the Spielberg office and with the casting people, so she's anxious to see the finished project. "I'm working on the script now [her own script, not theirs] and I've got eighty-eight pages. It's a powerful love story. Lena was so strong, and they were very compatible. He was very lost, always losing jobs, and Lena gave him a center. She knew his passion to go back [to the Pacific and the war]."

According to Ms. Viracola, Lena met the Basilone family only that one time in Massachusetts and never in New Jersey (as other sources insist she did). "They met up in Boston for the commissioning of the ship. The Basilones had been horrible to her. Raritan was resentful. I gather his sister wanted to run the show, getting all the limelight and the plaudits. There were a lot of self-serving people around."

To my knowledge, the widow did not attend the 1948 reburial at Arlington. "I don't know if she was invited," Viracola said. "I hear the mother [Dora] wanted Lena to come back to Raritan and live there, but that wasn't her style. She became a master sergeant and left the Marine Corps eventually and ran a company that was in air-conditioning and things like that and was involved in many things for the vets. People were drawn to Lena."

What about that line explaining why she never remarried, "I was married to the best"? "Yes," said the niece, "that quote is true. She also said, 'Great love only happens once.'"

Had she as reported handed over her ten-thousand-dollar government check as next of kin to the Basilone family? "Yes, she gave it to them. And when Lena was asked if she wanted to be buried next to John at Arlington, she said, 'I don't want anything to do with them.'" Was "them" the government or the family? "The family. They did not treat her well. And when she died Lena was buried in California wearing his wedding ring."

28

Sixty-five years after he earned the Medal of Honor fighting on Guadalcanal, sixty-three years after his death on Iwo
Jima, there remains within the Marine Corps controversy about
John Basilone. Not that anyone seriously disputes his heroism or
questions the Medal of Honor, but you encounter differences of
opinion about him, and he has his critics.

For instance, did Chesty Puller recommend Basilone not for
a Medal of Honor but for a lesser award, a Navy Cross? No,
reported Bob Aquilina, of the Marine Corps History Division,
who sent me Puller's formal recommendation of October 30, 1942
(just a week after the October 25 battle), for a Medal of Honor
for Basilone.

Aquilina also provided more information about what exactly
happened on Iwo. According to a dispatch from Marine combat
correspondent Henry Giniger, shortly after the landing Basilone
was "wounded fatally" when "he was about to lead his machine
gun platoon forward through a heavy barrage."

More descriptive is part of a cover story in the *Marine Corps
Gazette* of October 1963, which also brings into question the

account in Chuck Tatum's book of the famous blockhouse attack that first day on Iwo. It quotes former Marine corporal Ralph R. Belt (also cited in a disparate version by Tatum): "Basilone and I were both in the 27th Regiment—he was with C Company, I was in B Company. We landed on Red Beach 2. Right after we'd landed, my squad ran into a Jap block-house firing canister shells at the 26th Marines, and doing a lot of damage, too. There was a Marine standing on top of this pillbox, shouting for flame throwers and demolition men, I was a demolition man, and my buddy right alongside, PFC William N. Pegg, was a flame-thrower man. Before I had time to prepare demolition, Pegg moved to one side of the pill-box and knocked it out. He got a Silver Star. The Marine standing on top of the pill-box—shouting instructions, yelling for a machine gun, shaking a Ka-Bar knife at the Japs trying to get out—was Manila John. He would turn his back on the Japs to yell at us—wave his knife and laugh, then turn around toward them again—wave his knife and laugh right in their faces. I think Manila John was a great Marine. I'm very proud to have served with him in the Marines and on Iwo Jima. With the block-house out of the way, Manila John and his platoon fought their way across those bullet-torn sand dunes toward Airfield Number 1."

Corporal Belt then also corroborates the yarn about Basilone's guiding the tanks ahead before winding up his eyewitness account. "They had reached the edge of the airfield when the end came for Manila John a bursting mortar shell got him along with four others of his platoon." Later, crossing the airfield itself, "Pegg and I ran across a kid from our company by the name of Sorenson who had a very bad shoulder wound. A few feet away a corpsman was working on another wounded Marine. It was Manila John. He'd been hit bad. It looked like a mortar shell had landed right in front of him and ripped him wide open from his chin on down. As bad off as he was, he spoke to us—and he wore that grand smile of his. I have thought about that smile many, many times since. He died soon afterwards."

In 1992 a couple of newspaper reporters named Laurence Arnold and Regina de Peri Whitmer of the *Bridgewater (NJ) Courier-News* Sunday paper, for a feature about Basilone, got hold of a letter sent by a Lieutenant Hector R. Gai Jr. to his own sister on March 7, 1945, writing this about Iwo. "When a Japanese mortar struck Basilone's position, I was with him when he died on the south edge of [the airfield] Motoyama 1. He certainly did a hell of a fine job before he got it. He was only in action about two hours and a half.... John lived about an hour and a half but was in a coma. Surgery was the only thing and, of course, at that time it was out of the question. There wasn't any."

Aquilina also highlighted a copy of Basilone's posthumous Navy Cross citation signed by Forrestal and cited earlier. In part it reads—according to Corporal Belt, inaccurately—how Manila John, on top of the blockhouse, destroyed it single-handedly with grenades and demolitions.

As *Time* magazine reported in 1945, it was a mortar shell that killed Basilone. That story was also appended by the reference branch, as were other newspaper clips from the *Journal-American* in New York, a 1943 story bylined by Burris Jenkins Jr., headlined "Fought full regiment of Japs, Now he has Congressional Medal."

Regarding Corporal Belt, how just plain wacky is it that a veteran Marine machine-gun platoon sergeant in a firefight would be on the roof of an enemy blockhouse waving a Ka-Bar hunting knife around and taunting the Japanese instead of firmly on the ground commanding his gun crews and directing their fire? Tatum's earlier version seems more credible, that Basilone ordered demolitions man Belt and flamethrower Pegg to attack the bunker while his machine guns provided overhead covering fire.

Then again, as in Tatum's memory and book, was Basilone firing off a storm of bullets at the enemy in a fury, eyes blazing, or had he never fired a round just before he was hit? You can't have it both ways. Was his final action on the beach? Clearly not. Or inland on the approach to Motoyama Airfield #1? Probably there. The contradictions escalate with each different source. I'm not quite sure just which of the competing accounts is the most reliable. Some seem more bizarre than anything else with their obvious fabrications.

As far as Basilone's performance on Iwo is concerned, we have the official citation for his Navy Cross with attachments, including the signature of the commandant of the Marine Corps, who by that time late in the war, six months after Basilone died, was General Alexander Vandegrift, his commanding officer on the 'Canal and the very officer who in Australia in May 1943 presented Basilone with his Medal of Honor.

Here is the documentation for the Navy Cross on Iwo and the citation itself, starting with the recommendation for an award: "From the commanding officer, Company C, 1st Battalion, 27th Marines, 5th Marine Division, 24 April 1945," and sent upward through the chain of command all the way to Vandegrift:

> Subject: Navy Cross, recommendation for, case of Gunnery Sergeant John (n) Basilone (287506). USMC (Deceased). (A) Simple citation. (B) Statement of Witness.
>
> It is recommended that Gunnery Sergeant John Basilone be considered for the award of the Navy Cross. On 19 February, 1945, Gunnery Sergeant Basilone was serving in combat with 1st Battalion, 27th Marines, 5th Marine Division, on Iwo Jima, Volcano Islands.
>
> On this date, Gunnery Sergeant Basilone, moving forward in the face of heavy artillery fire, worked his way to the top of an enemy blockhouse which was holding up the advance of his company. Single handed, through the use of hand grenades and demolitions, he completely destroyed the blockhouse and its occupants. Later, on the same day, Gunnery Sergeant Basilone calmly guided one of our tanks, which was trapped in an enemy minefield, to safety, through heavy mortar and artillery fire. Gunnery Sergeant Basilone's courage and initiative did much to further the advance of his company at a time vital to the success of the operation. His expert tactical knowledge and daring aggressiveness were missed when he was killed at the edge of the airstrip by a mortar blast later the same day.

This was signed by Edward Kasky.

Rereading this "simple citation," a sort of preliminary sketching out of the facts for the authorities to review before writing and approving the formal citation itself and the award, I'm struck by several problems noted earlier in other accounts. Why would a machine-gun platoon sergeant be toting hand grenades and demolitions enabling him to knock out a blockhouse? Earlier stories seemed to indicate he destroyed the blockhouse from ground level, running toward it, not on its roof. And how is it that Basilone, just arrived on the scene, is able expertly to guide a tank through enemy minefields?

Then there is the statement of a single witness, PFC George Migyanko, dated April 24, two months after John's death: "I, George Migyanko, while serving with the 1st Battalion, 27th Marines, 5th Marine Division, saw Gunnery Sergeant John Basilone (287506), USMA, single-handedly destroy an enemy blockhouse which was holding up the advance of his company. Later in the day he led one of our tanks from a trap in a mine field in the face of withering artillery and mortar fire." End of statement.

That April 24 document was approved and forwarded to the secretary of the Navy on September 13, signed by H. G. Patrick, senior member of the board looking into the matter. Attached are other endorsements from lower-ranking officers of the 27th Marines, including Gerald F. Russell on April 25, T. A. Wornham on April 27, and K. E. Rocket on May 25. On June 27, 1945, it is the commanding general himself, "Howlin' Mad" Smith, who adds a fourth endorsement and sends the whole package on to the secretary of the Navy, via the commander in chief of the Pacific Fleet (Chester Nimitz, I would suppose) and to the commandant of the Corps. Next, on August 10, the commander, Pacific Fleet, sends along his approval to the secretary, again via the commandant, this letter signed by J. A. Hoover, deputy CINCPAC and CINCPON. On August 27 Vandegrift, who was by now the commandant, sends along his okay to Forrestal, the Navy secretary, noting, "recommended that Gunnery Sergeant Basilone be awarded the Navy Cross, posthumously."

There's a little more confusing bureaucracy at work here, it seems, since James Forrestal, SEC/NAV as they say, would not date until August 12, 1946, the official award of the Navy Cross, a year after the war ended. Who can explain that one except to suggest the office rubber stamp was incorrect in dating the sheet of paper with Forrestal's signature 1946 instead of 1945 when all the other material is dated? Clearly, in wartime, paperwork in the Corps or in the Department of the Navy was often sloppy.

Here, in any event, is the final version of the citation for his Navy Cross, verbatim:

> For extraordinary heroism while serving as a Leader of a Machine Gun Section of Company C, 1st Battalion, 27th Marines, 5th Marine Division, in action against enemy Japanese forces on Iwo Jima, Volcano Islands, 19 February, 1945. Shrewdly gauging the tactical situation shortly after landing when his company's advance was held up by the concentrated fire of a heavily fortified Japanese blockhouse, Gunnery Sergeant Basilone boldly defied the smashing bombardment of heavy artillery fire to work his way around the flank and up to a position directly on top of the blockhouse and then, attacking with grenades and demolitions, single-handedly destroyed the entire hostile strongpoint and its defending garrison. Consistently daring and aggressive as he fought his way over the battle-torn beach and the sloping, gun-studded terraces toward Airfield Number One, he repeatedly exposed himself to the blasting fire of exploding shells and later in the day coolly proceeded to the aid of a friendly tank which had been trapped in an enemy mine field under intense mortar and artillery barrages, skillfully guiding the heavy vehicle over the hazardous terrain to safety, despite the overwhelming volume of hostile fire. In the forefront of the assault at all times, he pushed forward with dauntless courage and iron determination until, moving upon the edge of the airfield,

he fell, instantly killed by a bursting mortar shell. Stout-hearted and indomitable, Gunnery Sergeant Basilone, by his intrepid initiative, outstanding professional skill and valiant spirit and self-sacrifice in the face of fanatic opposition, contributed to the advance of his company during the early critical period of the assault, and his unwavering devotion to duty throughout the bitter conflict was an inspiration to his comrades, and reflects the highest credit upon Gunnery Sergeant Basilone and the United States naval Service. He gallantly gave his life in the service of his country.

Among the multiple copies one is directed to "Public Info," and with a brief notation at the bottom, "Raritan, New Jersey . . . Buffalo, New York," I assume this meant that the media in those two cities, of John's rearing and his birth, were to be notified of the honor.

It is the accuracy of details in these battle accounts of Basilone's conduct that comes under criticism. But despite all the brass in Washington signing off on his Navy Cross, there remain to me some questions. We know Basilone was brave, a great Marine, a heroic man. But where did the blockhouse-busting grenades and demolitions come from? Was he on the blockhouse roof or down below? Was he really waving a hunting knife around? How was he sufficiently familiar with alien ground to guide that tank through the mines? Was he killed instantly by that mortar? Then why all those accounts of his living for hours, speaking with the corpsman, dictating messages to be passed on to brother George, and gradually bleeding to death? And what about that sole witness, the private who signed the citation recommendation? Where were the others? Questions remain.

Epilogue

Despite what Bertolt Brecht said, I believe having national heroes is healthy, giving us people to admire, role models, perhaps helping us to *be* somehow better than we are. Maybe heroes are just plain good for us; they make us feel better about ourselves, about the country, to know that among us are men and women who under pressure behave in exemplary ways and do things most of us don't even try. And it's not only wars that make heroes; newspapers and the local television stations regularly run features about "everyday heroes," urging nominations. There was even a time when America really *needed* a hero like John Basilone.

I'm neither a scholar nor a historian, just another old newspaperman who once fought in a war, but I remain fascinated and often puzzled by John Basilone, a professional Marine machine gunner in two climactic battles, one at the very start of a Pacific war we were losing and then in a second fight near the end of a war we knew we were going to win. He was a man already dead when I was a Catholic high school boy reading about him in the *Daily News,* and most of what I later knew of Basilone came from Marines and Marine Corps lore and the memories of old men in New Jersey, what they told me, the black-and-white photos at the Raritan library, when they drove me to the big bronze statue and took me to visit the little frame boyhood home, to see his hangouts.

I mentioned earlier a resemblance to the youthful Sly Stallone. Basilone *was* Stallone's Rambo, a real-life Rambo. And despite the wars and the years that separate the generations of Marines, I feel I knew a man I never met—because every Marine knew Manila John.

Even though . . .

More than sixty years after his death at age twenty-eight on Iwo Jima, Basilone remains an enigma. There are still questions about the famous decorations for his heroic battles. Some of these are insignificant points, matters of detail, an incorrect stat here, a confusion of names there, the chaos of battle, the tendency of loved ones to boast a little. Other questions were more substantive. This was the exasperating part of Manila John's story.

It goes without saying that neither sergeant, Mitchell Paige nor Basilone, campaigned for a decoration of any sort, never mind the top medal we have. Marines don't recommend themselves for awards; their superiors write them up.

The Navy Cross awarded posthumously on Iwo Jima is a strange affair, more complicated than any doubts about Guadalcanal. And being dead, Basilone can have no responsibility for what was subsequently written, said, or sworn to. The facts seem to be that Gunny Basilone, when confronted by a Japanese blockhouse, did precisely what the moment called for. He demonstrated initiative by getting a demolition assault team to send a man forward with a heavy explosive charge and another, the giant William Pegg, with the flamethrower, while Basilone's machine gunners gave them overhead covering fire.

Sergeant Basilone did his job perfectly, and so did the demo guy and the flamethrower, as did Basilone's machine gunners. The Japanese position fell to the combined Marine operation of explosives, flame, and machine-gun fire, and the stalled Marine drive inland got going, thanks in large part to Basilone's gutsy, intelligent leadership.

If that's the story, those the precise facts—and Chuck Tatum, there as a machine gunner, writes that they were—it is both rational and believable. If "Sergeant Basilone directed this operation 'by the book,' the way we practiced it at Pendleton and Camp Tarawa," then why conjure up a fantastic story about how Basilone scaled the roof and single-handedly destroyed the position with grenades? Or spent his time waving a hunting knife around, taunting and capering?

Basilone made the thing happen. It wasn't a solo performance, but it was heroic. Two other men backed up by his machine guns carried it out.

Then reread the official Navy Cross citation. The story of the tank in the minefield. Why pad the already impressive résumé? Did the Department of the Navy have so much invested in Basilone that he couldn't just die, he had to die gloriously, capable of superhuman feats? Maybe they had to make it up to America for permitting its hero to go back one more time to the battle. How else do you justify an official citation signed off by so many while so rife with apparent exaggerations?

Maybe, as has been charged, the Basilone of the war bond tour, with his handlers and packaged speeches and appearances, was to an extent a product marketed and merchandised by imaginative young officers doing PR for the Marine Corps. They were out to sell inspiration to a country that needed heroes, and Basilone must have looked like a good bet, a superior salesman. The kid out of Raritan was everyman from everywhere, an ordinary Joe, a small-town American; the darkly handsome, undefeated boxer Manila John, a poker-playing roughneck from the caddy shack, the guy with a knockout punch—and that marketable nickname. If this is true, none of it was Basilone's idea.

Basilone has surely been ill served even by people who loved him, family and friends, and by others, publicity professionals and inventive journalists, who damaged his reputation with fanciful stories and memoirs, their cartoon-styled exaggerations of feats of arms never performed, the hero lost behind his deeds.

The Basilone statue in Raritan, New Jersey, haloed by the sun.

But this is what makes him a legend and an American icon. Maybe we should just embrace the colorful lore, memorialize John Basilone as a Marine and honor his service, take him on faith, forget the disputation and the skeptical theories, mine and others, and just love the guy, saluting him with a well-earned and final Semper Fidelis. Always faithful. Perhaps we should leave it just as simple and as wonderful as that.

Bibliography

This bibliography was compiled from the author's notes after his passing. Any omissions or inaccuracies are, therefore, those of the editor.

Alexander, Joseph H. *Closing In: Marines in the Seizure of Iwo Jima.* Washington, DC: History and Museums Division, Headquarters, U.S. Marine Corps [Supt. of Docs., U.S. GPO, distributor], 1994.

Alexander, Joseph H., with Don Horan and Norman C. Stahl. *A Fellowship of Valor: The Battle History of the U.S. Marines.* New York: HarperCollins, 1997.

Doorly, Bruce W. *Raritan's Hero: The John Basilone Story.* Privately published.

Lansford, William Douglas. "The Life and Death of 'Manila John' Basilone." *Leatherneck.* October 2002.

Leckie, Robert. *Challenge for the Pacific: The Bloody Six-Month Battle of Guadalcanal.* New York: Da Capo, 1999.

———. *Helmet for My Pillow.* New York: Bantam, 1995.

Paige, Mitchell. *A Marine Named Mitch.* Santa Fe Springs, CA: Wylde & Sons, 1975.

Proser, Jim, with Jerry Cutter. *"I'm Staying with My Boys . . .": The Heroic Life of Sgt. John Basilone, USMC.* Hilton Head, SC: Lightbearer Communications, 2004.

Santelli, James S. *A Brief History of the 7th Marines*. Washington, DC: History and Museums Division, Headquarters, U.S. Marine Corps, 1980.

Shaw, Henry I., Jr. *First Offensive: The Marine Campaign for Guadalcanal*. Washington, DC: History and Museums Division, Headquarters, U.S. Marine Corps [Supt. of Docs., U.S. GPO, distributor], 1992.

Sledge, Eugene. *With the Old Breed, at Peleliu and Okinawa*. New York: Bantam, 1982.

Tatum, Charles W. *Iwo Jima: 19, February, 1945, Red Blood, Black Sand, Pacific Apocalypse*. Stockton, CA: C.W. Tatum Pub., 1995.

Tillman, Mary, and Narda Zacchino. *Boots on the Ground by Dusk: My Tribute to Pat Tillman*. New York: Modern Times, 2008.

United States Marine Corps, Historical Division. Lieutenant Colonel Frank O. Hough, USMCR; Major Verle E. Ludwig, USMC; and Henry I. Shaw Jr. *History of U.S. Marine Corps Operations in World War II: Pearl Harbor to Guadalcanal*, vol. I. Washington: GPO, 1958.

Illustration Credits

Index

THE
EXCHANGE

ALSO BY JOHN GRISHAM

A Time to Kill
The Firm
The Pelican Brief
The Client
The Chamber
The Rainmaker
The Runaway Jury
The Partner
The Street Lawyer
The Testament
The Brethren
A Painted House
Skipping Christmas
The Summons
The King of Torts
Bleachers
The Last Juror
The Broker
The Innocent Man
Playing for Pizza
The Appeal
The Associate
Ford County
The Confession
The Litigators
Calico Joe
The Racketeer
Sycamore Row
Gray Mountain

Rogue Lawyer
The Whistler
Camino Island
The Rooster Bar
The Reckoning
The Guardians
Camino Winds
A Time for Mercy
Sooley
The Judge's List
Sparring Partners
The Boys from Biloxi

The Theodore Boone Books
Theodore Boone: Kid Lawyer
Theodore Boone: The Abduction
Theodore Boone: The Accused
Theodore Boone: The Activist
Theodore Boone: The Fugitive
Theodore Boone: The Scandal
Theodore Boone: The Accomplice

JOHN GRISHAM

---•••---

THE EXCHANGE

After *The Firm*

---•••---

DOUBLEDAY

New York

Copyright © 2023 by Belfry Holdings, Inc.

All rights reserved. Published in the United States by Doubleday,
a division of Penguin Random House LLC, New York, and distributed in
Canada by Penguin Random House Canada Limited, Toronto.

doubleday.com

DOUBLEDAY and the portrayal of an anchor with a dolphin are registered
trademarks of Penguin Random House LLC.

Book design by Maria Carella
Jacket design by David Litman
Front-of-jacket photographs: Ascent/PKS Media Inc.;
narongcp; Alexander Spatari; feedough; all Getty Images

The Cataloging-in-Publication Data
is available at the Library of Congress.

ISBN: 978-0-385-54895-3 (hardcover)
ISBN: 978-0-385-54896-0 (ebook)

Manufactured in the United States of America

1 3 5 7 9 10 8 6 4 2

First Edition

BVG

THE
EXCHANGE

CHAPTER 1

On the forty-eighth floor of a glistening tower on the southern tip of Manhattan, Mitch McDeere stood alone in his office and gazed out the window at Battery Park and the busy waters beyond. Boats of all shapes and sizes crisscrossed the harbor. Massive cargo ships laden with containers waited almost motionless. The Staten Island Ferry inched past Ellis Island. A cruise ship packed with tourists headed out to sea. A mega yacht was making a splendid entrance into the city. A brave soul on a fifteen-foot catamaran zigzagged about, dodging everything. A thousand feet above the water no fewer than five helicopters buzzed about like angry hornets. In the far distance, trucks on the Verrazano Bridge stood still, bumper to bumper. Lady Liberty watched it all from her majestic perch. It was a spectacular view that Mitch tried to appreciate at least once each day. Occasionally he succeeded, but most days were too hectic to allow time for such loafing. He was on the clock, his life was ruled by it, just like the hundreds of other lawyers in the building. Scully & Pershing had over two thousand scattered around the world and vainly considered itself to be the premier international firm on the planet. Its New York partners, and Mitch was one, rewarded themselves with larger offices in the heart of the financial district. The firm was now a hundred years old and reeked of prestige, power, and money.

He glanced at his watch and the sightseeing came to an end. A pair of associates knocked and entered for another meeting. They met around a small table as a secretary offered coffee. They declined and she left. Their client was a Finnish shipping company having problems in South Africa. The authorities there had embargoed a freighter packed with electronics from Taiwan. Empty, the ship was worth about a hundred million. Fully loaded, it was worth twice that, and the South Africans were upset over some tariff issues. Mitch had been to Capetown twice in the past year and was not keen to return. After half an hour, he dismissed the associates with a list of instructions, and welcomed another pair.

At 5 P.M. sharp he checked in with his secretary, who was leaving, and walked past the elevators to the stairs. For short rides up and down he avoided the elevators to escape the mindless chitchat of lawyers he knew and didn't know. He had many friends in the firm and only a handful of known enemies, and there was always a new wave of fresh associates and eager junior partners with faces and names he was supposed to recognize. Often he did not, nor did he have time to pore over the firm directory and try to memorize them. So many would be gone before he knew their names.

Taking the stairs worked his legs and lungs and always reminded him that he was no longer in college, no longer playing football and intramural basketball and able to do so for hours. He was forty-one and still in decent shape because he watched his diet and skipped lunch at least three times a week while he worked out in the firm's gym. Another perk for partners only.

He left the stairwell on the forty-second floor and hustled to the office of Willie Backstrom, another partner, but one with the luxury of not billing by the hour. Willie had the enviable position of running the firm's pro bono programs, and though he kept up with his hours he did not send bills. There was no one to pay them. The lawyers at Scully made plenty of money, especially the partners, and the firm was notorious for its commitment to pro bono work. It volunteered for difficult cases around the world. Every lawyer was required to donate at least 10 percent of his or her time to various causes, all approved by Willie.

There was an even split down the middle of the firm on the issue of pro bono work. Half the lawyers enjoyed it because it was a welcome break from the stressful grind of representing high-pressure corporate clients. For a few hours a month, a lawyer could represent a real person or a struggling nonprofit and not worry about sending bills and getting paid. The other half paid lip service to the lofty notion of giving back but considered it wasteful. Those 250 hours a year could be better spent making money and improving one's standing with the various committees that determined who got promoted, who made partner, and who eventually got the boot.

Willie Backstrom kept the peace, which wasn't really that difficult because no lawyer, regardless of his or her ambition, would ever criticize the firm's aggressive pro bono programs. Scully even gave annual awards to its lawyers who went beyond the call of duty in service to the less fortunate.

Mitch was currently spending four hours a week working with a homeless shelter in the Bronx and representing clients who were fighting evictions. It was safe, clean office work, which was just what he wanted. Seven months earlier he had watched a death row client in Alabama utter his last words before being

3

executed. He'd spent eight hundred hours over six years trying in vain to save the guy, and watching him die was heartbreaking, the ultimate failure.

Mitch wasn't sure what Willie wanted, but the fact that he'd been called in was an ominous sign.

Willie was the only lawyer at Scully with a ponytail, and a bad one at that. It was gray and matched his beard, and just a few years before someone higher up would have told him to shave and get a haircut. But the firm was working hard to shed its fossilized image as a white-collar club filled with white men in dark suits. One of its radical changes was the ditching of a dress code. Willie grew hair and whiskers and went about his work in jeans.

Mitch, still in a dark suit but with no tie, sat across the desk as they went through the small talk. Willie finally got around to it with "Say, Mitch, there's a case down south I want you to take a look at."

"Please don't tell me the guy is on death row."

"The guy is on death row."

"I can't do it, Willie. Please. I've had two of those in the past five years and both got the needle. My track record is not very good."

"You did great work, Mitch. No one could have saved those two."

"I can't take another one."

"Will you at least listen?"

Mitch conceded and shrugged. Willie's fondness for death row cases was legendary and few lawyers at Scully could say no to him. "Okay, I'll listen."

"His name is Tad Kearny and he's got ninety days. A month ago he made the strange decision to fire his lawyers, all of them, and he had quite a team."

"Sounds crazy."

"Oh, he is. Off-the-charts crazy, probably legally insane, but Tennessee is pushing hard nonetheless. Ten years ago he shot and killed three undercover narcotics officers in a drug bust that went haywire. Bodies everywhere, total of five died at the scene. Tad almost died, but they managed to save him so they could execute him later."

Mitch laughed in frustration and said, "And I'm supposed to ride in on a white horse and save the guy? Come on, Willie. Give me something to work with."

"There's virtually nothing to work with, except insanity. The problem is that he probably won't agree to see you."

"Then why bother?"

"Because we have to try, Mitch, and I think you're our best bet."

"I'm still listening."

"Well, he reminds me a lot of you."

"Gee thanks."

"No, seriously. He's white, your age, and from Dane County, Kentucky."

For a second Mitch couldn't respond, then managed to say, "Great. We're probably cousins."

"I don't think so, but his father worked in the coal mines, same as yours. And both died there."

"My family is off-limits."

"Sorry. You caught a lucky break and had the brains to get out. Tad did not and before long was involved with drugs, both as a user and a dealer. He and some pals were making a big delivery near Memphis when they were ambushed by narcotics officers. Everybody died but Tad. Looks like his luck has finally run out."

"No question about his guilt?"

"Certainly not for the jury. The issue is not guilt but insanity. The idea is to have him evaluated by some specialists, our doctors, and file a last-minute Hail Mary. First, though, someone has to go in and talk to the man. Right now he's not accepting visitors."

"And you think we'll bond?"

"It's a long shot, but why not give it a try?"

Mitch took a deep breath and tried to think of another way out. To pass the time he asked, "Who's got the case?"

"Well, technically, no one. Tad has become quite the jailhouse lawyer and he filed the necessary papers to terminate his attorneys. Amos Patrick represented him for a long time, one of the best down there. You know Amos?"

"I met him once at a conference. Quite the character."

"Most death row lawyers are real characters."

"Look, Willie, I have no desire to become known as a death row lawyer. I've been there twice and that's enough. These cases eat at you and become all-consuming. How many of your clients have you watched die?"

Willie closed his eyes and took a deep breath. Mitch whispered, "Sorry."

"Too many, Mitch. Let's just say I've been there. Look, I've talked to Amos, and talked and talked, and he likes the idea. He'll drive you to the prison, and who knows, maybe Tad will find you interesting enough to have a chat."

"Sounds like a dead end."

"In ninety days it will certainly be a dead end, but at least we will have tried."

Mitch stood and walked to a window. Willie's view was westward, over the Hudson. "Amos is in Memphis, right?"

"Yes."

"I really don't want to go back to Memphis. Too much history."

"Ancient history, Mitch. Fifteen years ago. You picked the wrong firm and had to leave."

"Had to leave? Hell, they were trying to kill me down there. People were dying, Willie, and the whole firm went to prison. Along with their clients."

"They all deserved prison, didn't they?"

"I suppose, but I got the blame."

"And they're all gone now, Mitch. Scattered."

Mitch returned to his chair and smiled at his friend. "Just curious, Willie. Do people around here talk about me and what happened in Memphis?"

"No, it's never mentioned. We know the story but no one has the time to gossip about it. You did the right thing, got away, and started over. You're one of our stars, Mitch, and that's all that matters at Scully."

"I don't want to go back to Memphis."

"You need the hours. You're kinda light this year."

"I'll catch up. Why can't you find me some nice little foundation in need of pro bono counsel? Maybe an outfit that feeds hungry kids or delivers clean water to Haiti?"

"You'd be miserable. You prefer action, drama, the ticking clock."

"Been there, done that."

"Please. I'm asking for a favor. There's really no one else. And there's an excellent chance you won't get in the prison door."

"I really don't want to go back to Memphis."

"Man up. There's a direct flight tomorrow at one-thirty out of LaGuardia. Amos is expecting you. If nothing else, you'll enjoy his company."

Mitch smiled in defeat. As he stood, he mumbled, "Okay, okay," and headed to the door. "You know, I think I do remember some Kearnys in Dane County."

"Attaboy. Go visit Tad. You're right. He might be a distant cousin."

"Not distant enough."

CHAPTER 2

Most Scully partners, along with many of their rivals in Big Law, as well as countless money runners on Wall Street, scurried from the tall buildings around 6 P.M. and hopped into black sedans driven by professionals. The more important hedge fund stars sat in the spacious rear seats of long European cars they actually owned and were driven by chauffeurs on their payroll. The truly essential masters of the universe had fled the city altogether and lived and worked quietly in Connecticut.

Though he could afford a car service Mitch took the subway, one of his many concessions to frugality and his humble past. He caught the 6:10 train at South Ferry, found a seat on a crowded bench, and, as always, buried his face behind a newspaper. Eye contact was to be avoided. The car was packed with other well-heeled professionals headed north, none of whom had any interest in chatting. There was nothing wrong with riding the subway. It was quick, easy, cheap, and, for the most part, safe. The rub was that the other passengers were, in some fashion, Wall Streeters, and as such were either making plenty of money or on the verge of it. Private sedans were almost within reach. Their subway days were almost over.

Mitch had no time for such nonsense. He flipped through the newspaper, patiently squeezed even closer to other passengers as the car took on more riders, and allowed his mind to drift away to Memphis. He had never said he would never return. Between him and Abby, that promise did not have to be expressed. Getting away from the place had been so frightening that they could not imagine going back for any reason. However, the more he thought about it, the more intrigued he became. It was a quick trip that would probably lead nowhere. He was doing Willie a huge favor, one that would undoubtedly lead to a nice payback.

After twenty-two minutes, he emerged from underground at the Columbus Circle station and began the daily walk to his apartment. It was a splendid April evening, with pleasant skies and temperature, one of those postcard moments when half the city's population seemed to be outdoors. Mitch, though, hurried home.

Their building was on Sixty-Ninth Street at Columbus Avenue, in the heart of the Upper West Side. Mitch spoke to the doorman, collected the daily mail, and rode the elevator to the fourteenth floor. Clark opened the door and reached up for a hug. At the age of eight, he was still a little boy and unashamed to show his father some affection. Carter, his twin, was slightly more mature and already outgrowing the rituals of physical contact with his father. Mitch would have hugged and kissed Abby and asked about her day, but she had guests in the kitchen. A delicious aroma filled the apartment. Some serious food was being prepared and dinner would be another delight.

The chefs were the Rosario brothers, Marco and Marcello, also twins. They were from a small village in Lombardia in northern Italy, and two years earlier had opened a trattoria near Lincoln Center. It was a hit from day one and was soon awarded two stars by the *Times*. Reservations were hard to get; the current waiting time was four months for a table. Mitch and Abby had discovered the place and ate there often, anytime they wanted. Abby had the clout to get a table because she was editing the Rosarios' first cookbook. She also encouraged them to use her modern kitchen to experiment with new recipes, and at least once a week they descended upon the McDeere apartment with bags of ingredients and a near riotous approach to cooking. Abby was right in the middle of it, rattling away in perfect Italian as Carter and Clark watched from the safety of their stools near a counter. Marco and Marcello loved performing for the kids and explained their preparations in thickly accented English. They also chided the boys into repeating Italian words and phrases.

Mitch chuckled at the scene as he tossed his briefcase, took off his jacket, and poured a glass of Chianti. He asked the boys about their homework and received the standard assurances that it was all finished. Marco presented a small platter of bruschetta, placed it on the counter in front of the boys, and informed Mitch that he should not worry about homework and such because the boys were doing important work as taste-testers. Mitch pretended to be sufficiently chastised. He would check the homework later.

The name of their restaurant was, not surprisingly, Rosario's, and it was embroidered in bold letters across red aprons worn by the chefs. Marcello offered one to Mitch, who, as always, declined on the grounds that he could not cook. When they were alone in the kitchen, Abby allowed him to peel and chop vegetables, measure spices under her watchful eye, set the table, and handle the garbage, all grunt work she deemed acceptable for his talents. He had once elevated himself to the position of

11

sous chef but was rather harshly demoted when he burned a baguette.

She asked for a small glass of wine. Marco and Marcello declined, as usual. Mitch had learned years earlier that Italians, in spite of their prodigious production of wine and the presence of it at virtually every meal, actually drank little. A carafe of their favorite local red or white would satisfy a large family over a long dinner.

Due to her knowledge of Italian food and wine, Abby was a senior editor at Epicurean, a small but busy press in the city. The company specialized in cookbooks and published about fifty of them a year, almost all of them thick, handsome editions loaded with recipes from around the world. Because she knew many chefs and restaurant owners, she and Mitch dined out often and seldom bothered with reservations. Their apartment was a favorite laboratory for young chefs dreaming of success in a city crowded with fine restaurants and serious gourmands. Most of the meals prepared there were extraordinary, but since the chefs were free to experiment, there was the occasional dud. Carter and Clark were easy guinea pigs and were being raised in a world of cutting-edge recipes. If the chefs couldn't please them, their dishes were probably in trouble. The boys were encouraged to pan any dish they didn't like. Their parents often joked quietly about raising a couple of food snobs.

Tonight there would be no complaints. The bruschetta was followed by a small truffle pizza. Abby announced that the appetizers were over and directed her family to the dining table. Marco served the first course, a spiced fish soup called cacciucco, as Marcello found a seat. All six took a small bite, savored the flavors, and thought about their reactions. It was slow eating and this often bothered the kids. The pasta course was cappelletti, small ravioli in beef broth. Carter in particular loved pasta and declared it delicious. Abby wasn't so sure. Marco served a second pasta course of risotto with saffron. Since they were conducting research in a lab, a third pasta course of spaghetti in clam sauce was next. The servings were small, only a few bites, and they joked about pacing themselves. The Rosarios bickered back and forth about the ingredients, the variations of the recipes, and so on. Mitch and Abby offered their own opinions, often with the adults all talking at the same time. After the fish course the boys were getting bored. They were soon excused from the table and went upstairs to watch television. They missed the meat course, braised rabbit, and the dessert of panforte, a dense chocolate cake with almonds.

Over coffee, the McDeeres and Rosarios debated which recipes should be included in the cookbook and which needed more work. It was months away from completion, so there were many dinners to follow.

Shortly after eight, the brothers were ready to pack up and leave. They needed to hustle back to their restaurant and check on the crowd. After a quick cleanup and the usual round of hugs, they left with serious promises to return next week.

When the apartment was quiet, Mitch and Abby returned to the kitchen. As always, it was still a mess. They finished loading the dishwasher, stacked some pots and pans by the sink, and turned off the light. The housekeeper would be there in the morning.

———•—•———

With the boys tucked in, they retired to the study for a nightcap, a glass of Barolo. They replayed the dinner, talked about work, and unwound.

Mitch couldn't wait to deliver the news. "I'll be out of town tomorrow night," he said. It was nothing new. He was often gone ten nights a month, and she had accepted the demands of his job a long time ago.

"It's not on the calendar," she said with a shrug. Clocks and calendars ruled their lives and they were diligent with their planning. "Somewhere fun?"

"Memphis."

She nodded, trying and failing to hide her surprise. "Okay, I'm listening, and this better be good."

He smiled and gave her a quick summary of his conversation with Willie Backstrom.

"Please, Mitch, not another death row case. You promised."

"I know, I know, but I couldn't say no to Willie. It's a desperate situation and it's probably a wasted trip. I said I would try."

"I thought we were never going back there."

"So did I. But it's only for twenty-four hours."

She took a sip of her wine and closed her eyes. When they reopened she said, "We haven't talked about Memphis in a long time, have we?"

"No. No need to, really. But it's been fifteen years and everything has changed."

"I still don't like it."

"I'll be fine, Abby. No one will recognize me. All the bad guys are gone."

"You hope. As I recall, Mitch, we left town in the middle of the night, scared to death, certain the bad guys were after us."

"And they were. But they're gone. Some are dead. The firm imploded and everybody went to prison."

"Where they belonged."

"Yes, but there's not a single member of the firm still in Memphis. I'll ease in and out and no one will know."

"I don't like the memories of the place."

"Look, Abby, we made the decision a long time ago to live normal lives without looking over our shoulders. What happened there is old history now."

"But if you take the case your name will be on the news, right?"

"If I take the case, which looks doubtful, I won't hang out in Memphis. The prison is in Nashville."

"Then why are you going to Memphis?"

"Because the lawyer, or ex-lawyer, works there. I'll visit him in his office, get briefed, then we'll make the drive to the prison."

"Scully has about a million lawyers. Surely they can find someone else."

"There's not much time. If the client refuses to see me, then I'm off the hook and back home before you even miss me."

"Who says I'll miss you? You're gone all the time."

"Yes and I know you're miserable when I'm out of town."

"We can hardly survive." She smiled, shook her head, and reminded herself that arguing with Mitch was a waste of time. "Please be careful."

"I promise."

CHAPTER 3

The first time Mitch had stepped into the ornate lobby of the Peabody hotel in downtown Memphis, he was two months shy of his twenty-fifth birthday. He was a third-year student at Harvard Law and would graduate the following spring number four in his class. In his pocket he had three splendid job offers from mega firms, two in New York and one in Chicago. None of his friends could understand why he would waste a trip to visit a firm in Memphis, which was not exactly in the major leagues of Big Law. Abby was also skeptical.

He'd been driven by greed. Though the Bendini firm was small, only forty lawyers, it was offering more money and perks and a faster track to a partnership. But he had rationalized the greed, even managed to deny it, and convinced himself that a small-town kid would feel more at home in a smaller city. The firm had a family feel to it, and no one ever left. Not alive anyway. He should have known that an offer too good to be true came with serious strings and baggage. He and Abby lasted only seven months and were lucky to escape.

Back then they had walked through the lobby, holding hands

and gawking at the rich furnishings, oriental rugs, art, and the fabulous fountain in the center with ducks swimming in circles.

They were still swimming and he wondered if they were the same ducks. He got a diet soda at the bar and fell into a thick chair near the fountain. The memories came in a torrent: the giddiness of being heavily recruited; the relief that law school was almost over; the unbounded certainty of a bright future; a new career, new home, fancy car, fat salary. He and Abby had even talked of starting a family. Sure, he'd had some doubts, but they had begun to dissipate the moment he entered the Peabody.

How could he have been so foolish? Had it really been fifteen years? They were just kids back then, and so naive.

He finished his drink and walked to the desk to check in. He had reserved a room for one night in the name of Mitchell Y. McDeere, and as he waited for the receptionist to find his reservation, he had the fleeting thought that someone might remember him. The receptionist did not, nor would anyone else. Too much time had passed and the conspirators who'd chased him were long gone. He went to his room, changed into jeans, and left the hotel for a walk.

Three blocks away, on Front Street, he stood and stared at a five-story edifice once known as the Bendini Building. He almost shuddered at the memories of his brief but complicated time there. He recalled names and saw old faces, all of them gone now, either dead or living quiet lives elsewhere. The building had been renovated, renamed, and was now packed with condos advertising views of the river. He walked on and found Lansky's Deli, an old Memphis tradition that had not changed. He went in, took a seat on a stool at the counter, and asked for coffee. To his right was a row of booths, all empty in the late afternoon. The third one was exactly where he'd been sitting when an FBI agent appeared out of nowhere and began quizzing him about his firm. It had been the beginning of the end, the first clear signal that things were not as they seemed. Mitch closed his eyes and replayed the entire conversation, word for word. Wayne Tarrance was the agent's name, one he would never forget regardless of how hard he tried.

When the coffee was gone, he paid for it and left and walked to Main Street where he caught a trolley for a short ride. Some of the buildings were different, some looked the same. Many of them reminded him of events he had struggled to erase from his mind. He got off at a park, found a seat on a bench under a tree, and called the office to see what chaos he was missing. He called Abby and checked on the boys. All was well at home. No, he was not being followed. No one remembered him.

At dusk he wandered back to the Peabody and took the elevator to the top. The bar on the roof was a popular spot to watch the sunset over the river and have drinks with friends, usually on Friday afternoon after a hard week. During his first visit, his recruiting trip, he and Abby had been entertained there by younger members of the firm and their spouses. Everyone had a spouse. All the lawyers were men. Those were the unwritten rules at Bendini back then. Later, when they were alone, they had a quiet drink on the roof and made the calamitous decision to take the job.

He got a beer, leaned on a railing, and watched the Mississippi River wind its way past Memphis on its eternal voyage to New Orleans. Massive barges loaded with soybeans inched along under the bridge to Arkansas as the sun finally set beyond the endless flat farm fields. Nostalgia failed him. The days of such promise had vanished within weeks as their lives became an unbelievable nightmare.

There was only one choice for dinner. He crossed Union Avenue, entered an alley, and could smell the ribs. The Rendezvous was by far the most famous restaurant in town, and he had eaten there many times, as often as possible. On occasion, Abby had met him after work for their famous dry smoked ribs and ice-cold beer. It was Tuesday, and though always busy it was nothing like the weekends when it was not unusual to wait an hour for a table. Reservations were out of the question. A waiter pointed to a table in one of the many cramped dining rooms and Mitch took a seat with a view of the main bar. Menus were unnecessary. Another waiter walked by and asked, "You know what you want?"

"A full order, small cheese plate, tall beer." The waiter never stopped walking.

He had noticed many changes in the city, but there would always be one constant: the Rendezvous would always be the same. The walls were plastered with photos of famous guests, Liberty Bowl programs, neon signs for beer and soft drinks, sketches of old Memphis, and more photos, many from decades earlier. One tradition was to tack a business card to the wall before leaving, and there must have been a million of them. He had done so himself and wondered if there were any left from the lawyers at Bendini, Lambert & Locke. Since it was evident that no one ever bothered to remove a card, he suspected they were still there.

Ten minutes later the waiter presented a platter of ribs, cheddar cheese, and a side of slaw. The beer was as cold as he remembered. He ripped off a rib, took a large bite, savored it, and had his first pleasant memory of Memphis.

———•—•———

The Capital Defense Initiative was founded by Amos Patrick in 1976 soon after the Supreme Court lifted the ban on capital punishment. When that happened, the "death states" scrambled to spruce up their electric chairs and gas chambers and the race was on. They were still trying to out-kill one another. Texas was the clear leader with several states jockeying for second place.

Amos grew up dirt poor in rural Georgia and had known hunger as a child. His close friends were all black, and as a small kid he was angered by their mistreatment. As a teenager, he began to understand racism and its insidious effects on black people. Though he didn't understand the word "liberal," he grew up to become quite a radical. A high school biology teacher recognized his aptitude and steered him to college. Otherwise, he would have spent his life working the peanut fields with his friends.

Amos was a legend in the confined world of death penalty defense. For thirty years he had waged war on behalf of cold-blooded killers who were guilty of crimes that often defied description. To survive, he had learned to take the crimes, put them in a box, and ignore them. The issue wasn't guilt. The issue was giving the state, with its flaws, prejudices, and power to screw things up, the right to kill.

And he was tired. The work had finally beaten him down. He had saved many lives, lost his share along the way, and in doing so built a nonprofit that attracted enough money to sustain itself and enough talent to keep up the fight. His fight was fading fast, though, and his wife and doctor were badgering him to slow down.

His office was legendary too. It was a bad imitation of 1930s Art Deco that had been expanded and whittled down over the decades. A car dealer built it and once sold new and used Pontiacs along "Auto Row" on Summer Avenue, six miles from the river. With time, though, the dealerships moved on, fled farther east like most of Memphis, and left behind boarded showrooms, many of which were bulldozed. Amos saved the Pontiac place at an auction that attracted no one but him. His mortgage was guaranteed by some sympathetic lawyers in Washington. He cared nothing for style, appearances, and public perception, and he had little money for renovations. He needed a large space with utilities, nothing else. He wasn't trying to attract clients because he had more than he could handle. The death penalty wars were raging and the prosecutors were on a roll.

Amos spent a few bucks on paint, drywall, and plumbing, and moved his growing staff into the old Pontiac place. Almost immediately the lawyers and paralegals at CDI adopted a defensive attitude toward their sparse and eclectic workplace. Who else practiced law in a converted bay where they once changed oil and installed mufflers?

There was no reception area because there were no visiting clients. They were all on death row or some other unit in prisons from Virginia to Arizona. A receptionist was not needed because guests were not expected. Mitch rattled the bell on the front door, stepped into an open area that was once a showroom, and waited for human contact. He was amused by the decor, which was primarily posters advertising shiny new Pontiacs from decades earlier, calendars dating to the 1950s, and a few framed headlines of cases in which the CDI had managed to save a life. There were no carpets, no rugs. The floors were quite original—shiny concrete with permanent stains of paint and oil.

"Good morning," said a young lady as she hustled by with a stack of papers.

"Good morning," Mitch replied. "I'm supposed to see Amos Patrick at nine o'clock."

She had merely greeted him and had not offered to help. She managed a tense smile as if she had better things to do, and said, "Okay, I'll tell him, but it might be a while. We're in the middle of a bad morning." She was gone. No invitation to have a seat, certainly no offer of coffee.

And what, exactly, might constitute a bad morning in a law firm where every case dealt with death? In spite of the tall front windows with plenty of sunlight, the place had a tense, almost dreary feel to it, as if most days began badly with the lawyers up early and fighting deadlines across the country. There were three plastic chairs in a corner with a coffee table covered in old magazines. The waiting room, of sorts. Mitch sat down, pulled out his phone, and began checking emails. At 9:30, he stretched his legs, watched the traffic on Summer Avenue, called the office because it was expected, and fought off irritation. In his world of clock-driven precision, being half an hour late for an appointment was rare and expected to occur only with a suitable explanation. But he reminded himself that this was a pro bono matter and he was donating his time.

At 9:50, a kid in jeans stepped around a corner and said, "Mr. McDeere, this way."

"Thanks."

Mitch followed him out of the showroom and past a large counter where, according to a faded sign, they once sold auto parts. They went through a wide swinging door and into a hallway. The kid stopped at a closed door and said, "Amos is waiting."

"Thanks." Mitch stepped inside and got himself bear-hugged by Amos Patrick, a wild-looking character with a mass of unruly gray hair and an unkempt beard. After the hug they shook hands and exchanged preliminary chitchat: Willie Backstrom, other acquaintances, the weather.

"Would you like an espresso?" Amos asked.

"Sure."

"Single or double?"

"What are you having?"

"A triple."

"Make it two."

Amos smiled and walked to a counter where he kept an elaborate Italian espresso machine with an inventory of various beans and cups. The man was serious about his coffee. He took two of the larger cups—real, not paper—punched some buttons, and waited for the grinding to start.

They sat in a corner of his rambling office, under an overhead door that hadn't been lowered in years. Mitch couldn't help but notice that Amos's eyes were red and puffy. Gravely, he said, "Look, Mitch, I'm afraid you've wasted a trip down. I'm really sorry, but there's nothing you can do."

"Okay. Willie warned me."

"Oh no, not that. Much worse. Early this morning they found Tad Kearny hanging from an electrical cord in the shower. Looks like he beat 'em to the punch." His voice choked and went silent.

Mitch could think of no response.

Amos cleared his throat and managed to say, almost in a whisper, "They're calling it a suicide."

"I'm sorry."

For a long time they sat in silence, the only sound being the dripping of coffee. Amos wiped his eyes with a tissue, then struggled to his feet, retrieved the cups, and placed them on a small table. He walked to his remarkably cluttered desk, picked up a sheet of paper, and handed it to Mitch. "This came across about an hour ago."

It was a shocking image of a naked, emaciated white man hanging grotesquely from an electrical cord cutting into the flesh of his neck and looped over an exposed pipe. Mitch took one look, turned away, and handed it back.

"Sorry about that," Amos said.

"Wow."

"Happens all the time in prison, but not on death row."

More silence followed as they sipped espresso. Mitch could think of nothing to say, but the message was clear: the suicide was suspicious.

Amos stared at a wall and said softly, "I loved that guy. He was crazy as hell and we fought all the time, but I felt such sympathy for him. I learned a long time ago not to get emotionally involved with my clients, but with Tad I couldn't help it. Kid never had a chance in life, doomed from the day he was born, which is not unusual."

"Why did he fire you?"

"Oh, he fired me several times. It got to be a joke, really. Tad was street-smart and taught himself the law, thought he knew more than any of his lawyers. I stuck with him, though. You've been through it. It's hard not to get consumed by these desperate men."

"I've lost two of them."

"I've lost twenty, now twenty-one, but Tad will always be special. I represented him for eight years and during that time he never had a visitor. No friends, no family, no one but me and a chaplain. Talk about a lonely soul. Living in a cage in solitary with no one on the outside, only a lawyer. His mental state deteriorated over the years and the last few times I visited him he refused to say a word. Then he would write me a five-page letter filled with thoughts and ramblings so incoherent it should've been clear proof of his schizophrenia."

"But you tried insanity."

"Tried, yes, but got nowhere. The State fought us at every turn and the courts had no sympathy. We tried everything, and we had a fighting chance a few months ago when he decided to fire his legal team. Not a smart move."

"What about guilt?"

Amos took another sip and shook his head. "Well, the facts were not in his favor, shall we say? A drug runner caught in a sting with narcs, three of whom took bullets to the head and died at the scene. Not a lot of jury appeal. The deliberations lasted about an hour."

"So he did kill them?"

"Oh, yes, shot two in the forehead from forty feet away. The third one took a bullet in the chin. Tad, you see, was an expert shot. Grew up with guns everywhere—in every car and truck, every closet, every drawer. As a kid he could hit targets practically blindfolded. The narcs picked the wrong guy to ambush."

Mitch let the word rattle around the room for a moment, then said, "Ambush?"

"It's a long story, Mitch, so I'll give you a quick skinny. Back in the nineties there was a gang of rogue DEA agents who decided the best way to win the war on drugs was to kill the smugglers. They worked with informants, snitches, and other thugs in the trade and set up sting operations. When the delivery boys showed up with the goods, the agents simply killed them. No need to bother with arrests and trials and such, just vigilante justice that was bought hook, line, and sinker by the authorities and the press. Pretty effective way of putting the runners out of business."

Mitch was speechless and decided to drink his coffee and listen.

"To this day they've never been exposed, so no one knows how many traffickers they ambushed. And, frankly, no one cares. Looking back, it appears as though they lost some of their enthusiasm when Tad shot three of their buddies. Happened about twenty miles north of Memphis at a rural drop-off point. There were some suspicions, some of the lawyers were putting the pieces together, but no one really wanted to dig too deep. These were nasty, violent men of the law who made their own rules. Those who knew about it were only too happy to help with the cover-up."

"And you knew?"

"Let's say I suspected, but we don't have the manpower to investigate something this unbelievable. My wagon is fully loaded with deadlines elsewhere. Tad, though, always knew it was an ambush, and he was making some pretty wild accusations when he fired us. I think he was onto something. Again, the poor kid was so mentally unbalanced it was hard take him seriously."

"What are the chances it was not a suicide?"

Amos grunted and wiped his nose with the back of a sleeve. "I would bet good money, and I don't have much, that Tad didn't die by his own hand. I'll speculate and say that the authorities wanted to keep him quiet until they could kill him properly in July. And we'll never know because the investigation, if you could call it that, will be a whitewash. There's no way to find the truth, Mitch. Another one's gone and nobody cares." He sniffled and wiped his eyes again.

"I'm sorry." Mitch was somewhat surprised that a lawyer who had lost twenty clients to executions would be so emotional. Wouldn't you get callous and jaded after a few? He had no plans to find out. His time in this little corner of the pro bono world had just come to an end.

"And I'm sorry too, Mitch. Sorry you made the trip down."

"No problem. It was worth it to meet you and see your office."

Amos waved at the overhead door attached to the ceiling. "Whatta you think? Who else practices law in an old Pontiac place. Betcha don't have one of these in New York."

"Probably not."

"Give it a try. We have an opening, guy quit last week."

Mitch smiled and suppressed a laugh. No offense, but the salary would be less than his property taxes in Manhattan. "Thanks, but I've tried Memphis."

"I remember. The Bendini story was a big one around here for a while. An entire firm blows up and everybody goes to prison. Who could forget it? But your name was hardly mentioned."

"I got lucky and got out."

"And you're not coming back."

"And I'm not coming back."

CHAPTER 4

In his rental car, Mitch called his secretary and asked her to change his travel plans. He'd missed the morning nonstop to LaGuardia. Connecting flights would take hours and send him crisscrossing most of the country. There was a direct from Nashville at 5:20 and she got him a ticket. Getting to the airport would dovetail nicely with an idea he'd been kicking around.

The traffic thinned and Memphis was behind him before an unexpected wave of exhilaration hit hard. He had just dodged an awful experience, and the rogue DEA subplot was enough to give a lawyer ulcers, at best. He had taken one for the team, notched a huge favor with Willie Backstrom, and was fleeing Memphis again, this time without threats and other baggage.

With plenty of time, he stayed on the two-lane highways and enjoyed a peaceful drive. He ignored some calls from New York, checked in with Abby, and loafed at fifty miles an hour. The town of Sumrall was two hours east of Memphis, one hour west of Nashville. It was the county seat and had a population of

18,000, a big number for that part of the rural South. Mitch followed the signs and soon found himself on Main Street, which was one side of the town square. A well-preserved nineteenth-century courthouse sat in the center of the square with statues, gazebos, monuments, and benches scattered about, all protected by the shade of massive oak trees.

Mitch parked in front of a dress shop and walked around the square. As always, there was no shortage of lawyers and small firms. Again he wondered why his old friend would choose such a life.

———— • • ————

They met at Harvard in the late fall of Mitch's third year, when the most prestigious law firms made their annual trek to the school. The recruiting game was the payoff, not for hard work because that was the drill at every law school, but for being smart and lucky enough to get accepted to Harvard. For a poor kid like Mitch, the recruiting was especially thrilling because he could smell money for the first time in his life.

Lamar had been sent with the team because he was only seven years older than Mitch, and a more youthful image was always important. He and his wife, Kay, had embraced the McDeeres as soon as they arrived in Memphis.

There had been no contact in fifteen years. The internet made it easy to snoop around and see what folks were doing, especially lawyers, who as a breed, and regardless of their success or lack of it, enjoyed all the attention they could generate. It was good for business. Lamar's website was rather simple, but then so was his practice: the bland offering of deeds, wills, no-fault divorces, property transactions, and, of course, *Personal Injuries!!*

Every small-town lawyer dreamed of landing some good car wrecks.

There was no mention of such unpleasantries as Lamar's indictment, guilty plea, and prison sentence.

His office was above a sporting goods store. Mitch lumbered up the creaky steps, took a deep breath, and opened the door. A large woman behind a computer screen paused and offered a sweet smile. "Good morning."

"Good morning. Is Lamar around?"

"He's in court," she said, nodding behind her in the general direction of the courthouse.

"A trial?"

"No, just a hearing. Should be over soon. Can I help you?"

Mitch handed her a Scully business card and said, "Name's Mitch McDeere. I'll try to catch him over there. Which courtroom?"

"There's only one. Second floor."

"Right. Thanks."

It was a handsome courtroom of the old variety: stained wood trimmings, tall windows, portraits of white, dead, male dignitaries on the walls. Mitch eased in and took a seat on the back row. He was the only spectator. The judge was gone and Lamar was chatting with another lawyer. When he finally saw Mitch he was startled, but kept talking. When he finished he slowly made his way down the center aisle and stopped at the end of the row. It was almost noon and the courtroom was empty.

They watched each other for a moment before Lamar asked, "What are you doing here?"

"Just passing through." It was a sarcastic response. Only a lost idiot would be passing through such a backwater place as Sumrall.

"I'll ask again. What are you doing here?"

"I was in Memphis last night, had some business that got canceled. My flight is out of Nashville in a few hours so I made the drive. Thought I'd stop by and say hello."

Lamar had lost so much hair he was hardly recognizable. What remained was gray. Like a lot of men, he was trying to replace the thinness on top with the thickness of a beard. But it too was gray, as it usually is, and only added to the aging. He eased down the row in front of Mitch, stopped ten feet away, and leaned on the pew in front. He had yet to smile and asked, "Anything in particular you want to discuss?"

"Not really. I think about you occasionally and just wanted to say hello."

"Hello. You know, Mitch, I think about you too. I spent twenty-seven months in a federal pen because of you, so you're rather hard to forget."

"You spent twenty-seven months in a federal pen because you were a willing member of a criminal conspiracy, one that tried its best to entice me to join. I managed to escape, barely. You got a grudge, so do I."

In the background a clerk walked in front of the bench. They watched her and waited until she was gone, then resumed staring at each other.

Lamar gave a slight shrug and said, "Okay, fair enough. I did the crime and did the time. It's not something I dwell on."

"I'm not here to start trouble. I was hoping we could have a pleasant chat and bury the hatchet, so to speak."

Lamar took a deep breath and said, "Well, if nothing else, I admire you for being here. I thought I'd never see you again."

"Same here. You were the only real friend I had back in those days, Lamar. We had some good times together, in spite of the pressure and all. Abby and Kay hit it off nicely. We have fond memories of you guys."

"Well, we don't. We lost everything, Mitch, and it was easy to blame it all on you."

"The firm was going down, Lamar, you know that. The FBI was hot on the trail and closing in. They picked me because I was the new guy and they figured I was the weak link."

"And they were right."

"Damned right they were. Since I had done nothing wrong, I made the decision to protect myself. I cooperated and ran like a scared dog. The FBI couldn't even find me."

"Where'd you go?"

Mitch smiled and slowly got to his feet. "That, my friend, is a long story. Can I buy lunch?"

"No, but let's find a table."

———— • • ————

The first café on the square was crowded with "too many lawyers," according to Lamar. They walked another block and found a table in a sandwich shop in the basement of an old hardware store. Each paid for his own lunch and they sat in a corner, away from the crowd.

"So how's Kay?" Mitch asked. He assumed they were still married. His cursory internet sleuthing had found no records of a divorce in the past ten years. From time to time, Mitch would recall a face or a name from back then and waste a few minutes online digging for dirt. After fifteen years, though, his curiosity was waning. He took no notes and kept no files.

"She's fine, selling medical supplies for a nice company. Doing well. And Abby?"

"The same. She's an editor with a publishing company in the city."

Lamar took a bite of a turkey roll and nodded along. Epicurean Press, senior editor, a fondness for Italian food and wine. He had found some of her books at a store in Nashville and flipped through the pages. Unlike Mitch, he was keeping a file. *Scully partner. International lawyer.* The file existed solely for his own curiosity and had no other value.

"Kids?"

"Twin boys, age eight, Carter and Clark. Yours?"

"Wilson is a freshman at Sewanee. Suzanne is in high school. You landed on your feet nicely, didn't you Mitch? A partner in a major firm, offices around the world and all that. Living the fast life in the big city. The rest of us went to prison while you managed to get out."

"I didn't deserve prison, Lamar, and I was lucky to get out alive. Think of the ones who didn't make it, including your friends. As I recall, there were five mysterious deaths in about ten years. That about right?"

Lamar nodded as he chewed. He swallowed and washed it down with iced tea through a straw. "You vanished into thin air. How'd you do it?"

"You really want the story?"

"Definitely. It's been a big question for a long time."

"Okay. I have a brother named Ray who was in prison. I convinced the feds to release him in return for my cooperation. He went to Grand Cayman, met a friend there, and arranged a boat ride. A thirty-foot sloop, real nice. Not that I know much about boats. Abby and I sneaked out of Memphis with the clothes on our backs and went to Florida, near Destin. We rendezvoused with the boat and sailed off into the night. We spent a month on Grand Cayman, then sailed to another island."

"And you had plenty of money?"

"Well, yes. I compensated myself with some of the firm's dirty money and the feds let it slide. After a few months we got tired of the islands and began traveling, always looking over our shoulders. Life on the run is not sustainable."

"But the FBI was helping you?"

"Sure. I gave them all the documents they needed, but I did not agree to testify at trial. I was not going back to Memphis. As you know, there were no trials."

"Oh no. We fell like dominoes. They offered me three years for cooperation, or go to trial and face at least twenty. We all caved. The key was Oliver Lambert. They squeezed him till he choked. When he flipped we were all sitting ducks."

"And he died in prison."

"May he rest in peace, the bastard. Royce McKnight shot himself after he got out. Avery, as you probably know, got himself rubbed out by the Mob. The firm's final chapter is not pretty. No one returned to Memphis. No one was from there to begin with. Since we were all a bunch of disbarred and convicted felons, we scattered and tried to forget about each other. Bendini is not a popular topic."

Mitch stabbed an olive at the bottom of his salad and ate it. "No contact with anyone?"

"No, not at all. It was a nightmare. One day you're a hot-shot lawyer with a fancy pedigree and plenty of money, all the toys, then, bam, before you know it the FBI is raiding the place, flashing badges, making threats, grabbing computers, locking the doors. We fled in shock and scrambled to find good criminal lawyers. There were only so many in Memphis. For months we waited for the hammer to fall, and when it did our world came to an end. My first night in jail was horrific. I thought I was about to be attacked. I spent three nights before bonding out. Every day it seemed as if there was more bad news—someone else had flipped and was cooperating. I pled guilty in federal court in downtown Memphis, you know the courtroom, with

Kay and my parents in the front row, all crying. I thought about suicide every day. Then I shipped out. First stop was Leavenworth in Kansas. A lawyer in prison gives the guards and other inmates an easy target for abuse. Luckily, it was only verbal."

He took another bite and seemed tired of talking.

Mitch said, "I didn't intend to bring up the part about prison, Lamar. Sorry."

"It's all right. I survived and I got stronger. I was lucky because Kay stuck with me, though it wasn't easy. We lost the house and other stuff, but it's all just stuff. You realize what's important. She and the kids were tough and held on. Her parents were a big help. But there were so many divorces, so many ruined lives. I hit bottom after a year and made the decision that prison would not destroy me. I worked in the law library and helped a lot of guys. I also began studying for the bar exam, again. I was planning my comeback."

"How many of our former friends are practicing now?"

Lamar smiled and grunted as if to say *none*. "I don't know of anyone. It's virtually impossible with a felony conviction. But I had a spotless record in prison, waited my time, passed the bar exam, got plenty of recommendations, and so on. I was turned down twice, but the third time worked. Now I'm a small-town ham-and-egg lawyer trying to eke out sixty thousand bucks a year. Thankfully, Kay makes more than that so we can afford tuition." He took a quick bite and said, "I'm tired of talking. How did you go from a beach bum to a partner at Scully?"

Mitch smiled and drank some tea. "The beach bum part didn't last very long, got bored with it. It was okay for about a month, but then real life sort of returned. We left the islands and hiked around Europe for several months, living out of our backpacks and taking the trains. One day we found ourselves in this picturesque little town in Tuscany. Cortona, not far from Perugia."

"Never been to Italy."

"A beautiful town in the mountains. We walked past a small cottage just off the town square and saw a sign in the window. It was for rent, three hundred euros a month. We thought, What the heck. We had so much fun the first month, we signed up for another. The lady who owned the cottage also ran a bed-and-breakfast not far away, and she kept it filled with American and British tourists who wanted cooking lessons. Abby signed up and quickly became consumed with Italian cooking. Me, I was concentrating on the wines. Three months, then four, then five, and we leased the cottage for a year. Abby worked in the kitchen as a sous chef while I puttered around the countryside, trying to imitate a real Italian. We hired a private tutor for language lessons and went all in. After a year we refused to speak English around the house."

"Meanwhile I was in prison."

"Are you going to keep blaming me for that?"

Lamar folded the wax paper around the remnants of his wrap and shoved it aside. "No, Mitch. As of today I'm letting go."

"Thanks. Me too."

"So how did Scully and Pershing enter the picture?"

"After three years it was time to move on. Both of us wanted a career and a family. We settled in London, and, on a whim, I went to the Scully office there and asked around. A law degree from Harvard opens a lot of doors. They offered a position as an associate and I took it. After two years in London we decided to return to the States. Plus, Abby was pregnant and we wanted to raise the kids here. That's my story."

"I like yours better than mine."

"You seem content."

"We're happy and healthy. Nothing else matters."

Mitch rattled the ice in his empty cup. The wrap and the salad were finished, as was lunch.

Lamar smiled and said, "Several years ago I was in New York, a small business matter for a client. I took a cab down to 110 Broad Street, your building, and I stood outside and looked up at the tower, eighty floors. A spectacular building but only one of a thousand. International headquarters of Scully and Pershing, the largest law firm the world has ever known, but just another name on the crowded directory. I went inside and marveled at the atrium. Banks of elevators. Escalators running in all directions. Baffling modern art that cost a fortune. I sat on a bench and watched the people come and go, the frantic hustling of young well-dressed professionals, half of them on their phones, frowning, talking importantly. All sprinting at a breakneck pace to make the next dollar. I wasn't looking for you, Mitch, but I was certainly thinking about you. I asked myself: 'What if he saw me and walked over right now? What would I say? What would he say?' I had no answer, but I did feel a twinge of pride that you, an old friend, had indeed made the big time. You survived Bendini and you're now playing on a world stage."

"I wish I'd seen you sitting there."

"It's impossible because no one looks up. No one takes a moment to appreciate the surroundings, the art, the architecture. 'Rat race' is the perfect description of it."

"I'm happy there, Lamar. We have a good life."

"Then I'm happy for you."

"If you ever come back to the city, we would love to host you and Kay."

Lamar smiled and shook his head. "Mitch, my old pal, that'll never happen."

CHAPTER 5

It was almost midnight when Mitch stepped off the elevator and entered his apartment. The return trip was finally over and nothing had gone as scheduled. Delays ruled the evening: boarding, taxiing, taking off, even the cold dinner was served late. It took half an hour to get a cab at LaGuardia, and a wreck on the Queensboro Bridge wasted another forty minutes. His day had begun on time with a quiet breakfast at the Peabody. After that, nothing had gone as planned.

But he was home and little else mattered. The twins had been sleeping for hours. Normally, Abby would have been too, but she was on the sofa reading and waiting. He kissed her and asked, "Why are you still up?"

"Because I want to hear all about your trip."

He had called with the welcome news that the latest death row case had not materialized, and for that they were both relieved. He had not mentioned the detour to see Lamar Quin. She poured him a glass of wine and they talked for an hour. He assured her more than once that there was no nostalgia for the old days. They had left nothing in Memphis.

When he began to nod off, she ushered him to the bed-room.

———• •———

Five hours later, at exactly 6 A.M., the alarm clock pinged as always and Mitch crawled out of bed, leaving his wife behind. His first chore of the morning was to prepare the coffee. While it was brewing, he opened his laptop and found *The Commercial Appeal,* the Memphis daily. On the front page of the metro section the headline read: TAD KEARNY FOUND DEAD BY SUICIDE. The story could have been written by the warden himself. There was no doubt about the cause of death. No idea how the "convicted cop killer" found an electrical cord. Death row inmates were allowed two ten-minute showers per week, during which they were "unmonitored." Prison officials were scratching their heads, but hey, it's prison and suicides happen all the time. Tad was about to get the needle anyway and he'd fired his lawyers. Did anyone really care? The wife of one of the dead DEA agents was quoted as saying, "We're very disappointed. We wanted to be there and watch him take his last breath."

His last lawyer, Amos Patrick of Memphis, was contacted but had no comment.

The Nashville *Tennessean* was even less sympathetic. The condemned man had murdered three fine officers of the law "in cold blood," to coin an original term. The jury had spoken. The system had worked. May he rest in peace.

Mitch poured a cup of coffee, drank it black, and mumbled a prayer for Tad, then another one of thanks for dodging another messy, hopeless case. Assuming he had met Tad and somehow convinced him to sign on, Mitch would have spent the next ninety days scrambling to prove his client was legally insane. If he got lucky and found the right doctor, he would then frantically race to find a court that would listen. Every possible court had already said no to Tad. Every remaining strategy, and there were precious few, was a desperate long shot. Mitch would fly back and forth from New York to Memphis and Nashville, stay in budget motels, rack up thousands of miles with Hertz and Avis, and eat food that was a far cry from the delightful cuisine that came from Abby's kitchen. He would miss her and the twins, fall far behind with his paying clients, lose a month of sleep, and then spend the last forty-eight hours at the prison either yelling into the phone or staring at Tad through a row of bars and lying about their chances.

"Good morning," Abby said as she patted his shoulder. She poured a cup and sat at the table. "Any good news from around the world?"

He closed his laptop and smiled at her. "The usual. A recession is looming. Our invasion of Iraq looks even more misguided. The climate is heating up. Nothing new, really."

"Lovely."

"A couple of stories from down there about Tad Kearny killing himself."

"It's so tragic."

"It is, but my file is closed. And I've decided that my career as a death row lawyer is over."

"I think I've heard that before."

"Well, this time I'm serious."

"We'll see. Are you working late tonight?"

"No. I'll be home around six, I think."

"Good. Remember that Laotian restaurant in the Village, about two months ago?"

"Sure. How could I forget? Something Vang."

"Bida Vang."

"And the chef has a last name with at least ten syllables."

"He goes by 'Chan' and he's decided to do a cookbook. He'll be here tonight to destroy the kitchen."

"Wonderful. What's on the menu?"

"Far too much, but he wants to experiment. He mentioned an herbal sausage and fried coconut rice, among others. Might want to skip lunch."

Clark emerged from the darkness and went straight to his mother for a hug. Carter would be five minutes behind. Mitch poured two small glasses of orange juice and asked what was on tap at school that day. As always, Clark woke up slow and said little over breakfast. Carter, the chatterbox, usually handled both ends of the morning conversation.

When the boys agreed on waffles and bananas, Mitch left the kitchen and went to shower. At 7:45 on the dot, the three guys hugged Abby goodbye and left for school. When he wasn't out of town, and when the weather permitted, Mitch walked the twins to school. The River Latin School was only four blocks away and the walk was always a delight, especially when their father was with them. Near the school, other boys emerged, and it was obvious they had the same destination. They wore the uniform—navy blazer, white shirt, and khakis. The shoes were free of the dress code and were a startling mix of high-end basketball sneakers, L.L.Bean hiking boots, dirty buckskins, and traditional loafers.

Mitch and Abby still worried about their sons' education. They were paying for the best in the city, but they, like most parents, wanted more diversity. Unlike the rest of the world, River Latin was 90 percent white and all-male. However, as products of mediocre public schools, they realized that they had only one opportunity to educate their children. For the moment, they could not foresee changing schools, but their concerns were growing.

Without showing too much affection, Mitch said goodbye to the twins, promised to see them that night, and hustled toward the subway.

——— • • ———

As he entered the tower on Broad Street and walked through the soaring atrium, he paused to remember Lamar's story about his visit here. Mitch saw the chrome and leather benches against a glass wall and sat down for a moment. He smiled as he watched the ants marching, hundreds of well-dressed young professionals like himself eager to start the day and wishing the escalators would climb faster. It would indeed be a shock to a small-town lawyer with a laid-back practice.

He was glad he'd made the effort to see his old friend, but it would never happen again. Lamar had not offered a hand to shake as Mitch left. There were simply too many unpleasant memories.

And that was fine with Mitch.

He glanced at his watch and realized that about twenty-four hours earlier he had been sitting in the former showroom of a Pontiac dealership in a shady part of Memphis, waiting and waiting for a meeting he wanted no part of.

The sharp sound of the word "Mitch" interrupted his random thoughts and brought him back to reality. Willie Backstrom was walking over, thick briefcase hanging from a leather strip over his shoulder. Mitch stood and said, "Good morning, Willie."

"I've been here for thirty years and I've never seen anyone use those benches. You okay?"

"We're too busy to sit down. Seriously, how can you bill a client when you're sitting in the lobby?"

"Do it all the time."

They walked away and joined the crowd at a wall of elevators. Once they were packed inside and moving up, Willie said softly, "If you get a minute, stop by today and let's talk about Amos."

"Sure. You ever been to the Pontiac place?"

"No, but I've heard about it for years."

"I got the impression that a visiting lawyer can get a lube job while taking a deposition."

The top man at Scully & Pershing was Jack Ruch, a forty-year veteran still hitting it hard in the final months as he neared the finish line of his seventieth birthday. The firm mandated retirement at seventy with no exceptions. As a policy, it was wise but widely unpopular. Most of the older partners were renowned experts in their fields and were billing at the highest rates. When forced out, they took their expertise with them, as well as the long, trusted relationships with their clients. On the one hand it seemed shortsighted to set such an arbitrary deadline, but youth demanded it. Forty-something partners like Mitch wanted to see room at the top. The young associates were super ambitious and many refused to join big firms that did not clear the deck by shoving out the old guys.

So Jack Ruch was counting the days. His official title was managing partner, and as such he ran the firm much like a high-powered corporate CEO. It was a law firm, though, an organization of proud professionals, not a corporation, and the titles were much weightier. Managing partner it was.

JOHN GRISHAM

When Jack called, every lawyer in the building dropped
what he or she was doing because whatever he or she was doing
was not nearly as crucial as whatever Jack might have on his
mind. But he was a skillful manager and knew better than to
interrupt and throw his weight around. His email asked Mitch
to appear at his office at 10 A.M., "if convenient."

Convenient or not, Mitch planned to be there five minutes
early.

He was, and a secretary led him into the splendid corner
office suite at precisely 10 A.M. She poured coffee from a silver
pitcher and asked Mitch if he wanted something from the daily
platter of fresh pastries on the credenza. Mitch, mindful of Chan
and his band of Laotian sous chefs set to invade his kitchen in a
few hours, thanked her and declined.

They sat around a small coffee table in a corner of the
suite. From sixty floors up the views of the harbor were even
more impressive, though Mitch was far too focused to venture
a glimpse. Those who worked in Manhattan's tallest buildings
were adept at ignoring the views while visitors gawked.

Jack was tanned and fit and wearing another one of his fine
linen suits. He could pass for a man fifteen years younger and
it seemed a shame to show him the door. But he had no time
to dwell on a policy that he had agreed to thirty years earlier
and wasn't about to change. "I spoke to Luca yesterday," he said
rather gravely. Obviously, something heavy was going down.

In the vast universe of Scully, there was only one Luca.
Twenty years earlier, when American Big Law went on a merg-
ing binge and gobbled up firms around the world, Scully had
managed to convince Luca Sandroni to join forces. He had built
a sterling international firm in Rome and was widely respected
throughout Europe and North Africa.

"How is Luca?"

"Not good. He was not specific, rather vague actually, but he had a bad trip to the doctor's office and got some unwelcome news. He didn't say what it was and I didn't ask."

"That's awful." Mitch knew him well. Luca was in New York several times a year and enjoyed a good time. He had dined at Abby's table and the McDeeres had stayed at his spacious villa in central Rome. That the young American couple had lived in Italy and knew the culture and language meant a lot to him.

"He wants you in Rome, as soon as possible." Odd that he didn't contact Mitch directly with the request, but Luca was always respectful of the chain of command. By going through Jack, the message was being delivered that Mitch should drop everything and go to Rome.

"Of course. Any idea what he wants?"

"It involves Lannak, the Turkish construction company."

"I've done some work for Lannak, but not much."

"Luca has represented the company forever, a great client. Now there's another dust-up in Libya and Lannak's in the middle of it."

Mitch nodded properly and tried to suppress a smile. Sounded like another great adventure! In his four years as a partner he had established a reputation as a sort of legal SWAT team leader sent in by Scully to rescue clients in distress. It was a role he relished and tried to expand while guarding it as his own.

Jack continued, "As usual, Luca was light on the details. He still doesn't like the phone and hates email. As you know, he prefers to discuss business over a long Roman lunch, preferably outdoors."

"Sounds dreadful. I'm leaving Sunday."

CHAPTER 6

Scully & Pershing was known for its lavish offices wherever it ventured. Now in thirty-one cities on five continents and counting, because for Scully the numbers were important, it leased prime space in the most prestigious addresses, usually taller and newer towers designed by the trendiest of architects. It sent in its own team of decorators who filled each suite with art, fabrics, furnishings, and lighting indigenous to the locale. Enter any Scully office and your senses were touched by the look, feel, and expensive taste. Its clients expected as much. For the hourly rates they paid, they wanted to see success.

In his eleven years with the firm, Mitch had visited about a dozen of its offices, mainly in the United States and Europe, and, truthfully, the shine was wearing off. Each was different but all were similar, and he had reached the point of not slowing down long enough to appreciate the serious money on the walls and floors. After a while, they were beginning to blur together. But he reminded himself that the opulence was not for his benefit. It was all a show for others: well-heeled clients, prospective associates, and visiting lawyers. He caught himself mumbling like the other partners about the expense of maintaining such a facade. Much of that money could have trickled down to the partners' pockets.

Things were different in Rome. There, the offices, as well as every other aspect of the practice, were under the thumb of Luca Sandroni, the founder. For over thirty years he had slowly built a firm that was housed in a four-story stone building with no elevators and limited views. It was tucked away on Via della Paglia near the Piazza Santa Maria, in the Trastevere neighborhood of old Rome. All of the buildings around it were four-storied stucco with red-tiled roofs, and tastefully showed the wear and tear of being built centuries earlier. Romans, new and old, never cared much for tall buildings.

Mitch had been there many times and loved the place. It was a step back in time and a welcome break from the relentlessly modern image of the rest of Scully. No other office in the firm had such history, nor did they dare say *"slow down"* when you entered. Luca and his team worked hard and enjoyed the prestige and money, but they were Italians and refused to succumb to the workaholism expected by the Americans.

Mitch stopped in the alley and admired the massive double doors. An old sign beside them read: SANDRONI STUDIO LEGALE. The merger with Luca allowed him to keep his firm's name, a point he would not concede. For a moment, Mitch thought of the law offices he'd seen that week, from his own shiny tower in Manhattan, to the grungy Pontiac place in Memphis, to Lamar Quin's sleepy little suite upstairs above the town square, and now this.

He stepped through the doors and into a narrow foyer, where Mia was always sitting. She smiled, jumped to her feet, and greeted Mitch with the obligatory dramatic peck on both cheeks, a ritual that still made him a bit uncomfortable. They spoke in Italian and covered the basics: his flight, Abby, the boys, the weather. He sat across from her, sipped espresso that always tasted better in Rome, and finally got around to Luca. She frowned slightly but revealed nothing. Her phone kept ringing.

Luca was waiting in his office, the same one he'd had for decades. It was small by Scully standards, at least for a managing partner, but he could not have cared less. He welcomed Mitch with more hugs and kisses and the usual greetings. If he was sick, it wasn't apparent. He waved at a small coffee table in a corner, his favorite meeting place, as his secretary inquired about drinks and pastries.

"How is the beautiful Abby?" Luca asked, in perfect English with only a trace of an accent. His second law degree was from Stanford. He also spoke French and Spanish, and years earlier could handle Arabic, but had lost it through neglect.

As they caught up on the McDeere family front, Mitch began to notice a weaker voice, but only slightly. When he lit a cigarette, Mitch said, "Still smoking, I see."

Luca shrugged as if the smoking couldn't possibly be related to a health issue. A double window was open and the smoke made its way through it. Piazza Santa Maria was below and the sounds of the busy street life emanated upward. Mia brought coffee on a silver tray and poured it for them.

Mitch tiptoed through the minefield of Luca's family. He had been married and divorced twice and it was never clear if his current companion had lasting potential; not that Mitch or anyone else for that matter would dare to ask. He had two adult children with his first wife, a woman Mitch had never met, and a teenager with his second. A hot young paralegal broke up the first marriage, then ruined the second by cracking up and fleeing with their love child to Spain.

Amidst that wreckage, the bright spot was his daughter, Giovanna, who was a Scully associate in London. Five years earlier, Luca had finessed the firm's nepotism rules and quietly landed her a job. According to the firm gossip, she was as brilliant and driven as her father.

While his private life had been chaotic, his professional career was without a blemish. The Sandroni Studio Legale had been romanced by all the players in Big Law before Luca finally got the deal he wanted with Scully.

"I'm afraid I have a slight problem, Mitch," he said sadly. With years of practice he had flattened out almost every wrinkle in his accent, but "Mitch" still sounded more like *Meetch*.

"The doctors have run tests for a month now, and they finally agree that I have a cancer. A bad one. In the pancreas."

Mitch closed his eyes as his shoulders sagged. If there was a worse cancer he was not aware of it. "I'm so sorry," he whispered.

"The prognosis is not good and I'm in for a bad time. I'm taking a leave of absence while the doctors do their work. Maybe I'll get lucky."

"I'm so sorry, Luca. This is awful."

"It is, but my spirits are good and there are always miracles, or so my priest tells me. I'm spending more time with him these days." He managed a chuckle.

"I don't know what to say, Luca."

"There's nothing to say. It's top secret, classified and all that. I don't want my clients to know yet. If things deteriorate, then I'll gradually inform them. I'm already handing off some of my cases to the partners here. That's where you come in, Mitch."

"I'm here, ready to help."

"The most important matter on my desk right now involves Lannak, the Turkish contractor and a longtime client. An extremely valuable client, Mitch."

"I worked on one of their cases a few years back."

"Yes, I know, and your work was superb. Lannak is one of the largest construction companies in the Middle East and Asia. They've built airports, highways, bridges, canals, dams, power plants, skyscrapers, you name it. The company is family-owned and is superbly managed. It delivers on time and on budget and knows how to do business in a world where everyone, from a Saudi prince to a cab driver in Kenya, has his hand out looking for a kickback."

Mitch nodded along and noticed Luca's voice fading a little. On the flight to Rome he had read the firm's internal client memos on Lannak. Headquarters in Istanbul; fourth-largest Turkish contractor with estimated annual revenues of $2.5 billion; large projects around the world but especially in India and North Africa; an estimated 25,000 employees; privately owned by the Celik family, who seemed to be as closemouthed as a bunch of Swiss bankers; family fortune thought to be in the billion-plus range, but one guess was as good as the next.

Luca lit another cigarette and half-heartedly blew smoke over his shoulder. "Are you familiar with the Great Man–Made River project in Libya?"

Mitch had read about it but only knew the basics. His knowledge, or lack thereof, didn't matter, because Luca was in his storytelling mood. "Not really."

Luca nodded at the correct response and said, "Goes back decades, but around 1975 Colonel Gaddafi decided to build an underground canal to pump water from under the Sahara to the cities along the coast in northern Libya. When the oil companies starting poking around for oil eighty years ago, they found some huge aquifers deep beneath the desert. The idea was to pump the water out and send it to Tripoli and Benghazi, but the cost was far too much. Until they discovered oil. Gaddafi gave the project the green light, but most experts thought it was impossible. It took thirty years and twenty billion dollars, but damned if the Libyans didn't pull it off. It worked, and Gaddafi declared himself a genius, something he has a habit of doing. Since he then had dominion over nature, he decided to create a river. There is not a single one in the entire country. Instead they have seasonal riverbeds known as 'wadis,' and these dry out in the summer. Gaddafi's next breathtaking project would be to combine some of the larger wadis, reroute the flow of water, make a permanent river, and build a magnificent bridge over it."

"A bridge in the desert."

"Yes, Mitch, a bridge in the desert, with delusional plans to link one side of the desert to the other and somehow build cities. Build a bridge and the traffic will find it. Six years ago, in 1999, Lannak signed a contract with the government for eight hundred million dollars. Gaddafi wanted a billion-dollar bridge, so he ordered changes before construction started. In his newspapers he posed for photos with models of 'The Great Gaddafi Bridge' and told everyone it would cost a billion, all generated by Libyan oil. Not a dime would be borrowed. Because Lannak has done business in Libya for many years, they knew how chaotic things could be. Let's just say that Colonel Gaddafi and his warlords are not astute businessmen. They understand guns and oil. Contracts are often a nuisance. Lannak would not begin the job until the Libyans deposited five hundred million U.S. dollars in a German bank. The four-year project took six years and is now complete, which is a miracle and a testament to the tenacity of Lannak. The company met the terms of its contract. The Libyans have not. The overruns were horrendous. The Libyan government owes Lannak four hundred million and won't pay. Thus, our claim."

Luca put down his cigarette, picked up a remote, and aimed

it at a flat screen on the wall. Wires ran from the screen to the floor where they joined other wires that snaked away in all directions. The current demands of technology required all kinds of devices, and since the walls were solid stone and two feet thick, the IT guys did not drill. Mitch adored the contrast between the old and new: the latest gadgets wedged into a sprawling maze of rooms built before electricity and designed to last forever.

The image on the screen was a color photo of a bridge, a towering suspension bridge over a dried-up riverbed with six-lane highways running to and from. Luca said, "This is the Great Gaddafi Bridge in central Libya, over an unnamed river yet to be found. It was and is a foolish idea because there are no people in the region and no one wants to go there. However, there is plenty of oil and maybe the bridge will get used after all. Lannak doesn't really care. It's not paid to plan Libya's future. It signed a contract to build the bridge and upheld its end of the deal. Now our client wants to be paid."

Mitch enjoyed the conversation and wondered where it was going. He had a hunch and tried to control his excitement.

Luca stubbed out his cigarette and closed his eyes as if in pain. He punched the remote and the screen went blank. "I filed the claim in October with the United Arbitration Board in Geneva."

"I've been there several times."

"I know, and that's why I want you to take this case."

Mitch tried to maintain a poker face but couldn't suppress a smile. "Okay. Why me?"

"Because I know you can represent our client effectively, you can prevail in the case, and because we need an American in charge. The board's chairman, more formally known as the ruling magistrate, is from Harvard. Six of the twenty judges are American. There are three from Asia and they usually go along with the Americans. I want you to take the case, Mitch, because I probably won't be around to see it through." His voice faded as he thought about dying.

"I'm honored, Luca. Of course I'll take the case."

"Good. I talked to Jack Ruch this morning and got the green light. New York is on board. Omar Celik, Lannak's CEO, will be in London next week and I'll try to arrange a meeting. The file is already thick, thousands of pages, so you need to catch up."

"I can't wait. Do the Libyans have a defense to the claim?"

"The usual truckload of absurdities. Defective design, defective materials, unnecessary delays, lack of supervision, lack of control, unnecessary cost overruns. The Libyan government uses the Reedmore law firm out of London for its dirty work, and you will not enjoy the experience. They are extremely aggressive and quite unethical."

"I know them. And our claim is bulletproof?"

Luca smiled at the question and said, "Well, as the attorney who filed the claim, I'll say that I have complete confidence in my client. Here's an example, Mitch. In the original design, the Libyans wanted a superhighway approaching the bridge from both directions. Eight lanes, mind you. There are not enough cars in the entire country to fill eight lanes. And they wanted eight lanes over the river. Lannak really balked and eventually convinced them that a four-lane bridge was more than adequate. The contract says four lanes. At some point, Gaddafi reviewed the project and asked about the eight lanes. He went nuts when his people told him the bridge would have only four lanes. The King wanted eight! Lannak finally talked him down to six and demanded a change order from the original design. Expanding from four lanes to six added about two hundred million to the job, and the Libyans are now refusing to pay that. It was one major change order after another. To complicate matters, the market for crude oil cratered and Gaddafi ordered some stiff belt-tightening, which in Libya means everything gets reduced but the military. When the Libyans were a hundred million dollars in arrears, Lannak threatened to stop working. So Gaddafi, being Gaddafi, sent the army, his revolutionary goons, to the job site to monitor the progress. No one got hurt but things were tense. At about the time the bridge was finished, someone in Tripoli woke up and realized that it would never be used. So the Libyans lost interest in the project and refused to pay."

"So Lannak is finished?"

"All but the final punch list. The company always finishes, regardless of what the lawyers are doing. I suggest you go to Libya as soon as possible."

"And it's safe?"

Luca smiled and shrugged and seemed winded. "As safe as ever. I've been there several times, Mitch, and know it well. Gaddafi can be unstable, but he has an iron grip on the military and the police and there's very little crime. The country is full of foreign workers and he has to protect them. You'll have a security team. You'll be safe."

———•••———

For lunch, they strolled across the piazza to an outdoor bistro covered with large umbrellas. Without stopping, Luca smiled at the hostess, said something to a waiter, and by the time he arrived at his table the owner was greeting him with hugs and kisses. Mitch had eaten there before, and he often wondered why Luca chose the same place every day. In a city filled with great restaurants, why not explore a little? Again, though, he said nothing. He was an extra in Luca's world and thrilled to be included.

A waiter poured sparkling water but did not offer menus. Luca wanted the usual—a small seafood salad with arugula and a side of sliced tomatoes in olive oil. Mitch ordered the same.

"Wine, Mitch?" Luca asked.

"Only if you do."

"I'll pass." The waiter left.

"Mitch, I have a favor to ask."

At that moment, how could Mitch possibly say no to any request? "What is it?"

"You've met my daughter, Giovanna."

"Yes, we had dinner in New York, twice I think. She was a summer intern for a law firm. Skadden, I believe."

"That's right. Well, as you know, she's in our London office, fifth year there, and doing well. I've discussed the Lannak case with her and she's eager to get involved. She's been cramped in the office for some time, the ninety hours a week routine, and she wants some fresh air and sunshine. You'll need several associates for the busywork, and I want you to include Giovanna. She's very bright and works hard. You won't be disappointed, Mitch."

And, as Mitch vividly recalled, she was quite attractive.

It was an easy request. There was plenty of grunt work ahead—documents to read and categorize, discovery to decipher, depositions to plan, briefs to write. Mitch would supervise it all, but the tedium would be delegated to associates.

"Let's sign her up," he said. "I'll call and welcome her aboard."

"Thank you, Mitch. She will be pleased. I'm trying to convince her to return to Rome, at least for the next year. I need her close by."

Mitch nodded but could think of nothing to say. The food arrived and they busied themselves with lunch. The piazza was coming to life with midday traffic, as office workers left their buildings in search of something to eat. The foot traffic was fascinating and Mitch never tired of watching the people.

Luca stopped eating as a sudden pain stiffened his back. It passed and he smiled at Mitch, as if all was well.

"Ever been to Libya, Mitch?"

"No. It's never been on my list."

"Fascinating place, really. My father lived there in the thirties, before the war, back when Italy was trying to colonize the country. As you probably know, the Italians were not very good at the colonizing business. Leave it to the British, the French, the Spaniards, even the Dutch and Portuguese. For some reason the Italians never got the hang of it. We bailed out after the war, but my father stayed in Tripoli until 1969, when Gaddafi took over in a military coup. Libya has a fascinating history, one worth taking a look at."

Not only had Mitch never planned to visit the place, he had never been curious about its history. He smiled and said, "I'll have a PhD by next week."

"For the first ten years of my practice, I represented Italian companies doing business in Libya. I stayed there often, even had a little flat in Tripoli for a couple years. And there was a woman, a Moroccan." The twinkle was back in his eye. Mitch could not help but wonder how many girlfriends Luca had kept around the world in his day.

"She was a beauty," he said softly, wistfully.

Of course she was. Would Luca Sandroni waste time with a homely woman?

Over espresso and the obligatory Italian post-lunch cigarette, Luca said, "Why don't you stop off in London and see Giovanna? She'll be thrilled to be personally invited onto the case. And check on her, tell her I'm doing fine."

"Are you doing fine, Luca?"

"Not really. I have less than six months, Mitch. The cancer is aggressive and there's little I can do. The case is yours."

"Thank you, Luca, for the trust. You won't be disappointed."

"No, I won't, but I'm afraid I might not be around to see its conclusion."

CHAPTER 7

Two hours before he was to board the nonstop flight from Rome to London, Mitch abruptly changed plans and got the last seat on a flight to New York's JFK. There were pressing matters at home. Dinner with Giovanna could wait.

Confined to a narrow seat for eight hours, Mitch passed the time as always on long flights by diving into thick briefs so boring they usually led to a long nap or two. First, he reviewed the docket and current membership of the United Arbitration Board and read the bios of its twenty members. They were appointed by one of the many committees at the United Nations and served five-year terms, with a lot of time spent in Geneva and with generous expense accounts. A former member once told Mitch, over drinks in New York, that the UAB was one of the best gigs in the world for aging lawyers with international pedigrees and contacts. As always, its roster was chock-full of bright legal minds from every continent, most of whom had at one time or another passed through Ivy League law schools either to study or teach. Its business was done in English and French, though all languages were welcome and could be accommodated. Two years earlier, Mitch had appeared before the board and argued a case on behalf of an Argentine grain cooperative seeking damages against a South Korean importer. He and Abby spent three honeymoon-like days in Geneva and still talked about it. He won the case, collected the money, and sent a hefty bill to Buenos Aires.

Winning cases before the UAB was not that difficult if the facts fell into place. It had jurisdiction because the contracts, like the one for the bridge project between Lannak and the Libyan government, had a clearly written clause requiring both parties to submit their disputes to the UAB. In addition, Libya, like virtually every other nation, was a signatory to various treaties designed to facilitate international commerce and make the bad actors—and there was never a shortage of them—behave.

Winning was relatively easy. Collecting an award was another matter. Dozens of rogue states willingly signed whatever contracts and treaties were necessary to get the business, with no intention of paying the damages that became due at arbitration. The more Mitch read, the more he realized that Libya had a long history of trying to walk away from deals that looked promising at contract but went sour.

According to Scully's intelligence, the bridge was a perfect example of Gaddafi's erratic dreaming. He became enamored with the vision of a soaring structure in the middle of a desert and ordered it built. Then he lost interest and moved on to other important projects. At some point, someone convinced him it was a bad idea, but by then those pesky Turks were demanding serious money.

Luca's UAB claim ran for ninety pages, and by the time Mitch had read it once he was almost asleep.

———•—•———

The pressing matter at home was a youth baseball game in Central Park. Carter and Clark played for the Bruisers, a serious contender in the Under Eight division of the city's police league. Carter was the catcher and loved the dirt and sweat. Clark roamed the outfield and missed half the action. Mitch had almost no time to help coach the team, but he volunteered as the bench coach and tried to keep the lineup straight. It was a crucial task because if any kid, regardless of talent or interest, played one inning less than the others, his parents would be waiting in ambush after the game.

After a few light skirmishes with parents, Mitch was already plotting ways to interest the twins in individual sports such as golf and tennis. However, some of those parents were just as terrifying. Perhaps hiking and skiing might be more enjoyable.

The boys stood shoulder-to-shoulder in the foyer as Mitch inspected their uniforms. Abby was worrying about the time; they were already running late. They left in a rush and hurried along Sixty-Eighth Street to Central Park West. The teams were on one of the many fields of the Great Lawn, limbering up in the outfield as coaches yelled and parents huddled in the falling temperatures.

Hiding in the dugout presented its own challenges, but Mitch preferred it to the bleachers where the adults chatted nonstop about careers, real estate, new restaurants, new nannies, new trainers, schools, and so on.

The umpires arrived and the game began. For ninety minutes Mitch sat on the bench, surrounded by a dozen eight-year-olds, and managed to shut out the rest of the world. He kept the score book, made the substitutions, huddled with Mully, the head coach, chided the umpires, ribbed the opposing coach, and treasured the moments when his own sons sat beside him and talked baseball.

The Bruisers crushed the Rams, and at the final out the players and coaches lined up for the postgame handshaking rituals. The staff, Mully and Mitch, were determined to teach their players the virtues of sportsmanship, and they led by example. Winning was always fun, but winning with class was far more important.

In a crowded city with far too few fields and an abundance of kids, the games were limited by time, not innings. Another one was scheduled to start right away and it was important to clear the field. The victorious Bruisers and their parents walked to a pizzeria on Columbus Avenue where they commandeered a long table in the back and ordered dinner. The fathers had tall beers, the mothers chardonnay, while the players, all proud of their dirty uniforms, devoured pizza as they watched the Mets on a big screen.

Almost all the fathers were in finance, law, or medicine, and they were from well-to-do families from across the country. As a general rule they didn't talk much about where they were from. There was always plenty of good-natured talk about college football rivalries, favorite golf courses, and such, but the conversations rarely drifted to their hometowns. They were in New York now, on the biggest stage, living the big life, proud of their success, and they considered themselves real New Yorkers.

Danesboro, Kentucky, was another world and Mitch never mentioned it. He thought of it, though, as he watched his own boys laugh and chatter with their friends. He had played all the sports the small town had to offer, and he could not remember a single game when his parents were watching. His father died when he was just a boy, and afterward his mother worked in low-wage jobs to support him and his brother, Ray. She never had the time to watch a ball game.

What lucky kids these were. Affluent lives, private schools, and supportive parents who were too involved in their activities. Mitch often worried that his kids would be too pampered and too soft, but Abby disagreed. Their school was demanding and pushed the students to achieve and excel. Carter and Clark were, at least so far, well-rounded and being taught proper values both at school and at home.

———•—•———

Abby was startled at the news that Luca was gravely ill. She had met many Scully partners, probably too many, from all over the world, and Luca was by far her favorite. She wasn't keen on the idea of Mitch traveling to Libya, but if Luca said it was safe, then she wouldn't push back. Not that it would do any good. Since he made partner four years earlier, Mitch had become a seasoned traveler. She often went with him, especially when the destination was exciting. European cities were her favorite. Between her parents, her kid sister, and a collection of nannies, babysitting was rarely a problem. But the boys were getting older and more active, and Abby feared her globe-trotting days were about to be curtailed. She also suspected, though had said nothing, that her husband's success would mean even more time away from home.

Late that night, she brewed a pot of chamomile tea that was supposed to induce "slumber," and they cuddled and chatted on the sofa and tried to get sleepy.

Abby said, "And you're gone for a week?"

"Something like that. There's no clear agenda because we can't predict what might happen. Lannak has a skeleton crew still at the bridge, and we're told that one of their top engineers will be available."

"What do you know about bridge construction?" she asked with a chuckle.

"Nothing, but I'm learning. Every case is a new adventure. Right now I'm the envy of almost every lawyer at Scully."

"That's a lot of lawyers."

"It is, and while I'm dashing across the desert in a jeep looking for a magnificent bridge to nowhere, which just happened to cost over a billion dollars, the rest of my colleagues will be stuck behind their desks, worrying about their hourly billing."

"I've heard this before."

"And you'll probably hear it again."

"Well, your timing is good. My mother called today and they're coming for the weekend."

No, my timing is perfect, Mitch thought. In years past he would have blurted it out and stuck another pin into his wife's skin, but he was in the often uncomfortable process of reconciling with his in-laws. He had come a long way, but back at the beginning there had been so much territory to cover.

"Anything planned?" he asked, to be polite.

"Not really. I may have dinner with the girls Saturday and let my parents babysit."

"Do that. You need a night out."

The war had begun almost twenty years earlier when her parents insisted that she break off the engagement and ditch the McDeere guy. Both families were from Danesboro, a town so small that everyone knew everyone else. Her father ran a bank and the family had status. The McDeeres had nothing.

"Dad said he might take the boys to see the Yankees."

"He should take them to see the Mets."

"Carter would agree. And because of that, Clark is becoming a Yankee fan."

Mitch laughed and said, "I have a brother. I remember."

"How is Ray?"

"Fine. We talked two days ago, nothing has changed."

A week before they finished college, Mitch and Abby were married in a small chapel on campus, in front of twenty friends and no family. Her parents were so irate they boycotted the wedding, a slap so terrible it was years before she could discuss it with a therapist. Mitch would never truly forgive them. Ray would have attended the wedding had he not been serving time in prison. These days he was working as a charter boat captain in Key West.

Mitch's in-law rehab had now brought him to the point of being civil to them, dining with them, and allowing them to babysit their grandchildren. When they entered the room, though, walls went up around him and everything else was off-limits. They could not stay in the apartment. Mitch argued it wasn't large enough anyway. They could not inquire about his work, though it was evident that his partnership was providing a lifestyle far above anything in Danesboro. They could not and did not expect the McDeere family to visit them in Kentucky. Mitch wasn't going back anyway.

The law degree from Harvard had somewhat tempered their disapproval of their son-in-law, but only for a moment. The move to Memphis had been puzzling, and when things blew up there and Abby disappeared for months, they of course blamed Mitch and despised him all over again.

With time, some of the issues faded as maturity settled in. A therapist helped Abby begin the process of forgiving her parents. The same therapist realized Mitch was another story, but managed a slight breakthrough when he reluctantly agreed to at least be civil when they were in the same room. More progress was slowly made, driven more by Mitch's love for his wife than by the manipulations of the therapist. As so often happens in complicated families, the arrival of grandchildren softened the edges and shoved even more history aside.

"And your mom?" she asked softly.

He took a sip of tea and shook his head. "Still the same, I guess. Ray checks on her once a week, or so he says. I have my doubts." His mother was spending her final years in an assisted living facility in Florida. With dementia, she moved closer to the end each day.

"And what does one do in Tripoli?"

"I don't know. Ride camels. Play shoot-'em-up with terrorists."

"That's not funny. I went to the State Department website. According to our government, Libya is a terrorist state and they evidently hate Americans."

"Who doesn't hate Americans?"

"The State Department says it's sort of okay to go but take precautions."

"Luca knows more about Libya than the bureaucrats in Washington."

"I wish you wouldn't go."

"I have to go, and I'll be fine. Our bodyguards are quicker than the terrorists."

"Ha, ha."

Not too many years earlier, he would have blurted something like: *Well, I'd rather hang out with a bunch of Revolutionary Guards than see your parents.*

He smiled at the thought, then let it pass. After several thousand bucks in therapy, he had learned to bite his tongue.

Often, it was almost bleeding.

CHAPTER 8

There were no direct flights from New York to Tripoli. The marathon began in New York with an eight-hour trip through the night on Air Italia to Milan, then a two-hour layover before boarding an Egyptair flight to Cairo that was delayed for two hours, no excuses given. Cancellations and rebookings followed at a languid pace, and Mitch spent thirteen hours catnapping and reading in the Cairo airport while someone somewhere sorted out the mess. Or did they? The only bright spot was the fact that his time was not completely wasted. Lannak would eventually get billed for his hours.

When he left New York, at least half of the passengers seemed to be "Westerners," or, in other words, people who could generally be described as looking, dressing, speaking, and acting sort of like him. Most of those got off in Italy, and by the time Mitch boarded an Air Tunisia flight for the final leg, the plane was packed with people who were definitely not "Westerners."

He was not bothered by the fact that he was now in a distinct minority. Libya promoted its tourism and attracted half a million visitors a year. Tripoli was a bustling city of two million with business districts filled with domestic banks and corporations. Dozens of foreign companies were registered in the country, and in some sections of Tripoli and Benghazi there were vibrant international communities with British and French schools for the children of visiting executives and diplomats.

As he often did while traveling on the far side of the world, Mitch smiled at the thought that he was undoubtedly the only boy from Kentucky on the flight. And though he would never mention this, he was proud of his accomplishments and wanted more. He was as hungry as ever.

Almost thirty hours after leaving New York, he stepped off the plane at Mitiga International Airport in Tripoli, and shuffled along with the crowd in the general direction of Passport Control. Signs were primarily in Arabic, but there were enough in English and French to keep the traffic moving. Under the iron hand of Colonel Gaddafi, Libya had been a military state for thirty-five years, and like most countries ruled by intimidation, it was important to impress upon new arrivals the presence of heavily armed soldiers. They roamed the concourses of the modern airport in their smart uniforms, guarded the checkpoints, and with unpleasant scowls inspected every Westerner who walked by.

Mitch hid behind his sunglasses and tried to ignore them. Never make eye contact if possible. The same routine he'd learned long ago in the New York subway.

The lines at Passport Control were long and slow. The vast room was hot and unventilated. When a guard nodded at an empty booth, Mitch walked forward and presented his passport and visa. The customs officer never smiled; indeed, upon seeing that Mitch was an American, he managed to frown even harder. A minute passed, then another. Customs could be nerve-wracking enough for any citizen returning to his own country. Maybe there's a glitch in the passport. In a place like Libya, there was always the flash of horror that an American could be suddenly on the floor, handcuffed, then hauled away and detained for life. Mitch loved the thrill of the unknown.

The officer kept shaking his head as he picked up the phone. Mitch, without the sunglasses, glanced back at the hundreds of weary travelers behind him.

"Over there," the officer said rudely, jerking his head to the right. Mitch looked and saw a gentleman in a nice suit approaching them. He stuck out a hand, smiled, and said, "Mr. McDeere, I'm Samir Jamblad. I work with Lannak and also with Luca, an old friend."

Mitch felt like kissing him, which, in the sudden embracing and grappling that followed, seemed likely. Once properly hugged, Samir asked, "How was your flight?"

"Wonderful. I think I've been to at least thirteen countries since leaving New York."

They were walking away from the booths and crowds and security guards. "This way," Samir said, nodding to officers as they went. Luca had told Mitch not to worry about entry. He would take care of things.

Samir used the restricted doors, away from the crowds, and within minutes they were outside. His Mercedes sedan was parked near the crowded terminal and in a lane reserved for the police. Two officers leaned on a marked car, smoking, loitering, and appearing to guard nothing but Samir's fine sedan. He thanked them and tossed Mitch's bag in the rear seat.

"First time in Tripoli?" he asked as they left the airport.

"Yes, it is. How long have you known Luca?"

Samir smiled easily and said, "Oh, many years. I've worked for Scully and Pershing and other law firms. Companies like your Exxon and Texaco. British Petroleum, Dutch Shell. Plus some of the Turkish companies, Lannak being one."

"You're a lawyer?"

"Oh no. An American client once referred to me as a 'security consultant.' Sort of a facilitator, a corporate handyman, the go-to guy in Libya. I was born and raised here, all my life in Tripoli. I know the people, there's only six million of us." He laughed at his own effort at humor and Mitch felt compelled to join in.

Samir continued, "I know the leaders, the military, the politicians, and the government workers who get things done. I know the chief of customs back there at the airport. One word from me and they leave you alone. Another word from me, and you might spend a few days in jail. I know the restaurants, bars, good neighborhoods and bad ones. I know the opium dens and the brothels, good and bad."

"I'm not in the market."

Samir laughed again and said, "Yes, that's what they all say."

From the first impression—the handsome suit, polished black leather shoes, shiny sedan—it was apparent that Samir did indeed know his stuff and was paid well for it.

Mitch glanced at his watch and asked, "What time is it here?"

"Almost eleven. I suggest you check in, get settled, and let's meet for lunch around one in the hotel. Giovanna's already here. You've met her?"

"Yes, in New York, a few years back."

"She's lovely, yes?"

"Yes, as I recall. And after lunch?"

"All plans are tentative and subject to your approval. In Luca's absence, you are in charge. We have a meeting with the Turks at four P.M. at the hotel. You'll meet your security team and discuss the visit to the bridge."

"An obvious question. Lannak is suing the Libyan government for almost half a billion dollars, a claim that certainly looks legitimate. How much friction is there between the company and government?"

Samir took a deep breath, cracked a window, and lit a cigarette. The traffic had stopped and they were sitting bumper-to-bumper. "I would say not much. The Turkish construction companies have been in Libya for a long time, and they are very good. Much better than the Libyans. The military needs the Turks, the Turks like the money. Sure they fight and squabble all the time, but in the end business prevails and life goes on."

"Okay, second obvious question. Why do we need a security detail?"

Samir laughed again and said, "Because this is Libya. A terrorist state, haven't you heard? Your own government says so."

"But that's international terrorism. What about here, within the country? Why are we taking Turkish bodyguards to visit a Turkish construction site?"

"Because the government doesn't control everything, Mitch. Libya has a lot of territory but ninety percent of it is Sahara, the desert. It's vast, wild, sometimes uncontrolled. Tribes fight each other. Outlaws are hard to catch. There are still warlords out there, always looking for trouble."

"Would *you* feel safe going where we're going tomorrow?"

"Of course. Otherwise I wouldn't be here, Mitch. You're safe, or as safe as a foreigner can be."

"That's what Luca says."

"Luca knows the country. Would he allow his daughter to be here if he was worried?"

———•—•———

The Corinthia Hotel was ground zero for Western business-men, diplomats, and government functionaries, and the ornate lobby was hopping with corporate types in expensive suits. As Mitch waited to check in he heard English, French, Italian, German, and some tongues he couldn't identify.

His corner room was on the fifth floor with a splendid view of the Mediterranean. To the northeast he looked down on the ancient walls of the Old City, but he didn't gaze for long. After a hot shower he fell across his bed, slept hard for an hour, and woke up only with the aid of an alarm clock. He showered again to knock off the cobwebs, dressed for business but without a necktie, and went to find lunch.

Samir was waiting in the restaurant off the hotel lobby. Mitch found him at a dark corner table, and they had just been handed menus when Giovanna Sandroni arrived. They went through the rituals of hugging and pecking and when everyone was properly greeted they settled in and plunged into the small talk. She asked about Abby and the boys, and with some effort they agreed that their first meeting had been about six years earlier for dinner in New York. She'd spent a summer in New York as an intern in a rival firm. Luca was in town, and they met at, not surprisingly, an Italian restaurant in Tribeca where Abby knew the chef and there was talk of a cookbook.

Giovanna was full-blooded Roman, with the dark sad eyes and classic features, but she had spent half of her life abroad. Elite boarding schools in Switzerland and Scotland, an undergraduate degree from Trinity in Dublin, one law school diploma from Queen Mary in London, and another from the University of Virginia. She spoke English without a trace of an accent and Italian like a native, which, of course, she was. Luca said she was "picking up" Mandarin, her fifth language, which for Mitch was too frustrating to think about. He and Abby were still clinging to their Italian and often worried that it was slipping away.

Giovanna had been with Scully for five years and was on the inside track to a partnership, though an inside track would never be acknowledged by the firm. After the first year of associate boot camp the higher-ups usually knew who was a lifer and who'd be gone in five years. She had the brains, tenacity, and pedigree, not to mention the good looks that in principle counted for nothing but in reality opened many doors. She was thirty-two and single and had once been linked by the tabloids to a deadbeat Italian playboy who'd killed himself skydiving. That had been her only brush with fame and it was enough. As a member of a prominent family she was an easy target for gossip in Italy; thus, she preferred a quieter life abroad and had been in London for the past five years.

"How's Luca?" Mitch asked as soon as she settled in.

She frowned and got right to the point. His health was deteriorating, his prognosis was grim. They talked about Luca for almost fifteen minutes and practically buried him. Samir had known him for thirty years and almost teared up. They ordered light vegetables and green tea.

As they waited for the food, Samir pulled out a folded sheet of paper and held it so that it was obvious he had the floor. In his learned opinion, they should leave at dawn the following morning, around 5 A.M., when the city traffic was light. The bridge was a hard six-hour drive south of Tripoli. Assuming they arrived by noon, they could spend a maximum of three hours at the site before returning to the city. It was too dangerous to travel after dark.

"What kind of danger?" Mitch asked.

"Two hours out of the city, the roads are in bad shape and not safe. Plus, there are gangs and no shortage of bad characters. At the bridge, Lannak is breaking camp and almost finished with the job. The company is quite eager to close up shop. At least two of its engineers are still on-site and they will walk you through the design, history, problems, and so on. Luca thinks it's important for you to actually see some of the changes that were dictated by the Libyan government as the project went out of control. We have plenty of materials—architects' drawings, sketches, photos, videos, whatever—but the entire project is something you need to see. Luca has been there at least three times. We'll work quickly, then start the return to Tripoli."

Mitch asked Giovanna, "Have you reviewed Luca's summary?"

She nodded confidently and said, "I have. All four hundred pages, not quite a summary. He can be windy at times, can't he?"

"No comment. He's your father."

Lunch arrived and she removed a pair of bulky sunglasses. Mitch had already decided they were for fashion only and had nothing to do with improving her eyesight. She wore a long, black, loose dress that almost dragged the floor. No jewelry, no makeup, none needed. She said little, was sure of herself but deferential as an associate, and gave the impression that she could handle her side of the table in any discussion. They talked about the Great Gaddafi Bridge as they ate. Samir amused them with stories that had been circulating for years about the project, another boondoggle dreamed up by the Colonel. A man born in a tent. The stories, though, had never made it to print. The press was tightly controlled.

The best story, and perhaps the most likely, was that once the bridge was finished, the Colonel wanted to blow it up and blame the Americans. His engineers had been unable to redirect the flow of the nearest river. He sacked them all and stopped paying Lannak.

As first-time visitors to the city, and with a few hours to spare, they asked Samir if he could walk them through the Old City for a bit of sightseeing. He was delighted to show them around. They left the hotel on foot and soon entered the walled section of ancient Tripoli. The narrow streets were packed with small cars, delivery bikes, and rickshaws. A market was lined with stalls of vendors selling fresh meats and chickens, nuts roasting in hot pans, scarves, and all manner of clothing. The chorus of shouting and bantering, the honking horns and sirens, and the distant din of music combined to make a constant ear-splitting roar. Then, at 3 P.M., unseen loudspeakers erupted with the *adhan,* the afternoon call to prayer, and virtually every man in sight scurried away and headed to the nearest mosque.

Mitch had been to Syria and Morocco and had heard the *adhan* blare through the streets and neighborhoods five times each day. Though he knew little about the Muslim religion, he was fascinated with its traditions and the discipline of its adherents. Hustling off to church to pray in the middle of the day had never caught on in the States.

The markets and streets were suddenly much quieter. Giovanna decided to do some shopping. Mitch tagged along and bought a scarf for Abby.

CHAPTER 9

Any worries about being ambushed in the desert by warlords or bandits were allayed when Mitch and Giovanna met their Turkish security detail. There were four of them—Aziz, Abdo, Gau, and one whose name sounded like "Haskel." Their first names were such a challenge they did not offer their last ones. All Turks, they were large young men with thick arms and chests, and their bulky clothing was layered in such a way that it was evident they were concealing all manner of weaponry. Haskel, the unquestioned leader, did most of the talking in passable English. Samir was quick to point out a few things in Turkish, just to impress Mitch and Giovanna with his language skills.

They met in a small room in a warehouse half an hour from the hotel. Haskel pointed here and there on a large, colorful map that covered an entire wall. He'd been in Libya for four years, had been to the bridge and back dozens of times without incident, and was confident they were in for an uneventful day. They would leave the hotel at five the following morning in one vehicle, a customized delivery truck with plenty of axles and

fuel and other "protections." During lunch, Samir had let it slip
that the Lannak executives often zipped off to the bridge project
in a helicopter. Mitch thought of asking why one was not available for their legal team, but then thought better of it.

The truck driver would be Youssef, a trusted Lannak
employee and a bona fide Libyan. There would be checkpoints
and perhaps some minor harassment by local soldiers, but nothing Youssef couldn't handle. They would carry plenty of food
and water as it was best not to stop, unless of course nature
called. The trip had been approved by the government and so,
supposedly, their movements would not be monitored. Samir
would tag along just in case, though he was obviously not looking forward to another trip to the bridge.

He left Mitch and Giovanna at the hotel after dark and went
home. After greeting his wife and nosing around the kitchen, he
went to his small office, locked the door, and called his handler
with the Libyan military police. The debriefing lasted half an
hour and covered everything from what Giovanna was wearing
to the make of her cell phone, hotel room number, purchases at
the market, and her dinner plans. She and Mitch had agreed to
dine in the hotel at 8 P.M. and invited Samir to join them. He'd
begged off.

In his opinion, the visit to the bridge was a waste of time,
but typical of Western lawyers. Lannak was paying them by the
hour, so why not do some traveling, have some fun, get out of
the office, and see the eighth wonder of the world—a billion-
dollar bridge over a dried-up river in the middle of the desert?

——— • ———

With so many Westerners in the hotel, Giovanna decided
to ditch the local look and get dressed up. Her tight dress fell to

her knees and did justice to her splendid figure. She wore a pair of dangling gold earrings, a necklace, and some bracelets. She was Italian, after all, and knew how to dress. She was meeting a handsome American partner in her law firm, and there could be some tension in the air. They were a long way from home.

Mitch wore a dark suit with no tie. He was pleasantly surprised by her makeover and told her she looked lovely. They met in the bar and ordered martinis. Alcohol was strictly forbidden on Muslim soil, but the rulers knew how important it was to Westerners. Long ago, the hotels had convinced Gaddafi that to stay in business and show profits they needed to offer full bars and wine lists.

They carried their drinks to a table by a large window and took in the view of the harbor. Since he was curious about her background and deemed her far more interesting than himself, Mitch gently kept the conversation on her side of the table. She had lived half of her thirty-two years in Italy, the other half abroad. She was feeling the urge to go home. Her father's illness was a factor, and his death, heaven forbid, would leave a huge vacancy in Scully's Rome office. Luca, of course, wanted her by his side these days, and she was serious about making the move. She loved London but was tired of the dreary weather.

When the martinis were gone, Mitch waved to the waiter. With such an early departure the following morning, they could not indulge in a three-hour dinner, nor did they want heavy dishes of meats and sauces. They agreed on a light seafood stew and Giovanna picked a bottle of pinot grigio.

"How old were you when you left Rome?" Mitch asked.

"Fifteen. I was in the American school there and had traveled a lot, for a kid. My parents were splitting up and things were unpleasant at home. I was sent to a boarding school in Switzerland, an obscenely expensive getaway for rich kids whose parents were too busy to raise them. Kids from all over the world, a lot of Arabs, Asians, South Americans. It was a great environment and I had far too much fun, though I worried constantly about my parents."

"How often did you return to Rome?"

"Occasionally, but only for holidays. I took summer internships here and there to stay away from home. I blamed my father for the divorce, still do, but we've managed to work out a truce."

"What happened to your mother?"

She shrugged and smiled and made it clear that her mother was off-limits. Fine with Mitch. They were not about to discuss his parents. He asked, "Why did you choose college in Dublin?"

The wine arrived and they went through the ritual of opening, sipping, approving. After the waiter poured two glasses and left, Giovanna continued, "I had partied a bit too much in boarding school and my application was rather bland. The Ivies were certainly not impressed and they all said no, as did Oxford and Cambridge. Luca pulled a string or two and I got admitted to Trinity in Dublin. I didn't take rejection well and went off to school with a real chip on my shoulder. I studied hard and entered law school determined to turn the world upside down. I finished in two years, but at the age of twenty-three was not exactly ready to sit for the bar. Luca suggested I study in the States, and off I went to the University of Virginia for three delightful years. Enough about me. How'd you get into Harvard Law?"

Mitch smiled and took a sip. "You mean, how did a poor kid from a small town in Kentucky make it to the Ivies?"

"Something like that."

"Brilliant scholar, charismatic leader, you name it."

"No, seriously?"

"Seriously? I had a four-oh average as an undergraduate and

a near-perfect score on the law school admissions test. I was also from the coal county of Kentucky, a huge factor. Harvard doesn't get a lot of applications from that part of the world, and so the smart people in admissions thought I might be exotic enough. The truth is, I got lucky."

"You make your own luck in life, Mitch. You did well at Harvard."

"Like you, I had a chip on my shoulder, something to prove, so, yes, I worked hard."

"Luca said you finished at the top of your class."

Why would Luca want to repeat that? "No, not true. I was number four."

"Out of?"

"Out of five hundred."

It was almost nine o'clock and every table was filled with loud men talking at full throttle in more languages than Mitch cared to follow. A few wore robes and kaffiyehs but most were in expensive suits. In addition to plenty of alcohol going down, a lot of cigarettes were burning and the restaurant's ventilation was inadequate. Oil drove Libya's economy and Mitch caught snippets in English of markets, crude prices, and drilling. He tried to ignore it because he was dining with one of only two women in the room and his date deserved his attention. She was getting looks, seemed to know it, and seemed to accept them as if they were part of her world.

Giovanna wanted to talk about Abby and the twins and they did so for a long time as they toyed with the stew, which wasn't very good, and sipped the wine, which was okay but would have tasted much better in Lombardia. When they had covered Mitch's immediate family, Giovanna pushed her bowl away and said she needed some advice. She had been with Scully for five years, all in their London office, and she was determined to become a partner. Would her chances be better if she stayed in London? Or if she returned to Rome? And how long might it take? The average at Scully was the same as at the other major firms in Big Law, about eight years.

Mitch was tempted to go off the record and share the gossip he'd collected. She would probably make partner in average time if she maintained her current pace, and it didn't matter where she was located. However, being the daughter of Luca Sandroni would certainly open more doors in Rome. She was bright and driven and had the pedigree. And, the firm was committed to diversity and needed more women at the top.

He said it didn't matter. Scully was known for recognizing legal talent, either homegrown or poached, regardless of where they found it.

By the time they finished the stew and the wine they were both tired. Tomorrow would be an adventure. Mitch charged the dinner to his room. He walked Giovanna to hers, on the same floor, and said good night.

CHAPTER 10

He was fast asleep and had no idea of the time when he awoke in the darkness and grabbed the sheets because the bed was spinning. The sheets were soaked with water or sweat or something, he couldn't tell in the first few awful seconds when he tried to sit up and breathe. His heart was pounding and ready to explode. His stomach was churning and flipping and before he could find a light switch, the dinner of light seafood stew and the pinot grigio was burning its way up. He gritted his teeth, tried hard to swallow, but couldn't hold the surge and began vomiting off the side of the bed. He gagged and spat and coughed, and when the first batch was out he stared at the mess in the semi-dark and tried to think. It was impossible. It was all spinning—bed, ceiling, walls, furniture. His skin was oozing perspiration as his heart and lungs thundered away. He gagged and retched and puked some more. He had to get to the toilet but he was far too dizzy to stand up. He rolled out of the bed, fell into the vomit, and began crawling across the carpet to the bathroom where he turned on a light and unloaded again into the toilet. When his stomach was empty he leaned against the tub and washed his face with a hand towel and cold water. Hot sharp pains shot through his head and made him gasp. His labored breathing would not slow. His pulse felt like a jackhammer. He thought about another attempt at standing and moved slowly to all fours, then blacked out and fell to his side. He was sure he was dying.

His stomach exploded again and he retched into the toilet. When the wave passed he leaned on the tub and turned the knobs. He could smell himself and had to clean up. Lying on his back, he pulled down his boxers and pajama pants, then wrestled off his shirt. They were wet with sweat and reeked of rancid fish stew. He tossed them into the shower and would deal with them later. He managed to roll himself into the tub without breaking bones. The water was too cold so he turned a knob. It ran over his head and down his neck, and when the tub was half full he turned it off and soaked for a long time with his eyes closed. The spinning was relentless. He noticed a clock on the counter. 1:58. He had slept less than three hours. He closed his eyes again, massaged his temples, and waited for the dizziness to go away.

If it was food poisoning, then Giovanna would be just as sick. They ate the same stew, drank the same wine, started with the same martini. He should call her—she was only four doors away. What if she, too, was in the same shape? What if she was dying?

The problem was he couldn't walk. Hell, he was having trouble lying still in the lukewarm bathwater as his head spun like a top. He saw a thick white bathrobe hanging on the door and was determined to get it and cover himself. He slithered and wiggled his way out of the tub, found a towel and dried himself, then yanked the bathrobe off the hook and put it on. Nausea hit again and he stretched out on the cold tile floor and waited for it to pass. He would have vomited violently but his stomach was empty.

He crawled to a credenza, gently lifted the hotel phone, and punched the button for the front desk. There was no answer. He cursed, tried it again. No one. He cursed some more and thought about Samir, his one pal in town who could find a doctor, maybe a hospital. The thought of being put into an ambulance in Tripoli and rushed to a Third World hospital was terrifying, but then so was the idea of being found dead in a hotel so far from home.

He needed water but didn't see a bottle. Five minutes passed, then ten, and he vowed to make it to thirty because by then he would still be alive and getting better, right? His guts were suddenly on fire again and cramping. He leaned to one side and tried not to retch, but he couldn't hold back. The vomit was not last night's dinner; that was already on the floor. Now he was regurgitating blood and water. He called the front desk but no one answered.

He punched the number for Giovanna's room. After four rings she finally said, "Hello, who is this?"

"It's me, Mitch. Are you okay?" She sounded fine, maybe a bit sleepy. With his enflamed throat and dry mouth he sounded like a dying man.

"Well, yes, what's the matter?"

"You're not sick?"

"No."

"I'm in trouble, Giovanna. I think I have food poisoning and I need a doctor. The front desk doesn't answer."

"Okay, I'll be right there." She hung up before he could say anything else. Now, if he could only get to the door to unlock it.

———··———

For the next half hour, he lay on the bare mattress in his bathrobe and tried not to move or speak as Giovanna put cold towels on his neck and forehead. She had stripped off the sheets, blanket, and pillowcases, and piled them on the floor, covering some of the mess he'd made. Samir said he was twenty minutes away.

The nausea was gone, but his stomach and intestines still cramped and contracted. Mitch was in agony one moment, then drifting away to neverland the next.

Samir arrived in a rush, still growling at the desk manager, who followed him and did little but get in the way. He and Samir bickered in Arabic. Behind them were two uniformed medics with a gurney. They spoke to Mitch as Samir translated. They checked his blood pressure—too high. His pulse was 150. He was definitely dehydrated. Samir patted Mitch on the arm and said, "We're going to the hospital, okay, Mitch?"

"Okay. You're going with me, right?"

"Of course. We have a good hospital in the city. Trust me. Don't worry."

They rolled Mitch out of the room, down the hall, and to the elevators, with Samir and Giovanna close behind. Another medic was waiting in the lobby. The ambulance was at the front door. Samir said to Giovanna, "Ride with me. We'll follow." To Mitch he said, "I've called the right doctors. They'll meet us at the hospital."

Mitch kept his eyes closed and nodded. He would remember nothing from his first ride in an ambulance, except for the wailing siren.

With no traffic to contend with, they raced through the streets and within minutes wheeled him into the ER at the Metiga Military Hospital, a complex so modern it would look at home in any American suburb.

"A military hospital?" Giovanna asked.

"Yes, the best in the country. If you have money or connec-tions, you come here. Our generals get the best of everything in Libya."

Without the slightest concern, Samir parked in a no-parking zone. They hustled into the ER and followed the gurney. Mitch was taken into an exam room and tucked into a bed. Nurses and technicians scurried about, and after fearing the worst, he was relieved at the attention and level of care. Samir and Giovanna were allowed into the room. A Dr. Omran appeared bedside and took charge. With a wide smile and a thick accent he said, "Mr. McDeere, I, too, studied at Harvard."

Small world. Mitch managed his first smile in hours and relaxed as much as possible. With Giovanna's help, they tag-teamed through every bite they had eaten not only at dinner but also for lunch. While they talked, two nurses poked him with a needle and hooked him to an IV drip. They checked his vitals and drew a small vial of blood.

Dr. Omran seemed perplexed by the narrative but wasn't worried. "It's not unheard of for one person to get sick while the others are not fazed. It's unusual, but it happens." He looked at Giovanna and said, "There's still a chance you have the bacteria and might not feel well. It can hang around for a day or two."

She said, "No, I feel fine. No symptoms at all."

He spoke in Arabic to the nurses. A technician left to fetch something. To Mitch he said, "Let's try a couple of meds. One to calm the nausea and stop the cramping, another to ease the pain and maybe allow you some sleep."

Both sounded wonderful and Mitch smiled again. In an effort at toughness, he asked, "When can I get out of here?"

"You're being admitted, Mr. McDeere," the doctor said with a smile. "You're not leaving anytime soon."

And he was fine with that. He especially liked the part about the painkiller and a long nap. Cramps were still rolling through his guts. His head was still spinning. He had no desire to do anything but drift away for a few hours. He thought of Abby and the boys and knew they were safe. The last thing they needed was an urgent call from Libya with bad news. He would be fine in a few hours.

Giovanna said, "Mitch, it's almost four A.M. We were supposed to leave at five."

Dr. Omran said, "He's in no condition."

"Can we delay it twenty-four hours?" Mitch asked.

Samir and the doctor stared at each other, then both shook their heads. The doctor said, "I'm not sure I can release you in twenty-four hours. I want to see the blood work."

Samir said, "The trip is approved for today. I would have to go back and ask for another approval. As I've said, the government is getting stricter. For obvious reasons they are not thrilled with this claim by Lannak, and they are approving today's visit only to make themselves look good in court."

Mitch asked, "So, they might not approve another date?"

"Who knows? I think they will, but they'll delay a decision for a few days, just to make us wait. These are bureaucrats, Mitch. Tough guys."

Giovanna said, "I'll go, Mitch. I know the summaries, the checklist, everything. I can handle it. Let's do it and get it over with."

Mitch closed his eyes and endured another wave of cramps. At that moment, he had been in Libya long enough and couldn't wait to leave. He looked at Samir and asked, "And you still think it's safe?"

"Mitch, if I didn't believe so, we would not be here now.

As I've said, I've made the trip a dozen times and never felt threatened."

"And you'll go today?"

"Mitch, I work for you, your firm, and your client. You are in charge. If you want me to accompany the team, then I'll go."

Mitch grunted "Ahh!" and said through clenched teeth, "Diarrhea! Someone get the bedpan!"

Samir and Giovanna found the door and fled down the hallway. They waited and watched a few minutes as orderlies and nurses went in and out of Mitch's room. She finally said, "Let's go back to the hotel. I need to change."

———•—•———

The armored truck was waiting near the front entrance of the hotel. Youssef, the driver, was asleep behind the wheel. He was joined in the cab by the sixth member of the detail, Walid, another Libyan driver brought along in case Youssef needed a nap. He was facing a long day with at least ten hours at the wheel. The four Turks loitered near the street, all smoking, all dressed in desert fatigues and canvas boots.

Samir spoke to them as they waited, then walked away with his phone stuck to his ear. He met Giovanna in the lobby and said, "Dr. Omran thinks I should stay here today and help with Mitch. There might be some complications."

"Such as?"

"Maybe it wasn't food poisoning."

"And that's supposed to be reassuring?"

"You don't have to go, Giovanna. We can try again next week, or maybe in two weeks."

"You're not worried about this trip?"

For the fourth or fifth time, Samir said, "No. You have plenty of security and I'm sure it won't be needed."

"Okay, I'm off. You take care of Mitch."

He pecked her on both cheeks and said, "I'll meet you here for dinner tonight, okay?"

"Lovely. But let's skip the seafood stew."

They both laughed, and he watched her stride purposefully through the revolving door.

CHAPTER 11

The cab of the truck was like a cockpit with two captain's chairs for the drivers. A narrow passageway ran to the back so that the drivers could talk to the passengers if necessary. Unmarked crates of supplies were stacked near the rear door, with more loaded onto a deck above the roof. When Youssef was satisfied that everything was strapped down and secure, he took the wheel and shifted gears.

Giovanna and her bodyguards were in heavily padded chairs that could recline a few inches and were quite comfortable, at least on the paved city streets. Haskel, the leader, explained to Giovanna that the roads were not quite as smooth out in the country. According to him, the truck had been modified to haul Lannak engineers and executives from the city to the bridge and back, and had been used practically every day for years now. Youssef could make the drive in his sleep, which he often did.

Aziz offered her thick Turkish coffee, which smelled delicious as he poured it into a metal cup. Haskel handed her a twisted pastry of some sort, flaky around the edges with a distinct sesame aroma. He explained, "It's called a *kaak*. Very tasty."

Over his shoulder, Youssef said, "My wife makes them all the time for these trips."

"Thanks." She took a bite and smiled her approval.

The city's streets were still dark and empty and it was too early for even a hint of sunlight. Two narrow windows on each side of the cargo hold gave them glimpses of the city. Within minutes, Gau and Abdo were slumped in their seats, eyes firmly closed. After two sips of the coffee, Giovanna knew sleep would not be possible. She nibbled on the Libyan version of a biscuit and tried to absorb her surroundings. Two days earlier she had been at her desk in London, same as always, dressed to kill and not looking forward to another round of dull meetings. Now she was in Tripoli, in the rear of a converted truck, sitting with four heavily armed Turks, and venturing into the desert where she would inspect a billion-dollar bridge to nowhere. She was wearing loose jeans, hiking boots, no makeup whatsoever. She pulled out her cell phone. Haskel noticed this and said, "Service is okay for about an hour, then nothing."

"How do you speak with your construction people at the bridge?"

"A satellite system for phones and internet. You can use it when we get there."

She was worried about Mitch and sent him a text. She did not expect a response. She sent one to Samir, who quickly replied with the news that Mitch was feeling better. He, Samir, planned to spend the day at the hospital. She thought about Luca and decided to wait. Hopefully he was still asleep.

Aziz nodded off, leaving only Haskel to stand guard, though no security was needed at the moment. Boredom hit hard, and Giovanna opened an exciting office memo that purported to summarize the sorry state of modern Libya, or at least since

1969, when Gaddafi pulled off his coup and installed himself as dictator, ruler, and king for life. At the edge of the city, as the highway narrowed, she began to yawn and realized that she had slept less than three hours. Mitch had called near death at 2 A.M. and she had been wired ever since.

She checked her phone. No service. Only four hours to go.

———•—•———

The security guards at the checkpoint were regular Libyan Army. There were five of them, and they had been dead for an hour by the time Youssef made the long turn and the concrete barriers came into view. Their bodies were in the rear of a stolen truck that would soon be burned. Their uniforms were now being worn by their killers.

Youssef saw the guards and said, "Checkpoint. We may have to get out."

Haskel looked at Giovanna and said, "This is the main checkpoint and we usually get out so the guards can have a look inside. It's kind of nice to stretch our legs. There's a restroom of sorts, if needed. Don't worry."

She nodded and said, "I'm okay. Thanks."

The truck stopped. Two guards pointed with their rifles. Youssef and Walid got out and said hello. It was all routine. Another guard opened the rear door and motioned for the four Turks and Giovanna to get out.

"No guns!" the guard shouted in Arabic.

As usual, the Turks left their weapons on their seats and stepped into the sunlight. It was almost 9 A.M. and the desert was already hot. Two men in uniform climbed into the truck and looked around. Minutes dragged on and Youssef began glancing around. He did not recognize the guards, but then they rotated so often. Two of them stood close by with Kalashnikovs, their fingers close to the triggers.

The leader stepped out of the truck holding Haskel's automatic pistol. He waved it at them and yelled, in Arabic, "Hands up, high!"

The four Turks, two Libyans, and Giovanna slowly raised their hands.

"On your knees!" he shouted.

Instead of dropping to his knees, Youssef took a step in the wrong direction and said, "What is this? We have permission!"

The leader aimed the pistol at his face, and from three feet away, pulled the trigger.

———•———

Haskel had called his boss at the Lannak construction camp as they were leaving the city and said they were on schedule to arrive at 10 A.M. This had been standard operating procedure for the entire time the bridge had been under construction. Always plan the trip, nothing spur of the moment, always call ahead, and always call to announce the departure and arrival. Someone with authority was watching and waiting. Most of the highways were safe, but it was Libya, after all, a land of warring tribes that had thrived on conflict for centuries.

At 10:30, the camp called the radio in Youssef's truck, but there was no answer. Same at 10:45 and 11:00. If there had been a breakdown, which were not uncommon, the driver would have called the camp immediately. At 11:05, the camp received a call from the Libyan Army. The message was disturbing: Another truck had stopped at the checkpoint, only to find it deserted. The five army guards were missing, along with their two trucks and two jeeps. There was no sign of another vehicle. The army was sending helicopters and troops to the area.

The search revealed nothing, though it wasn't difficult to hide in the vastness of the Sahara. At 3 P.M., the Lannak executive in charge called Samir, who was at his office. He returned to the hospital to find Mitch napping again, and decided to wait an hour or so before delivering the troubling news.

By 5 P.M., Mitch had forgotten about his food poisoning and was on the phone with Jack Ruch in New York, who in turn had patched in Riley Casey, his counterpart in the London office. With so many details yet to be confirmed, it still seemed inconceivable that an associate of Scully & Pershing could be missing in Libya. But there had been no sign of Giovanna or any of the men with her for twelve hours. And no contact. The nightmare was evolving, and with each passing hour it became grimmer.

The most pressing issue was how to tell her father. Mitch knew he had no choice but to do so himself, and soon, before Luca heard the news from some other source.

At 6:30 P.M., Mitch called Luca in Rome and told him his daughter was missing.

CHAPTER 12

Viewed by most of the world as a pariah state, Gaddafi's Libya struggled to maintain normal diplomatic relations even with its friends. With its enemies, contact on sensitive matters was at best tricky and often impossible. The Turkish ambassador was the first to arrive at the People's Palace for a hurriedly arranged meeting. He spoke with a senior military adviser to Gaddafi and was told that the government was doing everything to find the missing team. Off the record, the ambassador was assured that the government was not involved in the abductions or kidnappings or whatever they were being called at the moment. He left the meeting unsatisfied and with more questions than when he arrived, but that was not unusual when dealing with the regime.

The Italians were next. Given their colonial history, they still maintained formal ties with the government and often did the dirty work for the Westerners who chose to deal with Libya because of its oil. The Italian ambassador spoke with a Libyan general on the phone and was fed the party line: the government was not involved, nor did they know who was, nor did they have any idea where the hostages had been taken. The Libyan Army was scouring the desert. The ambassador immediately called Luca, an acquaintance, and relayed the conversation. For some vague reason, the ambassador was confident Giovanna and the others would be found unharmed.

Neither the British nor the Americans used diplomats when dealing with Libya. After President Reagan bombed the country in 1986, an undeclared state of war had been in effect. After that, any contact with Gaddafi and his minions was complicated and fraught with intrigue. Further compounding the situation was the fact that no American was involved. Giovanna had dual Italian and British citizenship. Scully & Pershing was headquartered in New York, but it was a law firm, a corporation, not a person. Nevertheless, the U.S. State Department and its intelligence services were on high alert, watching the internet and listening to the chatter. And they were hearing nothing. Satellite images had yet to produce anything.

British spies in Tripoli were likewise scrambling for gossip. The details, though, were still vague, and their usually reliable sources knew virtually nothing.

As of 10 P.M. there was still no word from the kidnappers. No one knew what to call them because no one knew who they were. Terrorists, thugs, revolutionaries, tribal warriors, fundamentalists, insurgents, bandits—many descriptions were in play. Since the state controlled the press, there had been no confirmation of the story. Not a single word had been leaked to the Western media.

———•—•———

Samir spent the long, miserable afternoon and evening sitting with Mitch in his hospital room and walking around the parking lot with his phone stuck to his ear. Neither was pleasant. Mitch had been quite ill with what was probably food poisoning. Dr. Omran could find no other cause. The vomiting and diarrhea had finally stopped, because there was nothing left in his system. He was still afraid to eat and had no appetite. His physical problems, though, had vanished with the shocking news of the ambush. Now Mitch was just trying to get out of the hospital.

Samir's contacts with the military police had told him little. He had been assured it was not a government ploy to force Lannak out of the country minus, of course, the $400 million or so it was demanding for the damned bridge. His sources seemed to be in the dark like everyone else. He was suspicious, though, because he hated Gaddafi and knew his capacity for depravity was boundless. He kept such thoughts to himself.

———•—•———

At 11 P.M., Eastern Standard Time, Scully made the decision to extract Mitch McDeere from Tripoli. The firm had an insurance policy that provided emergency evacuation for any of its lawyers who might fall ill in a country with less than desirable health care. Libya qualified. Jack Ruch called the insurance company, which had already been notified and was standing by. He then called Mitch, for the third time, and they haggled over the details. Mitch wanted to stay because he didn't want to leave without Giovanna. On the other hand, he wanted to leave because he still felt awful and never wanted to set foot on Libyan soil again. He had talked to Abby twice and she was adamant that he get out as soon as possible. Ruch argued, in clear and forceful language, that Mitch couldn't do a damned thing to help find Giovanna and her security team and he'd be foolish to try.

At 6:30 A.M., Saturday, April 16, Mitch was placed in a wheelchair and rolled out of the hospital and into an ambulance. Samir stayed by his side, as did a nurse. Forty minutes later, they stopped on the tarmac in a section of the airfield not seen or used by the general public. Half a dozen corporate jets were parked and watched by armed security guards. A silver Gulfstream 600 was waiting. Mitch insisted on walking up the steps and boarding under his own power. A doctor and a nurse were waiting and immediately strapped him to a comfortable gurney. He shook hands with Samir and said goodbye.

His pulse and blood pressure were too high, but that was not unusual, given the excitement of the past hour. His temperature was slightly elevated. He drank a cup of ice water but turned down some crackers. The doctor asked if he wanted to sleep and he said yes, by all means. The nurse handed him two pills, with some more water, and he was snoring before the Gulfstream took off.

The flight to Rome was one hour and fifty minutes. He did not wake up until the doctor patted his arm and said it was time to disembark. With the help of one of the pilots, he managed to descend the steps and crawl into the rear of another ambulance.

At Gemelli Hospital in central Rome, Mitch was taken to a private room and examined again. Everything was normal and the doctor said he would be released before noon. After the nurses left, a Scully partner named Roberto Maggi entered the room and said hello. The two had met several times over the years but were not close. He had been with Luca all afternoon and they were, of course, in shock. Luca had not been feeling well before the news. Now, he was sedated and under the care of his doctor.

Mitch, wide awake and suddenly hungry, replayed every step he and Giovanna had taken in Tripoli. None of the information was helpful. He knew less about the abductions than Roberto. Evidently, the Libyan authorities were either still in the dark or simply not talking. As far as anyone knew, the kidnappers had yet to call.

Roberto left and promised to be back in a few hours to help Mitch with his discharge. A nurse brought a bowl of chopped fruit, a diet soda, and some crackers. Mitch ate slowly, then called Abby again and reported that he was resting comfortably in a nice hospital room in Rome and feeling much better.

She was watching cable news and monitoring the internet and had seen nothing out of Libya.

CHAPTER 13

The news blackout ended dramatically when the four Turks were found with their heads cut off. They were naked and hanging by their feet from a cable running between two storage buildings a mile from the bridge. Their flesh was slashed, burned, and bloodied, and it was safe to assume they had suffered greatly before being decapitated. Nearby was a large oil drum with a plank across its top. On the plank, in a neat row, were the four heads.

Haskel, Gau, Abdo, Aziz.

The Lannak security guard who found them early that morning did not attempt to match the heads with the bodies. Someone far smarter than him would be given that task.

There was no sign of Youssef, Walid, or Giovanna. No sign of the murderers. No note, no demand, nothing. The Lannak security guards at the bridge heard nothing, but the nearest one was at least a hundred yards away. There was little security left because the company was pulling people off the site and sending them home. The construction was practically finished. All closed-circuit cameras in the area had been dismantled.

The four beheadings would no doubt encourage the company to retreat even faster.

A Libyan official quickly sealed off the area and prohibited anyone from taking photos and videos of the scene. His orders from Tripoli were to keep everyone, including Lannak employees, away from the bodies. Such a gruesome sight would go viral in an instant and only embarrass the government. The story, though, could not be buried, and before noon Tripoli released a statement confirming the murders and kidnappings. There was still no word from the "terrorists." In its first effort at disinformation, the regime said the attack "was believed to be the work of a notorious tribal gang headquartered in Chad." The Libyan authorities vowed to find the outlaws and bring them to justice, after, of course, it found the other hostages.

———•—•———

Mitch was leaving the hospital in a car with Roberto Maggi when the call came. An associate in their Rome office had just seen the news out of Tripoli. The government was confirming the abduction of Giovanna Sandroni, along with two Libyan employees of Lannak. Their whereabouts were unknown. Their Turkish security team had been murdered.

They drove to Luca's villa in the Trastevere neighborhood, in south-central Rome, and found him sitting alone on the veranda under the shade of an umbrella pine, wrapped in a quilt and gazing at a fountain in the small courtyard. A nurse sat by the open double-doors. He smiled at Mitch and waved at an empty chair.

"It's good to see you, Mitch," he said. "I'm glad you're okay."

Roberto said, "I'll be inside, Luca," and disappeared.

Mitch asked, "How are you?"

He shrugged and took his time. "Still fighting. I've been on the phone all morning with my best contacts in Libya, and I'm not getting much."

"Could it be Gaddafi?"

"That's always a possibility. He's a madman and capable of anything. But I have my doubts. They just found five dead soldiers, Libyan Army, the guards at the checkpoint. All shot in the head, bodies burned. I doubt Gaddafi would kill his own men, but then one never knows."

"Why would he kill Lannak employees?"

"Intimidation, perhaps."

A well-dressed woman of about fifty appeared and asked Mitch if he wanted something to drink. He asked for an espresso and she walked away.

Luca ignored her and continued, "Gaddafi owes Lannak at least four hundred million dollars for his beautiful bridge in the desert. The price of oil is down. The Libyans are always out of cash because Gaddafi wants stockpiles of weapons. He just ordered forty more MiGs from the Russians." His voice trailed off and he lit a cigarette. He was pale and looked ten years older than he had two weeks earlier.

Mitch wanted to say something about Giovanna but couldn't bear to bring up the subject. His espresso arrived on a small tray and he thanked the woman.

When she was gone, Luca exhaled a cloud of smoke and said, "That's Bella, my friend."

Luca usually had a lady friend around.

He said, "Something told me not to let her go, Mitch. I didn't like the idea but she insisted. Giovanna's tired of London and I'm afraid she might be growing tired of the law. She wanted an adventure. She was home last Christmas and I talked too much, talked about the bridge Gaddafi built in the desert, and my client Lannak, a great company from Turkey. It was all cocktail talk, the way lawyers do, nothing confidential. I had no idea she would want to go there. And she couldn't, as long as I had the case. Then I got sick, called you, and here we are, Mitch. Here we are."

Mitch sipped his espresso and decided to just listen. He had nothing to add.

"How are you, Mitch?"

He shrugged and waved him off. With the body count now at nine—five burned bodies and four decapitations—it seemed almost silly to dwell on a bad case of food poisoning.

"I'm fine," he said. "Physically."

Luca had two phones on the table and one began vibrating. He picked it up, looked at it, said, "It's from the Libyan embassy in Milan. I need to take it."

"Of course."

Mitch walked inside and saw Roberto crouched over a laptop on a table in the kitchen. He waved Mitch over and said quietly, "There's a video that's going viral. Someone filmed the four dead Turks. The news stations are not showing it but it's everywhere else right now. You want to see it?"

"I don't know."

"It's graphic. Is your system still a bit fragile?"

"Let's see it."

Roberto slid the laptop around and hit a key. The video was shot with a cell phone and whoever took it was very close to the bodies. So close that he was told to stand back because of the blood that had pooled beneath each victim. It ran for thirty seconds and was abruptly stopped when someone began yelling in Arabic.

Mitch stood erect, felt another knot in his stomach, and said, "I wouldn't tell Luca."

"I'm not, but he'll probably see it anyway."

New York was six hours behind Rome. Mitch called Abby, who had been monitoring the news reports. So far there was nothing from Libya. Bad news from North Africa didn't sell well in the United States. However, the British and Europeans were far more interested. When the London tabloids got the story of a young British lawyer kidnapped in Libya by a ruthless gang that, at the same time, decapitated her bodyguards, the online reports ran wild. At the Scully & Pershing office in Canary Wharf, security was quickly beefed up, not out of fear of more terrorist attacks, but to protect the staff from an assault by the British press.

Mitch and Roberto had lunch with Luca on the veranda, though he ate almost nothing. Mitch, now ravenous, devoured everything in sight. It was clear that he was feeling much better and Luca said, "Mitch, I want you to go home. I'll call when I need you. There's nothing for you to do now."

"I'm sorry this happened, Luca. I should have been there."

"Be thankful you were not, my friend." He nodded at Roberto, who said, "We've gone back thirty years and reviewed every case involving Westerners taken hostage in Muslim countries. We're still digging. Almost all of the women survived and very few were mistreated. Their captivities ranged from two weeks to six years, but virtually every one got out, either by ransom, rescue, or escape. The men are a different story. Almost all were physically abused and about half did not survive. Forty that we know of are still captive. So, yes, Mitch, be thankful you had a good round of food poisoning."

"Is there a chance of a diplomatic resolution?" Mitch asked.

Luca shook his head. "Doubtful. We don't know the enemy as of now, but it's probably safe to say they don't care much for diplomacy."

"So it's rescue or ransom?"

"Yes, and we shouldn't dwell on rescue. That's always incredibly dangerous. The Brits will kick into high gear and want an elaborate military-style operation. The Italians will want to pay the money. Anyway, it's premature. Right now all we can do is sit and wait for the phone call."

"I'm sorry, Luca," Mitch said again. "We thought we were safe."

"So did I. As you know, I've traveled there many times. I love Libya, in spite of its instability."

"Samir felt sure we were safe."

"You can't trust Samir, Mitch. He's a Libyan agent and he reports to the military police."

Mitch swallowed hard and tried to keep a poker face. "I thought he worked for us."

"He works for anyone who'll pay him. Samir has no loyalty whatsoever."

Roberto added, "He was supposed to be with Giovanna, Mitch, but he found an excuse to stay at the hospital with you."

Mitch said, "Now I'm really confused."

Luca managed a smile and said, "Mitch, in Libya, you trust no one."

CHAPTER 14

Nothing changed in the twelve hours it took KLM to fly Mitch from Rome to Amsterdam to New York. There was one seat left on a direct flight to JFK, but it was back in coach and Mitch needed the legroom up in business class. He also needed easier access to the restrooms. His stomach was rumbling again and he feared a sudden eruption. After what his system had been through over the past four days, he left nothing to chance. Along the way he called Abby twice and caught up with family matters and neighborhood gossip. He called Roberto Maggi to check on Luca, who was resting. There was no word out of Libya, nothing from the kidnappers. He called his secretary and reorganized his schedule. Over the Atlantic, he took a sleeping pill that barely knocked off the edge but eventually led to a fitful thirty-minute nap. When he woke up, he made calls to his paralegal and two associates.

He tried not to think of Giovanna, though it was impossible. How were they treating her? Where were they hiding her? Was she getting food and water? Was she being interrogated, injured, abused? The law of the jungle accepted the torture and murder of armed men who had been trained with weapons and expected to do their own killing, but not an innocent civilian. Especially a young female lawyer who was just along for the ride.

The ride? Mitch simmered at the hubris and foolishness of dashing off to a country known for its instability and danger, and including Giovanna as a favor to her father. Of course, Luca had suggested the trip and assured him they would be safe, but Mitch was no rookie and could have insisted on other arrangements. He had asked himself, more than once, if a visit to the bridge was actually necessary. The answer was: probably not. Had he been overly excited about the adventure? Yes. He had never been to Libya and had been too eager to add it to his list of countries he'd visited.

Killing time in the Amsterdam airport, he had called Cory Gallant, Scully's chief of security. When Mitch joined Scully eleven years earlier he was unaware that it had its own little army of security experts. He learned that most firms in the world of Big Law spend a fortune not only to protect their partners but to investigate their enemies, even their own clients. Before leaving for Rome and Tripoli, Mitch had been briefed by Cory on the situation in Libya. Gallant had traveled to the bridge with Luca a year earlier. In his opinion, the trip was only slightly risky. It was in the best interest of the Libyans to protect all foreign businessmen and professionals.

Cory was waiting outside the baggage claim at JFK with a driver, a thick young man who took Mitch's bags and hauled them to a black SUV parked illegally near the cabs. He got behind the wheel as Mitch and Cory settled into the rear seats. A plexiglass panel separated them from the driver.

It was almost 8 P.M., Sunday, April 17, and the traffic out of JFK was brutal as usual.

After describing the joys of a twelve-hour journey, Mitch asked, "Any news from over there?"

"Not much."

"Not much? That sounds like more than nothing, which is what we had a few hours ago."

"There's been a development."

"Go on."

"There's another video. We found it about an hour ago on the deep web. The kidnappers videoed the decapitations."

Mitch exhaled and looked out the window.

Cory continued, "Live and in color. Horribly graphic. I saw it and I wish I had not. These are nasty boys."

"I'm not sure I want to see it."

"You don't, believe me, Mitch. Please don't watch it. It has nothing to do with Giovanna, other than the fact that she's being held by some sick and sadistic people."

"That's supposed to be comforting?"

"No."

The traffic was moving and they did not speak for a moment. Mitch asked, "Can you maybe describe it without going into too much detail?"

"They used a chain saw and made the others watch. The last one, a man named Aziz, saw his three buddies lose their heads before he lost his."

Mitch threw up both hands and said, "Okay, okay."

"It's the worst thing I've ever seen."

"I knew Aziz. I knew all four of them. We met the day before at the Lannak office in Tripoli and they briefed us on the trip. They had no worries at all, said they went to the bridge and back all the time."

Cory nodded sadly and said, "I guess they were wrong."

Mitch closed his eyes and tried not to think about Aziz,

Haskel, Gau, and Abdo. He tried not to think about the image of them hanging by their feet. His stomach flipped again as his pulse went haywire. He mumbled, "Sorry I asked."

"I've seen a lot, but this is something else."

"Got it. Any word out of Washington?"

"Our people there have talked to contacts at State, the CIA, NSA. Everybody's scrambling and nobody's hearing anything. For a lot of reasons we don't have a lot of good sources in Libya. Gaddafi has never been too friendly. The Brits have stronger contacts, as do the Italians, and, of course, she belongs to them. The Turks are raising hell. The situation is extremely volatile and unpredictable and no one is in charge. We can't just go barging in, as we so often do."

"How valuable is she?"

"Depends on who has her, I guess. If it's really some splinter group of terrorists or a renegade militia with big plans, then it'll be a demand for ransom. A few million bucks might be sufficient. But if it's Gaddafi, then who knows? He might use her as a bargaining chip to settle the lawsuit."

Mitch said, "Sure, she could save him some real cash."

"That's your department, Mitch."

"If it's Gaddafi, it's a pretty stupid move because Lannak will not settle. The company has been furious for two years because of non-payment. Now, with four of its security guards murdered, they'll want even more money. And the court will give it to them, in my opinion. Giovanna, of course, gets caught in the crossfire."

"Well, the early speculation out of Washington is that it's not Gaddafi. He may be crazy but he's not stupid. Anyway, we have a briefing at seven in the morning with our guys in Washington, a teleconference. Jack Ruch's office."

"I'm not going to be there at seven in the morning, Cory. Rearrange the schedule."

"Mr. Ruch said seven."

"I'm taking my sons to school in the morning and I'll be in the office around eight-thirty, my usual time. Sure, this is an important matter, but holding an urgent meeting at seven tomorrow morning, here in New York, will not do a damned thing to help Giovanna."

"Yes, sir. I'm sure Mr. Ruch will call you."

"Oh, he calls all the time and I usually do what he says."

———— . . ————

Carter and Clark were in their pajamas and enjoying an extra hour of television as they waited for their father. Mitch walked through the door shortly before nine and they raced to greet him. He picked them up, tossed them on a sofa, and went for their ribs. When both were laughing and yelling, Abby finally intervened with her usual concerns about the neighbors. When things were quieter, Carter seized the moment and asked, "Hey, Dad, can we stay up until ten?"

"No sir," Abby said.

"Of course you can," Mitch said. "And let's make some popcorn." Both boys raced toward the kitchen as Mitch attempted to kiss his wife.

"Popcorn for dinner?" she asked.

"It beats airplane food."

"Welcome home. There's leftover manicotti in the fridge."

"Rosario Brothers?"

"Yes, they were here last night. It may be the best manicotti I've ever tasted."

"We'll save it. I'm not that hungry and my system is, shall we say, unstable again."

"We have a lot to discuss."

"Indeed we do."

When the boys were wrapped in quilts and stuffing popcorn in their mouths, Mitch and Abby eased away and went to the kitchen. She poured two glasses of wine and gave her husband a proper kiss. "Any word?" she asked softly.

"Nothing on Giovanna."

"I assume you've heard about the video."

Mitch closed his eyes and grimaced. "Which one?"

"You know Gina Nelligan? Teaches art at the upper school."

Mitch was shaking his head. *No.*

"Her son is a junior at Purdue. He called home an hour or so ago, told her about the video on the deep web."

"The beheadings?"

"Yes. Have you watched it?"

"No. Don't plan to. Our security guy described it for me. That's enough."

"Did you know those men, the guards?"

"Yes, I met them the day before they were murdered. They were going with us to the bridge, along with two Libyan drivers and Giovanna. All of us in one secured vehicle."

"I can't believe it, Mitch. And that poor girl. They have no idea where she is?"

"Nothing, not a clue, but we expect that will change. She's worth a lot of money and her kidnappers will make contact at some point."

"You hope."

"Yes, no one is certain of anything right now."

"Well, I'm certain that you're not going back to Libya. Agreed?"

"Agreed."

"Let's go sit with the boys."

By nine-thirty the boys were yawning and Abby hustled them to bed. Mitch helped tuck them in and said good night. He turned off the television as she topped off their wineglasses. They sat together on the sofa and enjoyed the quiet.

She said, "As you might know, there's a lot of press, especially in the U.K. I've been online for hours trying to find whatever I can. Plenty of stories here and in Rome. Scully and Pershing is mentioned over and over, but so far I have not seen your name."

"Nor have I. My secretary and two paralegals are also searching."

"So you're worried?"

"I'm worried about Giovanna, of course. I take some of the blame for what's happened, Abby. It was my trip, my little fact-finding mission, one I asked for and was in charge of."

"I thought Luca told you to go."

"He suggested that I go but the decision was mine. He wanted his daughter to associate on the case because she was bored in London and looking for something more exciting. Looking back, the whole idea made little sense."

"Got it, but I was thinking more about us. Are you worried about the law firm?"

"Our safety?"

"Well, yes, I guess."

"No, not at all. More than likely the kidnappers are members of a tribal militia that roams the Sahara looking for trouble. They are far away and not that sophisticated."

"You hope."

Mitch took a sip of wine and rubbed her leg. "Sure, Abby, we're very much in the dark here. We should learn more tomorrow, and the next day. When it's time to worry, I'll let you know. Now, it's too early."

"I think I've heard that before."

CHAPTER 15

Whatever they were—criminals or terrorists—they had a flair for the dramatic. Four days after ransacking the checkpoint and murdering five army guards, and three days after taking a chain saw to the necks of the Turkish security team, and two days after releasing their video into the vastness of the deep web, they hung Youssef's body on a telephone pole next to a busy highway in Benghazi. He was found, head attached but with a gaping hole in it, bloody and stripped of all clothing, bound at the wrists and ankles, turning slowly at the end of a thick wire as the sun came up. A note was attached to his right ankle with a piece of string. It read: *Youssef Ashour, Traitor.*

The military police swarmed the area, blocked all roads and highways, and let him hang for hours as they waited for orders. Perhaps there would be another video of the murder that might yield some clues.

Samir went to the scene, confirmed that it was indeed Youssef, a man he'd known for years, and called Lannak, then Luca.

Only Walid and Giovanna were left, as far as anyone knew.

——— • • ———

Cory Gallant took the call at four in the morning, and after only three hours of light sleep had no trouble rolling out of bed and going to the office. He was waiting outside Mitch's office at eight-thirty when he arrived.

One look and Mitch knew the news was not good.

"There's been another development," Cory said abruptly.

"I'm beginning to hate the word 'development.'"

"Mr. Ruch is waiting."

On the elevator, Cory told Mitch everything he knew about Youssef, which was little more than the location and condition of his corpse. It had been found about nine hours earlier and, not surprisingly, there had been no word from the people who strung him up.

——— • • ———

Jack Ruch was irritated because he'd wanted the teleconference at 7 A.M., which did not fit with Mitch's schedule. Ruch still worked sixteen hours a day and was known for predawn meetings to prove his toughness. Mitch had lost all patience for such shows of machismo at Scully.

Ruch pointed to a conference table as he glanced at a large screen high on the wall. Nonstop cable news was covering an earthquake but, thankfully, it was muted. Nothing, yet, from Libya. A secretary poured coffee and Ruch said, "I assume Cory has given you the latest."

"I got the elevator version," Mitch replied.

"That's about all we have as of now." He glanced at the screen again as if expecting more news at any moment. The secretary left the room and closed the door. Ruch cracked his knuckles, looked at Mitch, and asked, "Have you spoken to Lannak this morning?"

"Not yet. It's first on my list."

"Get it done. They're rattled and very upset. Their in-house counsel is Denys Tullos."

"I know him."

"Good. I talked to him last night. The company is trying to get the four bodies back home and the Libyans are not cooperating, still pissed about the lawsuit. Everyone is. Lannak wants its money, and now it wants a lot more because of Libya's failure to protect foreign workers, something it has always promised. So, the lawsuit will probably be amended to seek more damages. When is it likely to go to trial?"

"Months, maybe a year from now. Who knows?"

"Okay. I want you to step on the gas, Mitch, and get this case before the judges. Lannak is a valuable client, paid us something like sixteen million in fees last year. Make plans to meet with them in the next week or so to make them feel better."

"Got it."

"How big is your team?"

"Well, I had two associates, including Giovanna. Now I'm not so sure. Roberto Maggi in Rome will stay on."

"Okay. We'll discuss personnel later. Right now we have a much bigger problem. A Scully associate has been kidnapped in Libya and we have to do everything possible to get her released. You know Benson Wall, our manager in Washington?"

"Yes, I've met him."

"Benson will join us in a moment by video. We have three partners in D.C. who worked in either State or CIA, so we have some contacts. Ever heard of an outfit called Crueggal?"

"Sounds like a breakfast cereal."

"Far from it. Cory."

Cory expertly took the handoff and didn't miss a beat. "You won't find the company on the internet or anywhere else. It's a bunch of ex-spooks and military intel experts who operate around the world as a super-security firm on par with MI6, Mossad, CIA, KGB, and so on. They tend to go where the trouble is, so they spend a lot of time in the Middle East. Without a doubt they are the best at handling a hostage situation involving a Westerner. They've had plenty of practice and a good record."

"And we've hired them?" Mitch asked.

"Yes."

Ruch said, "Because we operate globally, and go into some places that are not as safe as we'd like, we carry a lot of insurance, Mitch. Hostage negotiators, ransom, stuff like that."

"Military operations?"

"Not covered. And not expected."

Cory said, "The quickest way to get a hostage killed is to send in the dogs."

"The dogs?"

"Hotshots with guns and itchy fingers, cops or special ops or otherwise. Diplomacy, negotiation, and money work much better in these situations. Ever heard of K and R insurance?"

"Maybe."

"Kidnap and ransom. It's a huge industry and most big insurance companies offer it."

Ruch said, "We've carried it for years but it's a secret. We don't talk about it because the kidnappers might get excited if they know we're insured."

"So I'm covered?"

"We're all covered."

"For how much? What am I worth?"

Cory looked at Ruch and said nothing. The answer had to come from the boss.

"Twenty-five million," Jack said. "Costs us a hundred grand a year."

"Sounds like plenty. Just out of curiosity, what's a hostage like Giovanna worth on the open market?"

Cory said, "Who knows? Throw a dart. There is a strong rumor that two years ago the French government paid thirty-eight million for a journalist being held in Somalia, denied of course. Five years ago the Spanish paid twenty million for an aid worker in Syria. But France and Spain will negotiate. Britain, Italy, and the U.S. will not, at least not officially. And there is rarely a clear line between what is a criminal gang and what's a terrorist outfit."

Ruch said, "That's where Crueggal comes in. We've hired them, and we convinced our insurance company to use them as well."

"Who's our insurance company?"

"DGMX."

"DGMX? How creative."

"It's a sub of a big British insurer," Cory said.

"Anyway," Ruch said, tiring of the small talk, "we have Benson Wall and a man named Darian Kasuch on the line. He's an Israeli American who runs Crueggal worldwide."

He tapped the keyboard and a screen at the end of the table came to life. Two faces appeared. Benson Wall and Darian Kasuch. Both were about fifty years old. Both stared awkwardly at the camera on their end.

Ruch made quick introductions. Mr. Wall ran Scully's D.C. office with two hundred lawyers. He said little more than "Hello." Mr. Kasuch didn't even bother with that and took off with "There is no shortage of gangs that roam southern Libya, far away from Tripoli and Benghazi. They fight each other for territory but they all hate Gaddafi and at least two or three are usually planning a coup. As you know, he has survived eight attempts since he took power in 1969 and needs about ten thousand loyal soldiers to protect himself. When his enemies are not plotting to kill him, they meddle and make trouble as best they can. Kidnapping is common and it's a profitable way for the gangs to make a buck. They like to snatch oil field workers, maybe get lucky and get an executive with British Petroleum every now and then, and it's usually all about money. Having said that, there are some unusual aspects of this one that are disturbing. First is the appalling amount of bloodshed already on the ground. Ten dead so far."

Darian had close-cropped gray hair, tanned leathery skin, and the hard unblinking stare of a man who'd lived in dangerous shadows and seen his share of dead bodies. Mitch was glad they were on the same team.

He continued, "This is unusual for the work of a criminal gang, more typical of terrorists. The second point is that the latest victim, the truck driver, was found very close to Benghazi. The gangs seldom go near the big cities. These two factors alone indicate that we might be dealing with a new, more ominous threat."

He paused and Mitch asked, "So, you don't think it's Gaddafi?"

"No, and for several reasons. The most obvious is that his regime has dealt with foreign companies for the past thirty-five years without this type of violence. The Libyans need foreign workers and have done a good job of protecting everyone. Lannak has been there for twenty years without a serious incident. Why attack them now? Because the government is angry over the lawsuit? Doubtful. Lawsuits come and go and they always get settled. How many projects has Lannak completed in Libya?"

"Eight," Mitch replied.

"And how many times was the company forced to sue the government?"

"Five."

"And of that number how many were eventually settled?"

"All five went to trial and Lannak won them all. After the court orders were entered, the cases were settled."

Darian nodded slightly as if he, too, knew the numbers. "My point exactly. You take them to trial, you win an award, they stall and stall, then you convince the court to impose sanctions. The Libyans don't like the word 'sanctions' and they usually settle, right?"

"It's not quite that simple," Mitch said. "Some of the settlements were for a lot less than Lannak was entitled to. It's hardball litigation."

"Understood, but it's the way of doing business over there. The Libyans have been through it many times and know the routine. Why would they suddenly decide to start killing people? So, to answer your question, we have ruled out, for the moment, any involvement by the regime. It's too risky for them. They can't survive if foreign companies get scared and run away."

Darian was convincing and Mitch had nothing to argue.

He continued, "We have people on the ground in Tripoli and we're digging. We have a couple of suspects, but I'm not prepared to discuss them remotely. One problem right now is that half the spies and double agents in the world are snooping around Libya, desperate for intelligence. The Brits, Turks, Italians, even the Libyans. And of course the Americans can't wait to get in the middle of it. But we should have something to talk about by late afternoon. I can meet in our Manhattan office tomorrow at eight in the morning. Does that work?"

Everybody nodded and Jack said, "Yes, we'll be there."

————•——•————

It was raining when Mitch left the office that afternoon. Rain in the city usually made a mess of things, which was taken in stride by New Yorkers accustomed to surviving in all sorts of weather. Rain never bothered Mitch, except on game days. If the Bruisers had a game, then rain was catastrophic.

While he was on the subway, it had gone from a hard drizzle to a downpour, and there would be no chance of a game in Central Park. He entered their apartment at five-thirty and was met with the sad scene of Clark and Carter sitting side-by-side on the sofa, in full Bruiser uniforms, one holding a baseball, the other a glove, staring at the television. They were too deflated to say hello to their father.

"Rough bunch," Mitch whispered to Abby as he pecked her on the cheek.

"I suppose it's still raining out there."

"Pouring. No chance of a game."

"I really wanted to get them out of the house."

Carter tossed the baseball into a chair and walked over to hug his father. He appeared to be near tears and said, "I was supposed to pitch, Dad."

"I know, but that's baseball. Even the Mets get rained out occasionally. The game will be made up this Saturday."

"Promise?"

"I promise it will if it doesn't rain again."

"I guess you can take those uniforms off," Abby said.

"I have a better idea," Mitch said. "Leave the uniforms on.

Let's call the whole team, all the Bruisers, tell them to keep their uniforms on, and meet at Santo's for pizza."

Clark bounced off the sofa with a big smile.

"Great idea, Dad," Carter said.

"Tell them to bring umbrellas," Abby said.

CHAPTER 16

Giovanna was fourteen years old when her parents divorced. She loved them both and they adored her, their only daughter and youngest child, but when the marriage began to crack Luca and Anita thought it best to remove their children from the hostilities. They sent Sergio, their son, to a prep school in England and Giovanna to one in Switzerland, and when they were out of the way the parents fought some more, then grew weary of it and signed agreements. Anita moved out of the villa and gave up all claims to it. It had been in Luca's family for decades and Italian matrimonial law leaned heavily in his favor.

Anita took some money and a vacation home on Sardinia, and left Rome to try to put things back together. By the time she left, Luca had already arranged for his girlfriend, and future wife number two, to move in. The transition was another good reason for Giovanna to stay away.

She watched this from afar, grateful to be in Switzerland. She still loved her father, but at the time she didn't really like him. They had never been close, primarily because of his ambition to build the greatest law firm in Italy. His drive kept him at the office or on the road far too often. Her brother, Sergio, was so turned off by Luca's routine that he vowed never to become professional at anything. Currently he was living in Guatemala, drifting and painting street scenes in the city of Antigua.

Nor had she been close to her mother, Anita, who was a beautiful woman and watched with growing envy as Giovanna became just as beautiful. She competed with her daughter in fashion, style, weight, height, almost everything. Anita could not accept the realities of aging and grew more resentful as her daughter blossomed and grew taller and thinner. They had great mother-daughter times together, but there was always the undercurrent of competition.

When Anita realized her husband had a girlfriend, she was crushed and ran to her teenage daughter for support. Giovanna wasn't prepared to deal with such chaotic emotions and pushed her away. For a long time she avoided her father, but there was always the nagging suspicion that she really couldn't blame him for looking around. To get away from both of them, she embraced the idea of boarding school.

When Luca's second marriage blew up, Anita was elated and wished him even worse luck. Giovanna was turned off by her mother's gloating and tried to ignore both parents. During her last two years of boarding school she did not see either one. When they mentioned attending her graduation, she vowed to disappear and hide.

With time, most of the pain and anger dissipated. Luca, always quite the statesman, managed to patch things up with Giovanna. He was, after all, paying her college bills. When she started talking about law school, he was elated and made sure the right doors were opened. Anita found happiness in a serious boyfriend, a slightly older man with more money than

Luca. He was Karlo, a wealthy Greek, and he had been through enough marriages to understand the need for tranquility. He would never marry again, but he, like Luca, would always adore women. He insisted on meeting Luca, and eventually brokered a truce between the exes.

———·—·———

Luca and Anita sat on the veranda, under quilts and sipping tea as the sun set. The night air was chilly but pleasant. The wide doors were open and, just inside them, in the breakfast room, Karlo played backgammon with Bella, Luca's current companion. All spoke in low voices, and for long stretches of time the only sound was the tumbling of dice across the board. It was all so civilized.

As always, Luca had not been entirely forthcoming with Anita. He admitted he had pulled strings to get their daughter assigned to the Lannak case, but he had said nothing about encouraging Mitch to take her to Tripoli. Nor would he.

For Anita's benefit, he was projecting the image of the wise old veteran who knew Libya inside and out and was confident Giovanna would survive this ordeal. Whether or not this soothed her mother was not clear. Anita was high-strung, emotional, and overly dramatic. Perhaps age, along with Karlo's steady influence, had softened some of the edges and settled her down. Perhaps it was the pills she was taking in the bathroom. Whatever the reason, she had surprised Luca hours earlier with the phone call, said she was in Rome with Karlo and thought it was important for the parents to support one another. Could they stop by for a visit and maybe dinner? Luca thought it was a wonderful idea.

And so they sat together as the day turned to night, and

recalled warm and funny stories of their little girl. They did not dwell on what was happening to her now; that was too awful to contemplate. With long pauses in their conversation, time to reflect and remember, they dwelt on the past. And they had regrets. Their tumultuous breakup was entirely Luca's fault, and he had said so before. He'd made a mess of his family. His self-ishness had led to Giovanna's desire to leave home and get away from them. Contrition, though, was not his strong suit, and he would not apologize again. So much had happened since then.

———— • • ————

At least she was alive. And she was no longer being held in a tent in the desert. Her first two nights in captivity had been unpleasant; sleeping on a dirty mat on top of a dirty quilt that served as the floor; watching the sides of the tent ripple and shake in the howling wind; surviving on one bottle of water and nothing to eat; cowering when her masked kidnappers entered her little space. After that they wrapped a coarse fabric around her head and led her outside to a vehicle where they shoved her under boxes and began moving. They drove for hours, the only sounds being the engine and transmission grinding away. When they stopped she heard voices, the quick, sharp exchanges of men under pressure. When they stopped again the engine died and the men dragged her out quickly and led her a few steps to a building. She could see nothing, but there were sounds. The honk of a car horn. A radio or television in the distance. Then they untied her hands and left her so she could remove the shroud. Her new room had a floor that was not sand. There were no windows. There was a narrow bed of the size and design of a military cot and a small table with a dim lamp, the only light. In one corner there was a large tin pot where, she guessed, she was expected to relieve herself. The temperature was neither warm nor cold. The first night she assumed it was dark, though she had no idea. She slept off and on but hunger pangs kept her awake. Occasionally she heard muted voices in the hall, or whatever was out there.

A door opened and a veiled woman with a tray of food entered, nodded, and placed the tray on the table. She nodded again and left the room. The door lock clicked as she pulled it. A bowl of dried fruit—oranges, cherries, figs, and three thin slices of a bread that was similar to tortillas.

Giovanna ate like a refugee and drank half the bottle of water. The hunger pangs dissipated but she needed more food. Evidently, they had no plans to starve her to death. She hadn't thought much about their plans because of her hunger, but now that her body felt more normal her thoughts returned to the possibilities. None were pleasant. There had been no hint of physical or sexual assault. Other than a few grunts here and there, they had not spoken to her in the past twenty-four hours. She had heard no language other than Arabic, of which she knew almost nothing. Did they plan to interrogate her? If so, what did they hope to get? She was a lawyer. She could discuss their legal strategies, but it was difficult to believe that these guys cared much about the law.

And so she waited. With nothing to read, see, do, and no one to talk to, she tried to remember the most important cases in American constitutional law. First Amendment—freedom of speech: *Schenck, Debs, Gitlow, Chaplinsky, Tinker.* Second Amendment—right to bear arms: *Miller, Tatum.* Third Amendment? It was useless because it protected citizens from being forced to house soldiers, barely a footnote in history. The Supreme Court had never considered a challenge to the amendment. Fourth Amendment—unreasonable searches and seizures:

Weeks, Mapp, Terry, Katz, Rakas, Vernonia. The Fourth had always been laden with controversy.

She had aced Con Law at Virginia not too many years ago, primarily because she could memorize almost anything. During her final exam, she cited three hundred cases.

Law school was now far away. She heard voices and braced for a knock on the door. The voices faded and disappeared.

She had no idea what had happened to the others. After the horror of watching Youssef get shot in the face, she was thrown to the ground, handcuffed, blindfolded, dragged away, and thrown into the back of a truck. She was aware that other bodies were nearby—live bodies grunting, groaning, breathing. Probably the Turks. She lost all concept of time, but not long afterward she was removed and separated from the other hostages.

She could only hope and pray they were safe, but she had doubts.

CHAPTER 17

By 6:30 A.M. Mitch was well into his second cup of strong coffee and deep into the internet. For the third morning, he went from one tabloid to the next and marveled at how the Brits could make so much out of so little. The story itself was certainly newsworthy—an associate in the London office of the world's largest law firm kidnapped by murderous thugs in Libya—but the scarcity of real facts did nothing to throttle the breathless headlines, photography, and speculation. If the facts were insufficient to carry a story, others were simply created on the fly. The thugs were demanding ten million pounds in ransom, or was it twenty? There was a deadline three days away before Giovanna would be executed, or was it four? She had been spotted in Cairo, or maybe it was Tunis. She had been targeted because of her father's shenanigans with Libyan oil companies. A nut claiming to be an ex-boyfriend said she had always professed admiration for Muammar Gaddafi.

But the true sensation was, of course, all the dead bodies. Most of the tabloids continued to run photos of the four headless Turks hanging by their feet. Youssef, hanging by his neck, was still page-three news. Under the photo of him, one tabloid asked in bold print: COULD GIOVANNA BE NEXT? The titillating tone left little doubt that the reporter would not be disappointed by more tragic news.

The Italian press was slightly more subdued and had stopped running photos, other than a portrait of Giovanna. A few of her friends spoke to reporters and said nice things about her. Luca got more press than he could have dreamed of, though not the kind he wanted.

The Americans were preoccupied with their invasion of Iraq and the unexpected insurgency that was causing headaches. Casualties were mounting. Each day brought more bad news, and for a country accustomed to bad news in the Middle East, the kidnapping of a British lawyer was not enough for headlines. The stories were being reported but only in passing.

Scully & Pershing maintained a stone wall of silence. "Could not be reached for comment" was in many of the reports. The firm had issued a press release when the news of the abduction first broke, and its PR people were working around the clock to monitor events. Classified memos to every lawyer and employee went out daily. All said basically the same thing: Not a word to the press without authorization. Any leaks will be dealt with severely.

But what was there to leak?

The firm would not speak until it had something to say, and it would have nothing to say until Giovanna was home safe.

Abby wandered into the kitchen and, before uttering a word, went straight for the coffee. She sat down, took the first sip, then smiled at her husband. "Tell me only good news," she said.

"Yankees lost."

"No more bodies?"

"Not yet. Nothing new from the kidnappers. Scully and

Pershing gets mentioned, as does Luca Sandroni, but no one else."

Satisfied with the updates, she took another sip. Mitch turned off the television and closed his laptop. "What's on tap in your world today?"

"I haven't got that far yet. Meetings, always meetings. Marketing, I think. And you?"

"A briefing by our security consultant first thing this morning. I can't walk the boys to school."

"I'm happy to. A security consultant? I thought Scully had its own little spy shop."

"We do. It does. But this is far more serious and requires us to spend a fortune on an outside intelligence service, a rather shadowy outfit run by former spooks and retired colonels."

"And what might they brief you on?"

"It's classified, top secret and all that. Ideally, they would tell us who abducted Giovanna and where they are hiding her, but they don't know yet."

"They have to find her, Mitch."

"Everybody's trying, and that might be part of the problem. Maybe we'll learn something this morning."

"And can you tell me?"

"It's classified. Who's invading our kitchen tonight?"

"It's classified. Actually, no one. But we have some frozen lasagna from the Rosarios' last visit."

"I'm kinda tired of those two. When are you going to finish their cookbook?"

"Could be years. Let's take the boys out tonight."

"Pizza again?"

"No, let's make them pick a real restaurant."

"Good luck with that."

— • • —

The building was a 1970s high-rise with more brown brick than steel and glass, so dull that it blended in with a block of others, none of which were in any way attractive or imposing. Midtown was packed with such bland edifices, buildings designed only for the collection of rents with no regard for aesthetics. It was the perfect place for a mysterious operation like Crueggal to hide. Its main entrance on Lexington Avenue was staffed with armed guards. More of the same monitored a wall of closed-circuit screens.

Mitch had walked past the building a hundred times and never noticed it. He walked past it again, then turned onto Fifty-First, as instructed, and entered through a side door, one with a smaller number of pit bulls waiting to pounce. After being mug-shot and fingerprinted, he was met by a guard who could actually smile, and led to a bank of elevators. As they waited he scanned the directory, and of course there was no mention of Crueggal. He and his escort rode in absolute silence to the thirty-eighth floor where they got out and stepped into a small foyer with nothing to welcome guests. No firm name, no weird art, no chairs or sofas, nothing but more cameras to film the arrivals.

With time, they worked their way through the layers of protection and came to another thick door where Mitch was handed off to a young man in a non-polyester suit. They walked through the door and entered a large open space with no visible windows. Jack Ruch and Cory Gallant were chatting with Darian Kasuch in the middle of the room. Everybody said hello. Coffee was poured, pastries declined. They gathered around a wide table and Darian reached for a remote. He pushed a button and a detailed map of southern Libya appeared on a large screen. There were at least eight of them around the walls of the room.

He picked up a laser pointer and aimed the red dot at the region of Ubari near the southern border with Chad. "The first question is: Where is she? We don't have an answer because we have not heard a word from her abductors. The second question is: Who are they? Again, nothing definite. Ubari is highly unstable, and not friendly to Gaddafi. He's from up here." The red dot moved to the far north, to Sirte, then back to Tazirbu.

So far, he had told them nothing they did not already know. He went on, "For at least forty years the Libyans have fought with their neighbors, Egypt to the east, Chad to the south. In southern Ubari, there is a strong revolutionary movement, fiercely anti-Gaddafi. In the past five years a warlord named Adheem Barakat has managed to kill off many of his rivals and consolidate power. He's a hard-liner who wants Libya to become an Islamic state and kick out all Western companies and economic interests. He's also a terrorist who enjoys bloodshed. In that regard, he's one of many."

Darian tapped a key and the face of Barakat was suddenly glowering at them. Full black beard, sinister black eyes, white hijab, two bandoliers of shiny bullets draped over his shoulders and crossing over his chest. "Age about forty, educated in Damascus, family unknown. Fully committed to overthrowing the regime."

"So he can have the oil," Jack Ruch said.

"Yes, so he can have the oil," Darian repeated.

Mitch studied the face and had no trouble believing the man could order wholesale bloodshed. He shuddered at the thought that he had Giovanna somewhere in his possession. He asked, "And why do we believe he's the man?"

"We're not sure. Again, until they make contact we're just

speculating. However, last month Barakat attempted to blow up a refinery here, near the city of Sarir. It was a well-planned and tactically impressive raid involving about a hundred men, and it probably would've worked but for a breakdown in security. The Libyans were tipped off at the last minute and the army showed up. Several dozen were killed on both sides, though we never get the exact numbers. Not a word on the world news scene. Two of Barakat's men were captured and tortured. Under extreme duress, they talked before they were hung. If they can be believed, his organization now has several thousand well-armed gunmen operating on various fronts. They are committed to driving out foreign investment. Gaddafi has sold out to the West and so on, and this is motivating the revolutionaries. One of the captives said the bridge in the desert is still a target. We have an asset in Libya who confirms this. Barakat has been operating closer and closer to Tripoli, sort of daring Gaddafi to commit to a fight. He'll probably get what he wants."

Mitch was suddenly bored with the briefing. Crueggal could confirm almost nothing, and Darian was working too hard to impress Scully with information that was not reliable. Not for the first time in the past week, he caught himself longing for the old days when he could practice law without worrying about hostages and terrorism.

Jack Ruch, known for his lack of patience, said, "So, we're still just guessing."

"We're getting closer," Darian said coolly. "We'll get there."

"Okay, and when we know who has Giovanna, then what? Who makes decisions at that point?"

"That depends on what they want."

"Got that. Let's play hypotheticals. She has British citizenship, right, so what if the Brits decide to go in with guns blazing? But the Italians say no. The Libyans say yes. The family says no. The Americans, who knows? But does it really matter? She's in Libya, we think, and as long as she's there our options are basically zero, right?"

"It's fluid, Jack, it changes daily. We can't begin to make plans until we know a lot more."

Cory asked, "How many people do you have on the ground in Libya right now?"

"Contacts, agents, double agents, assets, runners, probably a dozen. All are being paid, bribed, whatever it takes. Some are old trusted assets, others have just been recruited. It's a murky world, Cory, with uncertain loyalties and fragile relationships."

Mitch drank some coffee and decided he'd had enough caffeine for the morning. He looked at the face of Adheem Barakat and asked, "What are the chances this guy has Giovanna?"

Darian shrugged and kicked it around for a moment. "Sixty-forty."

"Okay, and if he does have her, then what does he want?"

"The easy answer is money. A fat ransom to buy more guns and pay more soldiers. The other answer is more complicated. He may not want an exchange. He may do something dramatic, something awful, to announce his presence to the world."

"Kill her?"

"Unfortunately, that is a real possibility."

CHAPTER 18

In Giovanna's absence, Mitch needed an ambitious associate to step in and do the grunt work. There was no shortage of them at Scully; indeed, the firm hired three hundred of the brightest law grads each spring and marched them through the meat grinder of 100-hour workweeks and relentless deadlines. After a year, the blue-chippers began to emerge from the pack. After two years, those falling behind were jumping ship, but by then the veterans could spot the lifers, the future partners.

Stephen Stodghill was a fifth-year senior associate from a small town in Kansas who had excelled at the University of Chicago Law School. Mitch had a secret bias in favor of the small-town kids who were succeeding nicely in the big leagues. He asked Stephen to join the team and was not surprised when he jumped at the chance. There were no snide jokes about what happened to the last associate Mitch had picked. They were still trying to find her.

Giovanna's plight was on the minds of every Scully lawyer, all two thousand of them in thirty-one offices around the world. There was much concern and quiet talk as they went about their work, waiting. Always waiting for news of the next development. In the Atlanta and Houston offices, small groups of lawyers and employees met for coffee and prayer early each morning. A female partner in Orlando was married to an Episcopal priest who was thoughtful enough to stop by the office for a moment of prayer.

———•—•———

Mitch worked late on Thursday afternoon and met for an hour with Stephen to begin the arduous process of covering all aspects of *Lannak Construction versus The Republic of Libya*. The file was four thousand pages thick and counting. Scully had retained eight experts who were preparing to testify on such topics as bridge design, architecture, construction methods, materials, pricing, delays, and so on. The idea of an exotic case in a foreign country excited Stephen at first, but the fun wore off quickly as they plowed through the material.

Mitch left at seven and had a quiet evening with Abby and the boys. He returned at eight the next morning and found Stephen exactly where he had left him—at the small worktable in one corner of his office. When Mitch realized what had happened, he dropped his head as he shook it.

"Let me guess. An all-nighter?"

"Yes, I really had nothing else to do and I got into it. Fascinating."

Mitch had worked his share of brutal hours, but he had never felt compelled to pull an all-nighter. Such feats were common in Big Law, and were supposed to be admired and hopefully add to the legend of some gunner aiming for an early partnership. Mitch had no patience with it.

But Stephen was single and his girlfriend was an associate at another large law firm and suffering the same abuse. He wanted to propose but couldn't find the time. She wanted to get married but worried they'd never see each other. When they managed to meet for a late dinner they often nodded off after the first cocktail.

Mitch smiled and said, "Okay, a new rule. If you want to remain on this case you cannot work more than sixteen hours a day on it. Understood?"

"I guess."

"Then guess again. Listen to me, Stephen. I am now the attorney of record, and that means I'm your boss. Do not work more than sixteen hours a day on this case. Am I clear?"

"Got it, boss."

"That's more like it. Now get out of my office."

Stephen jumped to his feet and grabbed a pile of papers. On his way out he said, "Say, boss, I was fooling around last night on the internet and found the video, the one with the chain saw. Have you seen it?"

"No. Not going to."

"Smart. I wish I'd never seen it because I'll never forget it. That's one reason I stayed up all night. Couldn't sleep. Probably won't sleep tonight either."

"You should've known better."

"Yes, I should have. The screaming—"

"That's enough, Stephen. Go find something else to do."

———•·•———

Another day passed with no word from the kidnappers or those trying to find them. Then another. Mitch began each morning with a security briefing with Cory in Jack Ruch's office. By closed-circuit, they listened with increasing frustration to Darian's updates from North Africa. He did a credible job of filling twenty minutes with what-might-happen-next, but the truth was he was guessing.

Finally, there was high drama. On the night of Sunday, April 24, nine days after the abduction, a Libyan counterterrorism unit attacked a camp near the border of Chad. The area was a no-man's-land with few inhabitants, and those who did live there did so because they carried weapons and were either expecting trouble or planning more of it. The sprawling, hidden camp was rumored to be the headquarters of Adheem Barakat and his small army of revolutionaries. Given the vastness of the Sahara, surprise attacks were almost impossible to pull off and the Libyans did a lousy job of it. Barakat may have been warned by tribesmen on his payroll, or his sentries and their drones may have been on high alert. Regardless, the attack was met head-on and a fierce battle raged for three hours. Hundreds of Libyan commandos arrived in troop carriers while others were air-dropped from Mi-26 Russian-made helicopters. Two were shot down by shoulder-mounted Strela missiles, also made by the Russians. The Libyans were shocked at such firepower. Casualties on both sides were horrendous, and when it became apparent that the fight might go on until everyone was dead, the Libyan commander called for a retreat.

Tripoli immediately released a statement describing the mission as a precision strike by government forces against a terrorist group. It was a resounding success. The enemy had been routed.

At the same time, the government leaked a story that the real reason behind the raid was to rescue Giovanna Sandroni. It was intended as clear proof that Gaddafi was not involved in her abduction. He was trying to save her.

Mercifully, she'd been four hundred miles away.

——— • • ———

Mitch and Jack Ruch left LaGuardia on the 8:15 A.M. shuttle to Reagan National in Washington. They were met at the curb by Benson Wall, Scully's managing partner in D.C. A driver whisked them away in a black company sedan and just minutes after landing they were sitting in traffic above the Potomac. Their meeting with Senator Lake was at 10:30, so they had plenty of time. Lake was famously late for every other meeting, but for the ones in his office he expected punctuality.

Elias Lake was in his third term but still the junior senator from New York. The senior senator was elected in 1988 and was showing no signs of fatigue or vulnerability. Not surprisingly, Scully & Pershing had deep ties to both men, warm relationships built on the firm's ability to raise large sums of money and the senators' willingness to listen. With little effort, Jack could get either one on the phone at almost any reasonable hour, but the urgency of the Sandroni matter necessitated a face-to-face meeting. Senator Lake was a sub-committee chairman on Foreign Affairs, and in that position had become close to the current secretary of state. Also, Benson Wall had hired Lake's nephew three years earlier as an associate out of Georgetown. Jack and Benson agreed that their time would be better spent with Lake than with the senior senator from New York.

Four years earlier, Mitch had visited Capitol Hill for the first time. He had tagged along with another partner and a client, a defense contractor who had hired Scully to extract it from some unfair contracts. A certain senator from Idaho needed to be stroked. Mitch disliked Capitol Hill and saw it as a frantic place where little was accomplished. He had vowed to never go back.

Unless. Unless there was something as urgent as a kidnapped Scully associate and the firm was desperate for help.

He, Jack, and Benson arrived at 10:15 at the Dirksen Senate Office Building and went to the second floor where they were greeted by more security guards at the door of Lake's suite. They were shown to a small conference room where they waited a few minutes until an assistant chief of staff greeted them and said "The Senator" was running behind and tied up with other important matters.

At 10:40 they were led into his grand office where he greeted them warmly and showed them seats around the table. He was a pure New Yorker, from Brooklyn, and loved everything about his city. His walls were adorned with banners and pennants for all sports teams. No decent politician could play favorites and expect to be re-elected in New York. Lake was about sixty, fit, hyper, energetic, and always ready for a good scrap.

It was his office, his turf, so he would direct the conversation. "I appreciate your coming, fellas, but we could've done this by phone. I understand what's at stake."

Jack said, "I know. She's Italian and British, Senator, so she's not technically one of us. But she is. She's a part of Scully, and though we have offices around the world, Scully is and always has been an American firm. A New York firm. She spent one summer as an intern at Skadden, in the city. She has a law degree from Virginia. Her English is better than mine. We'd like for you, and the State Department, to consider Giovanna as one of us, practically an American."

"Got it, got it, got it. I spoke to Madam Secretary again yesterday. Believe me, Jack, they are taking this very seriously. Daily briefings here and over there. Contacts galore. Nobody is asleep here, Jack. But the problem is that nobody knows anything. Some nasty boys have their hands on her, but so far they're not talking. Am I right?"

Jack nodded and looked grimly at Benson.

The senator glanced at some notes and continued, "According to our people, and mind you our people are not exactly welcome in Libya so we have to rely on the Brits, Italians, and Israelis for intel, but what we're hearing is that some insurgent militia of desert rats run by a thug named Barakat is, more than likely, calling the shots. They have Ms. Sandroni but haven't made contact yet. As you know, there was some initial speculation that Gaddafi might be behind the abduction, but our people don't believe it."

Mitch felt as though he was sitting through another briefing by Darian Kasuch. Could he please hear something new?

Jack had cautioned him that the meeting would seem to be a waste of time, but Senator Lake could be crucial later on.

To impress them, the senator retrieved a classified memo from his desk. It was top secret, of course, so confidentiality all around. The raid two nights earlier, the one the Libyans were crowing about, was a total disaster for them. According to the CIA, which trusted the senator with all manner of sensitive material, the Libyan Army lost far more men than the enemy and had to pull back after a brutal counterattack.

More than likely, this had nothing to do with Giovanna, but since the senator had the information he felt compelled to share it. Confidentially, of course.

There were clocks on three of the walls, just so his visitors would know that his time was crucial, his days planned to perfection, and at exactly 11:00 a secretary knocked on the door. Lake pretended to ignore her and kept talking. She knocked again, opened it slightly, and said, "Sir, your meeting is in five minutes."

He nodded without interrupting his line of chatter and she withdrew. He talked on as if his visitors were far more important than the crucial meetings that followed. The first interruption was for show and designed to make the visitors feel uncomfortable and want to leave. The second interruption was just as scripted and occurred five minutes later when the chief of staff knocked as he entered. He held paperwork that could prove, if ever examined, that things needed to run on schedule and the senator was already late. The chief of staff smiled at Jack, Mitch, and Benson, and said, "Thank you, gentlemen. The senator has a meeting with the vice president."

Which vice president, Mitch wondered? VP of the Rotary Club? The nearest branch bank?

The senator kept talking as his visitors rose and headed for the door. He promised to stay on top of the situation and contact Jack if there were any developments. Blah, blah, blah. Mitch couldn't wait to leave.

Lunch was a sandwich in a cafeteria somewhere under the Capitol.

At 1 P.M. they met with a lawyer from the Office of the Legal Adviser to the secretary of state. He was a former Scully associate in the Washington office who had burned out and left private practice. Benson had hired him out of law school and they had maintained a friendship. He claimed to have strong contacts with the deputy secretary of state and was monitoring the hallway gossip. He found it hard to believe that a Scully associate could be abducted.

Crossing the Potomac on the way back to the airport, Mitch was a team player and agreed that the day went well. To himself, he vowed once again to avoid Capitol Hill if at all possible.

CHAPTER 19

The United Arbitration Board was headquartered on the fifth floor of the Palais de Justice in downtown Geneva. Its twenty judges came from around the world and served five-year terms, with the chance of being re-appointed for an additional term. Seats on the bench were quite prestigious, often lobbied for, and were doled out through the United Nations. The UAB's docket was a dizzying collection of civil disputes from all over. Governments fighting each other; corporations from different countries suing each other; individuals seeking vast sums from foreign companies and governments. About half the cases were heard in Geneva, but the board was quick to take its show on the road. Travel was first-class, as were the expense accounts. If Cambodia wanted to sue Japan, for example, it made little sense to require the lawyers and witnesses to set up camp in Geneva, so the board would pick a more convenient venue in Asia, preferably one near a fashionable resort.

Luca had filed Lannak's claim against Libya the prior year, in October of 2004, and requested a trial in Geneva. The chair of the board, known as the ruling magistrate, agreed.

Now she wanted a reschedule, a nuisance in every lawyer's opinion but not an uncommon one. Mitch was of the opinion that the board was curious about the case because of its sudden notoriety. Virtually all of the other cases on its docket were exceedingly boring disputes from the other side of the world. Nothing could match a half-billion-dollar fight that involved a bridge in the desert, four beheadings, several related murders, and the saga of a missing Scully associate. When Mitch first received the notice to appear for the reschedule, he thought seriously about asking for a postponement, which was standard practice. A thirty- to ninety-day continuance would have been granted. However, after conversations with Lannak, it was agreed that the hearing in Geneva would be a better time and place to meet and discuss the lawsuit.

Mitch and Stephen flew to Rome and visited with Luca in his villa. Two weeks had passed since Giovanna's abduction and there was still no word from her captors. The days were getting no easier for Luca. He seldom ate or slept and was losing weight. He was due for another round of chemo but simply wasn't up to it. He was bickering with his doctors and unhappy with the home nurses. He was, however, pleased to see Mitch and even had a glass of wine, his first in days.

With Roberto Maggi, the team spent two hours in Luca's home office going over strategies, then flew to Geneva where they met the men from Lannak: Omar Celik, the CEO and grandson of Lannak's founder; Denys Tullos, his chief lawyer and Mitch's principal contact; and Omar's son, Adem, a graduate of Princeton and the future owner of the company. They were not Muslim and enjoyed alcohol. After cocktails in the hotel bar, they walked to a restaurant and settled in for the evening. Joining them late was Jens Bitterman, a Swiss lawyer who was part of the team and handled the dealings with the UAB.

Omar had been close to Luca for over twenty years and was concerned about his friend. He had met Giovanna on a number of occasions as she was growing up. Several times Luca and his family had vacationed at the Celik beach estate on the Black Sea. Omar was, of course, angered by the fact that the Libyans owed him $400 million for the bridge, money he was determined to collect, but he was much more concerned about Giovanna's welfare.

In one of their many conversations, Denys Tullos told Mitch that the company was financing private security deep inside Libya in an effort to find her. Mitch relayed this to Darian Kasuch at Crueggal, who was not surprised. "Join the crowd," he said.

———•—•———

The hearing was scheduled for 2 P.M., Thursday, April 28. Mitch and his team spent the morning in a hotel conference room with the Celiks and Denys Tullos. They reviewed Luca's timetable and looked for ways to streamline the mountain of discovery still to be done. They debated the strategy of amending the lawsuit to include damages for the deaths of the four security guards and Youssef, all Lannak employees. Early on, Omar took control of the meeting and proved why he was regarded as a tough corporate boss who didn't back down. He had been fighting with the Libyans for over twenty years, and while he usually got paid he was fed up. No more projects there. He doubted the regime was responsible for the ambush and bloodshed because it had always promised to protect foreign workers, especially those with Lannak. It was clear to Omar that Gaddafi was losing control of much of his territory and could no longer be trusted. Omar certainly wanted the lawsuit expanded to cover the deaths, to hold the Libyan government responsible, but agreed with

Mitch that more time was needed. Walid would likely be found with his throat cut. No one could predict what would happen to Giovanna. At the moment there were too many unknowns to map out strategies.

After a sandwich for lunch they taxied to the Palais de Justice and went to the courtroom on the fifth floor. Waiting outside in the vast, empty hall were two reporters. One, with a camera hanging from his neck, was with a London tabloid, the other from a broadsheet. They asked Mitch if he had time to chat. He offered a polite no, kept walking, and entered the courtroom.

It was a wide, tall room with soaring windows, plenty of light, and enough seating for hundreds of spectators. But, there were none—only small groups of lawyers huddled here and there, whispering gravely as they watched each other from across the room.

The bench was an imposing piece of furniture, at least eighty feet long and made of some dark, rich wood that had probably been harvested two hundred years earlier. It stood six feet tall, and behind it were twenty leather rockers that swiveled and rolled. They were identical, deep burgundy in color, and exactly the same height so that the magistrates, when court was in session, looked down at the lawyers and litigants from positions of great knowledge and power.

All twenty were empty. A clerk led Mitch, Stephen, Jens, and Roberto to the plaintiff's table on one side of the room. They unpacked thick briefcases as if they might be there for hours. Across the way another team of grim-faced lawyers marched to their table and also unpacked. The Reedmore firm, from London, Libya's favorite firm, a notorious bunch of arrogant boys who seemed to relish their reputations as world-class assholes.

Reedmore had only 550 lawyers, not even enough to crack the top twenty-five in size, and limited its business to only a handful of countries, primarily in Europe. The firm had been in bed with the Libyan regime for many years. Luca said that was probably why they had such a sour outlook on life.

Along with its wealth of talent, ambition, skills, and diversity, one great asset of working at Scully & Pershing was its sheer size. It had been the largest firm in the world for a decade and was determined to stay on top. Its lawyers were known to often walk with a little swagger because of the firm's remarkable reach and depth. There had never been a bigger law firm. Size did not always equal talent, nor did it guarantee success, but in the world of Big Law, being number one was the envy of firms two through fifty.

The Reedmore lawyers were formidable foes and Mitch would never take them lightly, but at the same time he wasn't impressed by their aloofness. Jerry Robb was the attorney of record for the State of Libya. He'd brought with him a couple of younger guys, and all three wore matching, impeccably tailored navy suits. They seemed incapable of smiling.

However, since there was bad news at the other table, Robb felt compelled to pick at the scab. He walked over, stuck out a hand, and said, "Good afternoon, gentlemen." He was stiff as a board and shook hands like a twelve-year-old.

Nose up a bit, he said, "I spoke with Luca last week. I hope he's doing well, in spite of."

In spite of. In spite of the fact that he's dying of cancer and his daughter is being held hostage by some really unpleasant people.

"Luca's fine," Roberto said. "In spite of."

"Any word on Giovanna?"

Mitch refused to take the bait and shook his head. *No.*

"Nothing," Roberto said. "I'll tell him you asked."

"Please do."

Any further conversation would have been just as stilted, but a clerk by the bench began bellowing and Robb went back to his table. In English, the clerk called things to order. He sat down, and another one stood and did the same in French. Mitch glanced around the vast room. There were two pockets of lawyers seated far apart with a few clients sprinkled in between. The two British reporters were in the front row. He doubted anyone in the room spoke French, but the court had its procedures.

Three judges entered from behind the bench and took their seats. The ruling magistrate was in charge and she sat in the middle. Her two colleagues were at least twenty feet away. Seventeen of the thrones were empty. The reschedule docket did not warrant full participation by the board.

She was Madam Victoria Poley, an American from Dayton, a former federal judge who'd been one of the first women to finish at Harvard Law. It was acceptable to address her as Madam, Magistrate, Judge, Your Honor, or Lord. Anything else was problematic. Only lawyers from the British Isles and Australia dared use the word "Lord."

To her right was a judge from Nigeria. To her left was one from Peru. Neither wore headphones, so Mitch assumed there would be no delays for the interpreters.

Madam Poley welcomed everyone to the afternoon session and said there were only a few matters on the docket. She glanced at a clerk who stood, called the Lannak case, then proceeded to read its history, beginning with the filing of the complaint in October of the prior year. It would be next to impossible to make such a reading anything but dull, but the clerk's monotone cast a heavy pall over the courtroom. She went on, flipping pages as her voice grew flatter and flatter. Mitch's last thought before he fell into a coma was, I hope they don't do this again in French.

"Mr. McDeere," a voice called out, and Mitch snapped back to life. Madam Poley was saying, "Welcome to the court and please give my regards to Signor Luca Sandroni."

"Thank you, Your Honor, and he sends his regards as well."

"And Mr. Robb, always nice to see you."

Jerry Robb stood, bent slightly at the waist and made an effort at a grin, but said nothing.

"You may be seated and feel free to remain so." Both lawyers sat down.

Madam Poley said, "Now, a trial date has been scheduled for February of next year, almost a year away. I'll ask each of you if you can be prepared for trial by then. Mr. McDeere."

Mitch stayed in his chair and began by saying yes, of course, the plaintiff would be ready. The plaintiff had filed the complaint and it was always incumbent upon the plaintiff to push hard for a trial. A plaintiff rarely backed away from a trial date. Regardless of how much work was yet to be done, Mitch was confident he was on schedule. His client wanted a trial sooner than February, but that issue would be raised another day.

Madam Poley was curious about discovery and asked how it was going. Mitch thought it should be wrapped up in ninety days. There were more depositions to take, more documents to haggle over, more experts to pin down, but ninety days should be enough.

Mr. Robb?

He wasn't much of an actor and did a lame job of pretending to be surprised that counsel opposite would be so optimistic. There were at least six hard months of discovery left, maybe more, and a trial in less than a year was simply not possible. Using the standard defense playbook, Robb checked off a handful of reasons why much more time was needed. After rambling on for too long, he finished with "And I can only imagine how

JOHN GRISHAM

much more complicated our issues will become in light of recent events in Libya."

As if waiting for an opening, Madam Poley said, "Well, let's talk about recent events. Mr. McDeere, do you foresee amending your complaint to ask for additional damages?"

The answer was yes but Mitch wasn't about to say so in court. He feigned frustration and said, "Your Honor, please, the situation in Libya is fluid and can change dramatically on any day. I can't possibly predict what will happen and what the legal consequences will be."

"Of course not, and I understand your position. But, given what has already happened, it's safe to say that the issues will only become more complicated, right?"

"Not at all, Your Honor."

Robb saw an opening and jumped in with "Your Honor, please, you are indeed correct. Events beyond our control are muddying the water, so to speak. It's only fair that we agree on an extension of time and not force ourselves to rush to an unworkable deadline."

Mitch came back with "The deadline works, Your Honor, and I can promise the court that the plaintiff will be ready by February, if not sooner. I can't speak for the defense."

"Nor should you," retorted Robb.

"Gentlemen," Madam Poley said firmly before the debate dissolved into bickering. "Let's see how things play out down there and discuss it later. Now I'd like to move on and take up some of the issues already raised in discovery. By my count, the plaintiff has listed eight potential experts who might testify at trial. Six for the defense. That's a lot of testimony and I'm not sure we need that much. Mr. McDeere, I'd like a brief summary of each of your experts' testimony. Nothing fancy. Off the cuff."

Mitch nodded and smiled as if he would like nothing better. Roberto was quick off the mark and handed him some notes.

By the time he finished discussing his third expert, an expert in cement, he was certain all three judges were asleep.

CHAPTER 20

Two London newspapers ran stories about the hearing. *The Guardian,* on page two, back-filled with some history of the case and reminded its readers that there had been no "reported" contact with the kidnappers. It described the reschedule in Geneva as "boring" with little progress being made. The Board seemed reluctant to make decisions with so much uncertainty in the case. It ran a small stock photo of Giovanna, and a new one of Mr. McDeere walking into the Palais de Justice with Roberto Maggi at his side. Both were correctly identified as partners in the mammoth law firm of Scully & Pershing. They were seeking at least four hundred million dollars for their client from the Libyan government.

Mitch, once again over the Atlantic, studied the black-and-white of himself. He was not pleased at being identified but knew it was inevitable.

The Current ran a teaser on the front page—GADDAFI'S LAW-YERS SEEK DELAYS: NOTHING FROM GIOVANNA—and on page five attacked the "ruthless dictator" for not paying his bills. The slant was clear—Gaddafi was behind the killings and kidnappings because he was angered by the lawsuit. There was a photo of Mitch; one of Giovanna; and the same sad image of poor Youssef hanging by a wire.

———— · · ————

On May 1, Walid got what everyone expected. His killers chose to prolong his suffering by slashing his testicles and letting him bleed out. He was hanging by one foot from a tall cypress tree near a busy road, twenty miles south of Tripoli. A similar note was attached to his unencumbered foot: *Walid Jamblad, Traitor.*

A lawyer in the Rome office saw the news first and alerted Roberto Maggi, who in turn called Mitch. A few hours later a video was dropped into the deep web, another sick clip of thugs killing an innocent man for sport. Or maybe there was a reason, or a message. Roberto watched it and warned Mitch not to.

No one was left but Giovanna. Of course she was the prize, and there would be nothing simple about her destiny.

Mitch, Jack Ruch, and Cory Gallant endured another conference call with Darian at Crueggal. If he told them anything that wasn't obvious or that they didn't already know, it was not noted. After the call ended, and Mitch was certain there were no hot mikes or unflipped switches, he asked Jack, "And how much are we paying these guys?"

"A lot."

"That was another wasted half hour."

"Not exactly. Bill it to Lannak."

Mitch looked at Cory and asked, "You still believe in these guys? They've produced nothing so far."

"They'll come through, Mitch. I think."

"What's our next move?"

"We don't have one. We wait. Until we hear from Giovanna or the bad boys holding her, there's nothing we can do here."

Jack asked Mitch, "What's the latest from the arbitration court?"

"Not much. Nothing really. It's waiting too. The case is on hold as long as she's a hostage. Remember, it doesn't take much to inspire the court to find ways to delay itself."

"And Luca?"

"I talk to him every day. Some are better than others but he's hanging on."

"Okay. Time's up. Let's chat again in the morning."

———•—•———

On May 4, Riley Casey arrived at his office at his usual time of 8:30 A.M. He was the managing partner of Scully's London office and had been with the firm for almost three decades. Eleven years earlier, he had drawn the short straw and interviewed a young American lawyer in town looking for a job. A law degree from Harvard barely got him in the door. A nimble mind, quick wit, and good looks got him the job, and Mitch joined Scully as a thirty-year-old associate.

Six years after that, Riley hired Giovanna Sandroni, and, like most of the men in the office, had a secret crush on her. Secret but quite professional and, of course, unspoken. Riley was a happily married man who kept his pants on; otherwise, he would have already made a fool of himself. Having hired her, at Luca's quiet behest, he was watching with great pride as she developed into a fine lawyer, one who would probably run the entire firm one day.

Before he could have a drink of his morning coffee, his secretary entered without a word and handed over her cell phone. On the screen, the message read: "Unknown Caller. Tell Riley to check spam."

He looked at the screen, looked at her. Something wasn't right, and given the suffocating pressure around the office since Giovanna's abduction, every little aberration was treated cautiously. He motioned for her to walk around to his side of his desk. They looked at his large desktop computer. He went to spam, then clicked on an email from an unknown sender that had landed eleven minutes earlier. Both recoiled in disbelief.

On the screen was a large black-and-white photo of Giovanna, sitting in a chair, wearing a black robe and a black hijab that covered everything but her face. She was neither smiling nor frowning. She was holding a newspaper, the morning edition of *Ta Nea,* "The News" in Greek, and the largest daily in the country. Riley enlarged it and the date became readable— *May 4, 2005.* That very morning. The lead story was a farmers' strike and there was a photo of a row of tractors blocking a highway. Nothing about Giovanna, at least not on the front page above the fold.

Riley said, "You call tech and I'll call security."

—•—•—

Cory knew Mitch was an early riser, so he let him sleep until five-thirty before calling. Seconds later, Mitch was in the kitchen. First, he punched the ON button for the coffeepot, then he quickly opened his laptop. His first thought was, At least she's alive.

Cory said, "The Greek newspaper is validated, everything is as it seems. It's sold in Tripoli, but you have to know where to look. They picked up a copy of today's edition early this morning, took the photo, and sent it to London. As far as we can tell, it was not sent anywhere else."

"And no message from the sender?"

"Not a word."

Mitch took a drink of coffee and tried to clear his head.

Cory asked, "You think you should tell Luca?"

"Yes. I'll call Roberto."

———•—•———

The following morning, the news out of Athens was far more ominous. At 3:47 A.M., according to the alarm system, a bomb blew up in the mail room of the offices of Scully & Pershing, in the central business section of the city. Since no one was at work at that hour, there were no injuries. The bomb maker included incendiary combustibles designed not to knock down walls, but rather to spread fire, and an impressive one raced through the suite. With only four lawyers in Athens, it was one of Scully's smallest outposts, and their offices were engulfed and destroyed before the firemen arrived. The flames spread along the third floor as smoke poured out of the building from broken windows. Two hours after the alarm went off, the fire was contained and put out. By sunrise, the firemen were rolling up their hoses and retreating, though the cleanup would take days.

The managing partner was allowed into the building and led to the charred shell of what had been his rather plush suite of offices. The destruction was complete. Everything—walls, doors, furniture, computers, printers, rugs—was blackened and ruined. A few metal file cabinets had withstood the heat and smoke but were drenched with water. Their contents, though, were not valuable. All important files and papers were stored online.

By noon, the fire officials were calling it arson.

With that, the managing partner phoned New York.

CHAPTER 21

Epicurean Press occupied the bottom three floors of a turn-of-the-century brownstone on Seventy-Fourth Street, near Madison Avenue, on the Upper East Side. Above it, on floors four and five, the owner, an eccentric recluse who was pushing ninety, lived alone with her cats and her opera. She played records all day long, and as she aged and lost even more of her hearing, she gradually turned up the volume. No one complained because she owned the building, and also the ones on both sides. The editors on the third floor could sometimes hear the music, but it was never a problem. The brownstones of that era were built with thick walls and floors. She charged modest rent because, number one, she didn't need the money, and, number two, she enjoyed having nice tenants below her.

A perfect morning for Abby began with clear skies, a fifteen-minute walk with Clark and Carter to school, then a thirty-minute walk across Central Park to her office at Epicurean. As a senior editor, she was on the first floor and thus far away from the opera but close enough to the kitchen. The offices were small but efficient. Space was cramped, like most of Manhattan, but also because valuable footage had been given to the kitchen, a large, modern, fully equipped facility designed to accommodate visiting chefs working on their cookbooks. One showed up almost every day, and the air was perpetually filled with delicious aromas of dishes from around the world.

Giovanna had been abducted twenty-seven days earlier.

As always, Abby ducked into a trendy coffee shop on Seventy-Third for her favorite latte. She was waiting in line at about nine-fifteen, her mind on the day ahead, her boys at school, her husband forty-eight floors up and hard at work, and her eyes on her phone. The person behind her gently tapped her on the arm. She turned around and looked into the face of a young Muslim woman in a long brown robe with a matching hijab with a veil that covered everything but her eyes.

"You're Abby, right?"

She was startled and could not remember the last time, nor the first time, she had talked to a woman so completely covered. But it was, after all, New York City, home to plenty of Muslims. She offered a polite smile and said, "Yes, and you are?"

The man behind the Muslim woman was reading a folded newspaper. The nearest barista was loading a display case with croissants and quiches. No one was paying attention to anyone else.

She said, in perfect English with only a slight Middle Eastern accent, "I have news from Giovanna."

The eyes were dark, young, heavily made-up, and Abby looked at them in disbelief as her knees wobbled, her heart skipped, and her mouth was almost too dry to speak. "I beg your pardon," she managed to say, though she knew exactly what she had heard.

From somewhere inside her robe the woman pulled out an envelope and handed it to Abby. Five-by-seven, too heavy for only a letter. "I suggest you do as you're told, Mrs. McDeere."

Abby took the envelope, though something told her not to. The woman turned quickly and was at the door before Abby could say anything. The man with the folded newspaper glanced up. Abby turned around as if nothing had happened. The barista said, "What would you like?"

With difficulty, she said, "A double latte with cinnamon."

She found a chair, sat down, and told herself to breathe deeply. She was embarrassed when she realized there were beads of sweat on her forehead. With a paper napkin from the table she wiped them off as she glanced around. The envelope was still in her left hand. More deep breaths. She placed it in her large shoulder bag and decided to open it at the office.

She should call Mitch, but something told her to wait a few minutes. Wait until she opened the envelope because whatever was in there would involve him too. When her latte was ready, she took it from the counter and left the shop. Outdoors, on the sidewalk, she managed a few steps before stopping cold. Someone was, or someone had been, watching, waiting, following her. Someone knew her name, her husband's name, her husband's business, her walking route to work, her favorite coffee shop. That someone had not gone away, but was nearby.

Keep moving, she told herself, and act as if nothing is wrong.

The nightmare was back. The horror of trying to live normally while knowing someone was watching and listening. Fifteen years had passed since the Bendini mess in Memphis, and it had taken a long time to relax and stop looking over her shoulder. Now, as she dodged pedestrians along Madison Avenue, she wanted desperately to turn around and see who was watching her.

Five minutes later she opened the unmarked door of Epicurean Press on Seventy-Fourth, spoke to the usual lineup of friends and colleagues, and hustled to her office. Her assistant wasn't in yet. She closed her door, locked it quietly, sat at her desk, took another deep breath, and opened the envelope. In it was a phone and a sheet of typing paper.

To Abby McDeere. (1). The most disastrous thing you can do is involve your government in any way. That would guarantee a bad ending for Giovanna and possibly others. Your government cannot be trusted; by you or anyone else.

(2). Involve Mitch and his law firm, a firm with plenty of contacts and money. You, Mitch, and his firm can succeed and bring about a good outcome. Involve no one else.

(3). You know me as Noura. I am the key to Giovanna. Follow my instructions and she will be delivered. She is not being mistreated. The others deserved to die.

(4). The enclosed phone is crucial. Keep it close at all times, even when you sleep. I will call at odd hours. Do not miss a call. Use the same charger as your cell. The code is 871. The Menu has Photos, which you will find interesting.

Abby put down the sheet of paper and picked up the phone. Unmarked and about the same size as other cell phones, there was nothing distinctive or suspicious about it. She tapped 871 and a menu appeared. She tapped PHOTOS, and was instantly nauseous. The photo was of her, Clark, and Carter, less than an hour earlier, as they said goodbye on the sidewalk outside of River Latin School, four blocks from their apartment. She took another deep breath and reached for a bottle of water, not the coffee. She unscrewed the top, took a sip, and spilled water on her blouse. She closed her eyes for a moment, then slowly scrolled left. The next photo was an exterior shot of the brownstone in which she was now sitting. The next photo was an exterior shot of their apartment building, taken from Sixty-Ninth and Columbus Avenue. The next photo was a long-distance one of 110 Broad, where Scully & Pershing was headquartered. The last photo was of Giovanna, sitting in a dark room, wearing a black veil, holding a spoon, and looking into a bowl of what appeared to be soup.

Time passed but Abby was not aware of it. Her brain was a jumbled mess of rapid thoughts. Her heart pounded like a jackhammer. She closed her eyes again and rubbed her temples and became aware that someone was gently knocking on her door.

"In a minute," she said and the knocking stopped.

She called Mitch.

———•——•———

They were frozen, too stiff to move as they looked at the wide screen and waited for Abby's video to appear. And there it was: a close-up of the typed note to Abby from Noura. They read it quickly, then slower a second time. The camera moved to the mysterious phone on Abby's desk, next to the envelope it came in. After twenty-two seconds the video was over.

Mitch finally breathed and exhaled and walked to the window of Jack's office. Jack stared at his small conference table, too stunned to say anything. Cory, who had been operating under extreme duress since the bombing in Athens, stared at the blank screen and tried to think clearly. Without looking at Mitch he asked, "And there were five photographs on the phone?"

"That's right," Mitch answered without turning around.

"Tell her not to send the photos, okay?"

"Okay. What do I tell her?"

"Not sure yet. Let's assume they are monitoring everything

the phone does. Let's assume the phone can be used to track Abby wherever she goes, whether or not it's turned on. Let's assume the phone hears and records everything said around it, whether it's on or off."

As if he heard nothing, Mitch said, "They took a photo of my kids going to school this morning."

Cory shot a glance at Jack, who shook his head. The shock had not begun to wear off; indeed, they were still in the middle of the shock and everything was a blur.

Still speaking to the window, Mitch said, "My instinct is to walk out of this building right now, get a cab, go to the school, get my kids, take them somewhere safe and lock the doors."

"Totally understand, Mitch," Cory said. "Go if you must. We're not stopping you. First, though, we need to see the phone. Is your cell phone secure?"

"I don't know. You installed all that anti-viral stuff."

"And Abby's too?"

"Yes. We should be hack-proof, if anything is hack-proof these days."

Jack said, "I have an idea. The Carlyle Hotel is on Seventy-Sixth, near Park, close to Abby's office. Call Abby and tell her to meet you for lunch at the Carlyle. Bring the new phone. We'll get a conference room and look it over while you have lunch."

Cory said, "Great idea."

Mitch turned around and said, "So it's a go?"

"Yes."

Mitch pulled out his phone, called Abby, talked as though others might be listening, and said he would be in the neighborhood for lunch. Meet him at the Carlyle at noon. They would discuss whether or not to do something at the school. When he finished he asked Cory, "Could they possibly hack our phones and email? Are they listening to us?"

"Highly unlikely, Mitch. Everything is possible these days but I doubt it."

Jack asked, "And why would they? They don't care what you're doing for lunch or dinner. This is now all about money. If they were going to kill Giovanna it would've already happened, right Cory?"

"Probably, but who knows?"

"Look guys, the game has now changed. We've finally heard from the enemy and they want to talk. Talk means negotiation and that means money. What else can Giovanna do for them? Assassinate Gaddifi? Broker a Middle East peace deal? Find more oil in the desert? No. She has a price on her head and the question is how much?"

"It's not quite that simple, Jack," Mitch said. "There is also the question of how much damage we're willing to absorb before we knuckle under. Setting aside for a moment the killings so far, and there are eleven dead bodies by my count, we also have an office bombed in Athens and now they're right here in the city."

Cory said, "Let's not get ahead of ourselves. We're not in charge. They are, and until Noura reappears we can't do much."

"Oh really? Well, I plan to protect my family."

"Got it, Mitch. I don't blame you. Any ideas?"

"You're the security guy, right? What would you do?"

"I'm still thinking."

"Please hurry."

Jack said, "We should discuss Crueggal. Do they get involved?"

Mitch shrugged as if the question was not aimed at him. He returned to the window and looked at the streets below. Dozens of yellow cabs inched along in heavy traffic. In a few short minutes he planned to be in the backseat of one of them, barking instructions at the driver.

Jack asked, "Have you spoken to Darian lately?"

Cory replied, "Not since nine A.M. I begin every day with a fifteen-minute update from Darian in which he reveals nothing new. They're digging, waiting, and digging. We have to tell him, and soon. The enemy has made contact, Jack, which is what we've all been waiting for. Crueggal knows far more about this game than we do."

"And you trust them? I mean, their roster is loaded with ex-spies and CIA types. They pride themselves on having contacts in every cave around the world. What if someone has loose lips?"

"Not gonna happen. Darian's in the city. I'll call him and he'll meet us at the Carlyle."

"Mitch?"

"Until I know my kids are safe I won't be worth much, okay? Abby's a wreck."

Jack said, "Understood. Go meet her for lunch. We'll be there and make a plan."

CHAPTER 22

Mitch was waiting in the lobby of the Carlyle when Abby rushed in at ten minutes before noon. He waved her over and, without a word, they disappeared into Bemelmans Bar, one of the most famous in the city. At that hour, though, it was nearly empty. They sat on stools at the bar, face-to-face, and ordered diet sodas. Her eyes were moist and worried. Mitch tried his best to remain calm. By nature they were not excitable, but then they had never had their children threatened.

He motioned and she put her shoulder bag on the floor under her stool. Softly, he said, "There's a chance your new phone will track you wherever you go. Also a good chance it hears and records everything, whether off or on."

"I'd like to get rid of it. Have you called the school?"

"No, not yet." He nodded, stood, and motioned for her to follow him. They walked a few feet away and kept their eyes on her bag. Almost whispering, Mitch said, "We'll meet with the security folks upstairs in a few minutes. Maybe we'll figure out what to do."

Her jaws clenched and she tapped her teeth together. "I say we get the boys and get the hell out of the city, go hide somewhere for a few days."

"I like that. The problem is you can't leave. The phone might track you and you have to keep it in your pocket at all times. You're the link, Abby. They chose you."

"I'm honored." Her eyes suddenly watered. "Can you believe this, Mitch? They followed us to school this morning. They know where we live and work. How did we get here?"

"We're here and we'll get out, I promise."

"No promises, Mitch. You don't know any more than I do. I want to help Giovanna, okay, but right now my only concern is my two little boys. Let's go snatch 'em and run."

"Maybe later, but right now let's go upstairs and meet with the team."

——— • ———

The two conference rooms in the business center were taken, so Cory booked a suite on the third floor. He was waiting with Jack and Darian. Quick introductions were made. Abby knew Jack from the annual partners' Christmas dinner, a fussy black-tie party that almost everyone loathed. She had met Cory years earlier during one of the firm's security audits.

For obvious reasons, Abby was feeling vulnerable at the moment. In addition, she was suddenly in a meeting with a complete stranger and expected to discuss private matters. Always eager to take charge, Darian bulled right ahead and said, "It is important to walk through your confrontation with Noura."

Abby shot him a look and said, "I'm not sure I like your tone."

For a second all the air left the room. Mitch felt compelled to soothe tensions and said, "Look Darian, it's been a rough morning and we're a bit on edge. What, exactly, do you want to know?"

"Who said it was a confrontation?" Abby demanded.

Darian offered a quick phony smile and said, "You're right, Ms. McDeere. Bad choice of words."

"Okay."

"Mind if we see the phone?" he asked pleasantly.

"No problem." It was buried in the bottom of her large bag and it took a moment to fish it out. She placed it in the center of a small round table. Darian pressed his index finger to his lips to ask for quiet. He held it, examined its casing, and with a small screwdriver took the back off. With his phone he took photos and sent them to someone who worked for Crueggal. He opened his laptop, pecked away like a manic hacker, and stopped to admire whatever he had found. He half turned the screen around for the others to see. The trade name was "Jakl" and it was made in Vietnam for a company in Hungary. The list of specifications was in small print and ran on for pages. The message was clear: it was a specialized, complicated phone not intended for the average consumer. Darian returned to his rapid key-tapping and kept searching. His cell phone rang and he spoke in some coded dialect, then smiled and ended the call.

"It's not listening to us," he said with relief. "However, it does emit a tracking signal regardless of the ON/OFF switch."

Mitch asked, "So right now they know the phone is in the Carlyle Hotel?"

"They know the phone is within fifty yards of where it really is. They probably don't know it's up here and not in the restaurant."

Abby half snorted in disgust and shook her head.

Darian gave the phone to Cory, who held it so he and Mitch

could see the screen. He touched the Photos key, and there were the boys with their mother bounding off to another day of school. Mitch shook his head in disbelief at all five photos. When he'd seen enough, he said, "Okay, Abby, why don't you walk us through what happened with Noura?"

She looked at Darian and said, "Sorry I snapped. Things are a bit tense."

"No apology necessary, Abby. We're here to help."

Abby recalled every possible detail as Darian recorded her and everyone else took notes. He prodded with questions about Noura's appearance. Height—about the same as Abby's, five feet seven. Weight—who could tell with all the layers of robes. Age—young, under thirty, but again impossible to be sure with the heavy veil and all. Accent—perfect English with maybe a slight Middle Eastern accent. Anything memorable about her hands, arms, shoes? Nothing, everything was covered. Did Noura order food or drink? No.

As the interrogation went on, Jack stepped into the other room and began making calls.

When Abby had told them everything, she said, "That's it. Nothing else. I feel like I'm on the witness stand here. I'd like to spend some time alone with my husband."

Cory said, "Good idea. You two go downstairs and have lunch while we figure out the next steps."

Mitch said, "That's great, Cory, but the next step is our kids. Giovanna is important, but right now nothing matters but the safety of Clark and Carter."

"We're with you, Mitch."

"Right. And nothing is done without my approval, okay?"

"Got it."

—— • • ——

Thoughts of eating were impossible but it seemed imperative to at least order something. They chose salads and tea and could not help but glance around the lovely restaurant, Dowling's, to see if anyone was staring at them. No one was.

Though the wretched Jakl phone was wedged deep in the bottom of Abby's sizable shoulder bag, which itself was stuffed under her chair, they still spoke softly. The question was, Where? Not if, or when, or how, but where? They had to find a safe place to run and hide with the boys. Her parents' home in Kentucky, her childhood home, was a possibility, but would be too obvious. Abby's boss, the publisher of Epicurean, had a cottage on Martha's Vineyard. But then, virtually everyone they knew in the city had a getaway either in the Hamptons or upstate or somewhere in New England, and the list of options grew longer as they talked. It was easy to think of possible places; the difficulty would be in the asking.

Mitch doubted she would be able to leave the city. They had no idea when Noura might call again and Abby would be expected to drop everything for a meeting. Mitch was more than ready to flee with the boys and forget the office.

The head of River Latin School was Giles Gatterson, a veteran of the city's pressurized private school business. Mitch served on the Legal & Policy Committee and knew Giles well. He would call him later in the day and explain that they were in an unusual situation that was not covered by any of the rules. For safety reasons, they were taking the boys away for a few days, perhaps even a week. He would be as vague as possible and would not tell Giles the boys were being watched, followed, or threatened. No need to alarm anyone else at the school. He might be more forthcoming later, but not now.

For the $57,000 a year they paid in tuition per child, the school could damned well bend a little. The boys' assignments would be monitored in person by their parents and online by their teachers.

It was time to make a move. The only question was—Where?

———•·•———

In the restaurant, lunch was ignored. Up in the suite, it was never considered. Cory, Jack, and Darian sat around a small coffee table and walked through various scenarios. For the sake of argument, Darian broached the subject of notifying the FBI and CIA. Crueggal had close contacts with each and he was certain the information would be protected. He did not advocate any contact, but thought it appropriate to at least air it out. The obvious reason to say no was that Giovanna Sandroni was not an American. Jack believed strongly that neither agency would want to get involved, given the unstable relationship with Libya and the likelihood of a bad outcome. The CIA had blown enough operations in recent history to want to stay in its box. Darian agreed. During his long career in intelligence, he'd seen the CIA mishandle many crises, many of which it had created in the first place. He had no confidence in the agency's ability to either keep its nose out of it or to protect Giovanna if and when it got involved.

Jack decided there would be no contact with the U.S. authorities until later, if necessary. And he warned Darian and Cory there would be no action taken without the approval of the firm and Mitch McDeere.

They discussed Luca and whether he should be informed. It was a tough call because he was, after all, her father, as well as their esteemed partner. Any parent would certainly want to be involved in such delicate discussions. But Luca was ill and fragile and not at the top of his game. And, the kidnappers had chosen not to approach the family. Luca was a wealthy man by any measure, but he didn't have millions to toss around. Scully, being the greatest firm in the world, certainly did, or at least projected the aura of enormous wealth. Its lawsuits around the world sought billions in damages from big corporations and governments. Surely it could pay any ransom if money was the objective.

There was no playbook, no rules. Darian had worked through several kidnappings in his career, but each was radically different. Most had ended successfully.

They decided to wait twenty-four hours and discuss Luca again.

——— • • ———

Less than forty minutes after Abby and Mitch left for lunch, they returned to the suite and found that nothing had changed. Jack held a sheet of paper with notes scribbled all over it and said, "We have some ideas for the next twenty-four hours."

Mitch said, "Let's hear it."

"Okay, pick up the boys from school today as usual and we'll be close by." He nodded at Cory, who said, "We'll have guys on the ground, Mitch. Do you ever meet them after school?"

"Rarely."

"Abby?"

"All the time."

"Good. You get them today at three-fifteen and walk them home by the same route."

"I'll be at home," Mitch said.

"Get them packed for a long weekend, a very long one. Tomorrow is Friday and they're leaving town with you, Mitch. Abby, it's advisable for you not to leave the city at this time. It's the phone. You gotta stay close."

Abby didn't flinch but asked, "So you want them in school tomorrow?"

"Yes. We think they'll be safe."

Mitch said, "They'll go to school but they're leaving at noon. Abby and I will talk to the school tonight and explain things. She'll walk them to school in the morning. I'll sneak them out the back door at lunchtime."

Jack asked, "Got a destination, Mitch?"

"No, not really. Not yet."

"I have a good one."

"We're listening."

"My brother Barry retired from Wall Street ten years ago, made a fortune."

"I've met him."

"That's right. He has a nice home in Maine and it's very secluded. A place called Islesboro, a small island on the Atlantic coast near the town of Camden. You have to take a ferry to get there."

It certainly sounded safe and secluded enough, and Mitch and Abby both relaxed a little.

Jack went on, "I just talked to him. He summers there, stays about five months until it starts snowing. We go every August and enjoy the weather. He opened the house last week."

"And he has plenty of room?"

"The house has eighteen bedrooms, Mitch, plenty of staff. A couple of boats. The summer traffic hasn't arrived yet so there aren't too many folks on the island. Again, it's quite secluded."

"Eighteen bedrooms?" Mitch repeated.

"Yes. Barry likes to tell everyone that we have a large family. What he doesn't say is that he can't stand the rest of them. I'm his only ally. He and his wife use the house to entertain friends from here and Boston. It's a slightly older crowd who want to sit on the porch in the cool breeze and soak in the views while eating lobster and drinking rosé."

Cory added, "And we'll have a couple of guys there as well, Mitch. You won't see much of them but they'll be close by."

Mitch looked at Abby and she nodded. *Yes.*

"Thanks, Jack. Sounds good. I'll need an airplane."

"No problem, Mitch. Anything."

CHAPTER 23

After Carter and Clark were finally convinced that a weekend away from the city and on a remote island in Maine could be a great adventure, and that the Bruisers' game Saturday would probably be rained out, and that they would be staying in a mansion with eighteen bedrooms and two boats waiting at the dock, and that they would ride on a small private jet, then a ferry, and that their grandparents would be there to play with them, as would their father, and that their mother needed to stay in the city for some unclear reason, the boys were ready to go. They reluctantly went to bed, still chattering away.

The next conversation was just as complicated but forty minutes shorter. After swapping emails to arrange things, Mitch called Giles Gatterson of River Latin at exactly nine-thirty. He apologized again for the intrusion and they quickly dispensed with the preliminary chitchat. As vaguely as possible, he explained that one of his cases, an international one, had presented a "security concern" that necessitated an early and furtive departure from school for the boys the following day, and would likely keep them out of the city for a week or so. Giles was eager to help. The school was filled with the children of important people who traveled the world and ran into unusual situations. If questions were asked about the boys' absences, the company line was that they were suffering from measles and were quarantined. That should keep the curious at bay.

Abby made the next call, the third one to her parents in the past few hours. A private jet would fetch them in Louisville at 2 P.M. Saturday and fly nonstop to Rockland, Maine, where they would be met by a driver who would take them to the harbor in Camden.

As they talked, Mitch kept thinking about the eighteen bedrooms and was thankful that the summerhouse was large enough to put distance between himself and his in-laws. Only a threat from a terrorist organization could force him to spend a weekend with Harold and Maxine Sutherland. "Hoppy" and "Maxie" to the boys. His therapist would want to know how it happened, and he was already practicing his stories. The fact that he was still spending good money to deal with his "in-law issues" irked him to no end. But Abby insisted, and he did love his wife.

Oh well. His dislike of Hoppy and Maxie seemed rather trivial at the moment.

With the phone calls out of the way, an unforgettable day was finally coming to an end. Mitch poured two glasses of wine and they kicked off their shoes.

"When will she call?" Abby asked.

"Who?"

"What do you mean, 'Who'?"

"Oh, right."

"Yes, Noura. How long will she wait?"

"How am I supposed to know?"

"No one knows, okay? So what's your guess?"

Mitch drank some wine and frowned as if in deep and meaningful thought, calculating exactly what the terrorists were thinking. "Within forty-eight hours."

"And what do you base that on?"

"That's what they taught us in law school. I went to Harvard, you know?"

"How could I forget?"

He took another sip and said, "They've proven to be patient. Today is number twenty-seven, and the first contact. On the other hand, it's a lot of work holding a hostage. She's probably in a cave or a hole in a wall, not a good place. What if she gets sick? After a while the kidnappers will get tired of her. She's worth a lot of money so it's time to cash in. Why wait longer?"

"So it's all about ransom?"

"Let's hope so. If they were going to hurt her in some dramatic way it would've already happened. Probably, and according to our experts anyway. And what would they gain by it?"

"Because they're savages. They've managed to shock the world already. Why not do it in an even bigger way?"

"True, but the men they've killed were of little value, dollarwise. Giovanna's a different story."

"So it's all about money."

"If we're lucky."

Abby was not convinced. "So why did they bomb the office in Athens?"

"Something else we didn't cover in law school. I don't know, Abby. You're asking me to think like a terrorist. These people are fanatics who are half crazy. On the other hand, they're smart enough to put together an organization that can send an agent into a coffee shop down the street and hand you a package."

Abby closed her eyes and shook her head. Nothing was said

for a long time. Other than the occasional sip from a glass, nothing moved. Finally, she asked, "Are you scared, Mitch?"

"Terrified."

"Me too."

"I really want a gun."

"Come on, Mitch."

"Seriously. The bad guys have plenty of guns. I'd feel safer if I had one in my pocket."

"You've never held a gun, Mitch. Giving you one would endanger half the city."

He smiled and rubbed her leg. He gazed at a wall and said, "Not true. When I was a kid, my father took me hunting all the time."

She took a deep breath and considered his words. They had been in love for almost twenty years, and she had learned at the beginning not to be curious about his early years. He never discussed them, never opened up to her, never shared the memories of a rough childhood. She knew his father died in the coal mines when he was seven. His mother cracked up and worked low-wage jobs but had trouble keeping them. They moved often, from one cheap rental to another. Ray, his older brother, dropped out of school and pursued a life of petty crime. Mitch once spoke of an aunt he lived with before running away.

"We grew up in the mountains where every kid was hunting by the age of six. Guns were a part of life. You know Dane County."

She did. It was Appalachia, but she was a town girl whose father wore a suit and tie to work each day. They owned a nice home with two cars in the driveway.

"We hunted year-round, regardless of what the game warden said. If we saw an animal that might make a good stew, it was dead. Rabbits, turkeys, I killed my first deer when I was six. I could handle a gun—rifles, pistols, shotguns. After my dad died, Mom wouldn't let us hunt anymore. She was afraid we might get hurt and the thought of losing another son was too much. She gave away all the guns. So, yes, dear, you are correct in saying that if I had one now I'd probably hurt somebody, but you're wrong in saying I've never fired a gun."

"Forget the guns, Mitch."

"Okay. We'll be safe, Abby, trust me."

"I do."

"No one will be able to find us up there. Cory and his gang will be close by. And since it's in Maine I'm sure the house will be full of guns. Don't they shoot moose up there?"

"You're asking me?"

"No."

"Don't touch a gun, Mitch."

"I promise."

CHAPTER 24

Promptly at six the following morning, Cory rang the buzzer for the McDeere apartment and was welcomed by Mitch. Abby poured coffee at the breakfast table and offered yogurt and granola. No one was hungry.

Cory walked them through the plan for the day and gave each a little green phone that flipped open. He said, "These are cell phones that cannot be hacked or traced. Only five—these two, me, Ruch, and Alvin."

"Alvin?" Abby asked, obviously becoming irritated with the cloak-and-dagger stuff. "Have we met an Alvin?"

"He works for me and you probably won't meet him."

"Of course." She held her newest gadget and stared at it in frustration. "Yet another phone?"

"Sorry," Cory said. "I know your collection is growing."

"What if I make a mistake and pull out the wrong one?"

Mitch frowned at her and said, "Please."

She said to Cory, "I thought our cell phones cannot be hacked or tracked."

"That's right, as far as we know. These are just another layer of security. Stick with us, okay?"

"I'll shut up now."

"So, the plan is to leave the front door of the building at exactly eight A.M., as always, with Carter and Clark, just another walk to school. South on Columbus, west on Sixty-Seventh, two more blocks to the school. We'll be watching every step."

"Watching for what?" Mitch asked. "You don't really think these guys will do something stupid on a busy sidewalk."

"No, more than likely they will not. We want to see who's watching. It's doubtful Noura is working alone. It would take a team to follow Abby and the boys yesterday, take the photos, follow her across the park, and arrive at the coffee shop at about the same time. Somebody gave her the Jakl, a rather exotic gadget. She has a boss somewhere. These cells are not run by women."

"And what if by chance you notice someone following Abby today?"

"We'll do our best to track them."

"How many people do you have on the ground right now?"

"I'm not allowed to say, Mitch. Sorry."

"Okay, okay. Continue."

"You leave at the normal time, take the subway to work, nothing unusual. At ten I'll have a car nearby and I'll call with directions." He picked up his green phone, smiled, and said, "We'll use these. Hope they work."

"Can't wait."

"You'll return here, enter this building through the basement exit, get the bags, hustle back to the car. At eleven you'll enter the school through a side door off Sixty-Seventh, get the boys, and get out of there. I'll meet you at the Westchester airport. We'll hop on a cute little jet and thirty-five minutes later land in Rockland, Maine. Any questions so far?"

Mitch said, "You look exhausted, Cory. Are you sleeping?'

"Are you kidding? A Scully lawyer has been held hostage somewhere in North Africa for a month now. How can I sleep? My phone starts ringing at one A.M. when the sun comes up over there. I'm running on fumes."

Mitch and Abby looked at each other. "Thanks for all this, Cory," she said.

"You're under a lot of pressure," Mitch said.

"I am. We are. And we'll get through it. You're the key, Abby. They chose you and you have to make it work."

"I've never felt so lucky."

"And I'll be hunting moose," Mitch said with a laugh, one that was not shared by the others.

———— • • ————

The walk took seventeen minutes and went off without incident. Abby managed to chat with the twins and watch the traffic without glancing around. At one point she was amused by the thought that the boys had no idea how many people were watching them as they walked to school. Nor would they ever.

Cory and his team were almost certain Abby and the boys were not followed. He was not surprised. The threat had already been delivered the day before. Why take more photos? Five were plenty. But top security, as well as good spy-craft, dictated the surveillance. They probably would not get the chance to do it again.

Mitch arrived at the office and immediately called Luca in Rome. He sounded tired and weak and reminded Mitch that his daughter had been gone for a month. Mitch said he was in constant contact with their security advisers. The conversation lasted less than five minutes, and when it was over Mitch again felt it would be a mistake to tell Luca about Noura. Maybe tomorrow.

At 9:15, Cory called, on the green phone, and told Mitch that the surveillance had noticed no one trailing Abby and the boys. Mitch went to Jack's to debrief. At 10:00, he hopped in the rear of an SUV at the corner of Pine and Nassau. Cory was waiting. As they sped away, he couldn't help but nod off. Mitch smiled at the guy and felt sorry for him. He was also happy with the silence. He closed his eyes, took deep breaths, and tried to walk slowly through the events of the past twenty-four hours. Before coffee with Abby yesterday morning, no one in his world had ever heard of Noura.

At 11:10, Mitch emerged from the school with Clark and Carter. A gray sedan was waiting, with another driver. Forty minutes later, they stopped at the gate of the general aviation terminal at Westchester County Airport. A guard waved them through and they drove across the tarmac to a waiting Lear 55. The boys were wide-eyed and couldn't wait to take it up for a spin. Clark said, "Wow, Dad, is that our plane?"

"No, we're just borrowing it," Mitch said.

Cory was waiting outside the Lear, glancing at his watch. He welcomed the boys with a big smile and helped them aboard. He introduced them to the two pilots and strapped them into the thick, leather seats. Mitch and Cory sat facing the boys in club-style seating. A fifth passenger, Alvin, sat in the back. As they began to taxi, Cory fetched coffee for Mitch and cookies for the boys, but they were too busy gawking out the windows to take a bite. At 20,000 feet, Cory unlatched Carter from his seatbelt and led him to the cockpit for a quick visit with the pilots. The colorful display of switches, buttons, screens, and instruments was overwhelming. Carter had at least a hundred questions but the pilots were adjusting dials and talking on the radio and couldn't say much. After a few minutes, it was Clark's turn.

The excitement of flying on a fancy little jet made the trip seem even shorter, and before long they were descending. When it taxied and stopped at the small private terminal, a black SUV pulled alongside to collect the passengers and their luggage. The boys reluctantly climbed down and got in the SUV. For the next two days they would talk of nothing but flying airplanes when they grew up.

The date was May 13, a Friday, and coastal Maine was thawing out from another long winter. The picturesque town of Camden was coming to life and brushing aside the remnants of the spring's last snowfall. Its scenic harbor was already busy with fishermen, sailors, and a few summer residents eager to get to the islands and open their second homes.

One of Cory's men was holding a table at a restaurant on the water. When they arrived he disappeared, and Mitch wanted to ask how many were on the team. Sitting at the table and taking in the magnificent view of the harbor, the distant hills, and Penobscot Bay, Mitch could almost forget why they were there.

Away from their mother, and on some sort of vacation, Clark and Carter did not hesitate to order burgers, fries, and milkshakes. Mitch had a salad. Cory ate like one of the kids. Service was slow, or maybe they were on Maine time now, but they were in no hurry. The big city was far away and they would get back to it soon enough. It was Friday afternoon, and Mitch wanted a beer. Cory, though, was on duty and declined. Never one to drink alone, Mitch fought the temptation.

Twice during lunch Cory excused himself to take calls. When he returned each time Mitch was tempted to grill him for the latest news, but managed to control his curiosity. He assumed Corey was dealing with his team somewhere in the vicinity and probably not getting calls from Tripoli.

The ferry to Islesboro ran five times a day and took twenty minutes. At 2:30, Cory said, "We should get in line."

———— • • ————

The island was fourteen miles long and almost three miles wide in places. Its eastern end jutted into the Atlantic, with beautiful views from the rocky coast. Mitch and the boys were on the ferry's upper deck admiring the other islands as they passed. Cory walked over, pointed, and said, "That's Islesboro coming into view ahead."

Mitch smiled and said, "We are remote, aren't we?"

"I told you. It's a perfect place to hide for a few days."

"Hide from who?"

"I'm not sure, probably no one. But we're not taking any chances."

As they drew closer they began to see the mansions dotting the shoreline. There were dozens of them, most dating back a hundred years to the glory days of "summering" by the rich. Families from New York, Boston, and Philadelphia built fine homes to avoid the heat and humidity, and of course they needed plenty of bedrooms and lots of staff to take care of their friends, who often stayed for weeks at a time. The homes were still in use, still splendid, and a few had even attracted celebrities. The permanent population of Islesboro was five hundred, and most of the adults either worked "in the houses" or trapped lobsters.

They drove off the ferry and were soon on the only highway that ran the length of the island. Within ten minutes, they turned onto a narrow asphalt drive and passed a sign reading WICKLOW.

Mitch asked Cory, "Any idea where 'Wicklow' comes from?"

"It's the county in Ireland where the first owner was born. He got rich bootlegging Irish whiskey during prohibition, built this place, then died young."

"Cirrhosis?"

"No idea. It's been bought and sold several times and everyone kept the name. Mr. Ruch picked it up at an auction about fifteen years ago and did a renovation. Whacked off ten bedrooms on a different wing, according to Jack."

"So he's down to eighteen."

"Only eighteen."

They were soon arriving at a circular drive in front of a sprawling old house that belonged in a travel magazine. It was classic Cape Cod architecture: two levels with steep roofs and side gables, a wide centered front entry, weathered shingle siding painted a pale blue, gabled dormers, and four centralized chimneys. Beyond it was nothing but miles of the Atlantic Ocean.

Mr. Barry Ruch himself came through the front door and practically bear-hugged Mitch as if they were dear friends. They were not, at least not yet. Mitch had met him a few years earlier at a birthday party for his younger brother Jack. There had been at least fifty other guests and Mitch and Barry had barely spoken to each other. He was known as a quiet billionaire who loathed attention. According to an old *Forbes* story, Barry had made his money speculating in Latin American currencies.

Whatever the hell that meant.

Everybody shook hands and said hello. As trained, Carter and Clark stood as tall as possible and said, "Nice to meet you." Their father was proud of them.

Barry swept the whole group into the house through the front door and into the main foyer where they met Tanner, the butler-porter-driver-handyman and boat captain. He was also a part-time lobsterman who would always seem ill at ease in his navy jacket and white shirt. Thankfully, Mr. Ruch allowed him to wear khaki britches.

Tanner handled the luggage and room assignments while Barry showed the McDeeres to the den where a fire was roaring. He laughed about the last snowfall just two nights ago and promised there would be no more of the white stuff until October. Maybe November.

———•—•———

As the men talked about the weather and how Jack was doing as he neared retirement, Carter and Clark admired the massive stuffed moose head looking down upon them from the stone fireplace.

Barry noticed this and said, "I didn't kill him, boys, wasn't me. He came with the house. Tanner thinks he's been here for about thirty years. Probably from the mainland."

"Are there moose on the island?" Carter asked.

"Well, I've never seen one, but we'll go looking for them if you want. Tanner says the wind is dying down and a warm front is moving in. Let's wait a couple of hours, hop in the boat, and go for a ride."

The boys couldn't wait.

CHAPTER 25

Mitch's shot-in-the-dark prediction, allegedly based on his fancy education, was remarkably close. Noura did not wait forty-eight hours. She waited about forty-seven, and called Abby on the Jakl phone at 7:31 Saturday morning.

Abby was on her yoga mat in the den, stretching half-heartedly and trying to remember the last weekend when she had the apartment all to herself. She missed her guys and under different circumstances would not have been worried about them. She talked to Mitch twice Friday night, on the green phone, and was fully debriefed. The boys were having a grand time in Mr. Barry's mansion, while Mitch and the owner were smoking Cuban cigars and drinking single malts.

They felt perfectly safe. No one could possibly find them.

Selecting the proper phone from her collection assembled on the coffee table, always close at hand, Abby lifted the Jakl and said, "Hello."

"Abby McDeere, this is Noura."

What's the proper greeting to a terrorist on a rainy Saturday morning in Manhattan? Though in an odd way she was relieved to get the call, she refused to show any interest. Calmly she said, "Yes, this is Abby."

Evidently, terrorists didn't use greetings because Noura skipped them altogether. "We should meet tomorrow morning before noon. Are you available?"

Do I have a choice? "Yes."

"Walk to the ice rink in Central Park. At ten-fifteen, approach the main entrance. There's an ice-cream vendor to the left, on the east side. Stand there and wait. Your husband is a Mets fan, right?"

A kick in the gut could not have jolted her more. How much did these people know about them? "Yes," she managed to say.

"Wear a Mets cap."

Mitch had at least five of them hung on a rack in his closet. "Sure."

"If you bring anyone with you, we will know immediately."

"Okay."

"That would be a terrible mistake, Mrs. McDeere. Understood?"

"Yes, of course."

"You must come alone."

"I'll be there."

There was a long pause as Abby waited. She repeated, "I'll be there."

More silence. Noura was gone.

Carefully, Abby put down the Jakl, picked up the green phone, walked to her bedroom, closed the door, and called Mitch.

———— • • ————

Though obviously built to entertain adults, Wicklow showed signs of children passing through. At least one of the bedrooms had two sets of bunk beds, rainbows painted on the walls, outdated video games, and a wide-screen television. Tanner showed the boys around and they quickly gave the house thumbs-up. By dinner Friday, Tanner was their new best friend.

They slept until almost eight Saturday morning and followed the smells downstairs to the breakfast room where they found their father drinking coffee and talking to Mr. Cory. Miss Emma appeared from the kitchen and asked what they would like for breakfast. After much indecision, they settled on waffles and bacon.

Cory finished his omelette and excused himself. Mitch asked the boys how the night went and everything was awesome. They said they wanted bunk beds at home. "You can discuss it with your mother. She's in charge of furniture and decorating."

"Where's Mr. Barry?" Clark asked.

"I think he went to his office."

"Where's his office?"

"That way," Mitch replied, waving over his shoulder as if the office was far away but still under the same roof. "I don't want you guys roaming around the house, okay? We are guests and this is not a hotel. Do not go in a room unless you're invited."

They listened intently and began nodding. Carter asked, "Dad, why are the rooms so big here?"

"Well, it might be because Mr. Barry has a lot of money and can afford big houses with big rooms. Also, he invites guests to stay here for weeks at a time and I suppose they need plenty of space. Another reason might be that you guys live in a city where almost everybody lives in apartments. They tend to be smaller."

"Can we buy a mansion?" Clark asked.

Mitch smiled and said, "We certainly cannot. Very few people can afford a house like this. Do you really want eighteen bedrooms?"

"Most of them are empty," Carter said.

"Does Mr. Barry have a wife?" Clark asked.

"Yes, a lovely woman named Millicent. She's still in New York but will be here later this month."

"Does he have kids?"

"Kids and grandkids, but they live in California."

According to Jack, Barry was estranged from both of his adult children. The family had been bickering for years over his fortune.

The waffles and bacon arrived on platters, each large enough for a small family, and the boys lost interest in Mr. Barry. Mitch left them at the table and walked outside to a covered deck not far from the pier to the boat dock. Cory, of course, was on the phone. He put it away and Mitch asked, "What's the plan?"

"Let's stay here tonight, get the grandparents settled, then take off early in the morning for the city. That was Darian and he'll be there. We'll set up camp in the Everett Hotel on Fifth, across from the ice rink."

"How often do you remind yourself that we have no idea who we're dealing with, other than a woman named Noura?" Mitch asked.

"Once every thirty seconds."

"And how often do you ask yourself if Noura could be a hoax?"

"Once every thirty seconds. But she's not a hoax, Mitch. She found your wife in a coffee shop in Manhattan. They had her under surveillance. Hell, they were watching your entire family. She gave her that phone. She's not a hoax."

"And how much money will they want?" Mitch asked.

"Probably more than we can begin to imagine."

"So, do we expect Abby to negotiate?"

"I have no idea. We're not running this show, Mitch. They are. All we can do is react and pray we don't screw up."

———•·•———

Harold and Maxine Sutherland had never been to Maine but it was on their list. In their retirement they were having far too much fun checking off the places they had dreamed of and were now visiting. With no dogs or cats, a downsized cottage in the country, and a healthy bank account, they were the envy of their friends as they repacked their bags almost as fast as they unpacked them. Luckily, they were at home when Abby called Thursday afternoon and said it was urgent.

Tanner fetched them at the ferry and delivered them to Wicklow. Mitch and the boys greeted them at the door. Once again, Mitch was touched by how excited they were to see Maxie and Hoppy, who, of course, were even more excited to see their grandsons. Everybody helped with the bags and Tanner settled them into a fine suite across the hall from the bunk room. The boys couldn't wait to show their grandparents around Mr. Barry's mansion. After being there for twenty-four hours they felt like they owned the place and had forgotten their father's warning about roaming the halls. A late lunch was in order, and Mr. Barry appeared from some far corner of the house to dine with the McDeeres and Sutherlands. He was a gracious host and had the knack for making complete strangers feel welcome.

Mitch figured this came from years of hosting lots of friends at Wicklow, but he was also an easy soul to be around. A billion bucks in the bank probably added to his quiet, laid-back approach to life. But Mitch had met his share of self-made Wall Streeters, and many of them were to be avoided.

Mitch kept an eye on the boys. They had been taught by their mother to say little in the presence of adults and to mind their table manners. Mitch was thankful for her proper, small-town upbringing. Abby had been "raised right," as they say in Kentucky. To himself, he acknowledged this and thanked her parents.

So why did he find it so hard to forgive them? And to actually like them? Because they had never apologized for their slights and transgressions of twenty years ago, and, frankly, Mitch had stopped waiting. The last thing he wanted now was an awkward forced hug with a tearful "We're sorry." His therapist had almost convinced him that carrying such a heavy grudge for so long was hindering his growth as a mature person. It had become his problem, not theirs. He was the one being damaged. The therapist's mantra was: *Just let it go.*

Over lunch, common ground was soon found with fly-fishing. Barry had shucked the 80-hour workweeks years earlier and found solace in mountain streams all over the country. Harold had begun as a child and knew every creek in Appalachia. As the fish got bigger and bigger, Mitch found himself drifting away. He chatted with Maxine off and on. It was obvious they were concerned and wanted details.

Tanner appeared and suggested another boat ride. The boys beat him down to the dock. Mr. Barry retired into the depths of Wicklow to watch the Yankees game, a daily ritual.

Mitch led his in-laws into the library, closed the door, and explained to them why they were there. He gave only the barest of details, but it was enough to frighten them. The fact that terrorists were following their daughter and grandsons around Manhattan, and taking photos, was shocking.

They would hide in Maine with the boys for a month if necessary.

CHAPTER 26

The runway at Islesboro's small airport was only 2,500 feet long, too short for a jet. Early Sunday morning, Mitch and Cory took off in a King Air 200, a turboprop with small field capacity.

They left Alvin and one other guard behind at Wicklow. Mitch was convinced the boys were safely tucked away where no one could find them and he told himself to stop worrying. The day would be complicated enough without thinking of them. But there was no way not to.

An hour later they landed at Westchester, drove into the city, and by 10 A.M. were in a large suite on the fifteenth floor of the Everett Hotel, with a view of the Wollman ice rink in Central Park. Darian was there from Crueggal, along with Jack. Over coffee, Mitch gave Jack a full report on his brother and all the gossip around Wicklow, which wasn't much. Jack planned to retire July 31 and spend the month of August at Islesboro fishing with his brother.

The weather was cool and clear and Central Park was crowded. In the distance, they could see skaters circling the rink, but they were too far away to distinguish anyone. At 10:20, Mitch was certain he saw his wife walking down Fifth Avenue, on the park side. She was wearing jeans, hiking boots, and a brown barn coat she'd had for years. And a faded blue Mets cap.

"There she is," he said with a knot in his stomach. She disappeared into the park and they lost sight of her. Cory and Darian had argued over placing someone near the entrance of the rink to watch Abby, but decided not to. Cory thought there was nothing to gain by doing so.

At 10:30 she walked to the counter of an ice-cream vendor near the rink's main entrance. From behind large, dark sunglasses, she watched everyone while trying to appear nonchalant. It wasn't working; she was a wreck. The Jakl vibrated in her pocket and she pulled it out. "This is Abby."

"This is Noura. Leave the ice rink and walk to the Mall. Go past the statue of Shakespeare and to your left you'll see the one of Robert Burns, then a long row of benches. Stay to the left, walk about a hundred feet, and find a spot on a bench."

Minutes later, she passed the statue of Shakespeare and turned right onto the Mall, a long promenade lined with stately elms. She had made the walk countless times, and flashed back to their first winter in the city when she and Mitch had shuffled along, arm in arm, in a foot of snow with more falling. They had spent many long Sunday afternoons, in all seasons, sitting in the shade of the elms and watching the endless parade of New Yorkers outside for the day. When the twins arrived, they put them in a tandem stroller and pushed them up and down the Mall and all over Central Park.

Today, though, there was no time for nostalgia.

Hundreds of people were strolling along the Mall. Vendors sold hot and cold drinks. Loud carousel music echoed from speakers in the distance. As Abby walked she counted thirty steps, found an empty bench, and sat down as nonchalantly as possible.

Five minutes, ten. She clutched the Jakl in her pocket and tried not to look at everyone who passed. She was looking for a Muslim woman in full robes and a hijab, but saw no one of that description. A woman in a navy jogging suit pushing a baby stroller eased beside her. "Abby," she said, barely loud enough to be heard.

Both were wearing large sunglasses, but somehow they made eye contact. Abby nodded. She assumed it was Noura, though she could not identify her. Same height and build but that was all. The bill of an oversized cap sat low and covered her forehead.

"Over here," she said, nodding to her right.

Abby stood and said, "Noura?"

"Yes."

They walked together. If there was a baby in the stroller it wasn't visible. Noura turned right onto a sidewalk and they left the Mall. When they were away from everyone, she stopped and said, "Stare at the buildings. Don't look at me."

Abby gazed at the skyline of Central Park West.

Noura took her time and said, "The safe return of Giovanna will cost one hundred million dollars. The price is not negotiable. And it must be paid ten days from today. May twenty-fifth at five P.M. Eastern is the deadline. Yes?"

Abby nodded and said, "I understand."

"If you go to the police, or the FBI, or involve your government in any way, there will be no safe return. She will be executed. Yes?"

"Understood."

"Good. In fifteen minutes a video will be sent to your phone. It is a message from Giovanna." She turned the stroller and walked away. Abby watched her for a second—stylish Adidas jogging suit, red and white sneakers with no brand visible, goofy cap. She had seen only a portion of her face and would never be able to identify her.

Abby went the other direction and zigzagged northeast to Seventy-Second Street, then followed it east to Fifth Avenue. She entered the Everett Hotel, walked to the dining room, and asked for the table she had reserved earlier that morning. A table for three. She was meeting a couple of friends for brunch. When her coffee was served, she left the table and took the elevator to the fifteenth floor.

———•———

Darian connected the Jakl to a laptop with an eighteen-inch screen and they waited. And while they waited, each silently pondered the rather formidable task of somehow finding a hundred million dollars. As the shock began to wear off, it became evident that no one in the room had a clue.

The screen was blank for a few seconds, then there she was: Giovanna in a dark room wearing a dark robe or dress with a black hijab covering her head. She looked frail, even frightened, though she tapped her teeth together and tried to appear brave. A small candle burned on a table next to her. Her hands were not visible. She said, without smiling, "I am Giovanna Sandroni of the law firm of Scully and Pershing. I am healthy and well fed and I have not been harmed. Noura has now delivered the news. The price of my safe return is one hundred million U.S. dollars. This is not negotiable and if it is not paid by May twenty-fifth, I will be executed. Today is Sunday, May fifteenth. Please, I beg you, pay the money."

She was gone; the screen was blank again. Abby took the

Jakl, placed it in the bottom of her shoulder bag and took it to the bathroom. Mitch stood at a window and looked at Central Park. Darian was still staring at the screen. Cory studied his shoes. Jack sat at a breakfast table and sipped coffee. No one seemed capable of speaking.

Scully & Pershing was a law firm, not a hedge fund. Sure, its lawyers made plenty of money and the veteran partners were millionaires, at least on paper, but they were far from billionaires. Not even close. They had nice apartments in the city and pleasant weekend cottages in the country, but they didn't buy yachts and islands. The private airplanes they used were leased not owned, and every trip was billed to a client. The previous year the firm grossed just over $2 billion, and after the bills were paid and the profits were split, there was almost nothing left over. It was not uncommon for the firm to tap into its line of credit for extra cash during the slow months. Virtually every firm in Big Law did so.

Cory finally said, "We've asked ourselves if this is a hoax, if Noura is for real. This removes any doubt. She's part of a pretty slick operation over there with plenty of contacts here."

"Mitch, you're sure that's Giovanna?" Darian asked.

Mitch snorted as if the question was ridiculous. "No doubt."

Darian appeared ready to take charge, but Mitch would have none of it. It was a Scully matter and its partners would make the hard decisions. He turned from the window and said, "It's clear that our line of communication is rather limited. It's Noura and no one else, and I doubt she has the authority to negotiate. So, if we can't negotiate we're stuck with a nine-figure ransom that seems impossible. But we do not have the option of giving up. Does anyone doubt that in ten days these thugs will execute Giovanna in some spectacular fashion?" He glared at Jack, Cory, Darian, and he nodded at Abby. Everyone agreed.

"She has dual citizenship, British and Italian. What are the chances of asking those two governments to contribute to a ransom fund?"

Darian was shaking his head. "Slim. They don't negotiate with terrorists and they don't pay them ransom. Officially, at least."

"No one is negotiating, Darian. That's part of the problem. They're using Noura to deliver messages to Abby. Let's make it clear to both governments that in ten days there is a good chance that one of their citizens, one with a high profile, could be murdered, probably in front of a camera."

Jack asked Darian, "What do you mean 'officially'?"

He nodded and said, "The Italians made a large payment a few years ago to rescue a tourist in Yemen. They kept it quiet and still deny it."

"And you were involved?" Mitch asked.

He nodded but said nothing.

"So there is wiggle room with the governments," Mitch said and waited for a response. Darian shrugged but said nothing. He looked at Jack and asked, "When does the management committee meet?"

"Early in the morning. Emergency session."

"Great. I'm off to Rome. I have to tell Luca that they've made contact and are demanding ransom. I'll show him the video and try to allay his fears. Knowing Luca, he'll have ideas about where to find some cash."

—•—

To emphasize the urgency of the matter, and to prod the world's largest law firm into action, the terrorists firebombed another Scully office. The timing was perfect: exactly 11 A.M. Eastern Standard Time, half an hour after Noura met Abby.

It was another basic package bomb: reinforced cardboard holding tubes of highly combustible fluids, probably ammonium nitrate and fuel oil, though the authorities would never be certain because of the extensive damage. It was similar to the one used in Athens and was not designed to knock down walls, blow out windows, or kill people. Its purpose was to set off a roaring fire on a Sunday when no one would be in the shipping room of the Barcelona office. It was on the fifth floor of a new building with plenty of sprinklers. They kicked in immediately and minimized the blaze until the fire crews showed up. The Scully & Pershing suites were either fire-gutted or soaked with water, but there was little damage in the rest of the building.

Mitch was in a cab headed to JFK for the flight to Rome when Cory called with the latest. "Crazy bastards," he mumbled in disbelief.

Cory said, "No doubt, and we're easy targets, Mitch. Just look at our beautiful website. Offices in every major city and some minor ones as well. World's biggest firm, blah, blah, blah. It practically invites trouble."

"And now we'll spend a fortune on security."

"We're already spending a fortune on security. How am I supposed to protect two thousand lawyers in thirty-one offices?"

"Make that twenty-nine."

"Ha, ha, very funny."

CHAPTER 27

The firm's management committee consisted of nine senior partners, ranging in age from fifty-two to almost seventy, Jack Ruch being the oldest at sixty-nine. There was no additional compensation for serving on the MC and most partners tried to avoid it. However, someone had to take the ultimate responsibility for running the place and making the most difficult decisions. But, obviously, never in the firm's illustrious history had any partner been faced with such a momentous predicament.

Jack rousted them out of bed for a seven o'clock emergency meeting Monday morning. He immediately called for an executive session, meaning the two secretaries and Cory had to leave the boardroom. He asked a partner named Bart Ambrose to take minutes, and, though it was completely unnecessary and borderline irksome, he reminded them of the need for confidentiality. He began with a quick slide show of the photographs Noura had sent to Abby's new phone the previous Thursday morning: Abby and the boys, their apartment building, her office. He saved the best for last and revealed the long-distance photo of 110 Broad, the handsome tower in which they were now sitting.

"We're being watched," he said dramatically. "Watched, followed, photographed, and threatened. And now they're fire-bombing our offices on the other side of the world."

All breathing had ceased as they gawked at the images.

The photos were from Thursday. The McDeeres went into hiding on Friday. Noura, the messenger, made contact on Saturday, met with Abby McDeere on Sunday, and passed along the demand for a hundred million.

Gloom was added to fear as the other eight members of the committee realized just how much money was at stake and that the firm might be on the hook for some of it.

The room was still silent as Jack played the video of Giovanna on a wide screen. Only a few had actually met her, but all of them knew her father. The visual impact of a Scully associate held hostage was breathtaking. They had been apprised of the situation over the past month, but nothing had prepared them for the shock of seeing her gaunt face and hearing her strained voice.

Jack stopped the video but left an indelible image of Giovanna on the screen for them to contemplate. He told them that Mitch had landed in Rome about an hour ago and was on his way to see Luca.

When the questions began, they came in a flood and from every side. Why not involve the FBI and CIA? The firm had strong contacts at the State Department. What were the Brits doing, and the Italians? Was there a plan to try to negotiate? The firm had insurance that paid for highly qualified hostage negotiators, why not use them? How much did they know about the terrorist group? Had they even identified it? Had the bankers been called?

Jack was not expecting the committee to agree on a plan, or on anything else for that matter, so he proposed nothing. He answered the questions he could, deflected those he couldn't, argued when necessary, and in general let everyone blow off steam and try to impress the others. After a raucous first hour, the committee was split into three or four factions, with loyalties swinging back and forth. The loudest group wanted to go straight to the FBI and CIA, but Jack held firm. A couple didn't like the idea of Mitch operating like a lone wolf out there, without real supervision.

No one held back. Opinions rose up swiftly, then dissipated. Some of the facts got blurred. Tempers flared and cooled, but no insults were hurled. They were too professional for that and most of them had been close for decades. At one time or another every member of the committee thought of Giovanna and silently asked the question *What if that was me?* More than once, Bart Ambrose said, aloud, "She's one of us."

———•—•———

When, in Jack's opinion, the discussion had run its course, he moved the conversation to the issue of security. The executive session was adjourned and Cory re-entered the boardroom. He passed out copies of the preliminary report from the crime scene in Barcelona, complete with graphic photos of the firm's fire-gutted offices.

One benefit of being a player in Big Law was unlimited travel. A senior partner could go almost anywhere in the world, or at least anywhere a person of stature would want to go, and call it work, and with deductions galore. Stop by the Scully office, take a partner to lunch or dinner, maybe see an opera or a soccer match, and write off the whole trip. If there was business to discuss, then double-bill the client and stick him for the tickets as well. Barcelona had always been a favorite, and every member of the management committee had visited the stylish offices there. Seeing the place in charred ruins was difficult to absorb.

Cory outlined their emergency plans to beef up security and surveillance at every office. In his opinion, the terrorists, still unidentified, had hit Athens and Barcelona because the offices were soft targets. Not too secure, easy to get into, unsuspecting. For a bloodthirsty bunch, they were careful not to harm anyone. The fires were meant as warnings.

Where were the other soft targets? He mentioned Cairo, Cape Town, and Rio, but made it clear he was only guessing. This led to a meandering chat about which offices were safe and which weren't, all bordering on speculation. One partner had been impressed with the security in their Munich office. Another had just returned from Mexico City and was surprised by the lack of surveillance cameras. And so on. They were successful lawyers, proud of their intelligence, and felt compelled to share their thoughts.

Jack knew them well. After an exhausting two-hour marathon, he could filter what had been said and gauge what had not been said. And he knew that in the end Scully would come through. The question was—How much?

———•—•———

Roberto picked up Mitch at the airport in Rome and drove him to Luca's. During the forty-five-minute drive they covered a lot of territory. Luca was doing okay physically, or at least his condition was somewhat stable, and the news that the kidnappers had made contact and wanted a ransom lifted his spirits considerably. He didn't happen to have $100 million in his bank accounts, but he was confident that with some good negotiations the figure would come down. He was already working on the Italian politicians.

During the drive, Mitch played the video of Giovanna on his cell phone. Roberto's eyes instantly watered and he had to look away. He said she was like a little sister, and he hadn't slept well in a month. He wasn't sure if Luca should see the video. They agreed to discuss it later.

Luca was on the veranda, in the shade and on the phone. He looked even thinner but he was put-together as always. His light gray tailored suit hung loose. He managed to hug Mitch as he kept talking on the phone. His voice was stronger. Later, over coffee, he replayed his recent conversations. He was not a fan of the current prime minister but knew one of his deputy ministers. The goal was to convince the Italian government to come to the rescue of an Italian citizen. With cash. One of the more immediate problems was that Italy had a law on the books that forbade the government from negotiating with terrorists and paying ransom. Its rationale was simple: big checks paid to criminals only encouraged the kidnapping of more Italians. The British and the Americans had similar policies. Luca said they meant almost nothing. The prime ministers and presidents could pound the podium, denounce terrorists, and promise no ransom, but through back channels deals could be made.

The more pressing issue was confidentiality. How could Scully expect help from the Brits and Italians when their governments knew nothing about the demand for ransom?

The three—Luca, Mitch, and Roberto—had talked at length about amending the Lannak complaint against the Libyan government and asking for more damages. Lannak had lost four valuable employees. Giovanna had been held for a month now.

The defendant, the Republic of Libya, had implicitly agreed to provide safety for foreign workers.

The arbitration claim Luca had filed the previous October demanded $410 million in unpaid bills, plus $52 million in interest that had accrued over the past three years. Mitch believed strongly that they should amend the claim, pile on more damages for the bloodshed and kidnapping, and press hard for a settlement. When Luca and Roberto finally agreed, Mitch called Stephen Stodghill, his associate, who was still in New York, and who happened to be asleep at 4 A.M. on a Monday, and instructed him to amend the complaint in Geneva, then meet him in London.

At eleven o'clock Luca retired from the veranda for a quick nap. Mitch went for a stroll around the piazza and called Omar Celik in Istanbul. He was on an airplane somewhere near Japan. Mitch talked to his son, Adem, and informed him of their plans to increase the amount of damages. He did not mention the contact with the kidnappers or the ransom, but that would happen soon enough.

At noon, 6 A.M. in New York, Mitch called Abby and said good morning. Things were fine there. She had talked to her parents at least three times on Sunday and everyone was having a splendid time in Maine. They were not being missed by the boys. No word from Noura.

Luca had an appointment with his doctors at noon and was not available for lunch. Mitch and Roberto walked to a café on a side street away from the tourists. Roberto knew the owner and at least two of the waitresses. With deep frowns and in low voices they inquired about Luca's health. Roberto passed along the more optimistic version.

Even for an Italian, the ritual of lunch seemed like a waste of time. Who could relax and enjoy food? The two had no experience with hostage negotiations and felt helpless. And what would a professional do? The enemy was unseen, unknown. There was nothing to negotiate, no one to talk to. Noura was just a messenger with no authority. As lawyers they negotiated all the time, back and forth, give and take, as both sides grudgingly inched toward a solution neither really liked. Kidnapping, though, was a different monster because murder was in the equation. But how many professional negotiators had ever dealt with an enemy as savage and inhumane as this one? Chain saws? On video?

They barely touched their pasta.

After the table was cleared and they sipped espressos, Roberto said, "Luca is wealthy by any measure, Mitch, but most of it is old family money. His fine home here has been handed down. He owns the office building. The country home is near Tivoli."

"I've been there," Mitch said.

"He's meeting with a banker this afternoon to arrange a mortgage on everything he owns. He thinks it's around five million. He has liquid assets of roughly the same. He's putting it all on the table, Mitch. If I had serious money, I would do the same."

"Me too. But I hate for Luca to lose everything."

"He can't lose his daughter, Mitch. Nothing else matters."

CHAPTER 28

B y 2 P.M. Luca had knocked back two double espressos
and was ready for action. He greeted an important visitor
at the front door and escorted him to the veranda where
he introduced him to Roberto and Mitch. His name was Diego
Antonelli and, according to Roberto, he was a career diplomat
in the foreign service and had known Luca for many years. Supposedly, he could be trusted with secrets and had contacts in the
prime minister's office.

Mr. Antonelli seemed ill at ease and Mitch got the impression he felt too important to make house calls. A light rain began
so Luca invited everyone to his dining table where coffee and
water were served. He thanked Mr. Antonelli for coming and
said there had been a major development in the kidnapping.

Roberto took notes. Mitch listened as intently as possible.
He always appreciated Luca's Italian because it was slow and
thoughtful, easier to follow. Mr. Antonelli, who no doubt spoke
multiple languages, also spoke with perfect diction. Roberto, on
the other hand, began each sentence in a mad dash to get to the
end of it. Mercifully, he said little.

Luca told the story of the mysterious Noura and her contact with Abby McDeere in New York: the meetings, the photographs, the phones, and eventually the demand for ransom. The deadline was May 25, and, given their recent history, it was their belief that the terrorists would not hesitate to carry out the execution.

He made it clear that they had not contacted him or anyone else. They had chosen his law firm and had done so on American soil. In his opinion, it was not wise to involve the Italian police or intelligence services, nor those in Great Britain.

Antonelli took no notes, never touched his pen, nor his coffee. He absorbed every word as if filing away the details in perfect order. Occasionally, he glanced at Mitch with a mildly disdainful look, as if he really didn't belong at the table.

Luca asked him to inform the foreign minister, who should then inform the prime minister.

"How do you know she's still alive?" Antonelli asked.

Luca nodded at Roberto who slid a laptop into view, pressed a key, and there was Giovanna. When she finished and the screen went blank, Luca said, "That arrived yesterday in New York. It has been validated by our security."

"A hundred million dollars," Antonelli repeated but did not seem surprised. Nothing surprised him, and if something did no one would ever know it.

"The second question is, who are you negotiating with?" he said.

Luca touched his eyes with a tissue and took a deep breath. The image of his daughter had upset him for a moment. "Well, there are no negotiations. We don't know who the terrorists are. But we do know they have my daughter, they are demanding ransom, and they will not hesitate to kill her. That is sufficient for the Italian government to get involved."

"Involved? We have been expressly forbidden to interfere."

"There is nothing you can do except help with the ransom. She is an Italian citizen, Diego, and right now she has a high profile. If the government does nothing, and she is sacrificed, can you imagine the backlash?"

"It's against our law, Luca. You know the statute. It's been on the books for over twenty years. We do not negotiate with terrorists and we do not pay ransom."

"Yes, and the law has loopholes. I'll be happy to point them out. There are ten ways around that law and I know every one of them. As of now, I'm asking you to speak to the foreign minister."

"Of course, Luca. They are very concerned about Giovanna. All of us are concerned. But we've heard nothing until now."

"Thank you."

"May I ask if the British are involved?"

Luca was suddenly winded. He looked pale as his shoulders sagged. "Mitch."

"I'm going to London tonight. We have a large office there and many of our partners have experience in the government. Tomorrow, we will meet with the British officials and tell them exactly what we have just told you. We will ask them to contribute to the ransom fund. Our firm has kidnapping and ransom insurance in the amount of twenty-five million dollars and we've put the insurance company on notice. Our firm will kick in an additional amount, but we cannot handle the entire ransom. We need help from both the Italian and British governments."

In English, Antonelli said, "I understand. I will speak to the foreign minister this afternoon. That's all I can do. I'm just the messenger."

"Thank you."

"Thanks, Diego," Luca said softly. He suddenly needed another nap.

———•——•———

The second hostage raid was about as successful as the first.

After dark on Monday, May 16, two teams of Libyan commandos dropped from the sky and landed in the desert two miles south of the small, forlorn village of Ghat, near the Algerian border. They were met by a third team that had been on the ground for twenty-four hours and had trucks, equipment, and more arms.

Surveillance and informants had confirmed the "high likelihood" that the hostage was being held in a makeshift camp at the edge of Ghat. Adheem Barakat and about a hundred of his fighters were hiding there as well. They were being forced to move continually as the Libyan Army tightened the net.

Barakat's informants proved to be more reliable than the Colonel's.

As the three teams, thirty men in all, moved into position near Ghat, they were being closely monitored by enemy drones. Their plan was to wait until after midnight, crawl to within fifty yards of the camp, and attack from three sides. Their plans went haywire when gunfire erupted behind them. The convoy truck with the equipment and arms exploded and its fireball lit up the night. Barakat's men stormed out of the camp with Kalashnikovs blazing. The commandos retreated and regrouped in a gathering of date palm trees, saplings that were too thin to provide adequate cover. From there they managed to hold off the insurgents as gunfire came from everywhere. In the darkness, injured men screamed for help. Searchlights swept the area but only attracted more gunfire. When the grenade launchers found their range, the commandos were forced to retreat even more. Their captain picked up a signal from one of their drones, and, out of the range of gunfire, they found their way back to the trucks. One was still burning. One had been raked with gunfire and its tires were blown. They piled into the third truck and took off in a frantic, inglorious retreat. The carefully planned and rehearsed rescue of the hostage was a disaster.

They left eight of their own behind. Five were presumed to be dead. The other three were not accounted for.

Giovanna was awakened by an explosion, then listened in horror as the gun battle raged for an hour. She knew she was in a small dark room behind a small house at the edge of a village, but nothing more. They moved her every third or fourth day.

She listened and wept.

——— • • ———

For a variety of reasons, the Libyans chose not to report the attack. They had failed miserably again, been embarrassed by a ragtag band of desert fighters, and had lost men in the chaos. And they had rescued no one.

Adheem Barakat had plenty to crow about but remained silent. He had something far more valuable: three Libyan soldiers. And he knew exactly what to do with them.

CHAPTER 29

The Scully & Pershing office in London was in the heart of Canary Wharf, the modern business district on the Thames. Similar in ways to lower Manhattan, the area was filling up with a dazzling collection of soaring skyscrapers, no two even remotely alike. London and New York were slugging it out to be the financial center of the world, and for the moment the Brits were winning because of oil. The Arabs felt more welcome in the U.K. and parked their billions there.

Scully, with a hundred lawyers, leased the top third of an outlandish structure designed along the lines of a vertical torpedo. Critics and purists hated the building. Its Chinese owner was crying all the way to the bank. Every square foot had been leased for years and "the Torpedo" was printing money.

Mitch had been there many times, and on each visit he always stopped in the canyon-like lobby and smiled. He never wanted to forget the first time, eleven years earlier, when he walked through the doors and gazed upward. He and Abby had lived for three years in Cortona, Italy, then two years in London.

They had made the decision to rejoin reality, stop drifting, put down some roots, and start a family. With considerable effort, he had managed to obtain a thirty-minute interview for an associate's position, a mere courtesy that would not have been possible without the law degree from Harvard. Two longer interviews followed, and at the age of thirty he began his legal career for the second time.

The nostalgia came and went. He had more important matters at hand. He rode the elevator to the thirtieth floor, stepped off, and was immediately greeted by armed security guards who meant business. They demanded his briefcase, cell phone, and any other metallic items. He asked if he could keep his shoes and no one laughed. He explained that he was a partner in the firm and one of them said, "Yes sir, thank you sir, now move along." He was scanned by a new machine that blocked the hallway, and when no weapons or bombs were found he was released without being frisked. Hustling away, he shrugged it off and knew that in all the remaining Scully offices around the world the lawyers, secretaries, paralegals, clerks, and couriers were being inspected. The firm could not afford another bombing.

He met Riley Casey, the managing partner, who led him to a small conference room where Sir Simon Croome was enjoying a splendid breakfast. He did not stand or say hello, nor did he stop eating. With his white linen napkin he sort of waved at the chairs across the table and said, "Please have a seat."

Sir Simon had served in Parliament as a young man, spent thirty years on the bench at the High Court, advised a handful of prime ministers, and was a close friend to the current solicitor general. In his golden years he had been recruited by Scully to serve as "of counsel," a title that gave him an impressive office, a secretary, an expense account, and only a client or two to fool with. The firm paid him a hundred thousand pounds a year for his name and connections and allowed him, at eighty-two, to hang around, primarily for breakfast and lunch.

Mitch declined the offer of food but said yes to strong coffee, which he drank as he and Riley waited for Sir Simon to finish chewing and swallow. Scrambled eggs, link sausage, dark toast, a cup of tea, and a small glass of what appeared to be champagne.

The life of a legend who knew the right people.

Mitch had not seen the old guy in at least five years and was sad to see he was aging badly. And he was quite plump.

"The way I see it, Mitch, is that you have a fine mess on your hands." Simon thought himself funny and laughed too hard. Mitch and Riley were obliged to play along.

"I spoke with Jack Ruch last night, at length, and he filled in the blanks. Good chap." He shoveled in another bite of sausage. Mitch and Riley nodded along, confirming that Jack Ruch was indeed a good chap.

"The way I see it, the key here is the Colonel. Sure, he's unstable, always has been, but I do not believe for a moment he was involved in the abduction of Giovanna. I'm quite fond of her, you know, and I go back decades with her father. A real prince."

More nods to confirm that Luca was indeed a real prince.

"The way I see it, Gaddafi desperately wants to deliver the hostage. He'll be the hero, of course, something he craves as a megalomaniac. Keep in mind, though, Mitch, that we have something he doesn't. We have contact with the terrorists. We don't know who they are, and may never know, but they've come to us, not him."

"So we lean on Gaddafi?" Mitch asked.

"No one leans on Gaddafi. No one gets near him, except for his family. He has some boys from different wives and the whole clan is always in a row, much like my family but for different reasons, but he really listens to no one. Take that damned bridge. His engineers and architects knew it was a bad idea. One poor chap, an architect I think, called it foolish, and the Colonel had him shot. That curtailed the dissension and everybody got in line. Halfway through the project the Colonel finally realized that they couldn't find enough water to fill a bucket of piss and all the streams had dried up."

Mitch was impressed that Sir Simon knew so much about his case. He was also reminded that he had the annoying habit of beginning almost every sentence with "The way I see it."

"The way I see it, Mitch, is that we lean on the Libyan ambassador here and the one in Rome and ask them to get the damned lawsuit settled, and quick. They owe our client the money so hand it over. Have there been settlement negotiations?"

"None at all. We just amended our claim to add more damages. A trial is a year away."

"And the Libyans still use the Reedmore bunch?"

"Yes, Jerry Robb."

Sir Simon cringed at the thought of opposing counsel. "That's unfortunate. Intractable as ever, I presume?"

"He's certainly an unpleasant fellow, though we have not yet approached the stage of negotiating."

"Go around him. He'll do nothing but obstruct." He ripped off a bite of toast and pondered his next thought. "The way I see it, Mitch, this is a diplomatic matter. We chat with our Foreign Office boys and send them over to the Libyans. Can we arrange this, Riley?"

Finally asked to speak, Riley said, "We're on the phones now. We have a solid contact inside the Foreign Office and I have a call in to her. The prime minister is traveling in Asia, gone for a week. His office has been superb, calls almost every day for updates. Same for the Service. Giovanna has been a priority from day one, but there was no movement until now. Now we have a demand and a threat. But no one knows where it's coming from."

Mitch asked, "Can we expect money from the British government? We're passing the hat here, Mr. Croome."

"I understand. The way I see it, our government should come to the rescue. However, it would be expecting too much for the Foreign Office to chip in when they have no idea where the money is going. Our intelligence services are being shut out. We haven't a clue who the bad guys are. We're not even sure they exist. Could be an elaborate hoax for all we know."

"It's not a hoax," Mitch said.

"I know that. But I can just hear the foreign minister raising objections. We have no choice, though. We have to ask him for money, and quickly."

Riley said, "There is a law on the books that prevents these sort of maneuvers. Just to remind everybody."

"The way I see it, that law is there for the terrorists to read. Officially, we don't negotiate and we don't pay. But we do, in certain circumstances. This, gentlemen, is an exceptional circumstance. You've seen the tabloids. If something awful happens to Giovanna we'll all be sickened by it and never forgive ourselves. You cannot fail, Mitch."

Mitch held his tongue and took a deep breath. Thanks for nothing. That's the way I see it.

—•—

The best they could do in a pinch was a Third Secretary named Mona Branch. Her title placed her about halfway down the ladder at the Foreign Office and she was not the choice Riley had in mind. However, she was the first one willing to set aside thirty unscheduled minutes in a hectic day to have a chat with the two lawyers from Scully.

They arrived at the Foreign Office complex on King Charles Street at ten minutes before eleven, and waited twenty minutes in a cramped holding room as, they figured, Mona cleared her desk and made room for them. Or perhaps she and her colleagues were just having tea.

She finally stepped out and offered a pleasant smile as introductions were made. They followed her into an office even more cramped than the holding room and sat down across her cluttered desk. She uncapped a fine pen, arranged a writing pad, seemed poised to take notes, and said, "Ms. Sandroni is on our morning sheet, which means her abduction is a primary concern. The prime minister is updated every day. You said you have some information."

Riley, the Brit, would do most of the talking. He said, "Yes, well, as you know, there has been no contact with her kidnappers, or abductors, or whatever. That is, until now."

Her pen froze. Her mouth dropped open slightly though she tried hard to project the standard diplomatic blankness. Her eyes narrowed as she stared at Riley. "They've made contact?"

"Yes."

A pause as she waited. "May I ask how?"

"It happened in New York, through our office there."

Her spine stiffened as she laid down her pen. "May I ask when?"

"Thursday of last week. Again on Sunday. There is a demand for ransom and a deadline. With a threat."

"A threat?"

"Execution. The clock is ticking."

The gravity of this news began to sink in. Ms. Branch took

a deep breath as her officious mood changed. "All right, what can I do for you?"

Riley said, "It is imperative that we see the foreign minister immediately."

She nodded and said, "All right, but I need more information. The ransom, how much?"

"We can't go there. We are under strict instructions from the kidnappers not to do exactly what we are doing now. Run to the government. This must be kept as confidential as possible."

"Who are they?"

"We don't know. I'm sure the Foreign Office has its own list of suspects."

"The usual ones. Libya has no shortage of bad actors. But we can't negotiate with someone we don't know, can we?"

"Please, Ms. Branch. We need to have this conversation with the foreign minister."

The stone face returned as Ms. Branch accepted the inevitable, as difficult as it was. Her rank was too low. The issue was too important. She had no choice but to hand the matter off to her superior. With a proper nod, she said, "Very well. I'll see what I can do."

Riley pushed and said, "Time is crucial."

"I understand, Mr. Casey."

———— • • ————

For lunch they ducked into a pub, found a corner booth, and ordered pints of Guinness and bacon sandwiches. Mitch had learned years ago that alcohol with lunch seriously hampered his afternoon and made him sleepy. For the Brits, though, a couple of pints at noon worked like early morning espressos. The brew recharged their batteries and prepped them for the rigors of what the rest of the day had to offer.

As they waited for their food, they worked the phones. It was impossible to simply sit in a pub and sip ale when they could feel the pressure of the deadline. Riley called Sir Simon and recapped the meeting with Ms. Branch. Both agreed it was a waste of time. Sir Simon was hot on the trail of a former ambassador who could move mountains, and so on. Mitch called Roberto in Rome to check on Luca. They were having little luck with their contacts inside the prime minister's office. Penetrating the Italian foreign service would be just as tricky as finding an audience in London.

Halfway through their sandwiches, and as Riley ordered another pint while Mitch declined, Darian called with news out of Tripoli. Unconfirmed, of course, but Crueggal's sources were reporting another botched commando raid by the Libyan Army, somewhere in the desert near the Algerian border. Barakat got away. No hostage was found. Gaddafi was out of his mind and sacking generals right and left.

Darian's fear was that the Colonel would overreact and send in his troops for a full-blown war. Once the bombing started, the casualties would be enormous and the aftershocks unpredictable.

Mitch ordered a second pint. After a lunch that was much longer than planned, and after a round of coffee, he and Riley returned to the Torpedo and tried to do something productive. Mitch called Abby for the family update. He called his office and chatted with his secretary and a paralegal.

Riley appeared at his door with the news that there was movement at the Foreign Office. They had a 5 P.M. meeting with a Madam Hanrahan, a Second Secretary.

"How wonderful," Mitch mused. "We started with a Third

Secretary and now we've moved up to a Second. I presume the next one will be a First. Then, beyond that, where do we go? How many layers are there?"

"Oh Mitch. The Foreign Office has ten times more departments than Scully. We're just getting started. It could take months to see all the right people, and the more we talk the more dangerous it gets."

"We have eight days."

"I know."

CHAPTER 30

The 5 P.M. meeting with Second Secretary Madam Sara Hanrahan began at 5:21 and ended ten minutes later. She complained of a long day, looked frazzled, and really wanted to go home. In Mitch's opinion, which he shared with no one, she had the watery eyes of a drinker and they were probably intruding on her happy hour. She had been briefed by the Third Secretary, and felt strongly that "her government" could not possibly get involved in a ransom scheme when it had no role in the negotiations. She claimed to be an expert on Libya and knew all that was knowable about the abduction of Giovanna Sandroni. Her department was briefed every morning and had grave concerns.

For Mitch and Riley, the only successful part of the otherwise useless meeting was a promise by Madam Hanrahan to push the matter upward and to do so with haste.

Leaving her office, in the rear seat of a shiny black Jaguar with a trusted Scully driver at the wheel, Riley yanked out his phone, looked at the message, and mumbled, "This should be fun." He listened for a moment, grunted a few times, rang off, then said to the driver, "The Connaught Hotel."

"Seems we're having tea with Sir Simon. He's found an old friend."

The Connaught was a legendary London hotel in the heart of Mayfair. Mitch had never stayed there because he couldn't afford it and Scully wouldn't expense it. Its elegant bars offered the priciest drinks in town. Its restaurant had three Michelin stars. Its staff was a study in tradition and precision.

Sir Simon looked right at home in the main tea room, with a platter of fancy sandwiches on the table and a pot of tea ready to pour. He was with a friend, a dapper little man at least his age or older. He introduced him as Phinney Gibb.

Riley knew him and was immediately suspicious. As Sir Simon explained to Mitch, Phinney had been a deputy minister of some variety back in the Thatcher years and was still connected. One look at the old guy, though, and it was hard to believe he was connected to anything but his pearl-handled cane.

Mitch went silent as Sir Simon laid out a plan. Phinney could still work the back channels and had contacts in the prime minister's office. He also knew a ranking secretary in the Foreign Office. Mitch and Riley exchanged glances. They'd had a full day with important secretaries. And, on top of that, Phinney knew Libya's ambassador to the U.K.

Phinney was confident he could arrange a meeting with the prime minister's office. The goal, of course, was to convince the PM that the government should pay some of the ransom to rescue a British citizen.

Mitch listened hard, sipped tea that he had never learned to enjoy, nibbled on a cucumber sandwich, and worried once again that too many people were getting involved. And the more they met and the more they listened, the more time was being wasted. It was Tuesday evening. Six thirty-five. Two days down, eight to go, and the ransom pot was still empty, except for Luca's commitment.

Phinney prattled on about what a fine fellow the Libyan ambassador was. Riley asked if he could arrange a meeting the following day. Phinney would certainly try, but there was a good chance the ambassador was not in London.

———— • • ————

Inviting Samir Jamblad to Rome was a calculated risk. Under the guise of an old friendship, Luca asked him to come for a visit and he implied that it might be their last. Thirty years earlier they had often worked together and had enjoyed many long dinners together in Tripoli, Benghazi, and Rome. Luca had known back then that Samir was a government informant, as were many professionals and businessmen in Libya, and he had always been careful with his words. Now, desperate for information about his daughter, he hoped Samir might know something Crueggal and the others did not.

Samir arrived in time for dinner. Roberto Maggi met him at the door, introduced him to Bella, and escorted him to the veranda where Luca sat on a leather stool, his wheelchair nowhere to be seen. They greeted each other like old friends and got through the necessary chatter about the beautiful weather and so forth. Samir expected to find Luca pale and gaunt and he was not surprised. A server brought a tray with three small glasses of white wine. They sat on the table, untouched.

Luca nodded off. Samir glanced at Roberto, who frowned and kept talking about Italian football. A few minutes passed and Luca was still asleep.

"I'm sorry," Roberto whispered. He waved Bella over and said to her, "He needs to rest. We'll have dinner in the kitchen."

When Luca was gone, Roberto and Samir picked up their wineglasses and took a sip. Roberto said, "I'm sorry, Samir, but he's very ill. His doctors think he has less than ninety days."

Samir shook his head as he gazed across the rooftops of Rome.

"Of course, the stress of Giovanna's abduction is not helping things."

"I wish I could do something," Samir said.

The nagging question was: Should the Libyans know that the terrorists had contacted Scully? It had been debated back and forth between Luca, Mitch, Roberto, Jack, Cory, and Darian until there was no way to reach an agreement. Those who thought so argued that the Libyan government, or simply Gaddafi, could help facilitate a release and make himself look good in the process. Those who disagreed did so out of utter distrust of the Libyans. Who could possibly know what Gaddafi would do if he knew the kidnappers were demanding ransom in his own kingdom?

Compounding the issue was the apparent plan by Gaddafi to destroy Barakat and his forces, regardless of cost or casualties. If Giovanna got caught in the crossfire, then so be it.

Mitch had made the decision.

"Can you tell us anything new?" Roberto asked.

"I'm afraid not, Roberto. From what I gather, the military is convinced it's the work of Adheem Barakat, a nasty character with a growing army. But there's been no contact, as far as I know. As always, in Libya information is tightly controlled."

"Why can't the army liquidate Barakat?"

Samir smiled and lit a cigarette. "It's not that easy, Roberto. My country is a vast desert with many hiding places. Its borders are porous, its neighbors are rarely friendly and often treacherous. There are many warlords, tribes, gangs, terrorists, and thieves, and they've roamed the desert for centuries. It's impossible for anyone, including a violent dictator like Gaddafi, to exercise a firm grip."

"And the first commando raid was not a success."

"Not really, in spite of what was reported. Sounds like nothing went as planned."

"Was the goal to rescue Giovanna?"

"That's the rumor, but then most of the rumors started by the military are not reliable." Samir spoke like a disinterested man on the street, not a career informant.

"What happened in the second raid?"

"The second?" Samir asked with raised eyebrows, a lame effort to feign ignorance.

"The one last night, near the town of Ghat, on the Algerian border. Surely you heard about it, though evidently it's being buried by the government. Looks like the army walked into another trap and things went badly. No mention of Giovanna."

"Your intelligence is better than mine, Roberto."

"Sometimes. We pay a small fortune for it."

"I know only what I read in the newspaper, which is rarely accurate."

Roberto nodded along as if he believed him. "Here's the danger, Samir. The army doesn't know where she is and they still don't know who has her. They've tried two commando raids to rescue her and have nothing to show but casualties and embarrassment. They're desperate. Gaddafi could lose his mind and turn this into a full-scale war. If that happens then a lot of people will die. Including Giovanna."

Samir nodded along, agreeing with the logic. He said, "He loses his mind all the time. Sort of a habit."

Roberto lit his own cigarette, sipped his wine, and let a

moment pass. "There's a confidential matter, Samir. Of utmost importance and it has to be handled carefully."

"I'm at your service."

And the Colonel's as well. "Contact has been made. Not here, not with the family, but in New York, through the law firm."

Samir could not suppress a look of disbelief. He inhaled quickly as his head twitched slightly to the right, then he collected himself. "By the terrorists?"

"Yes. With a demand for ransom and a deadline for an execution. We have eight more days."

"Who are they?"

"We don't know. The communications are coming from a mysterious contact in New York. Quite brilliant, actually."

"How much ransom?"

"I can't say. A lot. More than Luca and our law firm can scrape together. I know you have contacts everywhere in Libya, Samir. Can you get a message to the right people?"

"And who are the right people?"

"The ones who make the final decisions about everything in Libya."

"Gaddafi himself?"

"If you say so."

"No, I have no link to the man, nor do I want one."

"But you can make it happen, Samir. The message is twofold. First, leave the terrorists alone until Giovanna is safe. Second, settle the Lannak lawsuit as soon as possible and on our terms."

Bella eased behind them and said, in Italian, "Gentlemen, dinner is served." Roberto acknowledged her but neither man moved.

"The lawsuit?" Samir asked.

"Yes. The government owes the money. It can pay now and close the matter, or it can spend a fortune in legal fees and pay the money three years from now. Settling the lawsuit now might possibly help to bring Giovanna home."

"I'm not sure I follow."

"The ransom, Samir. It's all about the money. We're trying to collect a lot of money and Lannak will be at the table."

"You want the Libyan government to pay the ransom?"

"Of course not. We want the government to honor its contracts and pay the money it rightfully owes to settle the lawsuit."

Samir stood and walked to the edge of the veranda. He lit another cigarette and for a long time stared into the distance, seeing nothing. After a few minutes, Roberto joined him. "We should have dinner, Samir."

"Okay. Perhaps my connections are not as strong as you think, Roberto. I'm not sure where to go with this request."

"We don't know either. That's why Luca wanted you here. He should feel better tomorrow."

——— • • ———

Mitch skipped dinner and went for a walk along Charlotte Street in Fitzrovia. He and Abby had lived in the upscale neighborhood back then and it was still their favorite part of London.

At the moment, though, he had no time to reminisce. The day had not been a complete waste but, so far, there seemed to be little to show for their efforts. There was no plan to meet the foreign minister or any of his senior advisers. Luca had made no progress on the same front in Rome. The Libyan ambassadors to both countries were either back home in Libya or globetrotting on official business. His law firm was supportive but seemed content to let him decide what to do. No one knew what to do.

There was no guide or playbook. No lawyer at Scully had ever been down this road. Luca was quite ill and not emotionally stable, and for good reasons. Healthy and clearheaded, he was the one person who would know precisely the next five moves. Jack Ruch was a steady hand, but as the hours passed he was becoming more and more deferential to Mitch, as if he wanted some distance in case there was a bad outcome.

Mitch was making decisions with insufficient intelligence and no real clue as to their effectiveness. They could well be wrong. A bad ending was too awful to dwell on.

As always, when he was troubled he called his best friend and talked to Abby for half an hour. Clark and Carter had been fishing with Tanner. Her parents were finding it difficult to make the boys study, but having a grand time. It was like a vacation. Barry Ruch had left the island for a few days and they had the big house to themselves.

CHAPTER 31

At dawn, Mitch checked out of the hotel and got into the rear seat of the same Jaguar as the day before. Fortunately, the driver wasn't much of a talker and the ride to Heathrow was quiet. At eight-fifteen, he boarded a Turkish Airlines flight to Istanbul, four hours nonstop. At customs there, he was greeted by a Lannak representative and led to an express lane where he was waved through with hardly a glance. He did look over his shoulder at the long lines behind him and was once again grateful he worked for an outfit like Scully. A black car was waiting near the terminal, and less than twenty minutes after touching down Mitch was on the phone as his driver zipped through traffic with little regard for speed limits and other annoyances.

Of course, a proud old company like Lannak would insist on being headquartered in a prestigious section of Istanbul's central business district. There were several in the sprawling city of eleven million. Maslak was arguably the best known, and it was there that Omar Celik built a forty-story tower in 1990 and claimed the top half for Lannak, the family's holding company.

Omar was away on business in Indonesia. In his absence, his son, Adem, was ostensibly in charge, though it was well known that his father kept virtually everything under his thumb. Adem was being groomed to take over one day, but Omar had many miles to go. Those close to him expected he would at least try to run things from the grave.

Adem was forty-four and had an American wife he'd met at Princeton, two teenage children in school in Scotland, and friends around the world. He and his wife fancied themselves an international couple and traveled extensively. Though they had an apartment in New York, Mitch and Abby had yet to entertain them. But they were on the list.

Adem welcomed Mitch to his splendid office on the thirty-fifth floor and inquired about lunch. It was almost 2 P.M. and Mitch had not eaten. Neither had Adem. They took the stairs up two floors and settled into the company's small private dining room where a waiter took their orders and served ice water. The other six tables were empty. After some more of the obligatory small talk, Mitch went through the latest about Giovanna. The terrorists had made contact. There was a demand for $100 million in ransom, a threat, and a deadline. The questions began and Mitch had anticipated every one of them. Lunch arrived and they ignored it as the discussion continued.

Mitch had no idea why "they" would use Noura. They chose Scully because it is accessible, well known, and wealthy. Squeezing money out of Scully would be far more productive than hounding Luca, but the ransom demand was much too high. The British and Italian governments had been given most of the details, but neither was eager to jump into the middle of a mess over which they had no control. Both had tentatively agreed to work their diplomatic channels to push the Libyans into a settlement, but such efforts moved at a glacial pace even on a good day. So far, everyone seemed convinced that the terrorists were willing to carry out their threats. The Libyans had badly botched two rescue efforts.

It was not a hoax. Using his cell phone, Mitch showed Adem the video of Giovanna asking for help. Its date and time had been validated by private security. Obviously, its location was unknown.

———•—•———

After lunch, they walked down the stairs to Adem's office and took off their jackets. Mitch handed over a brief memo outlining Lannak's losses and claims on the bridge project. Adem had seen it all before.

Mitch finally got down to business. "Our plan is to push hard for an immediate settlement. It's a long shot, but right now so is everything else. As your lawyer, it is my job to get as much money for you as possible. The question is—"

"What's our bottom line?" Adem said with a smile.

"What's your bottom line?"

"Well, we're owed four hundred and ten million dollars. That's our starting point. You believe you can prove that in court, right?"

"Yes. It will be hotly disputed by the Libyans, but that's why we have courtrooms and trials. I am confident we will win."

"And we are entitled to interest at five percent on the unpaid bills."

"Correct."

"And the balance due has been on the books for almost two years."

"Correct."

"Your figure for interest is fifty-two million." Adem sort of waved at the memo. The figures were clear.

Mitch said, "And we've amended our claim to cover damages for the security guards and the kidnapping. We're demanding half a billion dollars, all in. I don't expect to recover that much because the Libyans will claim they are not liable for the attack and murders. It's debatable. There has always been an implied promise of protection for foreign workers, but the arbitration board has never been too impressed with it."

"So the four families receive nothing?"

"Unlikely, but we'll try. I'm sure your company will take care of them."

"Oh, we will, but the Libyans should pay too."

"I'm prepared to argue that. I'll argue everything, Adem," Mitch said with a smile. "That's my job. But a trial could be months away, maybe a year or more. Meanwhile, your company is losing money at the going interest rate. There is value in settling now."

"You want to discount our damages?"

"Perhaps, but only if it will facilitate the settlement. That's where your bottom line comes in. There's also the real danger of getting nothing."

"Luca has made that clear."

"The arbitration board's ruling is nonbinding. It has no real teeth. There are ways to enforce the judgment and make the Libyans pay, but it could take years. We would demand more sanctions from the board, from the Turks, Brits, Italians, even Americans, but Gaddafi has lived with sanctions for many years. I'm not sure they bother him that much."

"We're finished with Libya," Adem said in disgust.

"Don't blame you."

"What's your advice, Counselor."

"Can you live with four hundred million?"

Adem smiled and said, "We would be delighted."

"We discount our claim to four hundred, but only for purposes of settlement negotiations. Lannak gets the first four hundred. With your permission, I'll ask for more, with any overage going into the pool for the ransom. In the meantime, you ask your government to lean on the Libyan ambassador to get some relief in Tripoli."

Adem was shaking his head. "We've done that, Mitch, repeatedly. Our ambassador to Libya has met on more than one occasion with Gaddafi's people and pled our case. No good. Our prime minister has met with the Libyan ambassador to Turkey here in the city and tried to twist arms. Nothing. We've been told that Gaddafi is embarrassed by his bridge project and blames everyone involved, including our company. You know he shot one of his own architects."

"So I've heard. Does he shoot his lawyers?"

"Let's hope not." Adem glanced at his wristwatch and scratched his jaw. "My father is three hours ahead of us, in Jakarta. He'll be home late tonight. I'll have to get his approval to discount our claim."

"Perhaps both of us should talk to him."

"I'll go first. I don't foresee a problem."

———•—•———

When traveling alone in an unfamiliar city, and with a few hours to kill, Mitch often hired a car and driver to at least catch a glimpse of landmarks and famous places, sort of hitting the high spots on the tourist maps. During his flight to Istanbul he had read travel guides on Turkey and was fascinated by the country.

He told Abby it definitely deserved another look, a place on their wish list.

But sightseeing was not possible. Wasting time seemed frivolous. In his hotel room he made a desk on a coffee table and worked his phones. Abby again, just to check in. Jack Ruch for the same. Roberto in Rome broke the news that Luca had been hospitalized with a fever, dehydration, and probably other symptoms and ailments. He was resting fitfully and being watched closely. Samir was in town and they had spent a few hours together. Diego Antonelli had called with little to report. He was obviously finding it difficult to find an ear inside the prime minister's circle. Cory was in New York and had just finished speaking to Darian, one of their daily updates. Nothing much to report from Libya except snippets regarding the latest commando raid that went badly. The government was still stonewalling the story. There were rumors that the Barakat gang had captured three Libyan soldiers. As always, there was no sign of Giovanna. In London, Riley Casey was still slogging his way up the endless ladder of the Foreign Service in search of someone with real authority. Sir Simon Croome was having lunch as they spoke with a bona fide Libyan, a businessman who'd been in the U.K. for decades and had made a mint. There was a chance this old friend and client could twist an arm or two and prod Tripoli into paying his bills and settling the Lannak claim. Mitch found the idea silly. The two old goats would probably drink their lunches, take long naps, then forget whatever they talked about.

After two fruitless hours on the phone, Mitch was deflated and fell asleep.

He rallied in time for dinner. Adem suggested a table at 10 P.M. in an Asian fusion place with a Michelin star, and Mitch was tempted only because his wife routinely expected him to bring back menus and notes from new restaurants. Not surprisingly, she knew a Turkish chef in Queens and they were discussing a cookbook. However, Mitch preferred to eat no later than eight and did not want a late night. Instead, they met in the Brasserie of the St. Regis Hotel, where he was staying. Adem had hinted that his wife might join them, and Mitch was relieved when she did not.

Over whiskey sours, Adem relayed a conversation he'd had with his father late that afternoon. Omar wanted blood from the Libyans, and he certainly wanted every dime he was due for the bridge, but he was a pragmatist. Four hundred million dollars in today's money might seem like a great deal years down the road. If Mitch could deliver that much, then anything above it was his to bargain with for Giovanna's return.

They shook hands, though both knew that a settlement was unlikely.

CHAPTER 32

At 11:55 Wednesday night, Abby was still awake and reading magazines in bed. She was tired of the quiet apartment and tired of living alone. She wanted to hug her twins, crawl in bed with her husband, and say farewell to all the horrible drama she had not asked for. Someone else could play the spy game.

The Jakl buzzed on the nightstand and startled her. It had not made a sound since Sunday morning. She picked it up and walked to a small table near the den where she placed it next to her cell phone. She tapped both phones. An app on hers would record the conversation without the Jakl knowing it, according to Darian.

"Hello."

"This is Noura. Are you alone?"

Don't you know the answer? Aren't you people watching us? "Yes."

"Do you have the money?"

"Well, no, but we're working on it."

"Is there a problem?"

Who knew how many people were listening on the other end? Be careful, measure every word. There is a language difference here and something might be misunderstood or taken the wrong way.

"Not a problem, just the challenge of finding that much money."

"That should be easy, I would think." A definite British lilt in the last phrase.

"Why would you think that?" Keep her talking.

"Rich lawyers, largest law firm in the world, offices everywhere. It's all right there on the website. Billings last year of over two billion."

Oh, the frustration of lawyers pounding their own chests. Abby said, "The firm has lost a couple of offices lately, in case you haven't heard."

"That's unfortunate, but it will continue until we have the money."

"I thought the money was for Giovanna's release."

"It is. Deliver the money and everything will be fine."

"Look, I'm not a member of the firm and I don't know what they're doing. I know my husband is in Europe right now trying to raise the money, but I don't know what's going on. I'm a book editor, you know?"

"Yes. There has been a change in plans." A pause. Say something, Abby.

"Okay, what kind of change?"

"There shall be a deposit, to show good faith." Another pause.

"I'm listening."

"Ten million dollars by noon Friday, sent from a bank here in New York."

Abby exhaled and said, "Okay. All I can do is relay this to my husband. I have no control over anything."

"Noon Friday. I will send instructions. I will also send a new video of Giovanna to prove she is in good hands."

Good hands? Same hands that held the chain saw?

———— • • ————

Jack Ruch finally yielded to the grumbling. It was irritating enough that the management committee had to meet daily for the crisis update, but to meet at 7 A.M. was too much. Jack pushed it back to 9:30 on Thursday, and called the executive session to order for the fourth day in a row. By then most of the members were secretly wondering if it was really necessary to meet every day, but it was a crisis like no other. No one had yet found the spine to question Jack. All nine were present.

He began with, "There's a new development. Our dear Noura made contact late last night with Abby, and informed her that a good-faith deposit is now part of the deal. Ten million by noon tomorrow, Friday."

The news settled heavily around the room. All eyes were on the table.

Jack cleared his throat and continued, "I spoke with Mitch an hour ago. He's leaving Istanbul and going to Rome, where Luca has been hospitalized."

Ollie LaForge asked, "And we still don't know who we're talking to, right? We're supposed to fork over ten million up front and hope for the best?"

"You got a better idea?" Jack shot back.

"Has Mitch had any luck since yesterday?" asked Mavis Chisenhall.

"If you're asking me whether Mitch has obtained any commitments for money, then the answer is no. But he's trying. That's all I can say."

Month in and month out, the firm kept about $15 million in extra cash on hand for emergencies and other contingencies. There was a larger reserve for the sacred year-end bonuses, but that money could not be touched.

Sheldon Morlock, one of the more influential partners on the committee, said, "There must be a way to negotiate with these people. What they're asking is outrageous and beyond our capacity. And, you can't convince me they'll walk away if they don't get every dime. Say we somehow scrape together only half the money. Are they going to say no?"

Jack said, "That's just it, Sheldon, no one knows. We can't predict. This is not a typical business transaction with rational people on both sides. They could kill her at any moment."

Piper Redgrave, the third woman on the committee, said, "Jack, are you saying we should hit the line of credit and borrow the money?"

"Yes, that's exactly what I'm saying. We should borrow twenty-five million because that's the extent of our policy. We give them ten tomorrow and say a prayer."

Bart Ambrose said, "I talked to Citibank, as instructed. They're ready, but they'll require personal guarantees from each of us."

There were groans, sighs, silent expletives, head-shaking in frustration. A two-thirds majority vote was required to borrow money.

Jack said, "That's nothing new. Any objections?"

"Are we voting?" Morlock asked.

"Yes. Anyone opposed to borrowing twenty-five million from Citi on our line of credit?"

All nine shot quick, fierce looks around the table. Morlock raised his hand, then lowered it. Slowly, Ollie LaForge raised his.

"Anybody else?" Jack asked with contempt. "Okay, the vote is seven in favor, two opposed. Right?"

There was no further discussion. They filed out of the conference room in silence and hurried to their own offices.

And that was the easy vote. Every dime would be reimbursed under the firm's insurance policy.

Or so they thought.

———•—•———

After the meeting, Jack called the insurance company for the update. Instead, he was put on hold and waited far too long. When the CEO said good morning, Jack was surprised. What he heard next was deflating. The claim was being denied on the grounds that Giovanna had been kidnapped and was being held by terrorists, as opposed to a criminal gang. The policy unequivocally excluded coverage for acts of terrorism.

"I can't believe this," Jack roared into the phone.

"It's right there in black and white, Jack," replied the CEO calmly.

Black and white. Since when were insurance policies clear about anything?

"Kidnapping is kidnapping," Jack said, trying to control his anger. "The damned policy covers kidnapping."

"Our sources tell us it's the work of a terrorist organization, Jack. So we are denying. I'm sorry."

"I don't believe this."

"Our counsel is emailing a denial memo as we speak."

"I guess I'll see you in court."

"That's up to you."

CHAPTER 33

Luca rallied somewhat after a few hours in the hospital. Some different meds stabilized his blood pressure. A drip rehydrated him. A stronger sedative sent him into a long, much-needed nap. The best medicine was the constant attention of a thirty-year-old nurse with a stunning figure and a short white skirt. Bella watched it all from a corner, shaking her head. Some men were hopeless.

Luca was attempting to put together a deal that involved a reclusive Italian billionaire he had known for a long time. Carlotti was his name and he was an heir to an old family fortune built on olive oil. His politics did not jibe with Luca's, but when it came to money the two had always managed to see past their differences. Carlotti was close to the prime minister and had bankrolled him for years. At Luca's urging, he had agreed to pressure the prime minister into an elaborate plan to funnel money from the Italian treasury into a ransom fund owned by a company in Spain, where Carlotti spent most of his time. He was reluctant because paying kidnappers was against the law in Italy but not in Spain. However, he adored Giovanna and would do anything to help her. The prime minister was reluctant because one more scandal would easily topple his fragile government. But, as Luca argued vehemently, a bad outcome for Giovanna could do even more damage. The prime minister was getting shoved into a no-win situation. Luca was confident he could skirt the law and bluff the prosecutors later if necessary. Mitch was uncomfortable with any conversation in which the word "prosecutors" was mentioned.

The next step was a conversation with Diego Antonelli, the deputy minister they had met Monday afternoon at Luca's. His office was in a nondescript government building in the Lateran section of eastern Rome, near a palace where some popes once lived, according to Roberto, who had the mildly annoying habit of pointing out minor points of historical interest to any non-Roman around him.

Mr. Antonelli had been less than cordial during his house call on Monday. Evidently, a meeting at 6:30 P.M. on a Thursday did not please him either. He made them wait twenty minutes and finally waved them into a small conference room near his suite. There were quick handshakes but no smiles.

"There is no record of this meeting," he began pleasantly, and actually looked around to see if anyone was eavesdropping. The door had been shut tight and locked. Mitch suspected there were bugs everywhere.

"If someone asks, the meeting never happened."

Not for the first time, Mitch questioned what he was doing. If an illegal bribe or payment was in the works, why was he in the room? Luca had hinted at finding enough loopholes in the law to get the ransom paid, but Mitch had thought that was solely the concern of Luca and his Italian buddies. Scully could not be a part of a conspiracy to circumvent the laws of any country. He shuddered at the thought of federal prosecutors in Manhattan having a rowdy time with those charges.

According to Luca, the purpose of the meeting was to confirm "the deal" with Antonelli, who would serve as the intermediary between Carlotti and the prime minister. From one of its discretionary funds, the Foreign Service would loan $50 million to a faceless corporation registered in Luxembourg and controlled by one of Carlotti's sons. A repayment agreement would be signed but buried. The money would then be wired here and there and parked in an account where it would sit at the ready.

Antonelli seemed less than enthusiastic about the deal and spoke only to Roberto, in Italian. That was fine with Mitch. He followed the conversation well enough, but would have preferred to miss all of it.

Antonelli asked, "And in your opinion, Counselor, this complies with all statutes and will not raise concerns at the Justice Ministry?"

"I see no problem," Roberto said confidently, though all three knew there was trouble at every turn.

"Well, the prime minister's attorneys will review it tonight. I suspect they may have a different opinion."

"Then I'm sure you'll inform Luca."

The meeting lasted less than ten minutes and both sides were eager to get out the door. Mitch left Roberto on the street and took the first cab to the airport. His secretary had juggled flights again and he was booked on one to Frankfurt, then JFK. In the back of the cab, he closed his eyes and dreaded the next ten hours.

What about the next five days? Not only was the ransom pot still empty, it had sprung a significant leak. Tomorrow's "deposit" of $10 million was the easy step, though Mitch was irritated that two members of the management committee had voted no. By yanking the rug out from under them, the insurance company not only acted in bad faith, an issue for another day, but it had upset all possible scenarios for pooling the ransom. The deal with Carlotti was precarious at best and illegal at worst and was probably already unraveling. Mitch would report it to Jack Ruch, who would no doubt call Luca and start yelling. Everyone was sympathetic and desperate to save Giovanna, but Scully was not about to start breaking laws in any jurisdiction. There was no movement from the British government, in spite of numerous Scully operatives pecking away at the Foreign Minister. Riley Casey had met with Jerry Robb of the Reedmore firm that afternoon to gauge any interest in a quick settlement of the Lannak lawsuit. Typical for Robb, the meeting was short, tense, and a total waste of time.

CHAPTER 34

Mitch had learned years earlier that jet lag was best shaken off with a long run through Central Park. He couldn't sleep it off, especially not with a clock ticking and his boys in hiding and his wife increasingly anxious. Abby joined him at dawn as they entered the park at Seventy-Second Street and fell in behind a crowd of early runners. They rarely talked as they ran, preferring instead to soak in the first rays of the sun and enjoy the coolness of New York in the spring. As the boys got older and life marched on, the long runs they cherished were becoming less frequent.

Back in their Cortona days, before children and careers and such, they ran every morning, through farms and vineyards and villages. They would often stop and chat with a farmer to see if they could understand his accented Italian, or stop at a sidewalk café in a village for a glass of water or a shot of espresso. Their favorite character was the owner of a small winery who often flagged them down to inquire about the odd American habit of voluntarily running down a road, in a sweat, going nowhere in particular. Several times he invited them into his small courtyard where his wife poured glasses of cold rosé and insisted they try slices of *buccellato,* a sugary cake with raisins and aniseed. Such mid-workout stops usually drifted into longer wine tastings and the joggers forgot about their mileage. After a few detours, Abby insisted they alter their route.

They circled the reservoir and headed home. The streets were coming to life with morning traffic. Another busy day in the city. They had no plans to be there after dark.

At 11 A.M., they took a cab to the Citibank office on Lexington Avenue near Forty-Fourth, and went up twenty-six floors to the office of Ms. Philippa Melendez, a VP of some variety and an expert on moving money. She led them to a conference room where Cory and Darian were having coffee. Within minutes Jack arrived, and the firm's ultimate authority was ready to sign. Philippa confirmed that the $10 million was on hand. All they had to do was wait for Noura.

She called at 11:30 and asked if Abby had her laptop. She had been told to bring it. The email arrived quickly with the wiring instructions. Cory's team of hackers would track the sending address to a cyber café in Newark, but the sender was long gone. Jack Ruch signed an authorization on behalf of the firm. All $10 million would go to a numbered bank account in Panama.

"Ready?" Philippa asked Jack. He nodded gravely, and Scully said goodbye to the money.

"Impossible to track?" Abby asked as they stared at her laptop screen.

Philippa shrugged and said, "Not impossible, but not practical either. It's going to a shell company in Panama, and there are thousands of them. The money is gone."

They waited eight minutes before the Jakl rattled again. Noura said, "The money has arrived."

The larceny had been quick, efficient, almost painless. They all took deep breaths and tried to adjust to the reality that a lot of money had just evaporated, with nothing, at the moment, to show for it. They said quiet goodbyes and left the office.

On the street, Abby and Cory got into a black SUV and headed uptown to the apartment. Mitch and Darian took another one and headed south to the financial district.

Abby's overnight bag was packed and waiting. At the kitchen table, she sent a text on the Jakl informing Noura that she would be away from the phone until noon Sunday. She left it, along with her cell phone, hidden in her closet. She slipped out of the apartment through a basement entrance and returned to the same SUV, where Cory was waiting. The driver left the city over the George Washington Bridge and disappeared into northern New Jersey. Cory was certain they had not been followed. In the town of Paramus they stopped at a small airport, boarded a King Air, and took off. Ninety minutes later, they landed on Islesboro, where Carter and Clark were waiting at the airfield to see their mom. It had been a week.

——— . . ———

At 12:30, Jack called the management committee to order for the fifth straight day. All nine were present. The mood was tense and gloomy. The firm had just lost ten million dollars.

He brought them up to date on the morning's activities then opened the door. Mitch walked in and said hello. They were pleased to see him and had plenty of questions. He briefed them on Luca's condition, gave an update on the Lannak claim in Geneva, and passed along the latest rumors out of Tripoli.

On the ransom front, there was little progress. The governments of Italy and Great Britain were still stonewalling and hoping the crisis would pass, or just go away. Since they were not involved with the negotiations and had no idea exactly who in hell they were dealing with, they were understandably reluctant to commit cash for the ransom.

Now that the kidnappers had collected a nice deposit, Mitch planned to ask them for more time. The deadline, as everyone well knew, was the following Wednesday, May 25. His gut told him this would be fruitless since they had shown no interest in negotiating.

After carefully painting the grim picture, Mitch moved on to more unpleasant business. As he paced back and forth in front of a large blank screen, he finally cut to the heart of the matter. They knew it was coming.

"It is imperative that this law firm commit its full resources to the safe return of Giovanna Sandroni. To do so will be to guarantee that the demands of her kidnappers are met in full, whatever the ultimate terms may be. As of now, it's ninety million dollars."

As senior partners, their average gross earnings the previous year were $2.2 million, third on the list of national rankings. They lived well, spent well, some saved more than others. Almost all were financially conservative, but a few were rumored to spend as much as they took home. On paper they were all millionaires, and in the not too distant past, maybe twenty years or so, they would have been considered the rich boys of Wall Street. Now, though, their incomes were dwarfed by the money runners—hedge funders, private equity guys, venture capitalists, currency speculators, bond boys—the new kings of the street.

The first comment came from Ollie LaForge, who oddly enough found some humor in the moment. He smiled as he chuckled and said, "You gotta be kidding."

Mitch knew better than to respond. He'd said enough and

the ensuing conversation was for the committee members. He sat down, not at the table, but against a wall.

Sheldon Morlock said, "I am not going to risk everything I've worked for and the financial security of my family by guaranteeing a bank loan in the amount of ninety million dollars. It's out of the question." He would not look at Mitch.

Piper Redgrave said, "I'm sure we all feel the same way, Sheldon, but no one will ever expect you to fork over that much money. The firm will own the debt, and I'm sure that with some belt-tightening here and there, and some sacrifice, we can muddle through it. Bart, what would the terms of the loan look like?"

Muddle through, Mitch said to himself. As if Scully's partners might skip a weekend in the Hamptons or even miss a Michelin star meal.

Bart Ambrose said, "Well, for now, it would be a line of credit for ninety million, three percent interest, something like that. If we go all in, we can convert it to a long-term note."

Bennett McCue said, "It won't be ninety mil, Sheldon. We'll have a nasty lawsuit with the insurance company but in the end they'll pay. That's twenty-five mil right there."

"It could take years," Morlock shot back. "And winning is not a sure thing."

Ollie LaForge said, "Look, I hate debt, you know that. I have none, never have. My father went bankrupt when I was twelve years old and we lost everything. I hate banks and you've all heard this speech before. Count me out." He still lived in a bungalow in Queens and took the train to work. And because of his tightfistedness he undoubtedly saved more money than anyone in the room.

Mavis Chisenhall was another tightwad. She looked at Mitch and asked, "Would you sign a personal guarantee, Mitch?"

The perfect question. One he was begging for. He got to his feet, pulled out a folded sheet of paper, tossed it to the center of the table, and said, "I've already signed it. There it is."

As they stared at it, he pulled out another, tossed it too on the table, and said, "And here's one from Luca. We're all in."

He studied their faces, though most were looking at their notepads. While he had the floor, he decided to try and close the deal. "Here's why this is important. There is a chance we might collect monies from other sources, but nothing is certain. We might get promises, but not in time. We need certainty, and the only way to have certainty at this point is to have the money in the bank. Only Scully can put it there. I'm leaving Sunday for London, then Rome, then who knows where else. I'm passing the hat, begging on street corners, whatever it takes. But if I fail, at least we'll have the money in the bank. All of it. I don't know if they'll give us more time. I don't know if they'll cut the ransom, settle for less. It's impossible to predict the next five days. But, it is possible to know we can pay the ransom."

When he finished, Jack nodded at the door and they stepped outside. He whispered, "Nice job. You should probably leave now. This may take some time."

"Okay. I'm off to your brother Barry's to see my kids."

"Hug the boys for me. I'll give you a call."

———•———•———

The driver took the Brooklyn Bridge and the traffic barely moved. It was a Friday afternoon in late May and half of Manhattan was headed for somewhere on Long Island. An hour later they arrived at Republic Airport, a small general aviation field outside the town of Farmingdale. Mitch thanked the driver, and as he drove away he realized he had not bothered to check the traffic behind him. What a lousy spy. He was so fed up with looking over his shoulder.

A pilot who appeared to be no more than fifteen took his bag, led him to a twin-engine Beech Baron, and helped him inside. It was snug but comfortable, a far cry from the Falcons and Gulfstreams and Lears that Scully often leased. Mitch didn't care. He was taking twenty-four hours off and about to spend time with his boys. The pilot pointed to a small cooler and Mitch thought why not. The weekend was starting. He popped a top and had a cold beer. As they taxied, Mitch called Roberto in Rome for an update. Luca was awake and griping about this and that. The nurses liked him better when he wasn't awake.

For almost two hours they flew at 8,000 feet. The weather was perfectly clear. As they descended along coastal Maine, Mitch gazed from above and was touched by the beauty of the ocean, the rocky shores, the quiet coves, and the quaint fishing villages. Thousands of small sailboats bounced across the azure water. They buzzed the picturesque town of Camden with its busy harbor, then aimed for Islesboro. At five hundred feet, Mitch saw a row of mansions on the water and picked out Wicklow. Clark and Carter were on the dock with Abby, and they waved as the Baron flew over. Half an hour later, Mitch was sitting by the pool watching the boys swim and chatting with his wife and her parents.

The week had been summer camp for the boys. Mr. and Mrs. Sutherland admitted they had been somewhat less than diligent with the lessons and homework. Bedtime, too, had been rather flexible, and with Miss Emma at their service in the kitchen the meals had been total kid food. Mitch and Abby could not have cared less. Given the stress they were under, any help from the grandparents was more than welcome.

Over drinks—white wine for Mitch and Abby, lemonade for the Sutherlands—they gently inquired as to how much longer they would be needed so far from home. This irritated Mitch, it didn't take much, because the safety of the boys was far more important than anything the Sutherlands might be missing back in Danesboro, Kentucky. He held his words and said maybe, perhaps, just a few more days.

May 25, to be exact.

They watched as Tanner walked to the end of the pier and met a lobster boat that had pulled alongside the dock for a home delivery.

"More lobster," said Mr. Sutherland. "We're eating it three times a day."

Maxine, a thoroughly humorless woman, added, "Lobster quiche in the morning. Lobster rolls for lunch. Baked lobster tails for dinner."

At the edge of the pool Carter was listening and added, "And don't forget lobster mac and cheese, my favorite."

Harold said, "Lobster bisque, lobster fritters, New England lobster dip."

"Sounds delicious," Abby said.

Maxine was happy not to be cooking every meal. "Miss Emma is wonderful, really."

Clark said, "Mom, you should do a lobster cookbook. Put Miss Emma on the cover."

"I like that," Abby said, trying to recall the dozens of seafood cookbooks she had already collected.

Barry Ruch appeared in shorts and deck shoes, a long cigar in one hand and a Scotch in the other. He had managed to stay away from Wicklow all week, and Mitch assumed he wanted no part of the babysitting. Or the grandparents. He smiled at Mitch and said, "Jack's looking for you."

— · —

Holding the green phone, Mitch walked along the pier and called Jack. When he answered it was clear the news was not good. It was almost six-thirty on Friday evening, and they had started their long day together at Citibank's offices, watching ten million evaporate.

Jack said, "We met for almost five hours, Mitch, and it was without a doubt my worst experience in forty years at Scully. Four of us voted to borrow the money, say to hell with it, save Giovanna, and worry about the future starting next week. The other five would not budge. Not surprisingly, Morlock became their mouthpiece. I have never been so disgusted. I lost some friends today, Mitch."

Mitch stopped walking and watched the lobster boat disappear. "I don't know what to say."

"Retirement's looking better."

"How many times did you vote?"

"I don't know. Several. But the bottom line is the same. I'm not giving names here, Mitch. In fact, this is all confidential. You're not supposed to know what happened in the executive session."

"I know, I know. I'm just, you know, stunned."

"You did your best, Mitch."

"And there's no way around the management committee?"

"You know our by-laws. Every partner does. You could force a recall, fire the committee, and so on, elect new members if you could find anyone willing to serve. Believe me, Mitch, with this issue on the table not a single lawyer at Scully would want to serve."

"So what happens next week if they murder Giovanna and video the whole damned thing for the world to see?"

"The usual. Point fingers, blame everyone else. The terrorists, the Libyans, the Turks, the foreign services. No one will ever know that we had the chance to ransom our way out of this mess. That will not be publicized. And with time I'm sure our colleagues will get over our loss and move on. Lots of eager young lawyers out there, Mitch. Giovanna was just another associate. They can all be replaced."

"That's pretty sick."

"I know. I'm pretty disgusted with this firm."

"I guess you should call Luca."

"That's for you, Mitch. You're closer to him than anyone else."

"No, Jack, sorry. You're the managing partner and it's your committee. But call Roberto, not Luca."

"I can't do it, Mitch. Please."

CHAPTER 35

She could tell by the way he walked back to the pool that the conversation had gone badly. Whoever was on the other end had delivered unpleasant news. He flashed a fake grin at Carter when he tried to splash water on him. Hoppy was telling Barry another story about catching salmon on a river in Oregon.

"You okay?" Abby whispered.

"Peachy." Which, of course, meant things just went south.

"The boys want a boat ride?" Tanner yelled.

To which Maxie jumped in with "Oh yes, we do a boat ride every afternoon as soon as the water settles down." The twins were climbing out of the pool, reaching for towels.

"Sounds like fun," Mitch managed to say. Nothing, at that moment, could be fun.

Maxie said, "You guys take them. We'll watch from the porch."

Tanner was already on the dock checking the engine. The boys bounded aboard without using the stepladder. Mitch and Abby were more careful. The air was cooler on the water and the boys were wet and freezing. Abby wrapped them in thick towels and they assumed their favorite spots on cushions near the bow while their parents settled into leather deck chairs. Mitch tried to relax with "Not a bad rig here, Tanner. All wood?"

"It's a classic. Made in Maine by a famous builder named Ralph Stanley. Thirty-six feet long. A beauty. Slow as molasses, though."

"Who cares?"

Before he shoved off, Tanner said, "A beverage is required on Friday afternoons."

"White wine, please," Abby said.

"Double bourbon," Mitch said. Tanner nodded and disappeared into the cabin.

"Double bourbon?" Abby asked with a frown.

"That was Jack Ruch. The management committee met for five hours today and voted not to borrow the money. As of now, the ransom account is empty. Ten million down the drain, nothing left. Giovanna's a step closer."

Her mouth fell open but she didn't speak. Instead, she looked across the water and saw nothing.

Mitch went on, "Jack is upset, says he lost some friends today."

"This is terrible."

"I know."

"Has he told Luca?"

"Not yet. You wanna call him?"

"I think not. I don't understand."

Carter bounced around the cockpit, disappeared into the cabin as if he owned it, and emerged with two small bags of popcorn. He smiled at his parents but did not offer them the snack. Then he was gone.

Mitch said, "These kids are out of control, you know?"

"Totally. I don't think my parents are exactly cracking the whip."

"And we do? I feel sorry for their teachers when they go back to school."

"And when might that be?"

Mitch thought for a second and said, "Another week. Are your folks okay with that?"

"They'll manage."

Tanner was back with the drinks on a proper tray. He served them, yelled at the boys, and shoved off. Sitting close together and facing the stern, Mitch and Abby watched Wicklow fade behind them. The hum of the engine muffled their voices.

"I don't understand," she said again.

"They're cowards, Abby. More concerned with protecting their assets than rescuing Giovanna. Put each one of them in her place, and they'd say hell yeah, borrow the money, get me outta here. The firm can absorb the loss, over time. But sitting in their nice offices in Manhattan they feel threatened and want to protect their money."

"The firm grossed how much last year?"

"Two billion plus."

"And more this year?"

"Yes, always more."

"I don't understand."

"You know, we've had eleven good years with Scully and never thought about leaving."

Tanner inched the throttle up a notch and the wake grew wider. They were nearing a cove with the Atlantic not far away. The water was deep blue and flat, but an occasional wave sent mist over the boat and refreshed everyone. With his left hand, Mitch reached over and took hers. With his right hand, he took a sip of bourbon and savored it as it wet his mouth and seeped down his throat. He rarely touched the hard stuff, but it was soothing at the moment.

"I'm sure you have a plan," she said.

"Oh, lots of them, and none are working. There's no playbook here. We're all guessing."

"Do you really think they'll do something awful to Giovanna?"

"Oh yes. Definitely. They're savages and they obviously crave attention. Look at all the videos. If they harm her, we'll get to see it."

Abby shook her head in frustration. "I think of her all the time. I'm living in a safe world with family and friends all around. I go anywhere, do anything I want, while Giovanna's buried in a cave praying that we'll come get her."

"I'm still blaming myself, Abby. The trip to the bridge would probably have been productive at some level, but it wasn't crucial. I couldn't wait to go, another adventure."

"But Luca insisted."

"He pushed hard, but I could've said no, or not at this time. Actually seeing the bridge would not have affected our representation of Lannak."

"You can't beat yourself up, Mitch. Blaming yourself is wasted energy and you have more pressing matters at hand."

"You don't say."

Barry skipped dinner with his house guests. Seemed as if a fancier party was underway at another mansion down the road, old friends from Boston were on the island and rounding up their pals for a long night. Tanner chauffeured him, dropped him off, and would collect him hours later when the last cigars and brandies were finished. Tanner worked long days, but, according to Hoppy, who was never shy about prying, the winter and spring months were slow and the staff caught up on their rest. When the big houses were open, usually from May to October, the owners and their guests came in waves, and eighteen-hour shifts were common.

Miss Emma, too, seemed to be in the kitchen around the clock. For dinner, she suggested they dine outside on the deck and watch the sunset. She and Miss Angie served lobster mac and cheese with fresh greens from the garden.

Fortunately, Hoppy was in a talkative mood and carried the conversation. Maxie chimed in when she could, and Abby worked hard to keep the mood light for the boys. Mitch was off his game and obviously distracted. The entire family was out of place and had been for a week. The boys were missing school. Mitch was living on airplanes and visibly stressed. Abby was ignoring her job. Hoppy and Maxie were supposed to be in Utah with friends and they were tired of Islesboro. And no one really knew when their secret little detour to Maine would be over.

One side benefit of it, though, was Mitch's kindness to his in-laws. They were pinch-hitting in a big way and he was truly appreciative.

After dinner, the Sutherlands hastily retired to their suite and locked the door. They wanted a quiet night, away from the kids. The McDeeres gathered in one of the dens to watch television on a big screen. A small fire crackled in the fireplace. Clark immediately found a spot between his parents on the deep sofa and curled up with his mother. The first movie was *Shrek,* but because they had seen it so many times they were soon bored with it. They couldn't decide on the next one until Abby mentioned an old classic, *E.T.* She and Mitch had seen it when it was released in 1982 on their second date. The twins objected for a few minutes, primarily because it was an old-fashioned movie, but within ten minutes were completely hooked. Carter said he was cold and joined them under the covers. Mitch soon dozed off, and when he woke from his nap he glanced at Abby.

She was drifting away too.

They were running on fumes, but the fatigue could not overtake the stress. They took turns catnapping until, typically, the boys were hungry again. Mitch wandered into the kitchen in search of popcorn.

CHAPTER 36

When Tanner opened the house at daybreak on Saturday, he found Mitch at the breakfast table, pecking away on his laptop. Notepads and memos were scattered about. Mitch said, "I wasn't sure how to make the coffee and didn't want to screw up the machine."

"I'll take care of it. Anything else?"

"No. I'll be leaving in a couple hours. Abby will leave tomorrow. We're hoping to retrieve the boys by the end of next week, if that's okay. We feel like we're imposing here."

"No, sir, not at all. This house was built for guests and Mr. Ruch enjoys your company. You have a very nice family, Mr. McDeere. Please don't feel rushed or anything like that. I promised the boys we'd go fishing this afternoon, if the weather holds."

"Thank you, Tanner. They're city boys and they're having a blast, an unexpected vacation. You're very patient with them."

"Good kids, Mr. McDeere. We're having fun. Emma will be along shortly for breakfast, but can I offer you anything?"

"No, thanks. Just coffee."

Tanner disappeared into the kitchen and began making noise. Mitch took a break and walked outside to enjoy the brisk morning. Then the calls began. The first was to Stephen Stodghill, who was already at the office. Mitch wanted two paralegals on standby. Jack Ruch was en route. Cory was in the city and still asleep, or he was until Mitch called. It was early afternoon in Rome, and Roberto had just left the hospital where Luca had been through another bad night.

Abby wandered in at seven in search of coffee. Miss Emma fixed them cheese omelets and they ate alone in the dining room. With each day being entirely unpredictable it was difficult to plan, but plans had to be made. Mitch would leave for New York in half an hour, then on to Rome. Abby would leave Sunday morning for the city and be in their apartment staring at that damned Jakl at precisely noon. They expected a call from Noura, and the great question would be: "Do you have the money?"

The answer would be: "Yes. What's next?"

Mitch showered and changed and peeked in on the boys. He wanted so badly to wake them and squeeze them, then go outside and play baseball. But the games would have to wait, hopefully for only a few more days.

A King Air was waiting at Islesboro Airport.

———•—•———

Lannak's claim against the Republic of Libya was for unpaid bills in the amount of $410 million, plus interest on the balance of $52 million. After the murders and abduction, Mitch had tacked on another $50 million for additional damages. It was a sum he chose arbitrarily and represented the "soft" part of the claim. The interest was also a moving target since it was accumulating daily. Of the original claim, the $410 million, about half included sums due that, at least in his opinion, were not disputable. These included "hard" charges for labor, supplies, cement, steel, equipment, transportation, professional fees, and so on. These were costs that were built into the project from day one and incurred regardless of how much Lannak and the Libyans bickered over change orders and design flaws.

During their many hours on airplanes, Mitch and Stephen had reviewed every invoice and labor timesheet. They had put together a four-page summary of expenses paid by Lannak that were indisputable. For fun, they labeled it: *Dossier GGBN84. Great Gaddafi Bridge to Nowhere.* Clark's baseball jersey was number 8. Carter was number 4.

In Jack's conference room, Stephen passed around current drafts of the dossier as Mitch stood by the window. Jack, Cory, and Darian looked at the drafts. Two paralegals sat in the hallway, outside the closed door, waiting for instructions. It was 11:45 on a gorgeous Saturday morning in late May.

Mitch was saying, "We've gone through all the numbers so you don't have to. The bottom line on page four sums it all up. We can argue that there are at least a hundred and seventy million dollars in unpaid bills that are beyond dispute. Needless to say, we think Lannak is due half a billion and I'm confident I can prove it in Geneva, but that's for another day."

Jack said, "So a partial settlement?"

"Exactly. We present this to the Libyans now, today even, and demand payment. And we make it clear that an expedited settlement could quite possibly facilitate the release of Giovanna Sandroni."

No one in the small audience seemed moved.

Jack laid down his copy and rubbed his eyes. "I don't get it. You're asking the Libyans to pay one-seventy to Lannak so we can pay the ransom."

"No. We're asking the Libyans to pay this amount because they owe this amount."

"Got that. But what about Lannak? They're going to chip in a pile of money because they're good guys?"

"No. Frankly, I don't know what they'll do, but they'll contribute something to the fund."

Darian said, "May I ask who else is contributing to the fund at this time? Anyone? We're ten million down with ninety to go, right?"

"Right," Mitch said. He glanced at Jack, who looked away. Neither Darian nor Cory knew that mighty Scully & Pershing had declined further participation in the ransom plot.

Mitch continued, "There are many moving parts, Darian. We continue to push hard in diplomatic circles, in Rome and London."

"The goal being?"

"The goal being to squeeze money from both governments to prevent the murder of a high-profile hostage. We've just learned that last year the Brits paid something like ten million pounds to get a nurse out of Afghanistan. It's technically against their law but sometimes laws get in the way of saving lives. We've asked the Brits and the Italians for twenty-five million each, and we know that both requests are being considered by the prime ministers."

"What about your insurance policy? Another twenty-five, right?"

"Wrong," said Jack. "The insurance company has denied coverage. We intend to sue but that'll take a few years. We have four days."

Cory gave Mitch a puzzled look and asked, "How did you learn of the nurse in Afghanistan?"

"Sources. It came out of Washington."

"Can we discuss it later?"

"Maybe. If there's time. It's not a priority at the moment."

Cory withdrew, chastened. The nurse was secret intel he was supposed to know about, not the lawyers at Scully.

Mitch said, "Anything else? The plan is to zip this to Roberto in Rome and Riley in London and crank up the pressure on the Libyan embassies there."

Jack shook his head and said, "It's a long shot, Mitch."

"Of course it's a long shot, highly unlikely and all that. I get it! Does anyone have a better idea?" Mitch immediately regretted his sharp tone. He was, after all, still addressing the managing partner. For the moment, anyway.

"I'm sorry," Jack said like a true friend. "I'm on board."

———— • • ————

The meeting moved from the conference room at Scully & Pershing to the cabin of a Gulfstream G450 parked at Teterboro Airport in New Jersey. When they were belted in—the same team minus the paralegals—the flight attendant took their drink orders and informed them they would land in Rome in seven hours. Lunch would be served when they reached altitude. Phones and Wi-Fi were all working. There were two sofas in the rear cabin for napping.

———— • • ————

Shortly after 7 P.M. in Rome, Roberto Maggi entered the Caffè dei Fiori in the Aventine neighborhood of southwestern Rome. Diego Antonelli lived around the corner and agreed to a quick glass of wine. He and his wife had plans for dinner later in the evening and he did little to hide his annoyance at being bothered on a Saturday. But bothered as he might be, he also appreciated the gravity of the moment. The government he served was being whipsawed by events beyond its control. It was compelled to protect an Italian citizen being held hostage, yet it was not allowed to know the details of the captivity and possible release. It could not negotiate. It could not consider a rescue. Only the Americans were in contact with the kidnappers, and that had become a source of great irritation.

They sat at a small table in the corner and ordered glasses of Chianti. Roberto began with "The Carlotti deal is off the table."

"That's good to hear. What happened?"

"Carlotti got cold feet. His lawyers convinced him he was risking too much by trying to circumvent our laws. He wants to help Luca, of course, but he also wants to avoid trouble. Plus, the American wing of my law firm was skittish. There are some nasty federal prosecutors over there and they'd love to catch a big law firm getting its hands dirty."

Diego nodded along, as if he completely understood the motivations of federal prosecutors in the United States. The wine arrived and they clinked glasses.

"There's something else," Roberto said.

"So you said." Diego glanced at his watch. Ten minutes in and he was ready to go.

"Our client is Lannak, the Turkish contractor."

"Yes, yes. I know the file. Arbitration. I talk to Luca."

"We have a plan to settle the claim, in part only, and quickly. Some of the money will go to the ransom. We want your boss to meet with the Libyan ambassador as soon as possible and urge him to urge Tripoli to settle the claim."

"A waste of time."

"Maybe, but what if a settlement leads to the release of the hostage?"

"I don't follow."

"Money. We take some of it and add it to the pot." Roberto removed a legal-sized manila envelope from his attaché case and handed it across the table. "Read it and you'll understand."

Diego took it without showing any interest. He sipped his wine and said, "I'll give it to my boss."

"The sooner the better. It's rather urgent."

"So I've heard."

CHAPTER 37

It was after 3 A.M. Sunday morning when the two vans
carrying the Scully team stopped in front of the Hassler Hotel
in central Rome. The weary travelers wasted no time getting
out, checking in, and heading up to their rooms. Mitch had
stayed there before and knew the Spanish Steps were just outside
the hotel's front door. His room faced east, and before crashing
he pulled back the curtains and smiled at the fountain and piazza
far below at the foot of the famous stairway. He missed Abby and
wished they could be enjoying the evening together.

The day promised to be long and stressful. Sleep could wait.
The team met at nine for breakfast in a private dining room.
Roberto Maggi joined them and reported that Luca was preparing to check himself out of the hospital and go home. It was
unclear what his doctors thought of it. The good news of the
morning was a phone call from Diego Antonelli an hour earlier
in which he reported that the prime minister himself had spoken
with the Libyan ambassador to Italy and pressed the need for a
quick settlement of the lawsuit.

Over the weekend, Roberto had spent time on the phone

with Denys Tullos, the chief legal adviser to the Celik family in Istanbul. Tullos passed along the encouraging news that Turkey's deputy foreign minister had dined the previous evening with the Libyan ambassador to Turkey. The principal item on their agenda had been Lannak.

Thus, the Libyan ambassadors in Italy, Turkey, and Great Britain were getting squeezed in various ways to expedite the settlement. What that meant back in Tripoli was anybody's guess. Roberto, with more experience in Libya than anyone else in the room, cautioned against even the slightest optimism.

Other than Mitch and Jack, no one else in the room knew how much, or how little, money had actually been committed to the ransom fund. Both had picked up the vibe from Cory and Darian that Scully wasn't doing enough to help with its considerable resources. If they only knew, and of course they would never know. Over the Atlantic, in the back of the jet, Mitch had asked Jack if he thought it was even remotely possible to go back to the management committee and beg again. Jack said no. At least not now.

———— • • ————

As Abby rode the elevator to her apartment she tried to dismiss her frustration with armed security, basement entries and exits, surveillance, black SUVs, and the whole silly espionage routine. She wanted her husband home and her kids back in school. She wanted normalcy.

And she wanted to take the Jakl phone and pitch it out the window onto Columbus Avenue where it would shatter into a hundred pieces and never be able to track her again. Instead, she placed it on the kitchen table as she made some coffee and tried to ignore it.

At 12:05, as Mitch predicted, Noura called, and for the first time tried to project a bit of warmth. "How was your trip?"

"Lovely."

"It's noon Sunday. The deadline is five P.M. Wednesday, Eastern Time."

"If you say so. I'm in no position to argue."

"Do you have the money?"

The answer had been rehearsed a dozen times. There was no way to logically explain the efforts underway to raise a hundred million dollars under such pressure. Noura and her fellow revolutionaries were probably naive enough to believe that a mammoth law firm like Scully could simply stroke a check and all would be well. They were right and they were wrong.

"Yes."

A pause as if there was relief on the other end. On Abby's end there was nothing but fear and dread.

"Good. Here are your instructions. Please listen carefully. You are to travel tonight to Marrakech in Morocco."

Abby almost dropped the phone. Instead she just stared at it. She'd been home for an hour. Her family was scattered. Her job was being neglected. Everything in her world was upside down and the last thing she wanted was to spend the next day on a plane to North Africa. "Okay," she mumbled. For the umpteenth time she asked herself, Why am I in the middle of this mess?

"British Air flight number 55 departs JFK this evening at five-ten. There are seats in business class but book one now. There is a three-hour layover at Gatwick in London, then eight hours nonstop to Marrakech. You will be monitored along the way but you will not be in danger. In Marrakech, take a taxi to La Maison Arabe Hotel. Once there you will await further instructions. Any questions?"

Only a thousand. "Well, yes, but give me a minute."

"Have you been to Marrakech?"

"No."

"I hear it's lovely. So decadent, so popular with you people."

Whoever "you people" were, it was obvious Noura did not approve of them. Westerners.

Two years earlier, Abby had tried to buy a cookbook by a Moroccan chef from Casablanca. He had a small restaurant on the Lower East Side and she and Mitch ate there twice. It was loud and rowdy, always full of Moroccans who loved to sit together at long tables and welcome strangers. They loved their country, culture, and food, and talked of being homesick. She and Mitch had discussed a vacation there. They read enough to know that Marrakech was filled with history and culture and attracted many tourists, primarily from Europe.

Abby said, "I'm sure this phone will work over there."

"Yes, of course. Keep it with you at all times."

"And I have to leave now?"

"Yes. The deadline is Wednesday."

"So I've heard. Do I need a visa?"

"No. There is a room reserved for you at the hotel. Do not tell anyone but your husband. Understood?"

"Yes, yes, of course."

"It is imperative that you travel alone. We will be watching."

"Got it."

"You must understand that this is an extremely dangerous situation. Not for you but for the hostage. If something goes wrong, or if a rescue is attempted, she will be shot immediately. Understood?"

"Of course."

"We are watching everything. One bad move and it will be disastrous for the hostage."

"Got it."

———— · · ————

Abby closed her eyes, tried to steady her shaking hands and take deep breaths. A jumble of thoughts rattled around. Her boys: they would be just as safe with her out of the country as in New York. Mitch: she wasn't worried about his safety but what if he said no to her trip? A no wouldn't bother her. Her job: tomorrow was Monday and she had the typical busy schedule for the week. The exchange: What might happen if the money did not materialize? She was already lying about having the ransom, but she had no choice.

And Giovanna. Nothing really mattered but "the hostage."

She called Mitch on the green phone but couldn't get through.

She opened her laptop and booked the flight; one-way because she had no idea when she might return.

———— · · ————

Against his doctors' wishes, Luca left Gemelli Hospital and rode in the front seat as Bella weaved through traffic. Once home, he asked for a caprese salad on the veranda, and he and Bella dined under the shade of an umbrella. He asked her to phone Roberto and invite him over, along with Mitch and Jack Ruch.

After another nap, Luca returned to the veranda and greeted his colleagues from New York. He wanted details of everything—every meeting, phone call, partners' conference. He was angry at the Italians for dragging their feet. He had never really trusted the British. He still thought Lannak would come through.

When the time was right, and when it was obvious that Jack

was not going to deliver the bad news, Mitch told Luca that his law firm had declined to borrow money to pay the ransom.

"I'm ashamed to say, Luca, that the partners ran for cover and said no."

Luca closed his eyes and for a long time everything was quiet. Then he took a sip of water and said, in a soft scratchy voice, "I hope I live long enough to see my daughter. And I hope I live long enough to face my esteemed colleagues and call them a bunch of cowards."

CHAPTER 38

Day 40. Or was it 41? She wasn't sure anymore because there was no sunlight, only darkness. Nothing to measure time. Even when they moved her she was shrouded and blindfolded and saw nothing but darkness. And they moved her constantly, from a lean-to that smelled of farm animals, to a cavern with sand for a floor, to a darkened room in a house with city noises not far away, to a dank underground cellar where rusty water dripped on her cot and made sleep difficult. She never stayed more than three nights in one place, but then she wasn't sure what was day or night. She ate when they brought her fruit and bread and warm water, but it was never enough. They gave her toilet paper and sanitary napkins but she had not bathed once. Her long thick hair was now matted and stringy from grease and dirt. After she ate, when she knew she would not be bothered for hours, she stripped and tried to clean her undergarments with a few ounces of water. She slept for long periods of time, the dripping water notwithstanding.

Her minder was a young girl, probably no more than a teenager, who never spoke or smiled and tried to avoid any eye contact. She was veiled and always wore the same faded black dress that hung like a bedsheet and dragged the ground. For humor, Giovanna nicknamed her "Gypsy Rose" after the famous stripper. She doubted the girl had ever taken her clothes off in the presence of a man. Wherever Giovanna went, Gypsy Rose went too. She had tried to engage her with simple words, but the girl had obviously been instructed not to talk to the captive. When it was time to move, Gypsy Rose would appear with a pair of oversized handcuffs, a blindfold, and a heavy black shroud. Not since the first days had Giovanna seen the face of a man. Occasionally she heard low voices outside her doors, but they disappeared.

She recalled from law school the *Gibbons* case. For over twenty years, Gibbons had been an inmate on death row in Arkansas, and as such was confined to an eight-by-ten-foot cell from which he was released one hour each day for exercise in the yard. He sued the state, claiming solitary confinement violated the Eighth Amendment's prohibition of cruel and unusual punishment. When the U.S. Supreme Court agreed to hear the case, it attracted an enormous amount of attention, primarily because of the thousands of prisoners living in solitary. Everybody piled on: death row lawyers, psychiatrists, psychologists, sociologists, law professors, prisoners' rights groups, civil libertarians, and penal experts. Virtually everyone agreed that solitary was cruel and unusual punishment. The Supreme Court felt otherwise and Gibbons eventually got the needle. The case became famous and made it all the way to the constitutional law casebook Giovanna purchased and studied at UVA Law.

After forty or forty-one days in solitary, she now understood. She could now qualify as an expert witness and explain in vivid testimony exactly how and why such confinement was unconstitutional. The physical deprivations were bad enough; a lack of food, water, soap, toothbrushes, razors, tampons, exercise, books, clean clothes, a hot bath. But she had made those adjustments and could survive. The maddening aspect of solitary was the lack of human contact.

And, as she recalled, Gibbons had a television, radio, buddies next door, guards who brought dreadful food three times a day, 2200 calories of it, two showers a week, unlimited visits with his lawyer, weekend visits with his family, and plenty of books and magazines. He still went insane but Arkansas killed him anyway.

If she was ever free again, she might consider shucking Big Law and working for a death penalty lawyer or a prisoners' rights group. She would welcome the opportunity to testify in court or perhaps before lawmakers and detail the horrors of solitary confinement.

Gypsy Rose was back with the handcuffs and they had the routine perfected. Giovanna frowned but said nothing, then touched her wrists together. Gypsy Rose slapped them on like a veteran beat cop. Giovanna leaned forward to take the blind-fold, a thick velvet cloth that smelled like old mothballs. Her world was black again. Gypsy put the hood over her head and led her from the cell. After a few steps, Giovanna almost stopped when she realized the girl's eyes had been moist. Gypsy Rose was showing emotion. But why? The horrible truth was that after caring for her prisoner for so long, she had feelings for her. Now, the captivity was over. After forty days the big moment had arrived. The prisoner was about to be sacrificed.

They stepped outside into cooler air. A few steps, then two men with strong hands lifted her into the back of a vehicle and sat close to her. The engine started, the truck began to roll, and soon they were bouncing along another sandy roadbed some-where in the Sahara.

Gypsy Rose had forgotten the morning bowl of fruit. After an hour, Giovanna was starving again. There was no ventilation in the back of the truck or whatever the vehicle happened to be, and Giovanna's face and hair were dripping with sweat under the thick shroud. At times, breathing was difficult. Her entire body was sweating. Her captors reeked of a pungent body odor she had been forced to endure many times now. The stink of desert soldiers who rarely bathed. She didn't smell too refreshing either.

As a hostage, she had logged thousands of miles over brutal roads without a glimpse of the outside. This ride, though, was different.

The truck stopped. Its engine was turned off. Chains rattled, and the men lifted her to the ground. It was hot but at least she was outside. There were voices all around her as something was being organized. One guard firmly held her right elbow; another one had the left. They led her this way and that way and then they were climbing steps, steep ones made of wood, though she could not see her feet. Her guards helped her climb by lifting her arms. She had the sensation of being with others who were also struggling to climb the steps. Somewhere above a man was mumbling in Arabic and it sounded like a prayer.

When the climb was over they shuffled along a wooden platform until they stopped. Dead still. Waiting.

Giovanna's heart was pounding and she could barely breathe. When they put a noose around her neck and yanked it tight, she almost fainted. Close by a man was praying. Another one was crying.

———·—·———

Once again, the killers chose to do it all on camera. The video began with the four victims already in place on the gallows with ropes around their necks and their hands cuffed behind them. From left to right, the first three were wearing uniforms of the Libyan Special Forces. They had been captured by Barakat's men in the second commando raid five days earlier near Ghat. The fourth person was to the far right and wore a skirt or a dress and not a uniform. Close behind each stood a masked warrior with an assault rifle.

The surname FARAS appeared at the bottom of the screen, and seconds later Faras was pushed by the gunman behind him. He fell forward, dropped fifteen feet, stopped abruptly as the rope jolted tight and shrieked just as his neck snapped. He jerked violently for a few seconds as his body slowly gave up. His boots were five feet above the sand. For good measure, a commandant of some variety stepped forward with an automatic pistol and pumped three slugs into his chest.

With each shot the next two soldiers shuddered and would have collapsed but for the nooses. They would fall soon enough. The woman on the end stood rigid and unmoving, as if too stunned to react.

Hamal followed, and at the age of twenty-eight the veteran solider with a wife and three children back home in Benghazi was murdered by a gang of insurgents. Moments later, Saleel took his last breath.

The camera refocused and zoomed in on the woman, SANDRONI. Seconds passed, then a minute with no movement anywhere, or at least none on camera. Suddenly, the unmistakable whine of a chain saw began, off camera.

The guard behind her stepped closer, loosened the noose, and removed it. He took her arm, and as she was being led away the video ended.

CHAPTER 39

I t was beneficial to have a real Roman in the group. Roberto Maggi knew all the restaurants, especially the famous ones with starred reviews and staggering bills. But he also knew the neighborhood trattorias where the food was just as enjoyable. With the clock ticking, no one was in the mood for a three-hour dinner early on a Sunday evening. He chose a place called Due Ladroni, "Two Thieves" in Italian, and they enjoyed a fifteen-minute stroll along Via Condotti. Of course Roberto knew the owner, a jolly Irish woman, and she had no trouble rearranging tables to accommodate the six of them outdoors.

Mitch was working through the menu when his green phone vibrated. It was Abby.

"I need to take this," he said as he stood. "It's my wife." He stepped around the corner, said hello, and absorbed the blow. She was expected in Morocco. She replayed her conversation with Noura, with all the details. It was almost 1 p.m. in New York. Her flight left JFK at 5:10. Should she go? What should she do? Would she be safe? His first reaction was to say hell no. It's dangerous. Think about the boys. But he realized his judgment was clouded by his last visit to North Africa. Abby had already blitzed through the internet and was convinced the trip would be reasonably safe. It was, after all, British Airways. The hotel was expensive, highly rated by travel magazines and websites. The more she surfed, the more attractive Marrakech became, though she would always feel vulnerable. She would not be the typical tourist.

Her confidence settled his nerves, but he was still bothered by the question of what might happen to his wife if they could not deliver the money. The pot was still empty. They wouldn't kidnap her, too. Not from a four-star hotel. And why would they? If Mitch and his team couldn't raise the money for one hostage, why bother with a second?

As they spoke, he ventured back to the table and said to Roberto, "I'll take the cioppino, fish stew." It was his favorite, then he remembered the fish stew in Tripoli. "Big news," he said to Jack and walked around the corner.

Abby had to go. No question. She had been chosen as the messenger from day one and it was her obligation to Giovanna to follow instructions. They agreed on the plan, and Mitch promised to call back in an hour. She began packing, though with no idea how long she might be away. The temperature was already above ninety in Morocco. Where were her summer clothes?

When Mitch returned to the table, the team was waiting. His report was stunning at first, then troubling. The idea that Abby was being directed to Morocco to facilitate an exchange was excellent news. What would she do, though, with no money?

Cory said little but was thinking it through. Mitch looked at him and asked, "What about security? For Abby?"

"Low to moderate risk. She's in a nice hotel, plenty of tourists from Europe. If she's asked to do something she's not sure of, then she says no. And we'll be there." He looked at Darian and said, "I think I should go, take a plane and a nurse. Check into a hotel nearby. Make contact with Abby. Monitor her movements. You have people in Morocco, don't you?"

"We do," Darian said. "I'll notify them."

"A nurse?" Roberto asked.

Cory nodded and said, "We have no idea what condition Giovanna's in."

Darian added, "It's always best to have a nurse, if possible. I'll stay here with the team."

"Of course."

"Jack, can we use the jet?"

Jack was not anticipating the question and hesitated only slightly, as if he didn't really want to let go of the airplane. "Sure. There are plenty available."

Other ideas came and went as they tried to enjoy dinner. The optimism ebbed and flowed. One moment they were excited about Abby's trip to Morocco, and the next moment they were once again fretting over the ransom.

After dark, and as they were strolling back toward the Hassler and trying to enjoy another beautiful Roman evening, Roberto's phone buzzed in his pocket. It was Diego Antonelli. Roberto held back from the others and listened intently as Diego rattled away in Italian. There were rumblings out of Tripoli. Somewhere in the depths of the regime a senior diplomat had been contacted by their embassies in Rome, London, and Istanbul, all urging the same course of action. The senior diplomat had Gaddafi's ear and an approval of the settlement was expected.

An hour later, Riley Casey called Mitch from London with similar news. Sir Simon Croome had received a call from an old friend in the Foreign Office. The rumor was that the Libyan ambassador to the U.K. had also been informed that his government had decided to settle the Lannak matter, all of it, and to do so promptly.

Mitch, Jack, and Roberto met in a dark corner of the Hassler bar to talk about their client. Assuming a settlement, and they were cautious enough to assume nothing, they needed a strategy to press Lannak into using the money for the ransom. Roberto, who knew them best because of their long history with Luca, thought it likely that the Celiks would go along, but only with some guarantee that they would eventually receive $400 million. All three lawyers knew that in litigation there were no guarantees. A lawyer who promised one was a fool.

Roberto wanted some answers. He asked Jack, "Can Scully be convinced to borrow the funds? I know you've tried, but can you try again?"

"Maybe, but I'm not optimistic about the firm right now."

"This is disturbing. Luca is devastated and he feels betrayed."

"With good reason," Mitch said.

"Would the committee vote differently if she were the child of an American partner?"

"Great question," Mitch mumbled.

"I don't know," Jack said. "But I doubt it. The majority are more concerned with protecting their own assets. Asking them to cosign and guarantee such a loan was just too frightening, I guess. I tried, Roberto."

"Luca's putting up ten million of his own money. He's mortgaged everything. He was expecting more from the firm."

"So was I. I'm very sorry."

———— • • ————

From the moment Abby entered the British Airways lounge at JFK, she was looking for whoever might be watching her. Not following, but "monitoring," as Noura said. Seeing no one suspicious, and fully aware that anyone on her tail would appear not the least bit suspicious, she relaxed, ordered an espresso, and found a magazine.

She had always enjoyed British Air and was pleased that it would take her all the way to Marrakech. She remembered, with some amusement, Mitch's circuitous route from New York to Tripoli only last month. It had taken thirty hours and three airlines. She would need only one and BA was a favorite. Business class was quite comfortable. The champagne was delicious. Dinner was edible, but then she had become such a food snob that nothing served on an airplane could ever be described as delicious.

She thought of her boys and the wonderful time they were having at Miss Emma's table, eating precisely whatever they wanted and getting little or no pushback from their grandparents. How many kids get lobster every day?

The layover in London's Gatwick Airport was three hours and twenty minutes. To kill time, she napped in a chair, watched the sunrise, read magazines, and worked on a Laotian cookbook. She noticed a North African gentleman wearing a white linen suit and blue espadrilles trying to hide most of his face under a straw fedora. The third time she caught him glancing at her she decided he was one of her "monitors." She shrugged it off and figured there would be tenser moments ahead.

CHAPTER 40

S amir called Mitch Monday morning and said he had good
news. Mitch invited him to breakfast with Roberto at the
Hassler, and the three of them met in the restaurant at
nine-thirty.

Mitch had been so out of step the past ten days that he wasn't
sure who was paying for what. He'd lost track of his expenses,
a sin for any big firm lawyer. The Hassler was costing someone seven hundred dollars a night, plus meals and drinks. He
assumed Lannak would eventually get the bills, but that didn't
seem entirely fair. The Celiks were not responsible for Giovanna's kidnapping. Scully might have to eat the expenses, which
was fine with Mitch because he was frustrated with the firm.

Samir was all smiles as they settled in. And he was quick to
announce, quietly, "A call from Tripoli this morning, my friend
in the Foreign Service. Late last night he heard that the government decided yesterday to settle the entire Lannak dispute and
to do so quickly."

Mitch swallowed hard and asked, "For how much?"

"Between four and five hundred million."

"That's quite a range."

"Excellent news, Samir," Roberto said. "Can it be done quickly?"

"My friend thinks so, yes."

They ordered coffee, juice, and eggs. Mitch glanced at his phone. A text from Abby. She had left Gatwick on time. Some new emails, none related to Giovanna and thus of little importance. He needed to call Omar Celik in Istanbul with an update. Settlement looked likely, but he decided to wait an hour.

He lost interest in breakfast.

———•—•———

An hour later all of the early euphoria over the likelihood of a quick settlement was shattered by a two-minute video that was sent by text message to two London newspapers, *The Guardian* and *The Daily Telegraph;* two Italian newspapers, *La Stampa* and *La Repubblica;* and *The Washington Post.* Within minutes it was raging through the internet. A Scully associate in Milan saw it and called Roberto.

In the hotel conference room Mitch hurriedly opened his laptop and waited. Roberto hovered over his left shoulder; Jack over his right. Darian stood nearby. They watched in muted disbelief as the three hooded soldiers, in full Libyan commando garb, were knocked forward from the makeshift gallows and twisted violently at end of their ropes. Faras, Hamal, Saleel. They jerked more with each shot to the chest.

Roberto gasped at the image of "Sandroni." Obviously a woman, in a skirt or dress, to the far right, standing bravely with a black shroud over her head and a noose around her neck. "Mother Mary," he mumbled, then said something in Italian that Mitch had never heard before. Seconds passed, then, mercifully, the noose was removed and she was led away, her life spared for the moment.

They watched it again. When Roberto recovered, he called Bella and told her to keep Luca away from his phone, computers, and television. He and Mitch would be there as soon as possible.

They watched it a third time.

Mitch immediately knew it would kill any interest the Libyans may have had in writing a fat check to Lannak and its lawyers. He was almost certain Samir had passed along the secret that the kidnappers had made contact with Scully. It was not a stretch to believe the regime blamed the whole mess on Scully to begin with.

The cold-blooded murder of three more Libyan soldiers, on Libyan soil no less, would most likely provoke the Colonel into a fit of rage and revenge. Settling an embarrassing lawsuit, a nuisance to him anyway, had just lost whatever importance it had. He was now being mocked on the world stage.

Mitch closed his laptop and both lawyers stared at their phones.

Samir called from his hotel to make sure they had seen it. He told Roberto that he could think of no possible way the video could help them. He feared even more for Giovanna's safety. He was talking to sources in Tripoli and would call if he heard anything of substance.

As the morning dragged on they worked their phones because there was little else to do. Jack had a long conversation with someone at the State Department in Washington, but it produced little worth discussing. Mitch talked to Riley Casey in London. Riley said not a soul at Scully & Pershing was working that morning. Everyone was staring at their computer screens, too stunned to do little more than whisper. Some of the women were crying. It was impossible to believe that the horrible image was really their colleague. Roberto was trying to find Diego Antonelli. Evidently, the Libyan diplomats who had been reluctant to talk over the weekend had suddenly lost interest in talking at all.

Cory was on a corporate jet headed to Marrakech to monitor Abby's movements. Mitch was fretting about what could go wrong there when she arrived with no ransom. Darian took a call from Tel Aviv. A source in Benghazi said that Gaddafi had unleashed his air force and was bombing suspected targets near the borders of Chad and Algeria. Extensive bombing, with entire villages being strafed and leveled. Not a single soul on a camel was safe at the moment.

Sir Simon called Mitch from London and in a voice that was much too cheerful explained that, in his opinion, the terrorists had played a masterful hand. The image of young Giovanna on the gallows, with three freshly murdered soldiers hanging nearby, had shocked the nation. He knew for a fact that the prime minister had seen the video three hours earlier and had summoned the foreign minister to 10 Downing Street. Doubtless, they were talking money.

Ten minutes later, Riley Casey called with the startling news that he, too, had been summoned to 10 Downing Street. The prime minister was demanding details. Mitch nodded at Jack, who said, "Go! And tell him everything."

At 6 A.M. Eastern Time, Jack called Senator Elias Lake at his home in Brooklyn and left a voicemail. Ten minutes later, the senator called back. An aide had just awakened him and sent over the video. Jack asked him to call the secretary of state with the plan to corral the British and Italian foreign services into a gang of three and find some damned money.

——— • • ———

With only a carry-on bag, Abby moved quickly through Menara Airport in Marrakech. She followed the signs, in Arabic, French, and English, to the taxi stand, and as she walked through the revolving circular doors she was hit with a jolt of hot, humid air. A dozen dirty taxis were waiting and she took the first one. She wasn't sure which language the driver might speak, so she handed him a note card with La Maison Arabe Hotel's address.

He said, "Thank you. No problem."

Fifteen minutes later she arrived at the hotel and paid him in U.S. dollars, which he gladly accepted. It was almost 6 P.M. and the lobby was empty. The receptionist seemed to be expecting her. A nice corner suite on the second floor had been reserved for three nights. Abby finally knew how long she was supposed to stay. She took the elevator to the second floor, found her room, and locked herself inside. So far, she had seen no one but the receptionist. She opened the curtains and looked out onto a beautiful courtyard. A knock at the door startled her and she instinctively said, "Who's there?"

There was no answer. She cracked the door without unfastening the chain. An impeccably uniformed bellman smiled through the opening and said, "A letter for you."

She took the letter, thanked him, and closed the door. In block letters on hotel stationery, someone had written, *Please join me for dinner in the hotel restaurant this evening. Hassan. Friend of Noura.*

She called Mitch on the green phone and they went through the latest developments. There was plenty of activity but little progress. He described the video and said that it had evidently negated all efforts to settle the lawsuit. The Libyans were in no mood to negotiate or do anything but find the terrorists. Mitch and the others believed that the U.S. secretary of state herself had spoken to her counterparts in the U.K. and Italy. Luca was feeling better and monitoring his phones. During the day, Jack had called every member of Scully's management committee and lobbied hard for approval of the loan agreement, but there was no movement. He surprised Abby with the news that Cory was also in Marrakech and would contact her soon.

Having Cory in town was certainly a relief.

She unpacked her carry-on and hung up two traveler's dresses, one white, one red, both wrinkle-free. The minibar had nothing but water and sodas and she needed something stronger. Morocco was staunchly Muslim with strict prohibitions against alcohol. It was also a former French colony and an historic melting pot of cultures, religions, and languages from Europe, Africa, and the Middle East. In Marrakech, somebody somewhere consumed over two hundred tons of alcohol each year. Surely she could get a glass of wine in the restaurant. She took a nap, then a long hot bath in a clawfoot tub, washed her hair and dried it, and put on her red wrap dress.

If she felt safe, why was there a knot in her stomach?

The restaurant was a grand dining room with a blue Persian-style ceiling and heavily draped tables. It was beautiful and small, with only a few tables distanced discreetly apart. It felt more like a private club.

Hassan stood as she approached, and flashed an impressive smile. "Hassan Mansour, Mrs. McDeere." She was afraid he would start the usual hugging and cheek-smacking but he was content with a gentle handshake. He helped her into her chair and took his across the table. The nearest diners were thirty feet away.

"A pleasure to meet you," she lied, only because she had to say something polite. Whoever he was and whatever he did, he was in bed with the enemy. Their relationship would last only hours and she was determined not to like him, regardless of how much phony charm he tried. He was about fifty, with short graying hair slicked back severely and small black eyes that were too close together.

The eyes took her in and liked what they saw. "How was your flight?" he asked.

No wedding ring but a diamond on the right pinkie. Fine designer suit, light gray in color, linen probably. Brilliant white shirt that contrasted nicely with his swarthy skin. Expensive silk tie. Matching pocket square. All the trimmings.

"Okay. The British know how to run an airline."

He smiled as if this was supposed to be humorous. "I'm in London a lot and I always enjoy British Air. And Lufthansa, two of the best." Perfect English with a slight accent that could be from anywhere a thousand miles south of Rome. She would bet serious cash his name was not Hassan Mansour and she didn't care. He was nothing but a facilitator, a connector between the money and the hostage. If she ever saw him again, maybe he would be wearing handcuffs.

"May I ask where you live? I'm sure you know a lot about me. Apartment, office, kids' school, important stuff like that."

He kept smiling and said, "We could spend hours batting questions back and forth, Mrs. McDeere, but I'm afraid there would not be many answers, not from me anyway."

"Who is Noura?"

"I've never met her."

"That's not what I asked. Who is she?"

"Let's say she is a soldier in the revolution."

"Certainly doesn't dress like a soldier."

A waiter appeared and asked if they wanted drinks. Abby glanced at a short wine list and said, "Chablis." Hassan ordered herbal tea. When the waiter was gone, he leaned forward a few inches and said, "I don't know as much as you might think, Mrs. McDeere. I'm not a member of the organization. I am not a soldier in the revolution. I am being paid a fee to broker a deal."

"You've seen the latest video, I'm sure. Released this morning."

He kept smiling. "Yes, of course."

"Giovanna with a rope around her neck. Three men in the process of being murdered. Chain saw noise in the background. Its timing was perfect and it was obviously intended to put even more pressure on Giovanna's friends."

"Mrs. McDeere, I had absolutely nothing to do with the events recorded in that video. Is your husband responsible for the actions of his clients?"

"No, of course not."

"Then I rest my case."

"Spoken like a real lawyer."

He smiled and nodded as if to concede that he was indeed a member of the profession. "We can discuss many things, Mrs. McDeere, but we're not here for social reasons."

"Right. Is it fair to assume that our deadline is still five P.M. Wednesday, May twenty-fifth?"

"That's correct."

She took a deep breath and said, "We need more time."

"Why?"

"Rounding up another ninety million dollars is not something we have much experience with. It's proving to be rather complicated."

"How much time?"

"Forty-eight hours."

"The answer is no."

"Twenty-four hours. Five P.M. Thursday."

"The answer is no. I have my orders."

She shrugged as if to say, *Well, I tried.*

"Do you have the money?"

"Yes," she said, with a confidence built on plenty of practice. The only answer was "Yes." Anything else could set in motion events that would become unpredictable. Just as quickly she added, "We have commitments. It may take a day or two to gather the money. I don't see how an extra twenty-four hours will harm your position."

"The answer is no. Are you having problems?" The smile was gone.

"No, not problems, just a few challenges. It's not a simple matter of getting the law firm to write a check. There are many moving parts that involve various entities."

He shrugged as if he understood.

The drinks arrived and Abby took her glass as quickly as possible without appearing desperate for the wine. Hassan toyed with his teabag as if time meant nothing. She had checked with the front desk and knew that room service was available. After five minutes with Hassan, the last thing she wanted was a long painful dinner with the man as they bobbed and weaved around topics they could not discuss. She had even lost her appetite.

As if reading her mind, he asked, "Would you like to discuss dinner?"

"No, thank you. I'm jet-lagged and need rest. I'll order room service." She took another shot of Chablis. He had yet to lift his teacup.

The smile was back as if everything was okay. "As you wish. I have some instructions."

"That's why I'm here."

Finally, he raised his dainty little cup to his lips and wet them. "As soon as possible, your husband travels to the island of Grand Cayman, in the Caribbean. I believe he knows the place.

When he arrives tomorrow afternoon, he presents himself to the Trinidad Trust in Georgetown and asks for a banker named Solomon Frick. He will be expected. Mr. Frick represents my client, and your husband will do exactly as he says. He will know immediately if anyone attempts to track the wires. Any hint that someone is watching, that someone being the FBI, Scotland Yard, Interpol, Europol, or any of the other boys who carry guns and badges, and bad things will happen to your friend. We've come this far without the interference of the police or military, and it would be a shame to do something stupid at this late stage of the game. If you have the money, Mrs. McDeere, Giovanna is practically free."

"We'd like to confirm she's still alive."

"Of course. She is alive and doing well and on the verge of going home. Don't allow a bad decision to lead to her demise." He reached into the pocket of his jacket and withdrew a folded sheet of paper. "Here are the instructions in more detail. Your husband is to follow them closely."

"He'll be traveling tomorrow, from New York to Grand Cayman."

Hassan offered the widest smile yet as he gave her the sheet of paper and said, "Mitch is not in New York, Mrs. McDeere. He is in Rome. And he has access to a private jet."

CHAPTER 41

Grand Cayman?

The Caymans are three tiny islands in the Caribbean, south of Cuba and west of Jamaica. Still a British territory, they cling to old traditions and still drive on the left. Large numbers of tourists are attracted to their beaches, scuba diving, and fine hotels. No taxes are levied on money earned there. Or stored there. At least 100,000 corporations, more than one per citizen, register in Georgetown, the capital. Billions of dollars are parked in huge banks where they accumulate even more billions in interest, tax-free of course. Highly paid tax lawyers work in nice firms and enjoy a splendid quality of life. In the world of international finance, the word "Caymans" means, among other things, a safe place to hide money, clean or dirty.

Grand Cayman, Little Cayman, Cayman Brac.

Mitch had tried to forget about all three.

It was the shadier side of the Caymans that attracted the Bendini firm years earlier, in the 1970s, when drug money was pouring into the islands. Bendini was laundering money for its own criminal clients and found some friendly banks on Grand Cayman. The firm even bought a couple of swanky condos on the beach for its partners to enjoy when they were down on "business."

"Tell me again, Abby, what he said. Word for word."

"He said, 'Tomorrow morning your husband goes to Grand Cayman. I believe he knows the place.'"

He knows the place.

Mitch paced around his room in his boxers, thoroughly baffled and ready to pull out his hair. How could anyone, especially a man like Hassan or whatever his name was, really know that Mitch had ever had any contact with the Cayman Islands? It had been fifteen years ago. He sat on the edge of his bed, closed his eyes, and began breathing deeply.

Some details were returning. When Bendini imploded, there were dozens of arrests and news reports. Mitch and Abby were hiding on a sailboat with his brother Ray near Barbados. Mitch was not being sought by the FBI, but the Chicago Mob damned well wanted to find him. Months later, when the McDeeres finally came ashore, Mitch went to a library in Kingston, Jamaica, and found the newspaper stories. In several, the Caymans were mentioned in connection with criminal activity by the Bendini firm. But Mitch's name was never in print, at least not in the reports he could find.

That was the one possible link: the Bendini firm, of which he was briefly a member, and some of its alleged wrongdoings in the Caymans. As old and as obscure as it was, how could Hassan have possibly found it?

Equally baffling was how he knew Mitch was in Rome, and that he got there on a private jet. Mitch called a partner in New York, a friend who was a pilot and aviation junkie. Without being specific, he asked how difficult it would be to track the movements of a private jet. No problem at all if you have the plane's tail number. Mitch thanked him and rang off.

But how could they know Mitch was on the plane?

Because they were watching Mitch.

He didn't tell Abby this because she would immediately think of the boys and freak out. If "they" were watching the McDeeres this closely, then how safe were they?

——— • • ———

For additional privacy, Jack moved their operations to a large suite on the third floor of the Hassler. He ordered some snacks, no alcohol, and the team nibbled on finger food as they waited anxiously to hear from Mitch. When he arrived they listened raptly as he replayed his conversation with Abby and described the events in Marrakech. Abby was staying in a lovely hotel, felt safe, and was eager to get on with it. The Hassan character was a smooth professional who seemed firmly in control. The fact that he knew of Mitch's history with the Caymans, and that he knew Mitch was in Rome and not New York, was nothing less than astonishing. The team was once again reminded that they were only reacting. The rules were being made by some nasty people far more informed and better organized than them.

Mitch and Jack decided they would leave Rome early the following morning and fly to New York. From there, Mitch would fly to Grand Cayman and arrive midday, Caribbean time. He called a Scully partner in New York and told him to contact their affiliated law firm on Grand Cayman and get a banking expert on standby. He called another partner and asked him to research the bank called the Trinidad Trust.

Darian talked to Cory, who was on the ground in Marrakech and had hired Moroccan security. One agent was now a guest of La Maison Arabe Hotel and was staying in a room two doors down from Abby. She was supposed to meet Hassan Mansour Tuesday for breakfast and an update. The Moroccans on their team would be watching for Mr. Mansour, a man they had so far been unable to track down. Darian warned Cory to caution the team that they were to take no chances. Just observe diligently and don't get caught doing it.

Just after 9 P.M., 3 P.M. on the East Coast, the senator came through with the news they had been waiting for. Elias Lake informed Jack, in deepest confidence of course, that the British foreign minister had brokered a deal with the Italians and Americans in which all three governments would chip in $15 million each for the ransom. The payments would originate from sources so hidden they may as well have been on Mars, and they would get routed through banks on four continents. In the end, though, they would arrive almost magically in the new account in a Cayman bank. And any poor soul curious enough to try and track where all the money came from would probably lose his or her mind.

Jack thanked the senator profusely and promised to call later.

Forty-five million was half of ninety, their goal. Add Luca's ten, and they were still far short.

An exasperated Darian said, "In the dirty world of American slush money, fifteen million is peanuts. The DEA pays that much to drug informants on a monthly basis."

Jack said, "She's not an American citizen."

"Right, and neither are the snitches down in Colombia."

For many hours over many days, they had debated whether the terrorists might bend. How much would they settle for if the entire $100 million could not be raised? It was difficult to imagine them walking away from a large pile of money. They had $10 million in hand. Another $55 mil was within their grasp.

Darian thought the current record was the $38 million paid by the French to a Somalian gang for a journalist, but since there was no centralized clearinghouse for international hostage taking, no one really knew. Sixty-five million was certainly an impressive sum.

The alternative, though, was too gruesome to think about.

Mitch stepped into another room and called Istanbul.

———•—•———

The Bombardier Challenger lifted off from Rome's Leonardo da Vinci international airport at 6 A.M. Tuesday, May 24. Both Jack and Mitch needed sleep, and the flight attendant prepared two beds in separate quarters in the rear of the cabin. First, though, Mitch had something to say. "Let's have a Bloody Mary, only one, and a chat. There's something you need to know."

All Jack wanted was a few hours' sleep, but he knew this was serious. They asked the flight attendant for drinks, and once they were served she disappeared.

Mitch rattled his cubes, took a couple of sips, and began, "Years ago, when Abby and I left Memphis in the middle of the night, literally running for our lives, we barely got out of town. My employer, the Bendini firm, was owned by the Mob, out of Chicago, and once I realized that I had to get out. The FBI was moving in and the sky was falling. The firm suspected I was whispering to the FBI and there were plans to eliminate me. By then I knew that the firm had a history of keeping its lawyers quiet. Once you joined the firm, you never left. At least five lawyers had tried in the decade before I got there. All were dead. I knew I was next. As I was planning my escape, I saw the opportunity to re-route some money. Some offshore funds that were hidden in a bank, on Grand Cayman, oddly enough, and

I knew how to wire it to other places. It was dirty money, firm money, Mob money. I was frightened and angry and facing a very uncertain future. My promising career was in the sewer, thanks to Bendini, and if I survived I was looking at a life on the run. So, as compensation, I took the dirty money. Ten million dollars of it. Whisked away by the magic of wire transfer. I sent some to care for my mother, some to Abby's parents, the rest I kept hidden offshore. Later, I told the FBI about it and offered to give most of it back. They didn't care. They were too busy prosecuting thugs. What would they do with the money? With time I guess they forgot about it."

Jack sipped his drink, thoroughly amused.

"After I went to work for Scully, in London, I contacted the FBI one last time. They had lost all interest. I pushed them and finally got a letter, a waiver, from the IRS. No taxes owed. Case closed."

"It's still sitting out there, offshore," Jack said.

"Still there, in the Royal Bank of Quebec, which happens to be just down the street from the Trinidad Trust."

"On Grand Cayman."

"On Grand Cayman. Those guys keep secrets, believe me."

"And by now it's a lot more than ten million."

"Correct. It's been earning interest for fifteen years, all tax-free. I've talked to Abby, and we think this is the perfect time to unload most of this money. For some reason, we've always felt like it's not really ours, you know?"

"Ransom?"

"Yes, we're kicking in another ten million. So, with another ten million from Luca, we're up to sixty-five, in addition to the first ten. Not a bad payday for a bunch of desert thugs."

"That's very generous, Mitch."

"I know. Do you think they'll take sixty-five?"

"I have no idea. They seem to love blood as much as money."

They were quiet for a long time as they enjoyed their drinks. Finally, Mitch said, "And there's something else."

"Can't wait."

"I called Omar Celik a few hours ago and I asked him for ten million. He adores Luca and Giovanna but I'm not sure his fondness translates into that much cash. So, I did a foolish thing. I guaranteed him we would recover the money in the lawsuit."

"That's pretty foolish."

"As I said."

"But I don't blame you. Desperate times call for desperate measures. What did he say?"

"Said he'd sleep on it. So, I doubled down and went even crazier. I threatened him, told him that if he didn't pitch in I'd withdraw as counsel and he'd be forced to hire a new firm."

"You don't threaten Turks."

"I know. But he kept his cool. I'll bet he comes through."

"That would be seventy-five million."

"The math is pretty simple, if nothing else is. Will they walk away from seventy-five million?"

"Would you?"

"No. Plus, they get rid of the hostage. She can't be an easy prisoner."

The booze blended nicely with the fatigue and jet lag, and an hour after takeoff, Mitch and Jack were in deep sleep 40,000 feet over the Atlantic.

CHAPTER 42

For morning coffee, Abby wore her white dress and no makeup. Hassan wore another fine linen suit of a soft olive color. Brilliant white shirt, no tie. They met at the same table, one she was already tired of. They ordered coffee and tea and told the waiter they would think about breakfast later.

Hassan, ever the charming pro, kept smiling until she said, "We need more time, an additional twenty-four hours."

A sudden frown and a shake of the head. "I'm sorry. That's not possible."

"Then we can't arrange the entire sum of ninety million."

A deeper frown. "Then things get complicated."

"Things are beyond complicated. We are collecting money from at least seven different sources and in multiple languages."

"I see. A question. If you have twenty-four additional hours, how much more money can you scrape together?"

"I'm not sure."

His small black eyes zeroed in like lasers. "Then, that says it all, Mrs. McDeere. If you can't promise more money, then I can't promise more time. How much do you have?"

"Seventy-five. Plus, of course, the deposit of ten."

"Of course. And it is in hand and your husband will be prepared to wire it tomorrow?"

The waiter was back and he slowly set the tea and coffee in front of them. He inquired again about breakfast, but Hassan rudely waved him off.

He glanced around, saw no one, and said, "Very well. I shall speak to my client. This is not good news."

"It's the only news I have. I want to see Giovanna."

"I doubt that's possible."

"Then there's no deal. No seventy-five million. No wire transfer tomorrow. I want to see her today and I'm not leaving this hotel."

"You're asking too much, Mrs. McDeere. We're not walking into a trap."

"A trap? Do I look like a person who could set a trap? I'm a cookbook editor from New York."

He was smiling again as he shook his head in amusement. "It's not possible."

"Figure it out."

She abruptly stood, picked up her cup of coffee, and left the restaurant with it. Hassan waited a moment until she was out of sight and pulled out his phone.

———•—•———

Two hours later, Abby was working at the small table in her room when the Jakl vibrated. It was Hassan with the grim news that his client was quite disturbed by the news that its demands were not being met. The deal was off the table.

However, it would be wise for Mitch to continue with his plans on Grand Cayman. Establish a new account at Trinidad

Trust, and wait for instructions. So, the deal was not off the table.

Mitch was somewhere in the clouds, and the jet's cell service was out of range.

———— • • ————

The Challenger touched down at Westchester at 7:10, almost exactly seven hours after leaving Rome. Two black sedans were waiting. One went north with Jack, who lived in Pound Ridge. Mitch took the other south into the city.

Moroccan time was four hours ahead of New York. He called Abby, who was holed up in her hotel room editing a cookbook. She replayed the morning coffee with Mr. Mansour and their subsequent conversation. Of course he was disappointed with the money, but then he had been prepared for such a development. He was coy, a real pro, and she could not read him. She had no idea if he would accept *only* $75 million more, but she had a hunch he had a bigger role in the negotiating than he let on.

An hour after landing, he entered his apartment on Sixty-Ninth, his home for the past seven years and a place he adored, and felt like a trespasser. Where was everybody? Scattered. For a moment, he longed for their old routines. The silence was haunting. But there was no time for melancholy. He showered and changed into casual clothes. He dumped dirty laundry from his bag and repacked it with clean clothes. He did not pack a jacket or tie. As he recalled, from fifteen years earlier, even the bankers down there avoided suits.

He called Abby again and reported that the apartment was still standing. They agreed that they both wanted their lives back.

The car was waiting on Sixty-Ninth Street. Mitch tossed his bag in the trunk and said, "Let's go." Driving against the traffic was easier and they were back at the Westchester airport in forty minutes. The Challenger was refueled and ready to go.

———•—•———

The waiting was beginning to grate. Four hours had passed since she had seen Hassan for coffee. Her room was getting smaller and now the housekeeper wanted to have it. She walked around the hotel and knew she was being watched. The clerk at the front desk, the concierge in his little nook, the uniformed bellman—everyone glanced at her nonchalantly, then did a quick second look. The small dark bar was empty at 2 P.M. and she took a table with her back to the door. The bartender smiled at her when she entered, then took his time easing over.

"White wine," she said.

With no other customers, how long does it take to pour a glass of wine?

At least ten minutes. She stuck her nose in a magazine and waited impatiently.

CHAPTER 43

His first trip to the islands, some fifteen years earlier, had been with Avery Tolar, his mentor and supervising partner, and they had flown from Miami on Cayman Airways with a load of rowdy scuba divers, all guzzling rum punch and trying to get plastered before landing. Avery made the trip down several times a year, and though he was married and though the firm frowned on womanizing, he chased the women hard. And he drank more than he should have. One morning as he nursed a hangover, he apologized to Mitch and said the pressure of a bad marriage was getting the best of him.

Over the years Mitch had trained his mind to shut out thoughts of the Memphis nightmare, but there were moments when it was impossible. As the Challenger descended through the clouds and he caught the first glimpses of the bright blue Caribbean, he had to smile at his luck in life. Through no fault of his own, he had been within an inch of either being killed or indicted, yet he had managed to wiggle free. The bad guys went down, and hard, and they deserved it, and while they were serving time Mitch and Abby were starting over.

Stephen Stodghill had flown from Rome to Miami to Georgetown and arrived four hours earlier. He was waiting outside customs with a cab and they headed for downtown.

Another memory. The first wave of warm tropical air blowing in through the open windows of the cab as the driver listened to soft reggae. Just like fifteen years earlier.

Stephen was saying, "Our lawyer's name is Jennings, British chap, nice enough. I met him two hours ago and he's up to speed. According to our people, he's a top guy here in the Caymans and knows all the banks and the ins and outs of transferring money. He knows Solomon Frick, our soon-to-be newest friend at Trinidad Trust. They probably launder money together on the side."

"That's not funny. According to my research, the Cayman bankers have cleaned up their act in the past twenty years."

"Do we really care?"

"We do not. Over dinner I'll tell you all about my first trip down here."

"A Bendini story?"

"Yes."

"I can't wait. Around Scully the legend is that the Mob almost got you. But you pulled a fast one and outfoxed the Mob. Is that true?"

"I outran the Mob. I didn't realize I was a legend."

"Not really. Who has time to tell war stories at a place like Scully? All they care is about billing fifty hours a week."

"We prefer sixty, Stephen."

The cab turned a corner and there was the ocean. Mitch nodded and said, "That's Hog Sty Bay, where the pirates used to dock their ships and hide on the island."

"Yeah, I read that somewhere too," Stephen said, with no interest whatsoever.

"Where are we staying?" Mitch asked, happy to forgo the tourist spiel.

"Ritz-Carlton on Seven Mile Beach. I've already checked in. Pretty nice."

"It's a Ritz."

"So."

"So, isn't it supposed to be nice?"

"I suppose. I wouldn't know. I'm just a lowly associate who'd normally be staying in cheaper joints but since I'm hanging with a real partner I get the upgrade though I still had to fly commercial. Economy, not first class."

"Your brighter days are ahead."

"That's what I keep telling myself."

"Let's go see Jennings."

"Here's his firm," Stephen said, handing over a file. "It's a British outfit, a dozen lawyers."

"Aren't all the firms down here British?"

"I guess. Wonder why we haven't bought one and added it to our letterhead."

"At the rate we're losing them we might need to expand."

Jennings was on the third floor of a modern bank building a few blocks from the harbor. They met in a conference room with a view of the ocean that would have been enticing if not for the three mammoth cruise ships docked in Hog Sty Bay. He was a stuffy sort who talked down through his nose and had trouble smiling. He wore a coat and tie and seemed to enjoy being better dressed than his American counterparts, neither of whom gave a damn. In his opinion, the best strategy was to establish a new account at Trinidad Trust, a bank he knew well. Solomon Frick was an acquaintance. Many of the banks on the islands refused to do business with Americans, so it was best to have Scully's London office open the account and keep everything away from the feds.

"Your tax people are notoriously difficult," he explained through his nose.

Mitch shrugged. What was he supposed to do? Rush to the defense of the IRS? When the money was collected, hopefully by the following morning, it would be transferred to a numbered account at the Trinidad Trust, pursuant to Mr. Mansour's instructions. From there, with one push of a button, it would be wired to some yet-to-be-determined account, and gone forever.

After an hour, they left his office and walked two blocks to a similar building where they met Solomon Frick, a gregarious backslapper from South Africa. A quick Scully background check on Frick raised a number of red flags. He had worked in banks from Singapore to Ireland to the Caribbean and was always on the move, usually with some debris scattered behind. However, his current employer, Trinidad Trust, was reputable.

Frick handed Mitch and Jennings the paperwork, which they reviewed and emailed to Riley Casey, who was at his desk in London. He signed where necessary and sent everything back to Frick. Scully & Pershing now had an account in the Caymans.

Mitch emailed his contact at the Royal Bank of Quebec, which was just down the street, and authorized the transfer of his contribution of $10 million. He watched the large screen on Frick's wall, and about ten minutes later his money hit the new Scully account.

"Your money?" Jennings asked, confused.

Mitch nodded slightly and said, "It's a very long story."

Mitch called Riley, who then called his contact in the Foreign Office. Stephen emailed Roberto Maggi with the wiring instructions. Luca's money was sitting in an account on the island of Martinique, another Caribbean tax haven. Luca had dealt with several of them and was no stranger to the offshore games.

As they waited, Mitch glanced occasionally at the screen and the sum of money he'd just said goodbye to. There was a measure of relief in parting with the dirty funds he should have never grabbed way back then. He remembered the exact moment he made the decision to do it. He had been where he was now—in a bank building in Georgetown, not five minutes away by foot. He had been frightened and angry that the entire Bendini conspiracy had robbed him of his future, and maybe his life as well. He had convinced himself that they, the firm, owed him something. He'd had the access code and passwords and written authority, so he took the money.

There was now a relief in knowing it might actually do some good.

He called Abby, who was six hours ahead, and they talked for a long time. She was bored, killing time, and waiting on word from Hassan. She had talked to Cory, on the green phone of course, and they agreed that no money would change hands unless Abby was convinced Giovanna was safe. Assuming, of course, she was still alive and the deal was still on.

The British slush money arrived at 3:25 and came from a bank in the Bahamas. Twenty minutes later, the Italian funds arrived from a bank on Guadaloupe in the French West Indies. The current tally was $50 million, including Luca's contribution.

Riley called Mitch from London with the intel that the American money would not arrive until Wednesday morning, unwelcome news. Since he had no idea who was sending it or where it was coming from, he could not complain.

Mitch had sent emails to Omar Celik and Denys Tullos in Istanbul but they had not responded. When it was time to leave,

Mitch called Jack in New York on the off chance that he'd had some luck with the Scully management committee. He had not. With some bitterness that was uncharacteristic, Jack explained that enough of them had fled the city to prevent a quorum.

———•—•———

At the Ritz-Carlton, Mitch shook off Stephen and promised to meet him at eight for dinner by the pool. He changed into shorts and a golf shirt, and walked two hundred yards down the busy street to a rental place they had just passed in the cab. He picked a red Honda scooter and said he'd have it back by dark. Scooters were everywhere on the island and he and Abby had enjoyed them years earlier, when they were in hiding.

The Georgetown traffic was unrelenting and he weaved through it trying to get out of town. He did not remember so much congestion. There were more hotels and condos, and strip malls offering fast food, T-shirts, cheap beer, and duty-free booze. Georgetown had been thoroughly Americanized. On the other side of Hog Sty Bay the traffic thinned and the scooter hummed along. He passed through Red Bay, left the city, and saw the signs for Bodden Town. The road followed the shore but the beaches were gone. The sea rolled gently in and splashed against rocks and small cliffs. With little sand to offer, the hotels and condos thinned too, and the views were impressive.

Grand Cayman was twenty-two miles long and the main road looped around all of it. Mitch had never had the time in his earlier visits to see much of the island, but at the moment he had nothing better to do. The salty air in his face was refreshing. Thoughts of Giovanna could be set aside for at least a few hours because the banks and offices were closed. He stopped at Abanks Dive Lodge outside of Bodden Town and had a beer at the bar at the water's edge. Barry Abanks had rescued Mitch, Abby, and Ray from a pier in Florida as they made their escape. He had sold his operation years earlier and settled in Miami.

Moving on, Mitch scootered east to the far coast and crept through the settlements of East End and Gun Bay. The road continued to narrow and at times two cars could barely pass. Georgetown was on the other end of the island, far away. On the leeward side he parked and walked to the edge of a cliff where other tourists had left their trash. He sat on a rock and watched the water churn below. At Rum Point, he had another beer, a Red Stripe from Jamaica, as he watched a large group of middle-age couples eat and drink at an outdoor barbecue.

When it was almost dark, he headed back to Seven Mile Beach. Stephen was waiting and it was time for dinner.

CHAPTER 44

Wednesday, May 25.

At 9 A.M. Abby entered the hotel's restaurant and asked for the same table. She followed the waiter to it and was mildly surprised because Mr. Hassan Mansour was not there. She took a seat and ordered coffee, juice, toast and jam. She texted Mitch just to say good morning and he responded quickly. She was not surprised that he was awake because he had not slept ten hours in the last month.

A well-dressed Moroccan couple sat at the nearest table. The gentleman was working for Cory and on her team. He glanced at her but did not acknowledge her presence.

Hassan finally came in and was all smiles and apologies. He had been delayed in traffic and so on, and wasn't the weather nice? He asked for tea and went on for a few minutes as if they were tourists. She ate dry toast and tried to calm her nerves.

"So, Mrs. McDeere, what is the status?" She had asked him at least three times to call her Abby.

"We're expecting two wires this morning, and they will tally things up to seventy-five million, as I promised."

A lame effort at a frown, but it was obvious Hassan and his clients wanted the money. "But the deal was for a hundred million, Mrs. McDeere."

"Yes, we are aware of that. You demanded one hundred and we tried our best to get it. But we're a bit short. Seventy-five is all we have. And, it is imperative that I see Giovanna before the money is wired."

"And you have an account at Trinidad Trust, as directed?"

"Yes," she said, playing along. She knew that he knew the answer. His banker, Solomon Frick, had informed him that the account had been opened, or that's what Jennings had told Mitch. Frick and his bank were waiting. Everything was set. The fortune was practically in hand, and Hassan was having a difficult time hiding his excitement.

"Would you like some toast?" she asked. There were four buttered slices on the small plate.

He took one, said "Thank you," and pulled it in half.

She said, "We have plenty of time. The deadline is hours away."

"Yes, it's just that my client still demands one hundred."

"And we cannot meet that demand, Mr. Mansour. It's quite simple. Seventy-five, take it or leave it."

Hassan actually grimaced at something, probably the idea of walking away. He sipped his tea and tried to appear concerned that things were falling apart. They ate for a few moments, and he said, "Here is our plan. I'll meet you in the lobby at four P.M. You will inform me that all of the wires are complete and your money is ready. We will then leave together, go to a safe place, and you will see Giovanna."

"I'm not leaving the hotel."

"As you wish."

———— • • ————

At 9:15 a wire transfer arrived from a bank in Cyprus. Ten million dollars, as promised by Omar Celik, from a Lannak subsidiary in Croatia. Mitch, Stephen, Jennings, and Frick all smiled and took a deep breath. Neither Jennings nor Frick knew the backstory. They had no idea where the money was going or what it was being used for. However, given the Scully lawyers' anxiety, it was obvious that time was crucial. Jennings, British to the core, suspected it was related to the Scully hostage the press had been salivating over, but he was much too professional to ask. His job was to simply advise his client and oversee the wires coming in and the big one going out.

Mitch called Riley Casey in London, not really expecting to learn anything, but just to inquire anyway and ask, "Where is the damned money from the Americans?" Not surprisingly, Riley had no idea what the Americans were up to.

At 10:04, a wire arrived from a bank in Mexico City. The last installment of $15 million had just landed, and now the question was what to do with it. Solomon Frick stepped into another office to call his client with the good news. Mitch called Abby with the same.

———•—•———

By 3:45, Abby was ready to go. She had been there for only two nights but it seemed much longer. She felt captive in the hotel, as nice as it was, but when you're afraid to leave the premises and you know you're being watched, the clock slows considerably.

At 4 P.M. she walked into the lobby and smiled at Hassan. Though no one was around he whispered anyway, "What is the status?"

"Nothing has changed. We have seventy-five million."

He frowned because he had to. "Very well. We will accept it."

"Not until I see Giovanna."

"Yes, well, to see her, you must leave the hotel."

"I'm not leaving the hotel."

"Then we have a problem. It's too risky to bring her here."

"But why?"

"Because you cannot be trusted, Mrs. McDeere. You were told to come here alone but we suspect you have friends in the vicinity. Is this true?"

Abby was too stunned to answer quickly and lie convincingly and her hesitation revealed the truth. "Well, uh, no, I don't know what you're talking about."

Hassan smiled and pulled out his phone, which appeared to be another Jakl. He stuck it in front of her and said, "You don't recognize this person?"

It was a shot of Cory leaving the front entrance of the hotel. Even with sunglasses and a cap he was recognizable. Nice work, Cory.

She shook her head and said, "Don't know him."

"Oh really," Hassan said with a nasty smile as he slid the phone back into his pocket and glanced around the lobby. It was still deserted. Softly he said, "His name is Cory Gallant and he works in security for the law firm of Scully and Pershing. I'm sure you know him well. He's here in the city with at least two local agents he thinks he can trust. So, Mrs. McDeere, we are not foolish enough to bring the lady here to the hotel. You can't be trusted either. The entire operation is on the verge of a terrible collapse. Giovanna's life is in danger. Right now she has a gun pointed at her head."

Stunned as she was, Abby tried to think clearly. "Okay, I was told to come alone, and I did. I had nothing to do with this guy showing up and I've never seen any local agents. You know

I traveled here alone because you watched me. I've done every-thing you've asked me to do."

"If you wish to see her, you must take a walk with me."

Among her many thoughts, the most prominent at that moment was: I'm not trained for this. I have no idea what to do next. Somehow, she managed to say, "I'm not leaving this hotel."

"Very well, Mrs. McDeere. Your refusal is putting Giovan-na's life at risk. I am offering to take you to see her."

"Where is she?"

"Not far. A pleasant walk on a nice day."

"I don't feel safe."

"How do you think Giovanna feels?"

With a gun to her head? There was no time to ponder or negotiate. She said, "Okay, I'll walk, but I'm not getting in a vehicle."

"I didn't mention one."

They left the hotel through the front entrance and turned onto a busy sidewalk. Abby knew the hotel was in the center of the city and near the medina, the original walled settlement that is the heart of Marrakech. From behind oversized sunglasses, Abby tried to see every face and every movement, but she was soon overwhelmed by the crowd. Wearing jeans and sneak-ers and carrying a bulky designer shoulder bag, she got a few looks, but there were other tourists, mostly Westerners, roaming about. She prayed that Cory and his boys were somewhere close behind, watching, but after his getting busted by Hassan she was not so confident.

Hassan said nothing as they strolled along. She followed him through an ancient stone entrance and into the medina, an incredible maze of narrow cobblestone streets packed with pedestrians and donkey carts. There were a few scooters but no automobiles. They drifted with the waves of human traffic, passing endless rows of stalls selling everything imaginable. Hassan weaved deeper into the maze, in no particular hurry it seemed. Abby stole a few looks behind her in a futile effort to see a landmark she might remember later, but it was impossible.

The medina had been centuries in the making and its markets, called souks, sprawled helter-skelter in every conceivable direction. They walked past souks for spices, eggs, textiles, herbs, leathers, carpets, pottery, jewelry, metals, fish, fowl, and animals, some dead and ready to eat, others alive and looking for a new home. In a large, dirty cage a pack of howler monkeys screeched but no one seemed to hear them. Everyone spoke loudly, some practically yelling, in a dozen languages as they haggled over prices, quantity, and quality. Abby heard a few words in English, a few more in Italian, but most of it was incomprehensible. Some of the merchants barked at the customers, who were quick to bark right back. In a crush of people, Hassan yelled over his shoulder, "Watch your bag. The pickpockets are aggressive around here."

In an open plaza they walked with caution near a row of snake handlers playing their flutes as their cobras danced from colorful urns. They slowed to admire a troop of acrobats and transvestite dancers. Young boys were boxing with heavy leather gloves. Street magicians were trying to draw enough people for the next show. Musicians strummed away on lutes and santirs. In one souk a dentist appeared to be pulling teeth. In another a photographer was coaxing tourists to pose with his beautiful young model. Beggars were everywhere and seemed to be doing a brisk business.

When they were hopelessly lost in the depths of the medina, Abby asked, above the din, "Where, exactly, are we going?"

Hassan nodded ahead but said nothing. Surrounded by

swarms of people, she did not feel completely vulnerable, but seconds later she felt lost and terrified. They turned in to another section, another narrow street with squat shabby buildings lining the cobblestones, and a souk for spice on one side and carpets on the other. From the open windows upstairs, colorful rugs hung by the dozens and shaded the stalls below. Hassan suddenly took her by the elbow, nodded, and said, "Over here." They stepped into a dark, tight passageway between two buildings, then through a door that was covered with a faded rug. Hassan shoved it open. They entered a room with walls and the floor made of rugs, then walked into another room, seemingly identical. A woman was placing a tea service on a small ivory table with two chairs. Hassan nodded at her and she disappeared.

He smiled, waved at the table, and said, "Will you join me for some tea, Mrs. McDeere?"

As if she could say no. Tea would not have been her beverage of choice at that moment. She sat in a chair and watched him slowly fill two cups with black tea. It even smelled strong.

He took a sip, smiled, and put his cup down. To his left he said, loudly, "Ali!" Two hanging rugs separated slightly and a young man stuck his head through the gap. Hassan nodded slightly and said, "Now."

The rugs slid farther apart to reveal a figure seated in a chair less than twenty feet away. It was a woman draped in black with a small hood covering her face. Her long light brown hair fell to her shoulders beneath the hood. Behind her was a tough guy also in black with a mask hiding his face and a pistol on his hip.

Hassan nodded and the man lifted the hood. Giovanna exhaled at the light, dim as it was, and blinked several times. Abby knew it was no time to be timid so she blurted, "Giovanna, it's me, Abby McDeere. Are you okay?"

Giovanna's mouth dropped open as she tried to focus. "Yes, Abby, I am okay." Her voice was weak and scratchy.

Abby said, *"Andiamo a casa, Giovanna. Luca sta aspettando."* Let's go home, Giovanna, Luca is waiting.

She replied, *"Si, okay, va bene, fai quello che vogliono."* Yes, just do what they want.

Hassan nodded and the carpets were quickly pulled back together. He looked at Abby and said, "Now, are you satisfied."

"I guess." At least she was alive.

"She looks nice, yes?"

Abby looked away, unwilling to dignify his question with a response. Keep her in a cage for forty days and I'm supposed to be impressed with how good she looks?

"The next move is yours, Mrs. McDeere. Please inform your husband."

"And when I do, and when you receive the money, what happens then?"

He smiled, snapped his fingers, and said, "We disappear, just like that. We leave from here and no one follows. You leave from here and no one follows."

"And I'm supposed to find my way out of here?"

"I'm sure you'll manage. Please make the call."

From her collection of phones, Abby selected her old cell and called Mitch.

———•—•———

Mitch put the phone back in his pocket, smiled at the others, and said, "All systems go."

Frick produced a one-page document and handed it to Jennings, who pored over every word, then handed it to Mitch, who did the same. Stripped of the verbiage, it was a simple authorization. Mitch and Jennings signed it.

Frick sat at his desk, opened his laptop, and said, "Gentlemen, please watch the screen. I am now transferring seventy-five million dollars from account ADMP-8859-4454-7376-XBU to account number 33375-9856623, both of said accounts in-house at Trinidad Trust, Grand Cayman office." As they watched the screen, the balance of the first account suddenly became zero, and a few seconds later the balance of the second account became $75,000,000.

CHAPTER 45

Hassan listened intently for a moment, then put his phone on the table. He poured himself more tea and asked, "For you?"

"No thanks." She had taken one sip. She doubted she would ever want another cup of tea.

Hassan removed another phone from another pocket and stared at the screen. Minutes passed slowly. He sipped even more deliberately. Finally, his first phone buzzed softly. He suppressed a smile, gathered both phones, and said, "The money has arrived. A pleasure doing business, Mrs. McDeere. I've never had a lovelier adversary."

"Sure. Whatever. A real pleasure."

He stood and said, "I'll go now. It's best if you wait a moment before leaving."

In a split second he was gone. He stepped between two hanging rugs on the other side of the room and vanished. Abby waited, counted to ten, got to her feet, listened silently, then said, "Giovanna. Are you there?"

There was no answer.

Abby yanked open the rugs and froze in horror.

"Giovanna!" she yelled. "Giovanna!" She pulled at other hanging rugs looking for another room, another exit, but found nothing. She stood and gawked at the empty chair, the empty room, and felt like screaming. But she couldn't hesitate. She had to find Giovanna and she couldn't be far away.

Abby managed to slip through more rugs and find the cramped passageway. She hurried through it and back to the cobblestone street where she stopped and looked around at thousands of people wandering in all directions. The vast majority were men in long robes of various colors, but white was dominant. At first glance she did not see a single woman robed in black.

Which way to go? Where to turn? She had never been so lost in her life. It was hopeless. She saw the top of the dome of a mosque and remembered passing near it earlier. Going toward it made as much sense as anything else.

She had lost the money and she had lost Giovanna. It was surreal, impossible to believe, and she had no idea what to do next. As she drifted with the crowd she realized she had to call Mitch. Perhaps he could stop the wire, get the money back, but she knew the truth.

A man was screaming at her, a wild-eyed, red-faced lunatic ranting in another language, angry at her for some reason. He blocked her path and stepped closer and stumbled. She realized he was drunk, but he did not stop his tirade. She turned to her right and picked up her pace. He stumbled again, then fell hard. She got away from him but was rattled even more. She kept moving, and when she saw a small group of people who were obviously tourists she kept close to them. They were Dutch, with neat backpacks and hiking boots. She followed along for a few moments as she tried to collect her thoughts. The Dutch found an outdoor café and decided to take a coffee break. Abby found a table nearby and tried to ignore them. She also tried to settle her nerves but realized she was crying.

Her nearest ally was Cory. With the green phone she called him and he answered immediately. "Where are you?" he snapped, obviously wired.

"In the medina, close to the mosque. Where are you?"

"Hell if I know. I'm trying to find my colleagues. We're close by, I think."

"They're watching you?"

"What?"

"Listen to me, Cory. The money has been wired and Giovanna has disappeared, again."

"Shit!"

"I'm afraid so. I saw her for a second and she is alive. At least she was moments ago. Mitch completed the wire, then she vanished. I blew it, Cory. She's gone."

"Are you okay, Abby?"

"Yes. Please come find me. I'm at an outdoor café near a row of stalls selling leather goods."

"Go to the Mouassine Mosque, the nearest one. There is a fountain on the north side. I'll find you there."

"Got it." Where the hell was north?

She walked across a crowded plaza and saw the dome in the distance. It was not as close as she thought.

A familiar sound rang in her bag and she realized she had forgotten about the Jakl. She stopped next to a stall selling cheese and looked at the Jakl. Of course they were still following her. It was Noura.

"Yes," Abby said.

"Listen to me, Abby. Turn to your left and walk past the large souk with brown pottery. Do you see it?"

"Where are you, Noura?"

"I'm here, watching you. Do you see the brown pottery?"

"Yes. I'm walking that way. Where's Giovanna, Noura?"

"In the medina. Stay on the phone. Next you'll see the small plaza with a row of donkey carts. Walk toward them."

"I am, I am."

Noura materialized from thin air and was beside Abby. "Just keep walking," she said and put her phone away. Abby returned hers to her bag. She glanced at Noura, who looked exactly as she had when they first met in the coffee shop a month earlier. Her face was completely veiled, her eyes barely visible. She wondered if it was the same person and realized there was no way to know. However, her voice sounded familiar.

"What's going on, Noura?"

"You will see."

"Is Giovanna okay? Tell me nothing has happened to her."

"You will see."

They walked past the donkey carts and onto a residential street that was quieter and slightly less crowded. A smaller mosque, Sidi Ishak, was in front of them.

"Stop here," Noura said. "To the right of the mosque, on the corner there, is a tiny souk for coffee and tea. Go inside."

Noura abruptly turned and walked away. Abby hurried down the street, past the mosque and into the store. In a corner, partially hidden, was Giovanna Sandroni, wearing the same jeans, jacket, and hiking boots she had worn the day she was abducted. She grabbed Abby and they embraced tightly and for a long time. The shopkeeper eyed them suspiciously but said nothing.

They stepped outside and onto the street. Abby called Cory, gave him the news, then called Mitch.

"Are we safe?" Giovanna asked as they walked back to the market.

"Yes, Giovanna, we are safe. And we're taking you to Rome. The airplane is waiting. Do you need anything?"

"No. Just food."

"We have food."

Abby glanced at an alley behind a row of stalls selling fruits and vegetables. A cardboard box was half filled with rotten produce and other garbage. She took a few steps toward it and dropped the Jakl into the mess.

CHAPTER 46

"Have you ever stopped to think about how much misery those bad boys can create with seventy-five million dollars?" Stephen asked.

"It's actually eighty-five, and yes I have," Mitch replied. "More people will be terrorized and killed. More bombs bought and detonated. More buildings burned. Nothing good will come from the money. Instead of being used for food and medicine, it'll be wasted on more bullets."

"You feel bad about that?"

"If I think of it in that context, yes. But I don't. We had no choice because there was a life at stake."

"I wouldn't worry about it either. As long as it's bad actors killing one another, who really cares?"

They were sitting at a small table on the shaded porch of a coffee bar overlooking Hog Sty Bay. One massive cruise ship was docked and another was visible on the horizon. They were nervous and staring at Mitch's phone in the center of the table.

It finally buzzed and Mitch grabbed it. From 4,500 miles

away, Abby said, "We've got her and we're going to the airport." He flashed a smile and gave Stephen a thumbs-up.

"Great. Is she okay?"

"Yes. She called Luca and can't wait to get home."

"I'll call Roberto." Mitch was choked up for a second, then said, "Great job, Abby. I'm so proud of you."

"I didn't really have a choice, did I?"

"We'll discuss it later."

"You have no idea. She disappeared after the money was wired. I'll tell you all about it."

"I'll see you in Rome. I love you."

Mitch pressed the OFF button and looked at Stephen. "They're going to the airport and headed for home. We did it."

Stephen shrugged and said, "Oh well, all in a day's work."

"Right. I'm calling Roberto and Jack. You call Riley in London."

"Will do. Where am I going from here?"

"You're going to New York. I'm going to Rome."

"Who gets the jet?"

"Not you."

"Figures."

"But I'll approve an upgrade to business class."

"That's nice. Thanks."

———•—•———

On the plane, the nurse finished a quick exam and found nothing wrong. Pulse, blood pressure, heart rate—all within normal ranges. She offered a sedative to help her relax, but Giovanna wasn't thinking about pills. She asked for a glass of very cold champagne. She drank half of it as they waited for clearance, then stretched out on the sofa and closed her eyes. Abby gently placed a blanket over her. As she tucked it tight around her legs, she realized Giovanna was crying softly.

When they lifted off, Abby smiled at Cory, who gave her a thumbs-up. They were in the air! Twenty minutes later, as they leveled off at 40,000 feet, Giovanna sat up and draped the blanket over her shoulders. Abby unbuckled her belt and sat close to her and said, "There's a small shower in the back."

"No. They moved me into the hotel last night and I was allowed to bathe for the first time in forty days. Try that sometime. My hair was nothing but knots and grease. My teeth were covered with a grungy film. I was gross from head to toe. I stayed in the bathroom for hours."

Abby was touching the sleeve of her shirt. "Looks clean."

"Yes, I wasn't allowed to wear this stuff. Did you see the videos?"

"Yes, some of them."

"They dressed me a like a monk, hijab and all. Last night they gave me this outfit back, all clean and pressed. Such nice boys."

"You said you were hungry."

"Yes, what's on the menu?"

"Sea bass or steak."

"I'll take the fish. Thanks. And more champagne."

———•——•———

Mitch was six hours behind them. Roberto had a car waiting for him at the Rome airport, along with strict instructions from Luca to come straight to his villa where a small party was underway. He arrived just after midnight, and practically tackled his wife when he saw her. After they finished a long embrace, he went for Giovanna. She thanked him repeatedly. He apologized repeatedly. He embraced Luca and thought the old guy looked ten years younger.

Along with Roberto and his wife, Cory, Darian, and Bella, there were about a dozen old family friends on the veranda and the mood was one of sheer euphoria and relief. They had feared the worst for so long, now it was time to celebrate the miracle. They did not want the night to end.

A friend who owned a restaurant around the corner arrived with another wave of food. Neighbors who complained of the noise were invited to join the revelry. "Giovanna's back!" someone yelled and the word spread.

———— • • ————

Mitch and Abby slept on a narrow bed in a guestroom, and awoke with mild, matching hangovers. Nothing that sparkling water and strong coffee couldn't fix.

One glance at his phone and he wanted to toss it. Dozens of missed calls, voicemails, emails, texts, all related to the release of the hostage. He and Roberto huddled and put together a quick media strategy. They wrote a press release that gave the most important fact—Giovanna's release and safe return—while avoiding all other details. They sent it to New York and London. Roberto would deal with the Italian newspapers. No one was getting near a television camera.

Mid-morning Luca appeared and joined them on the veranda. He said that Giovanna had agreed to follow the advice of his doctor and spend a couple of days in the hospital for tests and observation. She had lost at least twenty pounds and was dehydrated. He and Roberto would leave with her in half an hour.

Luca thanked Mitch and Abby again, and when he hugged them his eyes were moist. Mitch wondered if he would ever see him again.

Yes, he would. Once things were settled at home, he and Abby would return to Rome and hang out with Luca and Giovanna. He had made the decision to take some time off.

At noon, the Gulfstream left Rome again, bound for New York, where it would deposit Cory and Darian, then fuel up for a quick trip to Maine, where the McDeere family would be reunited and enjoy a long, lazy weekend.

Monday would be brutal. The boys were two weeks behind at school.

CHAPTER 47

As Mitch entered 110 Broad for the last time, he paused and drifted to his right where the designer benches sat empty, always empty, and the expensive and baffling paintings hung in plain view, ignored by all. He sat down and watched, just like his old pal Lamar Quin, as hundreds of young professionals raced upward with their phones stuck to their ears. The crowd was not as thick because the hour was late, almost 9:30 A.M., an unheard-of hour for arrivals in Big Law.

For the past week, Mitch had been going in later and leaving earlier, if he went in at all.

He finally made it to his office, where he checked on his storage boxes, then left without a word to his secretary. He might call her later.

Jack was expecting him at 9:45.

"Please thank Barry again," Mitch said. "For his incredible hospitality. We might go back in August."

"Well, I'll be there, Mitch. I'm leaving July thirtieth."

"I'm leaving now, Jack. I'm walking out, resigning, quitting, whatever you want to call it. I can't work here. I saw Mavis

Chisenhall yesterday in the cafeteria and she almost broke her neck trying to get away. Too ashamed to speak to me. I can't work in a place where people avoid me."

"Come on, Mitch. You're a hero right now, the man of the hour."

"Doesn't feel that way."

"It's true. Everyone knows what the management committee did, or didn't do, and the entire firm is upset."

"Scully lost its spine, Jack, if it ever had one."

"Don't do it, Mitch. Let some time pass. Everybody will get over it."

"That's easy for you to say. You're leaving."

"True. I just hate to see you go somewhere else, Mitch."

"I'm outta here, Jack. So is Luca. I talked to him yesterday and he's resigning. Giovanna too. She's moving back to Rome and will take over his office."

"Please, Mitch, don't overreact."

"And I'm keeping Lannak. They're fed up with Scully."

"Poaching clients already?"

"Call it whatever. You've done your share. I can think of a few you've snagged. That's the game in Big Law."

Mitch stood and said, "There are four boxes of my office junk on my desk. Could you have them delivered to my apartment?"

"Of course. You're really leaving?"

"I'm gone, Jack. Let's part as friends."

Jack stood and they shook hands.

"I'd love to see you and Abby and the boys in August. Barry's counting on it."

"We'll be there."

AUTHOR'S NOTE

The law firm of Scully & Pershing was founded in 2009 when I needed it to add flavor and authenticity to *The Associate,* that year's legal thriller. Big law firms are big targets for writers of fiction, and I've had my share of fun at their expense. Five years later, I retained Scully again in *Gray Mountain.*

It was the perfect place to put Mitch fifteen years after The Firm imploded in Memphis. Now, he's leaving again and I'm not sure where he'll turn up next.

I was once a lawyer in a small town, far removed from the world of Big Law. And since I've always tried to avoid big firms, I have no idea how they function. Typically, I did what I usually do when trying to avoid research. I called a friend.

John Levy is one of the senior partners of Sidley & Austin, a mammoth Chicago firm with offices around the world. He invited me to stop by for lunch and toss questions at him and some of his colleagues. I had a delightful time talking books and law with Chris Abbinante, Robert Lewis, Pran Jha, Dave Gordon, Paul Choi, Teresa Wilton Harmon, and, of course, Mr.

Levy himself. John is one of the finest lawyers I've had the plea-sure of knowing.

If asked to, I would swear on a Bible that Scully is not based on Sidley.

Thanks also to other friends: Glad Jones, Gene McDade, and Suzanne Herz.

A special thanks to the readers who have enjoyed *The Firm* over the years and been kind enough to write and ask: Will we ever see Mitch and Abby again?